GOING OUT

The Rise and Fall of
Public Amusements

DAVID NASAW

Harvard University Press

Cambridge, Massachusetts
London, England

Permission to reproduce the following images was kindly granted
by the Museum of the City of New York:

(p.16), Eden Musee, 1885
West 23rd Street
Photography by Adolph Witteman
The Leonard Hassam Bogart Collection

(p.17) A Night Scene on the Bowery, New York
Harper's Weekly, February 21, 1881
Museum of the City of New York, 92.50.184

(p.24), Proctor's (n.d.)
Photograph by Byron
The J. Clarence Davies Collection

(p.84), The Kaleidoscopic Tower, Luna Park, 1904
The Gottscho-Schleisner Collection

(p.156), Zucker and Loewe's Variety Arcade (n.d.)
Museum of the City of New York
The Byron Collection

Library of Congress Cataloging-in-Publication Data
Nasaw, David.
Going out : the rise and fall of public amusements /
David Nasaw.
   p. cm.
   Includes bibliographical references and index.
   ISBN 0-674-35622-5 (pbk.)
   1. Leisure—United States—History. 2. Amusements—
United States—History. I. Title.
GV53.N248   1993
790'01'350973—dc20   92-54515

To Dinitia

CONTENTS

ACKNOWLEDGMENTS

WORKS OF SCHOLARSHIP ARE IN ESSENCE collaborative endeavors. I have profited enormously from the assistance, encouragement, and critical insights of the large number of individuals who read portions of my manuscript and commented on papers derived from it.

An early presentation of my developing thesis on public amusements was delivered at Hebrew University in Jerusalem, Israel, where I was a Fulbright lecturer for the 1987–1988 academic year. Aryeh Goren was instrumental in arranging for my visit to Jerusalem and enormously supportive of the project at the outset. I have also profited from the comments of participants at seminars sponsored by the Wilson Center of the Smithsonian Institution; the Columbia University Seminar on American Civilization; the Social Science Research Council's Conference on the Landscape of Modernity; and the Organization of American Historians, where Robert Rydell and Mary Ryan commented on my presentation.

I have gained a great deal from conversations with Jean-Christophe Agnew, Robert Edelman, Roy Rosenzweig, David Rosner, Jon Wiener, and R. Jackson Wilson. Charles Musser graciously shared with me documents on the early phonograph conventions. Jamie Kaplan; Tracey Deutsch; John McTigue, Jr.; Andrea Finkelstein; and Beatrice Nasaw provided invaluable research assistance.

Jim Gilbert read a number of early drafts and, as always, was particularly encouraging and insightful in his criticism. George Custen and William Uricchio carefully read the final manuscript and made a number of apt suggestions. I am especially thankful to Michael Wallace and Steve Ross for agreeing to read my final draft on very short notice and providing extensive chapter-by-chapter commentaries on the entire manuscript.

Steve Fraser at Basic Books has from beginning to end been the perfect editor—enthusiastic, patient, and wise.

Dinitia Smith has read every word of every draft. Although I often resisted, she has taught me how to be a writer as well as a historian.

I wish to acknowledge the financial support of the American Council of Learned Societies, the College of Staten Island, and the City University of New York through the PSC-CUNY research award program.

CHAPTER 1

Introduction

THEY ARE ALL GONE NOW: THE MOVIE PALACES
with their majestic marquees climbing five stories high; the amusement parks with their acres of roller coasters, tilt-a-whirls, chutes, and carousels; the stately asymmetrical ballparks squeezed into residential neighborhoods. Once, these amusement spaces defined the city as a place of glamour and glitter, of fun and sociability. But they have vanished forever. The spectacular yet tawdry, wild, and wonderful Dreamlands only a subway ride away have been replaced by theme parks surrounded by parking lots. The inner-city baseball parks, accessible by mass transit, have been covered over by housing projects or industrial parks. The movie palaces have been torn down or multiplexed into oblivion. And the huge and heterogeneous crowds that gathered there have been dispersed. The audience at a shopping center theater; the spectators at suburban ballparks; and the visitors to theme parks, festival marketplaces, and enclosed shopping malls are, by comparison, frighteningly homogeneous.

The era of public amusements that was born in the latter decades of the nineteenth century has come to an end. We have lost not simply buildings and parks but also the sense of civic sociability they nourished and sustained. In the early twentieth-century American city, residents were segregated from one another at work and at home, by income, ethnicity, gender, and social class. But they were also, I will argue, beginning to share a common commercial culture and public amusement sites, where social solidarities were emphasized and distinctions muted. The world of "public" amusements was, in its "publicity," its accessibility, and its "wide-openness," as the *New York Times* characterized it in an 1899 editorial, a world like no other, situated in a magical corner of the city, where the city's peoples came together to have a good time in public.[1] There were no restrictions as to gender, ethnicity, religion, residence, or occupation in the new amusement spaces. Unlike the landsmen's lodges and union halls; the saloons and church socials; and the front stoops, parlors, and kitchens, the new entertainment centers held more strangers than friends. "Going out" meant laughing, dancing, cheering, and weeping with strangers with whom one might—or might not—have anything in common. The "crowd" replaced the select circle of acquaintances as the setting in which one sought and found amusement.

Only persons of color were excluded or segregated from these audiences, although they were overrepresented on stage—as darkies, strutters, and shouters in vaudeville and musical theater; as coons in popular song; as savages in world's fair exhibits; as buffoons in amusement park concessions; as mascots in baseball parks; as dim-witted children in the early silent movies; as rapists and beasts in D. W. Griffith's *The Birth of a Nation*. As I will argue throughout this book, neither the segregation of African Americans in the commercial amusement audiences nor their overrepresentation in parodic form were coincidental. To the extent that racial distinctions were exaggerated on stage, social distinctions among "whites" in the audience could be muted.

✦⇒◉⇐✦

This is a book about the rise of public amusements in the late nineteenth and early twentieth centuries and their decline and fall in the post–World War II decades. It is the story of the vanished world of phonograph and kinetoscope parlors; of vaudeville halls and ten-twenty-thirty-cent melodrama theaters; of world's fair midways; of amusement parks, ballparks, dance halls, and picture palaces.

In the 1870s and 1880s, "nightlife" was still the preserve of the wealthy few who patronized the first-class playhouses and of the "sporting" crowd that spent its evenings in "concert" saloons with live entertainment. Within only a few decades, however, the landscape of amusements—and their place in the everyday life of the city—changed dramatically. The city's muddied streets and gray edifices receded into the background, overwhelmed by the "Great White Ways" that studded the central business districts with their flashing lights advertising the newest, the most spectacular, the biggest shows in town. By 1900, New York City had more theaters than any city in the world. By 1910, the seating capacity of its playhouses and movie theaters approached two million. (In 1869, average daily attendance had been estimated at a little more than 25,000.) San Francisco in 1912 had five playhouses, eleven vaudeville houses, and sixty-nine moving-picture theaters with an estimated weekly attendance of more than half a million. (In 1870, there had been two playhouses and one opera house.) The increase in the number of theaters and seating capacities was just as great in other American cities, east and west.[2]

When we add to these numbers the world's fair, amusement park, and ballpark visitors, the enormity of the twentieth-century entertainment revolution becomes even clearer. The only world's fair held in the United States after the 1876 Centennial Exhibition in Philadelphia was the 1885 New Orleans World's Industrial and Cotton Exposition. Then, with dizzying regularity, the Chicago World's Fair of 1893 drew 14 million visitors; the Atlanta exposition in 1895, 1.3 million; Nashville in 1897, 1.8 million; Omaha in 1898, 1.5 million; Buffalo in 1901, 4 million; and St. Louis in 1904, 10 million. In 1870, there had been no amusement parks or baseball parks and only a handful of accessible picnic groves and beer gardens on the cities' outskirts. By the early twentieth century, there were enclosed baseball and amusement parks in every city and town in the nation, with visitors numbering in the tens of millions. Over twenty million men, women, and children visited Coney Island alone during the 1909 season, a number that, adjusted for population increases, is about 20 percent greater than the total number of visitors to Disney's Orlando and Anaheim amusement parks in 1989.[3]

⋆⇥═◑ ◐═⇤⋆

The rise of public amusements was a by-product of the enormous expansion of the cities. Commercial entertainments were, in this period at least, an urban phenomenon. Their rise and fall were inevitably and inextricably linked to the fortunes of the cities that sustained them.

Between 1870 and 1920, American cities flourished as never before. The urban population of the nation increased from under ten to over fifty-four million people. Per capita income and free time expanded as well. Between 1870 and 1900, real income for nonfarm employees increased by more than 50 percent, while the cost of living, as measured by the consumer price index, decreased by 50 percent. This increase in wages was accompanied by a steady decrease in work hours. The average manufacturing worker worked three and a half hours less in 1910 than in 1890; for many blue-collar workers, unionized employees, and white-collar workers, the decrease in the workweek was even more dramatic. It also was in this period that the Saturday half-holiday and the "vacation habit" arrived in the American city. Although, as we will see in chapter 6, most workers still had to finance their own vacations, increasing numbers of white-collar employees were beginning to take days, even a week or more, off during the warm-weather months.[4]

As Roy Rosenzweig and a generation of labor and social historians have argued, the quest for leisure time "reverberated through the labor struggles of the late nineteenth and early twentieth centuries. As a compositor told the U.S. Senate Committee on Relations Between Labor and Capital in 1883: 'A workingman wants something besides food and clothes in this country. . . . He wants recreation.'" "Going out" was more than an escape from the tedium of work, it was the gateway into a privileged sphere of everyday life. The ability to take time out from work for recreation and public sociability was the dividing line between old worlds and new. Peasants and beasts of burden spent their lives at work; American workers and citizens went out at night and took days off in the summer.[5]

Recreation and play were not luxuries but necessities in the modern city. As Daniel Rodgers has noted, the workday had been shortened by "squeezing periods of relaxation and amusement out of working hours, by trading long hours of casual work for shorter, more concentrated workdays." Instead of the older "interfusion of free and work time," there was now "an increasing segregation of work and play into distinct categories." The fear of idle time as the devil's workshop gave way to a reverence for play, promoted alike by middle-class reformers and working-class organizers. As the Yiddish *Tageblatt* advised its Jewish readers in the spring of 1907, "He who can enjoy and does not enjoy commits a sin."[6]

While all the city's workers, even its most recent immigrants, joined the assembling public for commercial amusements, it was the workers in white collars who constituted the critical element in the construction of the new "nightlife." As the white-collar sector of the work force increased in size in the late nineteenth and early twentieth centuries, so did the potential audience for the new public amusements. In 1880, there had been 5,000 typists and stenographers in the nation. By 1910, the number had increased sixtyfold to 300,000, while the overall clerical work force had risen from 160,000 to more than 1.7 million. From a negligible 2.4 percent of the total work force in 1870, the number of clerical and sales workers grew to a substantial 11 percent by 1920. In the big cities, the percentage of white-collar workers was even greater: 24 percent of the Chicago work force in 1920 were white-collar workers, a large number of them women.[7]

The city's white-collar workers were the most avid consumers of the commercial pleasures. Their work was increasingly regimented, concentrated, and tedious, creating a need for recreation. And, compared to that of blue-collar workers, it provided them with sufficient time, resources, and energy to go out at night. For factory, mill, and manual workers who had to get up at five in the morning to be at work by six, the consequences of a night "out" were considerable. Clerical and sales workers could, on the other hand, stay out late, get a good night's sleep, and still get to work on time.[8]

+►⚬☰⚬☰⚬◄+

The new amusements were "public" and "commercial" as well as urban. The terms, in this period at least, became almost interchangeable, as the city's showmen, learning the new calculus of public entertainments, lowered prices to welcome the largest possible audience to their establishments. Although in the long run, it was growth in the demand, not the supply, side that would prompt the expansion of commercial entertainments, the showmen played a considerable role in assembling the new urban public. To succeed in the show business (as it was called throughout this period), the amusement entrepreneurs had to do more than build theaters; they had to provide commercial amusements and amusement sites that were public in the sense that they belonged to no particular social groups, exciting enough to appeal to the millions, and respectable enough to offend no one.

Leisure time remained a contested terrain, an arena of social life of such critical importance that the city's social, political, cultural, and religious elites dared not abandon it to the whims of consumers and the marketplace. To keep their critics at bay and attract an audience from the diverse social groups in the city, the show businessmen had to mold and maintain a revised moral taxonomy of shows and audiences.

Vaudeville had to be certified as a decent entertainment for mixed audiences, with no relation to the male-only variety show that had preceded it; the amusement parks had to be promoted as "clean" outdoor shows for the whole family; the moving-picture theaters had to be distinguished from the penny arcades and peep shows. The envelope in which it was delivered mattered as much as the content of the show. An otherwise "indecent" act became "decent" when presented in an amusement site certified as "respectable." It was permissible to stare at gyrating belly dancers on the world's fair midways, if the dancers in question were performing "authentic" foreign dances; women in tights or tight-fitting bathing suits could appear on the vaudeville stage, if they were billed as acrobats or championship swimmers; holding onto a member of the opposite sex was acceptable at the amusement park, if it happened "accidentally" on the cyclone.

⋆⇀≡⊙⊏⋆⋆

No matter how hungry city folk might have been for cheap amusements or how eager the show businessmen were to provide them, the expansion in commercial amusements could not have occurred without accompanying advances in technology, in particular the electrification of the metropolis. In the chapters to come, we will follow the "invention" of new electric amusement machines that spoke, sang, showed moving pictures, and told stories. We begin, however, not with these scientific wonders but with the lighting of the city by electricity, the sine qua non for the expansion of urban "nightlife" in the late nineteenth and early twentieth centuries.

Incandescent lighting transformed the city from a dark and treacherous netherworld into a glittering multicolored wonderland. Nineteenth-century authors had described city streets after dark as sinister and filled with danger. The gas lamps did not "light" up the night as much as cast into shadow the disreputable doings and personages of slum, tenderloin, and levee. In *New York by Gas-Light*, first published in 1850, George Foster, the *New-York Tribune* reporter and bestselling author, described in lurid detail "the fearful mysteries of darkness in the metropolis—the festivities of prostitution, the orgies of pauperism, the haunts of theft and murder, the scenes of drunkenness and beastly debauch, and all the sad realities that go to make up the lower stratum—the under-ground story—of life in New York!"[9]

Fifty years after Foster wrote his account, Theodore Dreiser published *Sister Carrie*, an account of city life that turned upside down the sunshine/shadow, light/dark, day/night tropes used by Foster and other nineteenth-century authors. For Dreiser, it was in daylight, not after dark, that the city was at its grayest, cruelest, and most distressing. The coming of the night was a sign of promise, not depravity. "Ah, the promise of the night. . . . What old illusion of hope is not here forever repeated! Says the soul of the toiler to itself, 'I shall soon be free. I shall be in the ways and the hosts of the merry. The streets, the lamp, the lighted chamber set for dining are for me. The theatres, the halls, the parties, the ways of rest and the paths of song—these are mine in the night.'" Only after dark, when the "street lamps" shone brightly with their "merry twinkle," did joy return to the city as the "artificial fires of merriment" dispelled the gloom and chill, providing "light and warmth."[10]

The sparkling city that Sister Carrie traveled to was Chicago in 1900, when electric lighting was still new and wondrous. A Chicago journalist, writing in 1900, declared that "he had witnessed a profound change in the city's lighting, a revolution 'little short of marvelous. The field where but yesterday the flickering gas flame held full sway now blazes nightly in the glow of myriads of electric lamps, aggregating in intensity the illuminating power of 15,000,000 candles.'" By 1903, the new Commonwealth Edison of Chicago turbogenerator was producing over 5,000 times more energy than the dynamos that had powered Edison's 1882 Pearl Street station. Electricity had, in the words of the historian Wolfgang Schivelbusch, "begun to permeate modern, urban life."[11]

Unlike gas lamps, which were highly flammable, electric lamps could be kept on all night. The street lamps illuminated not simply the lamppost beneath but both sides of the street with a clear, bright white light, not the sooty gray of the gas lamps. The commercial lights of restaurants, shops, and theaters added the merry twinkle that gave the "nocturnal round of business, pleasure and illumination . . . we think of as night life . . . its own special atmosphere."[12]

The artificially illuminated streets provided city residents with an added incentive to leave their darkened or gas-lit flats to go out at night "when all the shop fronts are lighted, and the entrances to the theaters blaze out on the sidewalk like open fireplaces." As the journalist Richard Harding Davis wrote of Broadway in 1892, "It is at this hour that the clerk appears, dressed in his other suit, the one which he keeps for the evening, and the girl bachelor, who . . . has found her hall bedroom cold and lonely after the long working day behind a counter or at a loom and the loneliness tends to homesickness . . . puts on her hat and steps down a side-street and loses herself in the unending processions on Broadway, where, though she knows no one, and no one wants to know her, there is light and color, and she is at least not alone."[13]

Earlier in the nineteenth century, young people who walked the streets after dark would have been admonished for placing themselves in mortal danger of moral contamination. But the electric street lights had gone a long way toward purging "nightlife" of its aura of licentiousness. Although there were no accurate statistics to prove the case, it was taken for granted that the electric street lamps were removing much of the danger that had lurked in the dark. A 1912 article in *The American City* listed first among "the advantages accruing from ornamental street lighting [a decrease in] lawlessness and crime . . . 'A light is as good as a policeman.'. . . A criminologist of world-wide fame, and one who is considered an authority, says that he would rather have plenty of electric lights and clean streets than all the law and order societies in existence."[14]

Electricity was not simply providing power to light the urban landscape but was reconfiguring it into a fairyland of illuminated shapes, signs, and brightly colored, sometimes animated, messages and images—forty-foot green pickles, gigantic pieces of chewing gum, Roman chariots racing on top of a hotel. The lights of the city created "a new kind of visual text," a new landscape of modernity. They foregrounded the city's illuminated messages, its theaters, tall buildings, hotels, restaurants, department stores, and "Great White Ways," while erasing its "unattractive areas and cast[ing] everything unsightly into an impenetrable darkness. If by day poor or unsightly sections called out for social reform, by night the city was a purified world of light, simplified into a spectacular pattern, interspersed with now-unimportant blanks."[15]

The lights "marked" the city as a "sight" worthy of respect, even admiration. But they also focused attention on the city as a source of amusement. The lighting of the lights signaled that the workday was over and the time for play at hand. As the editorial in the February 1904 issue of *The Four-Track News* declared, "It is an old, old theme, and an oft told tale—but when the lights are on, and the season is in full swing, as it is now, any evening, that great thoroughfare, with its business activity, its wonderful social life, its rialto with its tragic comedians and its comic tragedians . . . when Broadway is really itself, it is a continuous vaudeville that is worth many times the 'price of admission'—especially as no admission price is asked. Where else is there such a free performance—such a festive panorama of gay life as Broadway 'puts up' when the lights are on."[16]

Electrification made going out at night not only safer and more exciting but easier and cheaper than ever before. The dynamos and generators that lit the street lamps also powered the trolleys that tied together the city and its neighborhoods. Between 1890 and 1902, investment in electric and cable cars quadrupled, track mileage tripled, and fare passengers doubled. In 1890, only 15 percent of all American streetcars had been electrified, and the remainder were connected to horses. By 1902, 94 percent were electric. The flat nickel fare and free transfers between lines made streetcar travel accessible to more city residents and workers.[17]

In connecting the city's business and residential districts, the electric streetcars fostered the growth—and transformation—of "downtown" into a central shopping and entertainment district. In Chicago, as Sam Bass Warner has written, the Loop, tied by electric streetcar to outlying neighborhoods, prospered as never before. "The downtown district became *the* city for Chicagoans. It was a place of work for tens of thousands, a market for hundreds of thousands, a theater for thousands more."[18]

The new "downtowns" were defined geographically by the convergence of the railroad and trolley lines and framed architecturally by the mammoth new terminals that welcomed out-of-towners into the heart of the city. The majority of those who resided temporarily in the nearby hotels had come for business purposes: to buy, sell, insure, inspect, or display their goods. Before, after, and sometimes even during business hours, however, they expected to be entertained. They were joined in this pursuit by white-collar workers who stayed "downtown" after work; by city residents who worked and lived in outlying residential neighborhoods but rode the streetcar to the theater district; and by suburbanites who were linked by electric "interurban" to the city and its nighttime pleasures. For all of them, the city was becoming as much a place of play as a place of work.[19]

CHAPTER 2

Dollar Theaters, Concert Saloons, and Dime Museums

THE EARLY NINETEENTH-CENTURY THEATER, like the city itself, was inhabited by rich, "middling," and working people thrown together into the same space, then divided by income, class, and race. The most expensive seats were the cushioned opera chairs in the boxes reserved for "the dandies, and people of the first respectability and fashion." Beneath the boxes in the "pit" (the area of the theater known today as the orchestra) sat the city's manual workers, sailors, artisans, tradesmen, butchers, and Bowery b'hoys in "red-flannel shirt-sleeves and cone-shaped trowsers," all, as Walt Whitman would describe them, "alert, well-dress'd, full-blooded young and middle-aged men, the best average of American-born mechanics." Above and behind the "pit" in the cheap balcony seats reigned the "gallery gods": the newsboys, apprentices, and assorted rowdies, who, though far away from the action on the stage, made their presence—and their displeasure—known by pelting the actors and the "better" classes below with pennies, rotten fruit, eggs, "apples, nuts and gingerbread" when offended by the show or offered less than they had bargained for.[1]

Though their choices were influenced by the size of their pocketbooks, most theatergoers sat where they pleased. Only African Americans and prostitutes were restricted to separate sections of the theater. In a world where many still believed moral character was both immutable and encoded in physical appearance, blacks who could not "pass" and prostitutes who advertised their trade by their use of makeup and costume had to be quarantined in separate sections of the theater so as not to degrade by their presence more "respectable" theatergoers.

Almost every theater, even the illustrious Park Theater in New York City, according to George Foster, writing in 1850, reserved its third tier of boxes for prostitutes and their customers. "Within a few feet and under the same roof where our virtuous matrons with their tender off-spring are seated, are . . . painted, diseased, drunken women, bargaining themselves away to obscene and foul-faced ruffians, for so much an hour." While Foster was clearly perturbed—or thought his readers would be—by the proximity of painted ladies and virtuous matrons, the seating arrangements served all parties. The prostitutes no doubt preferred their accommodations in the third tier, complete with separate entrance, exit, stairway, and bar, because it gave them the privacy they needed to transact business; the "respectable" folk in their box seats were, Foster's alarm notwithstanding, effectively shielded from the disorder above them—unless of course they chose to stare up at it; and the theater owners profited from knowing that whatever the attraction, they could be assured of selling out their third tier of boxes.[2]

The situation of African Americans, who were, like the prostitutes, required to sit in separate sections of the theater, was quite different. Black theatergoers, slave or freed, were assigned the worst seats in the house in the upper balcony or gallery. Unlike the prostitutes who, if offered a choice, would probably have remained in the third tier, African Americans who could afford better seats in the pit or the boxes would undoubtedly have preferred to sit there. Their sequestration in the upper gallery was not only a public badge of dishonor, but it placed them with the white rabble who behaved atrociously and made more than enough noise to drown out the actors below.[3]

Wherever they sat and whatever they had paid, audience members, with the exception of the African Americans exiled in the gallery, got their money's worth. To fill their houses, theater owners assembled programs with "attractions" to appeal to every taste in the audience. In the spring of 1839, for example, the playbill advertising *As You Like It* in Philadelphia's American Theater announced that the Il Diavolo Antonio and his sons would also be presenting "a most magnificent display of position in the science of Gymnastics," a Mr. Quayle would sing "the Swiss Drover Boy," La Petite Celeste would dance, followed by a

Miss Lee who would also dance, Mr. Quayle would then return to sing "The Haunted Spring," a Mr. Bowman would tell a "Yankee Story," and the entire company would conclude the evening "with *Ella Rosenberg* starring Mrs. Hield."[4]

This heterogeneous mixing of entertainments on the stage and social groups in the audience pleased no one entirely. The playwrights, critics, and managers were appalled by the extent to which the theater had become hostage to its heterogeneous audience; the box holders were disgusted by the rowdiness of pit and gallery; the pit was offended by the box holders' continuous chatter and inattention to the stage; the gallery was disgusted by the actors' fawning attention to the box holders; the actors were distraught at the prospect of satisfying what they perceived to be the divergent demands of gallery, pit, and boxes.

There were moments when the entire unstable mixture exploded into chaos, as in the Astor Place Riots of 1849, when the "people" in pit and gallery became so incensed at what they perceived to be English actor William Macready's aristocratic airs and insults to their nation, their manhood, and their class that they silenced him "by a storm of boos and cries of 'Three groans for the codfish aristocracy,' which drowned out appeals for order from those in the boxes." The theater had to be closed as "an avalanche of eggs, apples, potatoes, lemons, and ultimately, chairs hurled from the gallery . . . forced [Macready] to leave the stage in the third act." Two days later, under pressure from New York's elite theatergoers who were not about to grant victory to the "mob," Macready returned and this time completed his performance. Outside, a crowd of 10,000 gathered to protest. The militia was called to restore order, which it did, but only after 22 people had been killed, 150 hurt, and 86 arrested.[5]

Prompted no doubt by incidents like this one, mid-century prosperous theatergoers in cities large enough to support more than one playhouse separated themselves from the "rabble" by building new academies and opera houses with smaller galleries and higher prices. "One theater was no longer large enough to appeal to all classes. . . . One roof, housing a vast miscellany of entertainment each evening, could no longer cover a people growing intellectually and financially more disparate."[6]

After the Civil War, theater prices continued to rise, especially through the 1880s as touring productions became more and more elaborate. The result was a vastly different theater audience, one that no longer included as many of the city's working and "middling" populations. In Pittsburgh, according to Francis Couvares, the local theaters that had "catered to a working-class audience" had by the 1880s disappeared entirely. The theaters that survived and prospered, in Pittsburgh and elsewhere, were those cultivated by "newly class-conscious bourgeois patrons" who were happy to pay higher prices for a more refined show.[7]

By the mid-1880s, the average theater ticket price was a dollar, two-thirds of what the nonfarm worker earned in a day. Even the cheap seats in the melodrama and minstrelsy theaters cost far more than most city residents could afford. Balcony seats at Boston's Globe Theater in 1886 were priced at seventy-five cents to one dollar, with second balcony and gallery seats at fifty cents, this at a time when the average hourly wage in manufacturing was twenty cents and the average daily wage for unskilled laborers was under one dollar and fifty cents.[8]

⊷⊶⊜⊜⊶⊷

For those who could not afford or preferred not to go to the theaters in the 1870s and 1880s, there were other entertainment sites in the city, although not nearly as many as there would be in only a few decades. There were restaurants, lecture halls, and lodges; beer halls, bawdy houses, brothels, and dance halls; billiard rooms, picnic groves, and pleasure gardens just outside the city; and thousands of concert saloons and cheap variety theaters.[9]

The most popular of these were the concert saloons and variety theaters. The two terms were used almost interchangeably to refer to barrooms with free or cheap entertainment offered in adjacent backrooms, halls, or theaters. Some concert saloons were elaborately outfitted to attract slumming "sports" from uptown; others were simple barrooms with stages in front.[10]

The primary source of revenue in the concert saloons was selling alcohol, with prostitution an important side line. Free "entertainment" was offered as a come-on in adjacent halls, back rooms, or upstairs "theaters." The audience was exclusively male; the ambience was pure saloon—the floor filled with peanut shells and spilt beer; the air saturated with tobacco smoke; and the odor so rank that according to one newspaper story, a monkey that had "escaped from an animal act and died under the floor of the Casino Theater in Spokane . . . was not discovered until a year later when some repairs were being made."[11]

While the concert saloons offered something for every male taste—drink and camaraderie at the bar, gambling in the back rooms, sex in the boxes—the major source of entertainment was the stage show. In the smaller saloons, the "show" consisted of little more than local performers singing and dancing for tips on makeshift platforms opposite the bar. In the grander saloons, it could be as elaborate as any theatrical performance. Though most of the acts were simple song or dance numbers, every program had its bawdy or "purple acts": Adam or the boys in overalls would appear on stage, disheveled and smiling, to banter about their trysts in Eden or the hay. Most shows also included a turn or two of "legmania" dancers who wiggled their hips suggestively or kicked high to expose their "drawers." While there was a rough-and-tumble quality to the entertainment and the crowd, the ambience was more male than working class—unlike, for example, the English music hall, where audience, entertainment, and environment were decidedly male *and* working class. Concert saloons in the United States did not, for example, draw the bulk of their audience from factory, mine, or mill workers. Their prices were too high, they were inconveniently located far from working-class neighborhoods, and the stage shows were entirely in English and thus beyond the comprehension of most immigrants.[12]

Harry Hill's, the most famous of the New York City concert saloons, was, according to James McCabe, writing in 1882, "filled with a motley crowd. . . . The men represent all classes of society. Some are strangers who have merely come to see the place; others are out for a lark; and others still have come in company with, or to meet, some abandoned woman. . . . Among the men you will see prominent judges, city officials, detectives in plain clothes, men of prominence in other parts of the country, army and navy officers, merchants, roughs, and thieves." An 1883 Chicago guidebook observed similarly that the Chicago variety theaters were regularly patronized not only by "the lower class of society, but [by] journalists, professional men, bankers, railroad officials, politicians, and men of rank in society." The dividing line between those who patronized the variety shows and those who remained outside was not social class, but gender and "respectability."[13]

⌁⟫═◯═⟪⌁

If nightlife was, as we are arguing, largely the preserve of wealthy theatergoers and sports, where did this leave the city's respectable working and middling classes? At home, for the most part. Though workingmen continued to patronize their local saloons and celebrate special occasions at the union hall, firehouse, and landsmen's associations, they lacked the time and money to spend in theaters or concert saloons. The city's more prosperous middle classes, on the other hand, had the time and money to go out but preferred not to. The home—not the club, the saloon, the firehouse, or the theater—was the heart and soul of middle-class existence. Indeed, it was this "reverence for quiet, seclusion, and privacy," an emphasis on what Mary Ryan calls "entrenched domesticity," that both normatively and experientially distinguished the nineteenth-century middle class from the upper and lower classes.[14]

Middle-class families did not abstractly celebrate the virtues of domestic privacy; they lived them on a daily basis. While moral reformers chastised the poor and immigrant classes and attributed much of their distress to their proclivity for socializing in public, the model middle-class family sequestered itself within the confines of its home and kept its children in residence as long as possible. While the wealthy were "attending the operas, giving sumptuous balls, and even gambling, men and women together, in posh, private casinos," the middle class, as represented by the families Richard Sennett studied in Union Park, a Chicago suburb, confined its socializing to the home. In intentional contrast to the city's upper and lower classes, middle-class behavior was "sedate and ascetic . . . dull and unsensual."[15]

This did not mean that there were no organized leisure-time activities for the respectable classes. There were lyceums and lecture halls, libraries, churches, and church-affiliated associations, such as the YMCA, that sponsored musicals, concerts, travelogues, even an occasional magician or illusionist. There also was the museum, one of the few cultural institutions that was both accessible in price and respectable enough for the established middle classes to patronize.

Nineteenth-century American museums were quite different from those established in other parts of the world. As an English visitor wrote in 1870, a "'Museum' in the American sense of the word means a place of amusement, wherein there shall be a theatre, some wax figures, a giant and dwarf or two, a jumble of pictures, and a few live snakes."[16]

To establish their "bona fides" with the respectable public that they hoped to attract to their establishments, the museum owners posed as both educators and showmen. Visitors were greeted at the door of the museums by "lecturers" who guided them through the "scientific" and "historical" exhibits in the front of the establishment to the lecture hall, where the main show was presented. The stage show usually opened with a parade of "scientific oddities" presided over by a "lecturer" or

The Eden Musee in New York City was one of the nation's most prestigious museums, with a patronage that included respectable ladies and gentlemen like those posed in front of the building. This picture is from 1885. (*Museum of the City of New York.*)

"professor," who, pointer in hand, encouraged the audience to stare in the name of science at the dog-faced boys, bearded ladies, armless wonders, Fiji Islanders, Dahomean giants, and dwarfs assembled for their edification. The "freak" acts were followed by the "artists"—quick crayon-sketch masters, magicians, illusionists, mind-readers, sword-swallowers, glass-chewers, fire-eaters, and contortionists, especially prized by the museum managers, because they came cheaply and had no difficulty performing on tiny auditorium stages—and then by the variety acts: comics, Irish tenors, banjo players, acrobats, dancers, and "educated" animal acts.[17]

It was obviously not the quality of the entertainment that made the museum show acceptable fare for city folk who dared not enter a theater or concert saloon. It was the packaging and the environment in which the acts were presented. The museums barred liquor, smoking, prostitutes, and "blue" performers from their premises. As Barnum

This drawing of a night scene on the Bowery was published in *Harper's Weekly* in 1881. The barker in the dime museum doorway is trying to lure customers inside by pointing to the painting of the "freak" attractions over the sign. The attractions and the customers for this museum were quite different from those for the Eden Musee. (*Museum of the City of New York.*)

himself declared, "so careful is the supervision exercised over the amusements that hundreds of persons who are prevented visiting theatres on account of the vulgarisms and immorality which are sometimes permitted therein, may visit Mr. Barnum's establishment without fear of offence."[18]

While Barnum and his competitors tried their best to entertain the city's respectable classes, there were dozens of dime museums located in storefronts in the cheaper entertainment districts and the city's tenderloins that catered exclusively to the male-only population. On New York's Bowery, one of the largest and most notorious of the urban skid rows, there were "anatomical museums" with "lantern slides of horrifying venereal deformities" and museums featuring "living picture" exhibits with women in flesh-colored tights impersonating Lady Godiva, Lady Mephistopheles, or "bewitching female bathers in real water." These "Bowery museums," according to Luc Sante, author of *Low Life: Lures and Snares of Old New York,* were "the true underworld of entertainment, and their compass could include anything too shoddy, too risqué, too vile, too sad, too marginal, too disgusting, too pointless to be displayed elsewhere." Among the stars of their stage shows were egg cranks who ate dozens of raw eggs, foul-mouthed comics who recited limericks, tattooed ladies, and hootchi-kootchi dancers.[19]

Such was the state of urban entertainments in the 1870s and 1880s. For the city's drifters, transients, and unmarried manual laborers who lived or played in the city's tenderloins, there were skid-row museums and cheap honky-tonks. For the sporting crowd, the most visible and regular denizens of nightlife, there were concert saloons and variety theaters. For the prosperous who could afford them, there were high-priced playhouses and legitimate theaters. For a small minority of the city's respectable folk who for religious or moral reasons dared not enter the theater, there were the better dime museums. But for the vast majority of the urban population, working and middling classes alike, there were no affordable and "decent" places to "go out" at night.

CHAPTER 3

"Something for Everybody" at the Vaudeville Theater

I N LATER YEARS, THE VAUDEVILLE AND MOVING-
picture pioneers would claim that they had intentionally set out to
cater to the population of "decent" city folk who had been priced out of
the first-class theaters. Though their story has the advantage of narrative clarity, it greatly exaggerates their role in the development of commercial amusements. Vaudeville and the movies were not invented by
founders with a plan or a vision but by small businessmen who experimented with their products (their shows and theaters) until they began
to yield a profit. Almost all of the early vaudeville entrepreneurs came
from the lower end of the amusement business. Most had spent their
adult lives traveling with circus or variety troupes from town to town. A
few had owned concert saloons, honky-tonks, or dime museums.*

Benjamin Franklin Keith, who would become the most famous of
them all, had been a grifter, traveling with the circus selling novelties
like hand-held blood testers to the crowd outside the tent. In 1883,
road weary and with a small amount of accumulated capital, he opened
a storefront museum in Boston with a partner. Instead of locating it in

---

*Benjamin Franklin Keith, Edward Franklin Albee, and Tony Pastor began their show busi-
ness careers with the circus; Martin Beck and Percy Williams had traveled with variety
troupes; Alexander Pantages and John Considine had owned saloons and box houses on the
West Coast; Sylvester Poli had owned and operated wax museums and dime museums in
New York and New England.

an area of cheap amusements and cheaper saloons, where most of the smaller dime museums were sited, he chose Washington Street in the central business district near the city's major hotels, theaters, and restaurants. He purchased a few exhibits for the front of his storefront and improvised a stage in the back. When the storefront proved too small to hold all his attractions, he rented an upstairs room for his "theater." His July 6, 1884, bill, a typical one, featured "Miss Amelia Hall, a jolly fat Brooklyn Miss weighing 516 pounds," a "demon dwarf," German midgets who performed on the zither, a young lady invisible below her head and shoulders, the biggest frog in the world, a Punch and Judy puppet show, a troupe of Guatemalan musicians, comedians Weber and Fields, and a closing farce, "Murphy's Fat Baby."[1]

To make his show a bit more inviting and to attract the scores of passersby who were skirting his museum on their way to nearby offices, department stores, hotels, and legitimate theaters, Keith experimented in 1885 with what he called the "continuous." Instead of emptying the house after each performance, he kept the show going, bringing the opening act back on stage when the final one exited. As Keith knew from his days with the circus, nothing attracted a crowd like a crowd, and nothing was so depressing as an empty house. "Continuous" performances guaranteed that he would have an audience all day long.[2]

While he did better with his new format, Keith was still not filling his house on a regular basis. Had his establishment been located in a low-rent district filled with transients looking for cheap freak show entertainment, he might have done better with his "fat ladies" and "demon dwarfs," but the city folk who passed his establishment on Washington Street, the future site of the posh Adams' House, within a stone's throw of the Jordan, Marsh and Company department store and the exclusive Boston Theater, had different tastes. E. F. Albee, his manager at the time, suggested that Keith replace his variety show with a scaled-down version of Gilbert and Sullivan's operetta, *The Mikado*, then playing to full houses at premium prices in Boston's first-class theaters. Keith and Albee stole it (the operetta was not copyrighted in the United States), decorated the front of their theater like a Japanese garden, and advertised the show with the slogan, "Why pay $1.50 when you can see our show for 25¢?"[3]

There were, as Keith and Albee soon discovered, a large number of Bostonians who could not afford Gilbert and Sullivan at regular prices but were willing to climb the stairs to see a cut-rate version. Their scaled-down *Mikado* was so successful that it was sent on the road following its Boston run.[4]

Because operettas were expensive to mount, Keith and Albee continued to alternate them with variety programs. The new format proved so successful that by 1887, they were taking in enough money from their museum theater to lease the full-size Bijou Theatre next door and a dime museum in Providence, where Keith had once owned a broom store. From Providence in 1888 to Philadelphia in 1889 to New York in 1893 and onward to dozens of cities through the Northeast and Middle West, they applied the same formula—with the same success. Wherever they opened a theater, they found an audience awaiting them.[5]

Popular prices remained the key to success in the early vaudeville business. When in 1887, Keith and Albee took over the Bijou Theatre in Boston, they charged ten cents for every seat in the house, while the nearby Hollis Street and Globe theaters were charging a dollar to a dollar and a half for orchestra seats and fifty cents to a dollar for balcony seats.[6]

In the 1890 "catalogue" for his "Gaiety Musee and Bijou Theatre," Keith explained his rationale for charging "popular" prices in his vaudeville halls. "I have stood on the sidewalk mornings and afternoons, watching the people go by; I have seen shoppers walking aimlessly along, their trading over, trying to kill time until the hour for taking their suburban trains; I have seen young men and women unemployed who have glanced in upon various theatre entrances, and their faces have told either the desire for matinee performances upon off days, or prices at other times within their reach. Then I asked myself what could be done with the Bijou at cheap prices. If I were to sell an orchestra chair for twenty-five cents, four times a day, it would be just as lucrative to me as if sold once for a dollar."[7]

To reach the widest possible public at the least possible cost, the vaudeville managers advertised regularly in the daily newspapers. Each ad highlighted the price of tickets and listed every act on the bill, from the headliner to the midget dogs. As Roger Brett has written about the Keith organization in Providence in the 1880s, "at a time when other theaters considered a two column by four inch ad to be large enough for any show, Keith doubled and quadrupled that size." Keith and Albee bought advertising in every newspaper in the community. They advertised the opening of their new Pawtucket theater in the local

Vaudeville theaters like this one presenting "continuous vaudeville" for five and ten cents a seat could be found on the shopping and entertainment streets of most large and small American cities. Note the baby strollers parked next to the entrance on the right. (*Library of Congress, Prints and Photographs Division.*)

English-language papers and in the German, French, and Italian papers.[8]

In return for paid advertising, the newspapers opened their pages to entertainment "news" and "reviews." By the middle 1890s, one could not pick up a newspaper anywhere in the country without coming

across notices, ads, reviews, interviews, features, and photographs of
the stars and shows that were appearing that week in the major vaudeville halls. Most of this material had been written beforehand by press
agents and publicists. The newspapers published it, often exactly as
they received it. Even the "reviews" contained catch phrases taken
directly from the press releases. The weekend before Edmund Day
opened at Keith's Theater in Pawtucket, Rhode Island, in January
1904, identical articles appeared in the *Olneyville Times,* the *P. V.
Gleaner,* the *Bristol Phenix,* the *Herald-News* in Taunton, Massachusetts, just across the border, and the *Providence Bulletin.* In the days to
come, similar versions of the same story would appear in the *Providence Telegram, News,* and *Journal,* the *Pawtucket Gazette* and *Times,*
and the local French-, German-, and Italian-language papers.[9]

To city folk who could afford no other form of live theatrical entertainment, vaudeville must have appeared as a godsend. For a dime,
they received hours of entertainment from dozens of acts, including at
least one "headliner." And the vaudeville theater was open six days a
week, from noon to near midnight, extending the temporal boundaries
of the leisure world from nighttime into daylight. Unlike the first-class
theaters with their Wednesday matinees and select audiences of
wealthy "matinee girls," the afternoon shows attracted a heterogeneous
population of men, women, and children who were invited to steal time
away from work or family responsibilities to take in the show. In New
York City, F. F. Proctor who had leased a theater on 23rd Street, a short
walk from the Ladies' Mile department stores, specially advertised
what he called his "Ladies Club Theater," which opened at 11:00 A.M.
According to the vaudeville historian Joe Laurie, Jr., Proctor "slogan-
ize[d] the town with thousands of one-sheets, snipes, and newspaper
ads, all shouting 'After Breakfast Go to Proctor's.'"[10]

To attract an audience large enough to keep their theaters filled all
day, the vaudeville managers had to include "something for everybody"
on their programs. As Edward Albee explained in his own pretentious
prose, "In the arrangement of the ideal vaudeville program, there is
one or more sources of complete satisfaction for everybody present, no
matter how 'mixed' the audience may be. In vaudeville 'there is always
something for everybody,' just as in every state and city, in every county
and town in our democratic country, there is opportunity for everybody, a chance for all."[11]

In providing "something for everybody," vaudeville borrowed from
every nineteenth-century popular entertainment form: blackface

Proctor's 23rd Street vaudeville theater was within walking distance of the Ladies'
Mile department stores in Manhattan. Note the line of women customers waiting
to enter the theater for a matinee performance starring Lillian Russell. (*Museum
of the City of New York.*)

sketches, sentimental ballads, soft-shoe dances, and banjo players from
the minstrel show; acrobats and animal acts from the circus; skits,
satires, and full-costume "flash" acts from musical comedy; one-act
playlets from the legitimate theater; magicians, mind readers, and curio
freaks from the dime museums; monologists from the medicine show;
classical musicians from the symphony hall; opera singers from the
opera hall; sports stars from the boxing rings and baseball stadia. In
rapid succession, female impersonators, song and dance men, operatic
sopranos, jugglers, dancing bears, storytellers, pantomimists, masters of
prestidigitation, strongmen, whistlers, puppeteers, banjo players, acrobats, and comedy teams tumbled on and off the stage. If you weren't a
fan of "The Freeman Sisters in their New Vocal Sketch entitled 'Flirta-
tion,'" you simply had to wait ten or fifteen minutes until they left the
stage to be followed by Gus Williams and his "Dutch Character Songs
and Sayings." If you were bored by "Del Bartino, the great fire king, in
a new and novel fire act, entitled 'The Devil's Care,'" all you had to do

was sit back and await "Miss Flora Story, the queen of the African harp."[12]

Though many of these acts skirted the thin edge of indecency, few went beyond it. As Robert Snyder has argued, "vaudeville's exuberant, irreverent, sensual style of music, drama, and comedy" was far from puritanical. Vaudeville's comics, dancers, music, and sketches "sometimes directly, sometimes indirectly" challenged prevailing standards of moral purity and restraint. But this was all done, as it were, on the sly, never publicly acknowledged or even hinted at by the entrepreneurs who presented the acts or the audiences who cheered them on.[13]

The vaudeville managers, on the contrary, plastered the town with their good intentions. Visiting journalists and critics were lectured on the stringent oversight exercised by managers and directed to dressing-room signs such as the one Edwin Royle reproduced in his 1899 *Scribner's* article:

NOTICE TO PERFORMERS.

You are hereby warned that your act must be free from all vulgarity and suggestiveness in words, action, and costume, while playing in any of Mr. ———'s houses, and all vulgar, double-meaning and profane words and songs must be cut out of your act before the first performance. . . .

Such words as Liar, Slob, Son-of-A-Gun, Devil, Sucker, Damn, and all other words unfit for the ears of ladies and children, also any reference to questionable streets, resorts, localities, and bar-rooms, are prohibited under fine of instant discharge.

——— ———,

General Manager[14]

This outpouring of publicity not only drew attention from what was actually occurring on the stage, but also it congratulated the vaudeville audience on its good taste and moral sensibilities. Audience members, still unsure as to whether or not they should be paying their dimes and quarters to see variety acts in cheap theaters, were reassured that in doing so they were certifying their inclusion in a new and expanding respectable public for respectable amusements.

Much of this publicity was directed at women who were doubly prized by the vaudeville impresarios: as customers and as icons of decency. Women remained, at the turn of the century, the emblems and guarantors of middle- and working-class respectability, even though many were, at this precise historical moment, challenging the notion that the only proper amusements for the "gentler sex" were those that were sponsored by church or confined to the home.[15]

The presence of women has often been taken as a sign of embourgeoisement, of the transformation of raw and rough working-class amusements into more genteel, middle-class recreations. This was certainly the message that the show businessmen wanted to convey with their "ladies welcome" and "family entertainment" signs. But the effect of the women on the commercial amusements they patronized was both less and more than this. Their presence did not guarantee that off-color remarks, jokes, and skits would be removed. What it did do was mark the theater as a suitable arena for respectable folk to spend time in. The primary distinguishing mark of the "refined" vaudeville was not the show on stage but the women in the audience. A mixed audience was by definition a respectable one, a male-only one, indecent.

To attract women to their entertainments, the vaudeville impresarios arranged special matinees, advertised "Ladies Invitation Nights" where women were admitted for free, and showered them with a variety of gifts, from coal, flour, and hams, to bonnets, dress patterns, and dresses. But gifts were not enough to convince "respectable" women that they were indeed welcome in the vaudeville theaters. The show businessmen had to remove the prostitutes who had been a visible and accepted part of nineteenth-century concert saloons, honky-tonks, variety halls, and theaters. No respectable woman could visit a site where she might encounter or, worse yet, be taken for a streetwalker.[16]

Smoking had to be regulated because the smoke permeated the vaudeville hall with noxious odors and because it signified that the space it filled was for men only. Drinking also had to be controlled. Tony Pastor was the first show businessman to ban liquor from his theater in 1881 (though he conveniently kept a refreshment stand next door). Through the latter nineteenth and early twentieth centuries, other vaudeville impresarios followed his lead by restricting drinking to intermissions or removing bars from the premises entirely.[17]

The vaudeville managers succeeded in attracting large numbers of women to their shows because they kept their prices low *and* made the women feel comfortable inside. Even young shop girls and sales ladies who had to fight with their parents or scrimp and save to support an occasional night out were joining the crowd at the vaudeville hall. Louise Montgomery found that the subject of "leisure time [was] one of the greatest causes of family clashing" among Chicago's working girls and their mothers, because the girls demanded "a freedom in the use of their evening hours" that their parents were reluctant to grant them.[18]

Women who lived with roommates in boarding houses had more freedom to "go out" than those who remained at home but less money to pay their own way. Many had to "date," or, as one contemporary writer put it, play the "sex game," making implicit bargains with men who paid for a night out at the theater in return for "limited sexual favors."[19]

Women who would not have imagined accompanying their male friends or husbands to the saloon volunteered to go with them to the vaudeville hall. Mothers attended the weekday matinees with or without their children in tow. Suburban shoppers in town for the day took time out from their chores to visit the "continuous run" theaters within walking distance of the department stores. The recreation surveys undertaken after 1910 reported, some in a rather surprised tone, that women made up a significant portion of the vaudeville audience. They comprised one-third of the audience in New York City in 1910. Women and children made up 48 percent of the audience in San Francisco in 1912, 45 percent in Milwaukee in 1914, and comparable percentages in other cities.[20]

The vaudeville impresarios had begun by assembling an audience out of the vast numbers of city folk who could afford no more than ten to twenty-five cents for an evening's entertainment. Each "act" on the bill had its own special constituency. The animal acts appealed to the younger children, the slapstick comedians to the older boys and young men, the female singers to the lady shoppers. New kinds of acts could be added to bring in new customers.

To attract the male-only saloon crowd, vaudeville managers announced the scores of important home-town games and invited baseball players, wrestlers, tennis players, airship pilots, even the winners of Six Day Bicycle races to celebrate their victories on the vaudeville stage. Female swimmers were especially prized because they could appear in their swimsuits, further enhancing their appeal to the sporting crowd. As the manager of the Keith theater in Philadelphia reported in October of 1902, "A bunch of young and shapely girls is a good thing in any variety show." Boxers were also big attractions. City folk who would never have dreamed of attending an actual match could for a quarter sit in a comfortable seat in a "clean" theater and watch John L. Sullivan, Jack Johnson, Jim Jeffries, and other champions act in specially devised playlets or sing, dance, joke, and spar a few rounds on the vaudeville stage.[21]

In this era before moving pictures and radio, only vaudeville and the daily papers could bring celebrities before the public. The newspapers identified and marked individuals for celebrity; the vaudeville theaters capitalized on the marking by parading the notorious across their stages to tell their stories or reenact the events that had made them famous. Evelyn Nesbit, whose husband had murdered architect Stanford White, was a big vaudeville attraction, as were the "Shooting Stars," Lillian Graham and Ethel Conrad, who had achieved celebrity by placing "bullets in the leg of W. E. D. Stokes, a social registerite." Alexander Pantages who operated a circuit of theaters west of the Mississippi supplemented his regular variety program with local outlaws such as Ed Morrell, the youngest member of the Evans-Sontag gang in California, just released after sixteen years in prison, and "Convict 6630—The Man Who Sang Himself Out of the Penitentiary," an ex-forger named George Schroder.[22]

The celebrity acts extended the vaudeville audience laterally by bringing in customers who read the daily papers. The vaudeville impresarios also wanted to extend it upward to new and more prosperous social groupings. To accomplish this, they recruited and booked what they referred to as their "gold-brick" or "dignity" acts. F. F. Proctor tried to attract upscale lady shoppers by signing Italo Campanini, a famous operatic tenor, to appear at his 23rd Street theater. Keith and Albee preferred as their "gold bricks" such stars of the legitimate stage as Mrs. Drew and Maurice Barrymore, who read, recited, and performed in specially condensed one-act playlets and sketches. As it became apparent that the "gold bricks" were, in Keith's words, attracting "the attention of a desirable class of patrons," more were added to the vaudeville bills, among them entertainers as varied in their talents as the "greatly respected and admired performer on the women's club and garden circuits," Mrs. Alice Shaw, who whistled; Edouard Remenyi, a concert violinist, who "at his opening bill" performed "Hearts and Flowers," the "Melody in F," and "Mendelssohn's Spring Song"; and stars from European stages, the opera, the classical concert hall, and the ballet, all of them only too happy—for the right price—to condense their art into fifteen-minute vaudeville turns.[23]

By incorporating the "gold bricks" into their program, impresarios distanced vaudeville further from the male-only variety shows and concert saloons. As the *Dramatic Mirror* exclaimed rather breathlessly in 1897, "By winning over to the varieties some who have acted only in serious drama the distinctions between theaters of various quality have been lessened, and art begins to tell for what it is, a democracy being instituted that can work no harm to a right cause." Although the vaudeville halls, even the highest priced, continued to charge much less than the first-class playhouses and musical comedy theaters, the social distance between the two decreased. It was no longer unthinkable, as William Morris proudly reported in 1909, for "the same audiences who on Monday nights patronize a two dollar Broadway opening" to attend a vaudeville performance on Tuesday—"and with considerable pleasure."[24]

To enhance their own status further—and that of their "shows"—the vaudeville impresarios built their own "palaces," as luxurious as any in the land. As the promotional pamphlet celebrating the 1894 opening of B. F. Keith's "New Theatre" in Boston exclaimed, "It may be stated at the outset that [this theater] is the handsomest, most solidly constructed, most elaborately decorated, and most sumptuously appointed amusement establishment on the face of the earth." Inside the theater was a "'Bureau of Information' [with] telephone, messenger-call, writing desk with all appurtenances, directories, time-tables, guide books, etc."; a main foyer "which is unquestionably the most magnificent apartment connected with any amusement establishment in the world"; an orchestra reception room; three "sumptuously furnished apartments reserved exclusively for the use of ladies"; a men's smoking room "constantly supplied with all the leading daily papers"; and, on the balcony, a second grand reception room and ladies' parlor, complete with writing desk.[25]

Like the "dignity" acts, the palaces were intended to raise the status of vaudeville and its audience by enveloping what was still a relatively cheap variety show in luxury so extravagant patrons could forget that they were paying half of what it cost to attend the legitimate theater. Keith's Philadelphia hall was proudly referred to as the "million-dollar theater." The pamphlet celebrating the opening of the New Boston Theatre in 1894 reminded audience members—if they hadn't already grasped the point—that "money has been expended here with lavish prodigality."[26]

A decade earlier, in 1884, Keith and Albee had attracted a better class of customers to their dime museum by featuring *The Mikado*. Now, in 1894, they used the same strategy and offered performances by members of the Boston Symphony orchestra to bring Boston's social elites into their vaudeville palace. According to the critic Walter Prichard Eaton, the plan worked wonders, as Mrs. Jack Gardner, the leading socialite, hired a box to hear the orchestra. "What Mrs. Jack did was the signal. Keith's became not only respectable but quite the thing. . . . In the 1890s, middle-class and suburban Boston regarded it as the last word in magnificence, as well as morally and socially respectable. They flocked to it by the thousands."[27]

While Eaton's words must not be taken literally, the palaces did extend the vaudeville audience to include a range of theatergoers who would not, under other circumstances, have set foot within a vaudeville hall. The vaudeville entrepreneurs in the beginning had charged popular prices because their audiences could not or would not pay more. The construction of the new palaces changed all that. Keith and Albee, who had set a top price of twenty-five cents in their first Boston, Providence, and Philadelphia theaters, raised prices for orchestra and box seats in their Boston and Philadelphia palaces to a dollar, then a dollar and a half.

By moving up in class—and in price—what was now known as "big-time" vaudeville opened the door in the early 1900s to countless cut-rate variations, including "small-time," "ten-cent," "nickel," "family," and "tab" theaters. Just as vaudeville's founders had attracted an audience by lowering prices far below those of the first-class legitimate and musical-comedy theaters, so did a second generation of vaudeville impresarios compete with the older, established ones by charging half of what they did: a quarter for their best evening seats, a dime for matinee and gallery seats. Small-time theaters were built on the secondary shopping and entertainment districts to make them accessible to the city's less prosperous residents and workers. As we will see in chapter 14, many of these small-time theaters would in the later 1900s and early 1910s be converted to "combination" houses that alternated full programs of moving pictures with their live acts.

The small-time vaudeville owners and managers called their establishments family theaters to emphasize that they were not only respectable enough but also cheap enough for the entire family. Like their big-time counterparts, the popular-priced theaters offered customers a full bill of entertainment in a "clean" theater. The only real difference between the expensive and the popular-priced shows, except of course for the price, was that the ten-cent theaters were usually (but not always) smaller and less ornate, with bills containing fewer headliners and more moving pictures.[28]

The vaudeville entrepreneurs had cast their net wide, and although they had not yet reached a large number of the city's poorer working-class and immigrant populations, they had succeeded in assembling a huge and heterogeneous audience for their shows. According to the historian Albert McLean, Jr., "the rising class of white-collar workers" continued to make up the largest segment of the vaudeville audience. Even in the cheapest "vaudeville and moving picture shows" on Manhattan's Lower East Side, investigators in 1910 classified the audiences in six of the eight theaters they visited as "middle class" or "mixed," rather than "poor" and used such terms as "fairly well dressed," "fairly prosperous," and "respectable" to describe them. The San Francisco survey of "public recreation" completed in 1911 similarly reported that the audiences in the vaudeville houses were neither "predominantly 'rich' or 'poor'," but "fair-to-do" and "struggling."[29]

The only groups excluded from or segregated within the vaudeville audience were the city's African Americans.* Ethel Waters, who performed in Keith and Albee's Alhambra Theater at Seventh Avenue and 126th Street, recalled in her autobiography that "colored people could buy seats only in the peanut gallery." As far as its theaters were concerned, "125th Street was still a white boulevard." Many African Americans boycotted vaudeville theaters that sequestered them with newsies and rowdies in an upper or second balcony that was never cleaned and accessible only from a back entrance off a dark and dangerous alleyway. In his guidebook on building, managing, and operating a vaudeville theater, Edward Renton suggested that impresarios who wanted to attract more "negroes" should design their halls with one balcony instead of two. "It is well to remember that in some cities the better classes of the negroes have declined to patronize a 'second balcony' reserved for them exclusively and served from a separate ticket-

---

*In this chapter, we consider African Americans solely as audience members. While excluded or segregated from the vaudeville audience, however, they constituted a significant part of the performers on stage. In chapter 4, we will return to African Americans in vaudeville and focus on the performers.

window. Therefore, the better plan is to divide the balcony front and rear and provide a separate ticket-window and stairs for the negro patrons."[30]

The vaudeville entrepreneurs were succeeding in attracting a huge and varied audience because they had secured for their theater and "show" a privileged place in a revised moral taxonomy of public amusement sites and activities. Respectability was correlated not with class background, income, education, or ethnicity but with race, appearance, dress, and deportment. As Warren Susman has argued, in this period of cultural transition what mattered most, at least according to the advice literature, was neither character nor inner moral qualities, but personality, one's ability to get along and make oneself "pleasing to others" by proper grooming, dress, and "good manners."[31]

A decent person was someone who looked and acted decently. The well-dressed dandy or sport who made too much noise, spit on the floor, or appeared drunken in public was, no matter what his social background or education, not decent and, as such, not welcomed in the vaudeville theater. Lower-level white-collar workers, even manual workers, on the other hand, were welcomed into the vaudeville theaters as long as they dressed and acted decently. As Henry James had said of New York hotel society, the token of admission to the vaudeville theater was the "condition" that one "be presumably 'respectable,' be, that is, not discoverably anything else."[32]

Edward Renton, in his book on vaudeville theaters, cautioned managers to instruct box-office attendants to refuse tickets to drunken men and women, avoid seating the "mechanic in overalls . . . where he may be conspicuous," and direct "individuals who are likely to smell 'garlicky' or be poorly dressed" away from the better seats. In the larger vaudeville halls and palaces, ushers, dressed in pseudomilitary garb, patrolled the aisles to enforce minimal rules of deportment. Signs and underlined program announcements further instructed audiences not to snack, chat, drink, smoke, boo or cheer too loudly, or walk the aisles while the show was in progress.[33]

Ushers and written rules, no matter how strict and censorious they might have been, never quite succeeded in transforming the vaudeville halls into churches, school libraries, or concert halls. Nor were they supposed to. Though Keith and Albee were happy to have their theaters referred to as the "Sunday School Circuit," they were well aware that Sunday Schools did not attract many paying customers. While the women might have taken off their hats in the auditorium and the boys softened their cheers and jeers, few vaudeville patrons behaved as if they were in church or school. The "restraint of emotion in the theater," which Richard Sennett has identified as the hallmark of the middle-class audience, was not only absent but also actively undermined in the vaudeville theaters. Instead, vaudeville provided its patrons with the opportunity to display their emotions in public.[34]

In its "something for everyone" democracy, in its exaltation of good, "clean," but not too "clean" fun, in its unholy assortment of the crude and the classical, in the short attention span it required of its audience, even in its racism, vaudeville was becoming a quintessential American institution. As Edwin Milton Royle concluded in his essay on vaudeville in *Scribner's Magazine* for October 1899, "Vaudeville is very American. It touches us and our lives at many places. It appeals to the business man, tired and worn, who drops in for half an hour on his way home; to the person who has an hour or two before a train goes, or before a business appointment; to the woman who is wearied of shopping; to the children who love animals and acrobats; to the man with his sweetheart or sister; to the individual who wants to be diverted but doesn't want to think or feel; to the American of all grades and kinds who wants a great deal for his money. The vaudeville theater belongs to the era of the department store and the short story. It may be a kind of lunch-counter art, but then art is so vague and lunch is so real."[35]

CHAPTER 4

"The Best Smelling Crowd in the World"

V AUDEVILLE WAS THE ERA'S MOST POPULAR form of live entertainment, but it was by no means the only one. Live drama, melodrama, musical comedy, and revues of every kind prospered as never before in the late 1890s and early 1900s, their expansion fueled, as vaudeville's had been, by a spectacular increase in the number of popular-priced theaters. Between 1890 and 1900, the combined seating capacity of New York City's theaters more than doubled. Between 1880 and 1900, the number of shows touring the nation, many after runs in New York, increased from about fifty to over 500.[1]

Vaudeville's commercial success had revealed the existence of a huge, heterogeneous public for "clean," popular-priced amusements. What *Theatre Magazine* wrote of the "average New Yorker" in 1904 could be applied to city folk elsewhere. They were taking their "amusement seriously. It [was], indeed, part of [their] regular life."[2]

Those who continued to regard the theater as the devil's workshop were not as vocal or as influential as they had been in the mid-nineteenth century. Theatergoers no longer had to make excuses to others or themselves for "going out" at night. The reconfigured moral taxonomy of public amusements was most visibly reflected in theater architecture. Earlier nineteenth-century theater owners, as if ashamed of their product, had hidden it from public view. Auditoria were lo-

New York City's Casino Theatre was designed in 1882 as a concert hall, but it quickly became one of the city's premier showcases for light opera and burlesque. Note the attraction boards set up on the street all around the theater to draw pedestrians' attention to current and future productions. (*Courtesy of The New-York Historical Society, New York, N.Y.*)

cated on the second floor of multiple-use buildings, with only a placard out front to point the way to the stairs. Designed like banks or courthouses or, as an English observer noted of New York's Park Theater, with exteriors that were almost "prisonlike" in their austerity, mid-nineteenth-century American theaters had concealed their contents so effectively that one New York critic complained that theatergoers needed a guide to find them.[3]

One of the first theaters designed to attract attention to itself was the Casino Theatre, built in 1882 on Broadway and 39th Street, still the northern frontier of civilized nightlife in Manhattan. Instead of disguising the fact that the Casino was a palace of pleasure, the architects highlighted the building's function as conspicuously as they could. As the *New-York Tribune* critic noted at the theater's opening, the Moorish architectural forms "and the soaring round towers and bold outlines of the exterior are sure to strike the eyes of all visitors to the vicinity of Broadway and 39th Street."[4]

The Casino was a harbinger of facades to come. Through the 1890s and early 1900s, theater entrances would be studded with hundreds of twinkling, colored light bulbs, blazing a welcome onto the street and "advertising in permanent form the character of the transient delights and attractions within."[5]

Live theater prospered at the turn of the century because a new generation of theater impresarios was learning the calculus of commercial amusements. Frederic Thompson, the future owner of Luna Park, who had relocated to Buffalo for the 1901 world's fair, was astonished at the lack of business acumen exhibited by theater owners who "still catered to the carriage trade to the exclusion of the mass middle-class audience which had grown up around them." Thompson estimated that by keeping their prices well above a dollar, Buffalo's theater owners were excluding 75 percent of their potential audience. In New York City, alone, he "counted as many as three million New Yorkers" who were priced out of the city's musical comedy and dramatic theaters, because they could not afford two-dollar orchestra seats and had "too much self respect to go up in the gallery." When Thompson opened his own massive theater in New York City, the Hippodrome, he set prices at twenty-five cents to a dollar to accommodate this crowd of city folk.[6]

Theater owners across the country were, like Thompson, recognizing that it was far better to lower prices and play to full houses than to keep prices high and theaters half-empty. A new species of theater, the "ten-twenty-thirty," the name taken from the ticket prices that ranged from thirty cents for the best seats in the house to a dime for the upper balcony, symbolized the new order of public amusements. According to the journalist Marian Spitzer, the "ten-twenty-thirties" filled the same role at the turn of the century as moving pictures would in 1925. "Thousands attended the [full-priced] theater then, but hundreds of thousands attended the 10-20-30."[7]

The "ten-twenty-thirties" relied heavily on "blood and thunder" melodramas with big visual climaxes. Heroes, heroines, and villains were readily identifiable; plots turned on barely concealed "tricks and artifices"; only dialogue with "bounce to it" was permitted; actors and actresses punctuated every line with overdrawn gestures. Audiences were almost literally led by the hand through the dramas, signaled when to giggle with delight or sigh in distress.[8]

In San Francisco, where impresario after impresario had failed to turn a consistent profit at the Grand Opera House, Walter Morosco in 1894 cut prices dramatically, assembled a resident stock company to perform weekly melodramas, and filled the house for the next five years and 5,635 performances. In Chatterton, Illinois, the old—and failing—opera house was transformed into a "ten-twenty-thirty" in 1896. "The gallery-gods and their best girls," working people who had previously been restricted to the upper balconies, now "took possession of the orchestra and the parquet." In Toledo, Ohio, the Burt Theater was converted to "ten-twenty-thirty" melodramas in 1905 with great success. That season, 488 performances of 64 plays were presented with an average monthly audience of over 45,000.[9]

In many cities, enterprising theater owners, recognizing the potential in the "untapped market for low-cost entertainment," assembled stock companies to perform new and standard works at popular prices. By the early 1900s, stock had become so popular—and profitable—that a number of vaudeville impresarios, F. F. Proctor, Keith and Albee, and Sylvester Poli among them, had assembled companies that bore their names.[10]

The proliferation of popular-priced theaters made it easier than ever before for city folk to see live theater. In Chicago, where the population increased by 24 percent between 1896 and 1909, the seating capacity of the popular-priced theaters (those with seats priced at ten or fifteen cents) increased by 118 percent. The figures for Denver, Philadelphia, and other cities were similar.[11]

Small- and medium-size cities that had in the 1880s been starved for

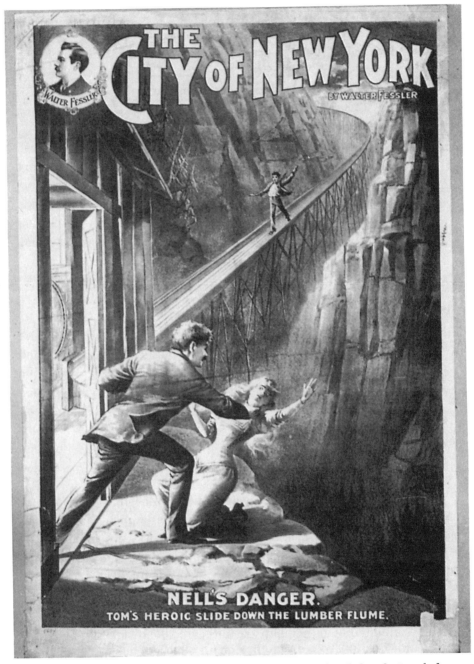

Huge posters like these were used to advertise the "blood and thunder" melodramas that were standard fare at the cheap theaters. These posters, originally printed in color, are from 1897. (*Library of Congress, Prints and Photographs Division.*)

live entertainment were by the late 1890s and early 1900s visited by dozens of theatrical troupes all year long. In Boonville, Missouri, the Stephens Opera House, which had been renovated in 1901, hosted "a succession of Broadway successes" and perennial touring favorites: *The Wizard of Oz;* James J. Corbett, the former heavyweight champion, in *Gentlemen Jim;* and "Beautiful Edna May, starring as a Salvation Army Lassie in *The Belle of New York*," who according to one local author was "still cherished [a half century later] for her musical lament, 'I tell them to follow, follow Jesus, but they always follow, follow me.'"[12]

-+*➡◯⫥*+-

Like the vaudeville audience, the audiences for the popular-priced live theaters, stock companies, and "ten-twenty-thirties" were made up in large part by the city's new and expanding ranks of lower-level white-collar workers. These groups of city residents formed a large part of the "decent" folk the show businessmen were trying to attract with "respectable" entertainment at popular prices. As *Theatre Magazine* observed in 1903, the rapid expansion of the cheap stock companies had been fueled by the patronage of small clerks "on a salary of $25 or $30 a week." While the experts had proclaimed the stock system dead, a new generation of companies was drawing "huge audiences from that large, intelligent, and ever growing class of people to whom fifty cents for an evening at the theater means a considerable outlay." When, in 1912, George Bevans and his team of sociology majors from New York City colleges surveyed "How Workingmen Spend Their Spare Time," they found that the clerical workers spent more time at the dance halls, the movies, and the theater than men in any other job classification. Sixty-six percent of the 135 men employed in clerical positions reported that they had gone to the theater that week. The sociologist Louise Marion Bosworth in her 1907–1909 study of 450 Boston working women found that "sales" and "clerical" workers spent more of their income on "recreation" than did professionals, waitresses, or factory and kitchen workers. Louise More included only one white-collar family in her budget study of twelve "typical" working families, but it spent more on amusements than the other eleven (sixteen dollars for weekly trips to the theater and an unnamed sum for family trips to Coney Island).[13]

The Cleveland Foundation's recreation survey also found that white-collar workers went out most often. D., the son of Eastern European Jewish immigrants, had gone to shows only "once a month" when he worked in factories. Since assuming the position of "chief clerk and assistant head in the planning department," however, he had begun to go out "once or twice a week." F., another Eastern European immigrant who had become the "head of the order department" of a "large business house in Cleveland," similarly went "to two or three shows a week."[14]

The shows these clerks and "assistant" department heads saw in their local "ten-twenty-thirties" were not unlike those being performed at ticket prices ten times higher in the downtown opera halls and play-houses. If there was a hierarchical division between the high-priced and the popular-priced audiences, it was not based on the contents of the shows. The only discernable difference was in timing. It took a season or two for current productions to reach the cheaper theaters. Theater historian Glenn Hughes's listing of Broadway openings in 1903 reads like the standard repertory of the popular-priced stock companies and "ten-twenty-thirties." "Farce followed melodrama, and sentimental comedy followed farce: *Mice and Men, The Earl of Pawtucket, A Fool and His Money, My Wife's Husbands, Under Cover, Are You My Father?, Raffles, The Marriage of Kitty, What's the Matter with Susan?*—these titles tell the story."[15]

Wherever they looked, in vaudeville, musical comedy, or melodrama, Yiddish and English, the critics found an excess of theatricality and a deficiency in intelligence. "The Bowery stage," F. H. McLean commented in an 1899 report for the University Settlement Society, was "coarse and nasty," but that "coarseness and nastiness" was no worse than "the plays dealing with the relations of the sexes which have much vogue in some of the uptown theaters." The Twentieth Century Club of Boston reached the same conclusions after its exhaustive study of "The Amusement Situation" in Boston: "A large proportion of the entertainments" in the high-priced theaters were "of a strikingly vulgar character, approaching burlesque or vaudeville."[16]

According to Walter Prichard Eaton of the *New York Sun*, early twentieth-century city dwellers were so hungry for entertainment and so fearful of being "bored" at home that they were buying tickets to anything, no matter how poorly written, staged, or acted. *Theatre Magazine* complained in 1904 of "theatrecitis" and of the "theatromaniac" who was incapable of making distinctions between different types of amusement. "To him 'Götterdämmerung' and the Siamese twins are equivalent in their respective capacities to make the hour flee. Giving 'Macbeth' no captious preference to Barnum's trained giraffes, neither does he rate the subtile satire of Henrik Ibsen below the popular platitudes of Hall Caine. He ascribes the same quantity of merit to these several forms of art, rejecting none, affecting all. He looks upon, and partially denominates, every performance given at an opera house, an ordinary theatre, or musical hall as a 'show.'"[17]

George Jean Nathan, a bit more acerbic than most, represented the critical consensus when, in the moving conclusion of *The Popular Theatre,* he admitted that all his previously held notions about the theater had been mistaken. The theater, even in its highest priced, most elegant, and exclusive Broadway showplaces, was, he confessed, no more nor less than "a place for light amusement . . . simply, plainly—and in the soundest critical definition—a place where a well-educated, well-bred, well-fed man may find something to divert him pleasurably for a couple of hours." The early twentieth-century theater was not to be confused with or measured against the "university, the studio and the art gallery." It was more akin to "the circus, the rathskeller, and the harem." Theatergoers did not seek enlightenment, instruction, or uplift, but "horse-play, belly laughter, pretty girls, ingenious scenery, imported ladies of joy and eminent home talent, insane melodramas, lovely limbs, lively tunes, gaudy colours, loud humours, farce, flippancy, fol-de-rol."[18]

It is difficult from our vantage point to evaluate criticisms as unrelenting and negative as those leveled by the turn-of-the-century analysts. While the prevailing theme of "declension"—that standards were in a state of rapid and irreversible decline—was not unique to this generation, their near unanimity and the vitriol with which they laced their attack is testimony to some sort of historical change.

The critics were probably wrong to characterize theater audiences as uniformly illiterate or unintelligent. But they had grasped an essential fact about the new amusements. They demanded little or no preparation or mental concentration from their audiences. The excessive theatricality, the bombast and spectacle, broad humor and coarse characterizations were designed to bypass the intelligence entirely. Education and taste on the part of theatergoers were entirely superfluous. Money and usually not very much of it provided all the "access" one needed to enter the theater and enjoy the show.*

The best marker of this change may be found in the new and abundant use of the term "show" to describe theatrical products and "the show business" to refer to the industry that produced and profited from them.† The term itself covered a myriad of entertainment forms. A "show" could be made up of several discrete acts as in vaudeville, one extended (if not always coherent) narrative, or a combination of narrative and acts as in musical comedy. The contents of the "show" were easily transplanted from genre to genre. Scaled-down, one-act versions of the dramatic repertory were imported onto the vaudeville stage. Boxers played themselves in melodramas and starred in musical comedies. Classical musicians sang outdoors at amusement parks. Cowboys left their Wild West shows to rope and ride their way across Broadway stages. Comedians, dancers, and singers moved gracefully from vaudeville to musical theater to legitimate stage to movie screen and back again.[19]

⭤

The marking of diverse entertainments as "shows" obscured the differences between audiences, but it did not obliterate them. Taking in a show at the vaudeville hall or "ten-twenty-thirty" was a different type of experience with a different significance for lower-level white-collar workers than for prosperous theatergoers. The rapid increase in white-collar positions, many of them filled by the daughters and sons of immigrants and blue-collar workers, had, as we will see, generated enormous confusion over class boundaries. The white-collar workers who "went out" in such great numbers at the turn of the century may have done so not simply to have fun but also because they experienced in the world of commercial amusements a temporary resolution of that confusion.

---

*As Pierre Bourdieu has so masterfully argued in *Distinction: A Social Critique of the Judgement of Taste,* trans. Richard Nice (Cambridge, Eng., 1984), individuals whose middle-class standing is based entirely on their possession of "cultural" as opposed to "financial" capital are "disposed" to privilege the place of "culture" in daily life. This was the case with the majority of American theater critics who were well-educated and endowed with "taste" rather than property or financial capital.

†The exact derivation of the term is difficult to locate. It was first used in the United States around the 1880s, with the article "the" preceding "show," as in "the show business."

Eric Hobsbawm in *The Age of Empire: 1875-1914* devotes an entire chapter, "Who's Who or the Uncertainties of the Bourgeoisie," to the theme of white-collar confusion. In England at the turn of the century, he has written, "the boundaries between the bourgeoisie and its inferiors were . . . far from clear. . . . The real difficulty arose with the enormous expansion of the tertiary sector—of employment in public and private offices—that is to say of work which was both clearly subaltern and remunerated by wages (even if they were called 'salaries'), but which was also clearly non-manual. . . . The line between this new 'lower-middle class' of 'clerks' and the higher ranges of the professions . . . raised novel problems," especially in the United States, where, according to Hobsbawm, the "new petty bourgeoisie of office, shop and subaltern administration . . . were, by 1900, already larger than the actual working class."[20]

The explosive growth of white-collar employment in the late nineteenth and early twentieth centuries played havoc with class identities. Were the new clerical and sales employees workers in white collars or a middle class of wage earners? There was no simple answer to this question. Borrowing Erik Olin Wright's terminology, we can conclude only that the new white-collar workers occupied "contradictory locations" in the class structure. Like the proletariat, they lacked assets in capital; but like the established middle classes, their material interests were not always in harmony with those of manual workers.[21]

In the final analysis, it is perhaps fruitless, as Ilene DeVault suggests in her study of Pittsburgh's clerical workers, to try to place the white-collar workers in either the working or middle classes. "The collar line," she argues, "was not so much a social chasm as it was a social estuary, a site for the mingling of economic groups and social influences. . . . In fact, these early clerical workers themselves could choose between these identities, opting for whichever one best fit their own purposes in a given situation."[22]

These ambiguities over social boundaries were exacerbated by the movement of immigrant children into clerical and sales positions, upsetting what had been for most of the nineteenth century a fairly straightforward labor market segregation of "natives" in white collars and immigrants and ethnics in blue collars. In Worcester, Massachusetts, where only 5 percent of Irish Americans had white-collar positions in 1880, fully one-quarter had such jobs at the turn of the century. The same was true in Chicago, where by 1900, according to James Gilbert, "the foreign-born or native-born with foreign-born parents filled [white-collar] jobs in approximately the same percentage as they constituted the population."[23]

The designation of lower-level white-collar work as women's work had a similarly disruptive effect on social boundaries. The movement of women workers into offices and retail stores created additional room at the top of the white-collar pyramid for male "middle managers" and what Alfred Chandler has called "lower management." But the feminization of clerical work also played havoc with the social significance of white collars for lower-level clerks and office workers. "Working alongside women in a sense decreased the status of male clerical workers," further damaging the presumption that donning a white collar signified that one had ascended from the working to the middle class.[24]

For urban Americans in general, and white-collar and ethnic workers in particular, the world of commercial amusements represented a privileged sphere of daily life outside the mundane social world with its confusions and contradictions. Everywhere else—at home, in their neighborhoods, and at work—they straddled the social divisions of class and ethnicity. Only in the playgrounds furnished by the show businessmen could they submerge themselves in a corporate body, an "American" public, that transcended these divisions.

For second-generation immigrants caught between their parents' immigrant cultures and urban America, this refuge from social tensions was particularly welcome. As I have argued elsewhere, the children of immigrants found their own way in the new culture, effectively "Americanizing" themselves on the streets and in the city's amusement centers. They spoke English in public, played stickball and potsies, spent their nickels and dimes at the candy store, the vaudeville hall, and the nickelodeon, and whenever possible, mingled with "Americans" in the downtown shopping and entertainment districts. This process of "Americanization" through participation in the city's public amusements did not cease at the boundaries of adult life. Many second-generation immigrants, as Kathy Peiss writes of New York's working women, "came to identify 'cheap amusements' as the embodiment of American urban culture." "Mass culture," as Lizabeth Cohen has written of Chicago's ethnic communities, "provided an ideal vehicle for expressing independence and becoming more American." Just as the young boys advertised their inclusion in the new culture by memorizing batting averages, and the young girls by wearing fancy hats with ostrich-plume feathers, second-generation immigrants displayed their familiarity and comfort with American culture by attending the vaudeville hall, the "ten-twenty-thirties," and as we will see in subsequent chapters, by going out to the amusement park, dancing the new "animal" dances, and regularly taking in the picture show in their neighborhood theaters and the downtown movie palaces.[25]

⊹⊱══◐══◑⊰⊹

The new amusements and amusement spaces afforded residents of divided cities the experience of belonging to social groupings that were totalizing rather than divisive, or, to employ the anthropologist Victor Turner's terms, generous rather than snobbish, inclusive rather than exclusive. Going out provided a momentary escape not simply from one's particular class and ethnic group but also from a society differentiated along these lines to "an alternative and more 'liberated' way of being socially human."[26]

Though individual audiences remained segregated by class and income, with the prosperous attending the downtown theaters that charged a dollar or more for orchestra seats, and the clerks and stenographers going to the "ten-twenty-thirties," they were all part of a larger national public for commercial amusements. The bills, fliers, posters, marquees, and newspaper advertisements that carried the magic words, "Straight from Broadway," confirmed for theatergoers that no matter how distant they might be from the two-dollar seats on the "Great White Way," no matter where they had come from or were returning to after the show, they were, for an hour or two at least, part of what the journalist Edwin Slosson would later identify as that "ordinary American crowd, the best natured, best dressed, best behaving and best smelling crowd in the world."[27]

CHAPTER 5

The "Indecent" Others

W HILE THE DOORS OF COMMERCIAL AMUSE-
ments were opening far wider than ever before, not everyone
was being welcomed inside. "Decency" remained the essential element
in determining who would and would not be permitted within the public amusement sites, but decency in the abstract was too evanescent a
notion. To sustain its integrity and utility, it had to be concretized
through reference to an immutably "indecent" other. This was the role
assigned to African Americans.

Racial segregation and racist parody were not invented by turn-of-
the-century showmen. They became constituent elements in commercial amusements because they were already endemic in the larger society and because they provided a heterogeneous white audience with a
unifying point of reference and visible and constant reminders of its
privileged status.*

"White" immigrants and ethnics who dressed appropriately, acted
decently, and had the price of admission were welcomed inside the

*While Asians and Asian Americans were also parodied on stage and segregated or excluded
in some western theaters, they were never as significant a factor in the amusement world.
Most of their leisure time was spent in their own communities; seldom did they venture outside them or attempt to patronize commercial amusements. They were, for this reason, not
affected to the same degree as the African Americans by segregation or exclusion.[1]

commercial amusement centers. As Henry James discovered in 1904 on his return to the United States after a twenty-year absence, the "aliens" were everywhere being rapidly Americanized or, as he put it, magically lifted to a new "level," "glazed . . . over . . . by a huge white-washing brush." Even the Italians, he found, had lost their "colour," which of all the European "races," they had "appeared . . . most to have." James's use of metaphors of color to describe the Americanization of the "alien" was particularly apt. For what most distinguished the European Americans from the African Americans was the former's ability to lose their "colour."[2]

Two years after James revisited America, Ray Stannard Baker, the magazine reporter and sometime muckraker, made his own tour of the country. In the articles and book he published about his journey, Baker made explicit what had been implicit in James's musings about ethnicity and race. He noted that, while the "mingling white races," "the Germans, Irish, English, Italians, Jews, Slavs," were being rapidly assimilated into the "nation we call America," the Negro was still not "accepted as an American. Instead of losing himself gradually in the dominant race, as the Germans, Irish, and Italians are doing, adding those traits or qualities with which Time fashions and modifies this human mosaic called the American nation, the Negro is set apart as a peculiar people." Like "blacks in South Africa, and certain classes in India," Negroes were becoming increasingly segregated, "a people wholly apart—separate in their churches, separate in their schools, separate in cars, conveyances, hotels, restaurants."[3]

This segregation of public facilities was, Baker asserted, a recent development. "Conditions are rapidly changing. A few years ago, no hotel or restaurant in Boston refused Negro guests; now [in 1907] several hotels, restaurants, and especially confectionery stores, will not serve Negroes, even the best of them." North and South, segregation had grown apace with the growth of the cities—and their African-American populations. As C. Van Woodward would assert a half-century later, segregation in the South "did not appear with the end of slavery, but toward the end of the [nineteenth] century and later." It was "essentially an urban, not a rural, phenomenon [that] appeared first in towns and cities and grew as they grew."[4]

Though segregation had by the early 1900s become national policy, reinforced by the 1896 *Plessy v. Ferguson* decision that permitted states and municipalities to establish "separate but equal" public facilities for African-American citizens, there remained significant differences between northern and southern cities. In the North, African Americans did not have to move to the back of trolleys and streetcars, and the segregation of theaters, restaurants, and hotels was generally prohibited by law. Unfortunately, these laws did not stop individual proprietors from establishing their own segregation policies—nor did they mandate that municipal and state judges punish them for doing so. As a result of regional variations and the uneven (sometimes nonexistent) enforcement of antidiscrimination statutes, southern migrants to northern cities never quite knew where they stood. Early twentieth-century Chicago, as James Grossman has written, "had its own racial rules, but [unlike southern cities] they were unwritten and ambiguous."[5]

One generally accepted rule was that first-class downtown theaters had to be segregated. When African-American investigators working for the Chicago Commission on Race Relations in 1919 and 1920 tried to purchase theater tickets on the main floor of one of Chicago's premier playhouses, they were informed that the only remaining seats were in the gallery. "White" customers behind them on line were, however, given their choice of seats. One theater manager, when queried about the behavior of "Negroes," replied that it was not the "conduct of the Negroes [that] was objectionable, but their mere presence."[6]

No matter how wealthy, educated, or distinguished black citizens might be, they had to sit in the upper galleries. Even on Broadway, African Americans who wished to see the black comedy team of Bert Williams and George Walker performing *In Dahomey* had to undergo the humiliating experience of entering the theater by a back entrance and taking seats in the upper galleries. Though such segregation was expressly illegal, the *New York Times* explained, it was necessary because white theatergoers did not enjoy sitting alongside blacks.[7]

African Americans did not, of course, passively condone such discrimination. In issue after issue of *Crisis,* the weekly W. E. B. Du Bois edited for the National Association for the Advancement of Colored People, there were stories about legal actions initiated to enforce antidiscrimination statutes. G. O. Cochran sued a theater proprietor in Los Angeles for refusing "him admittance to the first floor on the ground of color" and won fifty dollars plus court costs. Mary Scott, a white woman, and Hattie Jones, who worked for her, sued the Chicago theater manager who told them that they could only sit together in the gallery, not in Mrs. Scott's box, because "white patrons did not care to sit in boxes with colored people." Though such cases occasionally

resulted in decisions for the plaintiffs, the fines levied were seldom sufficient to force any permanent change in seating policy.[8]

African Americans protested against discrimination in white-owned
theaters but realized that the only alternative to patronizing segregated
white theaters was to build their own. As a group of black businessmen
explained in August 1901, "It has long been a source of exasperation to
the leaders of colored society in Chicago that they could not secure box
or orchestra seats in any of the theatres, no matter how much they
were willing to pay or how soon they got in line before the box office
window. . . . This fact has led to the plan of having a colored theatre in
Chicago, controlled by colored people and catering only to colored
patronage." In 1904, Robert Motts opened the Pekin Theatre on
Chicago's South Side with a multitalented stock company of African-
American actors, playwrights, and musicians. The Pekin Stock Company produced an entirely new musical show every two weeks—each
with up to twenty original numbers. Motts's venture proved so successful that within a few years white theater owners had "opened several
theaters on State Street, catering to black patronage and located only a
few blocks south of the Pekin."*[10]

Though few cities could duplicate Chicago in the variety of live
amusements offered by and for African Americans, most large cities by
1910 had at least one black theater. In Jackson, Mississippi, where the
manager of the Century Theatre had "refused to book Negro troupes
and made Negro patrons use the fire escape to reach the gallery," a
group of black businessmen in 1905 opened the American Theatre in
the building that housed the American Trust and Savings Bank, "a
Negro institution." In New Orleans, a black company subleased the
Elysium Theatre to present Billy Kersands' "black" minstrel show. The
theater remained segregated under the new management, but it was
"the white people [who were] treated with secondary consideration,
only having one side of the upper balcony set aside for them, while the
Negroes have the entire orchestra, half of the balcony, the whole pit
and all of the boxes with the exception of one."[11]

In southern cities, the theater-building campaign proceeded with
such alacrity that Salem Tutt Whitney, a black producer and performer,
commented in 1910 that, while Booker T. Washington could hardly

---

*These few blocks on South State Street would later become famous as the "Stroll,"
described by Langston Hughes in 1918 as "a teeming Negro street with crowded theaters,
restaurants, and cabarets. And excitement from noon to noon."[9]

have been thinking of show business when he "maintained that the South is the natural field of endeavor for the colored man . . . a trip through the South will convince one that there had been no more rapid progress along any line than in things theatrical. Every town of importance has its colored play-house, and for the most part they are well attended. From empty storerooms and lots in the walls there have grown many creditable theatres with all the modern equipment, capable of seating from 500 to 1,000 persons."[12]

There were other "ethnic" and "national" theaters in cities across the country, but they were seldom as well-attended as the African-American ones. The Irish in Philadelphia could, if they chose, buy tickets for the "Mae Desmond Players" or travel downtown to see the latest Broadway road show; Russian Jews could patronize cheap English-speaking theaters as well as neighborhood Yiddish houses. Black audiences did not have the luxury of such choices. They patronized the black theaters because they refused to accept segregation in the "white" ones.[13]

✦⟩══◯══⟨✦

The segregation of African Americans comprised one element in their designation as "indecent" others. Equally important was their representation in parodic form on stage. What Douglas Gilbert has written of the early variety theater remained true in vaudeville and musical comedy in the 1890s and early 1900s. "Most of the comedy . . . was racial" or what we would today call ethnic. Reading through vaudeville programs from the early 1900s, one is struck by the way ethnicity and race were used to identify acts. Singers, sketch artists, dancers, comedians, and acrobats were listed on the "bills" as Irish, Hebrew, colored, blackface, or German. The designation referred not to the performers' ethnicity but to the "type" of act they presented. Each "type" spoke its own language, dressed in readily identifiable costumes, and had its own routines. The Irish knockabout comics engaged in a particularly physical brand of comedy, tough-guy routines, dances, and songs. Dutch and German comics dressed in peaked cap, short pants, and large wooden shoes. The "Hebrews" sang and told their stories in "stage" Yiddish.[14]

Some comic teams mixed different types together on stage. Makey and Stewart appeared at Keith and Albee's Union Square Theater on November 24, 1902, "made up" as a "Hebrew" and an "Irishman." The Marx Brothers combined three different stage "ethnicities" in their act. Groucho began in vaudeville playing the Dutch role, which he later

This pen-and-ink drawing, originally published as an illustration for Edwin Royle's 1899 article on vaudeville in *Scribner's,* was entitled "German Dialect Comedians." Audiences would have known immediately from the costumes that these performers were playing "Germans." (*Library of Congress, Prints and Photographs Division.*)

altered only because it was too difficult for him to tell rapid-fire jokes in a "Dutch" accent; Harpo played the knockabout, slapstick Irishman; Chico, the happy-go-lucky Italian. There was a strange reality to the interplay among these ethnic types. As in real life, the "Hebrews," "Irish," and "Italians" fought, misunderstood, and mistrusted one another—but the bickering was "in famiglia" and the "act" usually ended with harmony, if not camaraderie, restored.[15]

Though the ethnic comedic types were immediately identifiable, it was impossible to confuse the stage parody with the real-life immigrant. The presence of ethnics in the audience obligated immigrant impersonators to behave with some degree of sensitivity. Most of the ethnic audience members, already well Americanized, laughed uproariously at the "greenhorn" caricatures, because, in doing so, they were celebrating their new status as urban Americans. Still, there were set limits beyond which those caricatures could not proceed. When those limits were exceeded, the ethnic community, or its most vocal defenders, could be expected to take immediate and direct action, threatening theater managers and performers with negative publicity, boycotts, or worse. The reports from the Keith-Albee managers contain, as Robert Snyder has indicated, "repeated references to cuts of ethnic spoofs and nastier expressions such as 'kike,' 'wop,' and 'dirty little Greek.'" In Chicago, representatives of the Jewish community "agitated . . . over the burlesque Hebrew types seen on the stage" and demanded "the suppression of the stage Jew."[16]

Sharing the vaudeville bill with the ethnic types were the native-born rubes, hicks, and hayseeds; the "gentlemen" in top hats; and the tramps, hoboes, and newsies. The hayseed acts were especially popular with vaudeville audiences who were only too pleased to see their cultural "superiority" acted out on stage. No matter how "green" the immigrants in the audience, they were always more sophisticated than the country bumpkins on the stage. Vaudeville audiences also joined together to hoot the daffy "gentleman" acts like that of Ed Wynn, who made his stage entrance with a pipe in his mouth, a bulldog on a leash, and the college cheer, "Rah, rah, rah. Who pays my bills? Pa and Ma." A different, more sympathetic laughter greeted the tramp and hobo characters. W. C. Fields did his tramp juggler routine on vaudeville stages for years with great success. He was but one of hundreds of hobo performers to appear in vaudeville, musical comedy, and later, like Charlie Chaplin, in silent movies.[17]

The cruelest and most popular of the comedic caricatures were the "coons" or "darkies" whose lineage reached back more than half a century to the antebellum minstrel show, where "stage Negroes" had been played exclusively by whites in blackface.* There were a variety of black comedic characters: the "dandy" preening and bragging about his thick lips, wooly hair, and smart clothes; the imbecile sputtering nonsense and forever "spooked" by hobgoblins; the lazy fool doing all he could to avoid work; the imposter maladroitly impersonating "white" doctors, lawyers, or politicians; and, toward the close of the century,

---

*Well into the twentieth century, whites in blackface would continue to score enormous commercial successes within and outside vaudeville. No African-American performer would ever make as much money or win as much fame as Eddie Cantor, Al Jolson, and Sophie Tucker, to mention only the most famous of the many performers who spent much of their careers in blackface.

the razor-wielding "coon" who was as foolish as his predecessors, but sexual and dangerous as well.

These negative qualities attributed to "blackness" on stage served to unite the audience in a celebration of its own "whiteness." As David Roediger reminds us, "Blackface minstrels were the first self-consciously 'white' entertainers in the world. The simple physical disguise—and elaborate cultural disguise—of blacking up served to emphasize that those on stage were really white and that whiteness really mattered. . . . All whites could easily participate in minstrelsy's central joke, the point of which remained a common, respectable and increasingly smug whiteness under the makeup."[18]

The blackface performers who migrated from minstrelsy to vaudeville and musical comedy in the 1890s and early 1900s played the same kinds of shuffling, bumbling, preening characters. So, tragically, did the African-American comedians, singers, and dancers who began to appear on the vaudeville stage in the middle 1890s and were required to portray—in a more "authentic" fashion—the "darky" characters constructed by white performers in blackface. Bert Williams and George Walker, the first African Americans to play the "big time" in New York City, billed themselves as "The Two Real Coons" to distinguish themselves from white performers in blackface. Other African-American performers, many of whom had toiled for years on backwater minstrelsy circuits, followed Williams and Walker onto the vaudeville stage. Some, like Williams and Walker, attempted to "give style and comic dignity to a fiction that white men had created and fostered." Others distanced themselves from the caricatures they acted out by exaggerating the parody. Billy Kersands claimed to have the largest mouth in the world. Ernest Hogan, who billed himself as "the Unbleached American" and wrote, published, and performed his own "coon" song, "All Coons Look Alike to Me," incorporated watermelon eating into his act.[19]

It is impossible to overstate the popularity of such black misrepresentations in the 1890s and early 1900s. African-American caricatures were a staple of the vaudeville bill, black musicals were playing on Broadway and touring the first-class theaters of the country, and "coon" songs were the hottest-selling item in sheet music. According to James Dormon, "Over six hundred [coon songs] were published during the decade of the 1890s, and the more successful efforts sold in the millions of copies. To take but a single example, Fred Fisher's 'If the Man

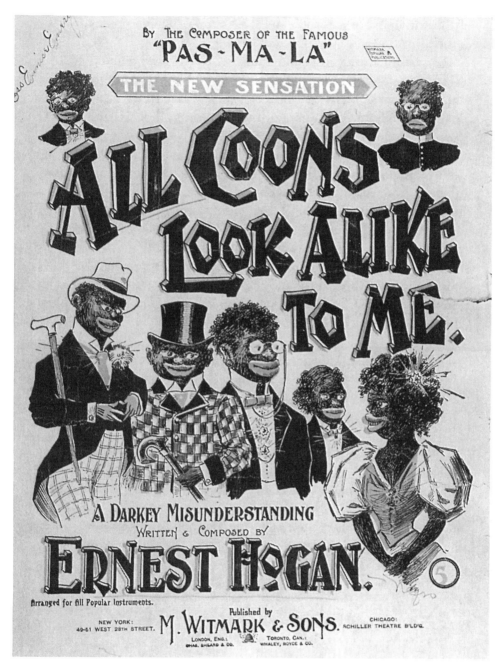

This sheet music cover is for Ernest Hogan's 1896 hit song, "All Coons Look Alike to Me." (*Manuscripts, Archives, and Rare Books Division; Schomburg Center for Research in Black Culture; The New York Public Library; Astor, Lenox, and Tilden Foundations.*)

in the Moon Were a Coon' sold over three million copies in sheet music form, and this was not exceptional."[20]

The intent to caricature and humiliate blacks was evident not only in the coon song lyrics (most often written by whites) but in the illustrations for the sheet music as well. The comic black figure had existed for a long time before the coming of the coon songs, but, according to J. Stanley Lemons, "the treatment of blacks in illustrations [had] presented them as humans." Not so the sheet music of the 1890s that pictured them with animal features. Like the trading cards issued by a number of advertising companies in the late 1880s, the sheet music illustrations showed "blacks with big mouths, big ears, oversized hands and feet, sloping foreheads (meant to indicate limited intelligence), and behaving in exaggerated and ridiculous fashion."[21]

The lyrics were even more explicit in portraying African-American inferiority and indecency. As in the past, "coons" were represented as ignorant, indolent, and dishonest, but increasingly in the early 1900s, they were depicted as bullying and violent as well.[22]

> *I'm the toughest, toughest coon that walks the street,*
> *You may search the wide, wide world my equal never meet;*
> *I got a razor in my boot, I got a gun with which to shoot,*
> *I'm the toughest, toughest coon that walks the street.*[23]

The lyrics of the coon songs, Dormon suggests, conveyed an unmistakable message: "Blacks are potentially dangerous; they must be controlled and subordinated by whatever means necessary. They must also be segregated: set apart, for it was also clear in the coon song lyrics that they wanted to be white—to break down the most important barrier of all—the boundary separating 'us' from 'them.'" The longing to be white included a longing for the power that would come with "whiteness," the power to employ and humiliate white men:

> *I've got a white man working for me,*
> *I'm going to keep him busy you see.*[24]

and to bed white women:

> *I've got a big brunette, and a blond to pet,*
> *I've got 'em short, fat, thin and tall.*[25]

By the early 1900s, African-American performers singing coon songs, dancing cakewalks, and playing the comedic "darky" roles had become so popular and so in demand that white performers who had previously had vaudeville all to themselves began to demand their removal from the stage. A few African-American stars responded by spending more time in Europe and Australia, where, they claimed, there was no race prejudice. However, most black performers, not unused to such bigotry, continued to accept whatever billings came their way regardless of the hostility exhibited by the white performers.[26]

The prejudice of white vaudevillians and the tastes of white audiences strictly circumscribed the performance boundaries of African-American stars. No more than one "colored" act could appear on any vaudeville program at the same time; African Americans (with few exceptions) had to perform in blackface, speak and sing in dialect, wear funny costumes, sing "coon" songs, and end their acts with a cakewalk or some other kind of "darky" dance. While other performers, no matter what their ethnicity, were permitted to regularly "make up" as "blacks," "Hebrews," "Irish," the only groups blacks were allowed to parody were "darkies" and occasionally the Chinese. As a writer in the *Philadelphia Tribune*, a black newspaper, complained in 1907, white people "don't care to see a black man imitate the white folk, but they have nothing to say about George Primrose, Billy West, George Thatcher, Lew Dockstader, George Wilson and a number of other white men, who have got rich by blacking their faces and imitating the Negro." Only in the black theaters were the black performers permitted to imitate whites.[27]

Though many black performers were talented dancers and singers as well as comics, their value on the vaudeville stage resided almost exclusively in their ability to make their white audiences laugh at them. As Theodor Adorno and Max Horkheimer argued, perhaps in exaggerated fashion, in *Dialectic of Enlightenment*, "To laugh at something is always to deride it. . . . A laughing audience is a parody of humanity. . . . Their harmony is a caricature of solidarity." Bert Williams described the source of his audiences' pleasure in much the same terms. He was convinced that his success on stage depended on his humiliation, his always "getting the worst of it." Williams played what he called "the 'Jonah man,' the man who, even if it rained soup, would be found with a fork in his hand and no spoon in sight, the man whose fighting rela-

This sheet music cover is from 1914. Unlike earlier representations of carefree "darkies," this caricature has a sinister, brutish quality to it, representing the "Free and Easy" African American as a potential danger to civilization. (*Manuscripts, Archives, and Rare Books Divisions; Schomburg Center for Research in Black Culture; The New York Public Library; Astor, Lenox, and Tilden Foundations.*)

tives come to visit him and whose head is always dented by the furniture they throw at each other."[28]

Although Williams, like Adorno and Horkheimer, claimed to be speaking of "laughter" in general, not whites laughing at blacks, there can be little doubt that the element of derision in the laughter of the white audience viewing black performers was of a different quality than it would have been had the audience been integrated. Adorno and Horkheimer scorned the "solidarity" of the modern audience as a "caricature," but they did not deny that it was a form of solidarity. The "white" audience assembled to laugh at blacks came away from the experience with a sense of solidarity united by their shared distance from the objects of ridicule.[29]

Other ethnic groups had some success in banning tasteless and offensive slurs, but African Americans could not threaten a boycott (they were too small an audience to matter), take direct action, or exert much political pressure. Their only recourse was to call on white theater managers, song publishers, and performers to be more sensitive; their only media for doing so were the columns of black newspapers like the *Indianapolis Freeman* and journals like *Crisis*.

As Sylvester Russell wrote in the *Indianapolis Freeman* in 1904, song publishers and performers had stopped using the words "sheenee" and "dago" to avoid offending Jews and Italians. There was, however, no such sensitivity when it came to "nigger," "darky," and "coon." "Colored song writers have never insulted any of the white races. Why then should the song publishers accept a manuscript that would insult the Colored race? The best class of cultivated white people of the North do not appreciate the word 'nigger.' The ignorant 'stick-weed' variety performer who thinks he pleases in forcing this word upon the public is very much mistaken. . . . Colored people regard this word as an insult and an injustice to their race. There is no humor in the words 'common nigger.'"[30]

More prevalent—and ultimately more damaging from the point of view of African Americans—was the widespread adoption of "coon" to refer to blacks. The term, which, David Roediger claims, had once been a common word for "white country persons," had by the early twentieth century been transformed into a racist slur. Where black performers had used the word "just to amuse or to cause laughter," white audiences had adopted it to insult the entire "race," a writer for the *Indianapolis Freeman* argued in early 1909. "A show goes to a country town—some low down, loud mouth 'coon shouter' sings 'Coon, Coon,

Coon,' or some other song that has plenty of the word 'coon' in it, with an emphasis on the word 'coon.' The people, especially the children, are educated that a colored man is a 'coon.' What was meant for a jest is taken seriously. Before the show came people were afraid to call a black man a 'coon.' ... But now they think it's alright and he won't mind because it's all in fun and it's in all the songs. In this way and many other ways too numerous to mention, 'coon' songs have done more to insult the Negro and cause his white brethren, especially the young generation to have a bad opinion of good Negroes as well as bad Negroes, than anything that has ever happened. ... Certain slang and nicknames should be abolished, even if it costs bloodshed—the same as it did to abolish slavery."[31]

No matter how vigorous the protests of black journalists and activists, the comedic "darkies" and "coons" remained an integral part of the vaudeville and musical-comedy show because they served a vital purpose. They provided a heterogeneous "white" audience with a symbol of the racial "other" and, in so doing, helped to cement it into a sort of "herrenvolk" democracy. Everyone in the audience, whether rich or poor, new immigrant, old immigrant, or native-born of native parents, was redefined as "white" by participating in collective, derisive laughter at the superstitions, the stupidities, the misuse of language and logic, the sentimentality and inherent childishness of the "blacks" cavorting on the stage before them.

⋅⋗⟹⟸⋖⋅

African Americans, alone among the American peoples, were considered to be not only lacking in respectability but also constitutionally incapable of acquiring it. For H. G. Wells, visiting the United States in 1904, this fact of American life was virtually inexplicable. Try as he might, he could not understand the attitudes of white Americans toward "colored" people, especially as many of these "colored" people were, he discovered, "quite white" and had "the same blood," the same Anglo-Saxon blood, flowing in their veins as the oldest, finest southern planter families. Wells was particularly confused by the difference between the way southern European immigrants and African-American "natives" were treated in the city's public spaces. Though many of the blacks had patrician white ancestors, they were shunned and segregated. European "immigrants," on the other hand, who shared no biological or cultural heritage with American whites, were afforded every social courtesy and right. Wells confronted his southern hosts with his confusion, "These people [the blacks] . . . are nearer your blood, nearer your temper, than any of those bright-eyed, ringleted immigrants on the East Side. Are you ashamed of your poor relations? Even if you don't like the half, or the quarter of negro blood, you might deal civilly with the three-quarters white."[32]

North and South, Wells's questions were met with the same sorts of answers, all testifying to the "mania" with which whites explained and defended segregation. "One man will dwell upon the uncontrollable violence of a black man's evil passions . . . another will dilate upon the incredible stupidity of the full-blooded negro . . . a third will speak of his physical offensiveness, his peculiar smell which necessitates his social isolation." More than once, Wells was told stories about light-skinned blacks who married "pure-minded, pure white" women who gave birth to children "black as your hat. Absolutely negroid." Anecdotes such as these about "the lamentable results of intermarriage" were used not simply as an argument "against intermarriage, but as an argument against the extension of quite rudimentary civilities to the men of color. 'If you eat with them, you've got to marry them,'" Wells was told. There was no acceptable compromise, no halfway point between miscegenation and segregation.[33]

What this thinking on the part of whites meant for African Americans was obvious. There was no escape from biological destiny, no way blacks could change their appearance, rid themselves of what Wells's hosts had called their "evil passions" or their "peculiar smell." The "taint" of black blood was such as to render attempts at respectability foolhardy. To sacralize public amusement spaces and sanctify their audiences as decent, African Americans had to be excluded or segregated within them. No exceptions could be permitted.

CHAPTER 6

The City as Playground:
The World's Fair Midways

"NIGHTLIFE" WAS THE MOST CONSPICUOUS, but not the only, realm of commercial leisure to overflow its boundaries in the 1890s and early 1900s. The "vacation habit" that arrived in America in this period would support the expansion of a host of new leisure-time activities and amusement sites, from world's fair midways to amusement and baseball parks.° Vacations were not, of course, new for the city's social elites who regularly left the metropolis during the warm weather to travel to Europe, the mountains, or the seashore. But they were for its less privileged residents who were beginning to adopt what the journalists referred to as "the vacation habit."[1]

Edward Hungerford described the new trend in an August 1891 article for *Century* magazine, "All classes and conditions of men enter the streams of population which from the middle of May to the middle of October ebb and flow through the land. Every social grade, every occupation, is represented. The rich and the well-to-do middle classes appear most conspicuously, but the currents are swelled by small tradespeople, by pensioners on limited legacies. . . . Then come the work-people, who in one way and another manage to move with the

°In this chapter, we will look only at the world's fair midways. In chapters 7 and 8, we will turn our attention to the amusement and baseball parks.

rest. Your colored barber, when trade begins to slacken in the large town, informs you that he is thinking of taking a little vacation. The carpenter and joiner sends his wife and babies a hundred miles away to spend weeks or months on a farm that takes boarders. Factories . . . empty their armies into the open fields . . . Professional men, college students, teachers, seamstresses, and fresh-air fund beneficiaries pour forth to the mountains, the seaside, the lakes, where they spend their summer outings in rest or in various forms of service."[2]

Hungerford exaggerated. The only factories that were emptying "their armies into the open fields" were those that had closed down for the season and laid off their workers. For most city folk in the nineteenth century, the warm weather signaled no relief from the daily cycle of work and rest. Summer and winter, working people expected to labor at least five and a half days a week. Vacations, when they came, were unpaid and unwelcome.*

Though journalists and reformers preached that "men and women in all vocations need[ed] rest and change" and settlement house workers raised money to send a handful of working girls to the countryside, the vast majority of vacationers came from the ranks of the self-employed, professionals, and white-collar workers. Teachers and self-employed professionals had always saved money for vacations. They were in the early 1900s joined by white-collar employees in government offices, banks, financial houses, and insurance companies, and salesmen and saleswomen from the larger department stores. The department store managers, in particular, encouraged their workers to take a week's unpaid holiday. Vacations boosted morale, created favorable publicity for the stores, and were of minor cost or consequence as they occurred during the slow season. A few department stores gave employees who had been steadily at work for the past fifty-one weeks a week's vacation *with* pay; senior employees got even longer vacations.[4]

When Abraham Cahan's fictional character David Levinsky arrived at Rigi Kulm, the most luxurious hotel in the Catskills, he found alongside the well-to-do manufacturers and professionals "a considerable number of single young people, of both sexes—salesmen, stenogra-

---

*It would be another fifty years before factory workers could expect a "paid" vacation. In their 1924 study of Muncie, Indiana, the Lynds found that only 12 of the 122 working-class families they interviewed had taken an annual vacation for two years in a row; another 12 had taken a vacation in one, but not both, of the previous two years. As late as 1939, the United States, unlike almost every European nation, had still not enacted legislation guaranteeing "vacation or holiday benefits for industrial wage-earners."[3]

phers, bookkeepers, librarians—who came for a fortnight's vacation."
On his weekend trip to the Coney Island hotel district in the 1890s,
Theodore Dreiser joined a crowd, that although dissimilar in ethnicity—there were probably no Russian Jews among them—was also representative of "New York's great middle class of that day." He shared
the ferry to Coney with "the clerk and his prettiest girl, the actress and
her admirer, the actor and his playmate, brokers, small and exclusive
tradesmen, men of obvious political or commercial position, their
wives, daughters, relatives and friends."[5]

While the countryside and the seashore remained the favored vacation spots of those who could afford a week's vacation, more and more
Americans of moderate means were beginning to spend their summer
holidays in the cities. In a 1904 *Ladies Home Journal* article on "The
Best Two Weeks' Vacation for a Family," Mrs. George Archibald
Palmer glowingly recounted her family's "vacation in New York." "Each
of the fourteen days yielded recreation, entertainment and instruction. . . . Those who had prophesied that a New York vacation would
wear us out saw us return with renewed strength, high spirits and a
firm conviction that there could be no better way to do it." In a companion article on "The Best Two Weeks' Vacation for a Girl: How Girls
with Little Money Enjoyed Their Holidays," one writer described her
"City Park Vacation"; another, her metropolitan holiday "By Way of the
Trolley Cars."[6]

The cities and their environs were heavily promoted as vacation
spots by tourist boards, hotels, railroads, and traction companies, all of
which regularly took out newspaper ads or circulated their own publications extolling the joys of summer in the city. *The Four-Track News*,
one of the country's first travel magazines (in later years, it would prosper as *Travel*, then *Holiday*) published by the Passenger Department
of the New York Central and Hudson Railroad, interspersed among its
travelogues on Java, Fiji, and Niagara Falls, stories about Chicago and
its drainage canal and New York City and its picturesque immigrant
quarters. Visitors to the cities were fed a steady diet of urban adventure
stories before they even reached the metropolis. Once in town, they
were assisted and advised by visitor's guidebooks, weekly tourist guides,
and hotel personnel specially trained to guide "strangers" through the
streets of the city.[7]

The city could never be marketed like other vacation resorts, domestic or foreign. But it had its charms, its attractions, and its "sights" to

see. It was also much, much cheaper for the new breed of vacationer—the "clerks, bureaucrats, and others of modest means" who were now for the very first time "able to go on excursions."[8]

Because the cities had not entirely shed their nineteenth-century aura of sin, crime, and degeneracy, potential visitors had to be reassured that their passage through the streets would be a safe one. As William R. Taylor has pointed out, tourist guidebooks evoked "the moral geography of the city." They located, as a warning meant to be heeded, the immoral districts, but did so in a way that reassured readers that by avoiding these districts they could avoid all danger.[9]

The city's diversity was presented as an attraction. The guidebooks, travel magazines, and tour guides pointed proudly to the city's myriad populations and types, its parks, shopping districts, building styles, and neighborhoods, including those inhabited by the "other half." *The Four-Track News* offered among its articles extolling New York City a feature on the Sub-Treasury Building, the Metropolitan Museum of Art, and the city's immigrant quarters, where the tourist might be granted the "pleasure" of "shaking hands with the Old World." The Chicago guidebooks, as James Gilbert has written, "boasted of Chicago's ethnic diversity" and advised tourists how they could sample the city's diversity from within the protective environs of downtown. The railroad terminals, hotels, theaters, restaurants, and downtown streets, tourists were informed, exhibited abundant specimens of new immigrants speaking exotic languages.[10]

One came to the city not just to see the sights but also to become part of the heterogeneous crowds, to join in the spectacle of urban life. As the anonymous author of "A Vacation on Fifth Avenue" wrote in *Outlook* in May 1906, "It is not the things which Fifth Avenue contains that give it its greatest interest—it is the moving, pulsating life which it bears along in its great current. It is like a splendid river filled with all sorts of craft engaged in ministering to the pleasure or the needs of the world." To walk the streets of the city and partake in its pleasures was to embark on one's own journey along that "splendid river."[11]

--*≡◎⇌*--

The city was being reconceived as a place of play as well as of work. Still, compared to Europe, the mountains, and the beaches, the American city was still regarded by many as less a tourist attraction than a place to flee in the summer months. That perception would change dramatically with the construction of the world's fair midways and later, the amusement and baseball parks, which would contribute enormously to the city's allure as a warm-weather amusement center.

The world's fairs were paeans to progress, concrete demonstrations of how order and organization, high culture and art, science and technology, commerce and industry, all brought together under the wise administration of business and government, would lead inevitably to a brighter, more prosperous future. Even the most high-minded of the fair's organizers, investors, and directors understood however that attracting visitors was an essential precondition to educating them. As the official history of the St. Louis exposition admitted, though reluctantly, visitors came to the fairs "to be amused, instruction . . . being secondary. . . . The educational features, of course, should be paramount, and perhaps they are, but the incontestable truth remains that without a great amusement feature, the light frivolity that ministers to the masses, an exposition cannot hope to succeed."[12]

The first of the major American fairs, the Philadelphia "Centennial Exposition" of 1876, had been, at least compared to those that would follow, a remarkably solemn occasion. Visitors lined up to pay their respects to the "wonders of the age": the Corliss Engine, the world's largest steam engine, ready-made shoes, elevators, canned foods, Fleischmann's dry yeast, Westinghouse air brakes, telephones, sewing machines, and typewriters—all products of America's developing scientific and technological prowess.[13]

To maintain the appropriate focus on the exposition's moral and educational missions, the Philadelphia fair directors banned amusements from the fairgrounds. Unfortunately, they could do nothing about the unofficial "Centennial City" (also known as "Shantyville" or "Dinkeytown") that sprung up, unplanned and unwanted, directly across the street, where, within view of the stately exhibition halls and manicured lawns, a small army of hustlers, showmen, saloon keepers, and performers provided fairgoers with a taste of peanuts, beer, and sideshow "attractions" (including learned pigs, a five-legged cow, "the Man-eating Feejees," and a 602-pound fat lady).[14]

Unlike the sponsors of the Philadelphia exposition, the directors of the Paris Exposition of 1889 had no qualms about mixing the edifying and the amusing on their fairgrounds. Parisian fairgoers could visit the Galerie des Machines, if they wished, but they could also spend the day climbing the Eiffel Tower, laughing at themselves in the Hall of Mirrors, riding wooden horses down a roller-coaster track, or visiting the reproduction of the Bastille, transformed 100 years later into an amusement concession. In large part because of the mixture and quantity of exhibits (space was granted to nearly 62,000 exhibitors), the Paris Exposition was an enormous success. The Philadelphia Exposition had taken pride in its ten million visitors; over thirty-two million would visit the Paris Exposition.[15]

The World's Columbian Exposition in Chicago in 1893 and subsequent American world's fairs would take a position halfway between Philadelphia, which banned amusements, and Paris, which fully integrated them on the fairgrounds. While the American fair directors recognized the necessity for incorporating amusements in their expositions, they worried that the amusements would detract from the fair's more noble purposes. Their solution was to include an entertainment "district" on the exposition site but segregate it in a "midway" geographically distinct from the rest of the fairgrounds.

The contrasts between the two fair "districts," the edifying and the entertaining, could not have been greater. In the main exhibit areas, known respectively as "The White City" in Chicago in 1893, "The Little City of the Beautiful" in Omaha in 1898, "The Rainbow City" in Buffalo in 1901, and "The Ivory City" in St. Louis in 1904, building styles, materials, exterior coloring, design elements, and decorative motifs were coordinated by central planning directors or committees. These "Cities on a Hill" were, in the words of visitors, commentators, and recent historians, stately, orderly, dignified, majestic, monumental, imperial, classical, cosmopolitan, correct, uniform, and harmonious. They were cities without crime, without poverty, without decay, urban utopias made possible through the judicious application and administration of science, technology, learning, and high culture.[16]

The midways were different matters entirely. There was no attempt at uniform design or orderly presentation. Exhibitors were free to use any building materials, designs, styles, or exterior decorations they chose. The result was a jumble of shacks, sheds, stalls, tents, and booths, some wooden, some canvas, of every conceivable color and design. "What was lacking in stability was made up by the artist, in stucco, gilding, and paint," wrote the authors of the official history of the St. Louis fair. "Minarets, towers, domes, peristyles, monuments, arcades, balconies, arches, and in fact all manner of ostentatious designs and devices to produce impressive architectural effects were employed." All was spectacle: the overdecorated buildings; the billboards, posters, and garish signs; the barkers shouting their wares in front of their exhibits; the "attractions" behind the canvas; the electric lights overhead. "Here," wrote Mark Bennitt in his *Illustrated Souvenir Guide to the Pan-American Exposition* in Buffalo, "is a business street—the strangest in the world—where all business is pleasure."[17]

The Chicago Midway was a mile-long amusement strip with restaurants, rides, ethnic villages, and stage shows starring singers, dancers, comics, and novelty performers who during the winter made their living on vaudeville or musical comedy stages. Here were the "ethnological" villages, the most popular of all, the "street in Cairo," with Fahreda Mahzar, or "Little Egypt, the Darling of the Nile," the "bewitching bellyrina" of the "Dance du Ventre." Interspersed among the villages were restaurants and food stalls, rides, and a variety of shows and exhibits, including Hagenbeck's animals, strongman Bernarr Mac-Fadden in white tights demonstrating his new exercise machines, James J. Corbett starring in *Gentleman Jim*, Houdini escaping from locked boxes, and "the stuffed horse Comanche, only survivor of Custer's last stand."[18]

There were also dozens of booths featuring the latest "automatic" amusement machines. Midway visitors could witness, for a nickel, the magic of Edison's talking machines, the zoopraxoscope that projected Muybridge's photographs of horses running, raccoons walking, and a dog's heart beating, and the "electro-Photographic Tachyscope" that "reproduced . . . the natural motion of objects and animals . . . with a degree of truth and accuracy that is absolutely bewildering. . . . Fee, One Nickel in Slot." Thomas Armat, a bookkeeper, who, as we will see, would in 1895 invent one of the earliest and best moving-picture projectors, claimed that his interest in moving pictures dated from his visit to the Chicago Midway, where, for a nickel, he had peered into the Anschutz Tachyscope and seen an elephant walking.[19]

Compared to anything that had come before it, possibly excluding the Paris Exposition of 1889, the Chicago Midway was stupendous. Compared to the midways that would succeed it, it was only a beginning. As the world's fairs rolled on from Chicago to Atlanta in 1895, Nashville in 1897, Omaha in 1898, Buffalo in 1901, and St. Louis in 1904, the amusement sections of the expositions grew in relative size and profitability. Midway exhibitors learned that by charging twenty-five cents for a fifteen-minute show, they could make a lot more than if they had collected a dollar for a two-hour show. Variety was the spice of show business and the right kind of amusements—brief, light, and frivolous—could be almost addictive.

Midway visitors passed in and out of succeeding shows until they dropped from exhaustion or were defeated by lack of funds. Each amusement only whetted the appetite for more. Had any of the exhibits been entirely satisfying the chain would have been snapped. But that never happened. The shows were sufficiently entertaining and insufficiently satisfying to leave their customers always asking for more.

In Omaha, in 1898, the midway concessions proved so lucrative that a group of local businessmen and concessionaires pooled their resources to keep the midway open for a second season. Unfortunately, the midway without a fair attached proved to be a financial disaster. Too many fairgoers believed in the balanced meal approach to pleasure: they abjured the "sweets" along the midway until they had dutifully filled up with the main courses offered in "The Little City of the Beautiful." With the edifying exhibits in the fair proper withdrawn, they stayed away entirely.[20]

In Buffalo in 1901, the demand for amusement space on the fairgrounds was so great that a "Midway Annex Company" was formed to build a second midway outside the official amusement district, known as the Pan. Among the most successful of the Pan exhibitors was Frederic Thompson, the future designer and owner of Luna Park on Coney Island and the Hippodrome in Manhattan. Thompson had worked at every world's fair since Chicago. In Buffalo, he created his masterpiece, the "Trip to the Moon," an early twentieth-century *gemeinkunst* with a live narrator, a cast of midgets in uniforms, recorded sounds, projected images, elaborate stage settings, lighting effects, and simulated motion in simulated vehicles to create the illusion of space travel and a moon landing. The dramatic illusion was heightened by the participation of the customers, who, on entering the airship Luna, were transformed from visitors into actors with their own parts to play in the extravaganza. Here was the ultimate tourist spectacle, where the visitor not only viewed but also became part of the sight, part of the show, simultaneously insider and spectator.[21]

By the time the world's fair came to St. Louis in 1904, the fair directors had abandoned entirely the conceit that the midway was a "sideshow" to the main exhibitions. They placed their amusement district, the Pike, smack in the middle of the fairgrounds, with its own entrance onto the street. While the official guidebooks and histories of the fair, with few exceptions, downplayed the centrality of the Pike (the official history devoted 34 of its 3,851 pages to it), local businessmen

This reproduction of a "stereopticon" slide shows the Pike, the main amusement street at the St. Louis world's fair, crowded from end to end with visitors. Nowhere else on the fairgrounds were the crowds this thick. (*Library of Congress, Prints and Photographs Division.*)

invested between five and ten million dollars of their own money in amusement concessions.[22]

The sideshow business, once the province of small-time hustlers, drifters, and traveling showmen, had become a respectable investment. In St. Louis, one of the largest and most profitable of the exotic villages was a re-created model of Jerusalem on 11 acres, with 22 streets, 300 structures, a wall "of the same height and aged tone as the one on the yellow hills of the Holy Land," and "one thousand inhabitants of Jerusalem . . . conveyed to the Exposition by chartered steamer, sailing from Jaffa." The exhibit, which cost almost a million and a half dollars to construct, had been paid for by a group of local investors whose Board of Directors read like a *Who's Who* of Business in St. Louis.[23]

⊷⊏⊐⊷

The world's fairs succeeded admirably in their primary task of bringing millions of visitors to their host cities. (While the official attendance figures were probably exaggerated, if we follow James Gilbert and estimate the number of fair patrons by dividing the total paid admissions in half, we still end up with almost 14 million fairgoers in Chicago, 1.5 million in Omaha, 4 million in Buffalo, and almost 10 million in St. Louis.) As the official guide to the St. Louis fair exclaimed in particularly overblown prose, "Admission price was an open sesame to whatever desire or fancy might conceive; for a period caste and class distinction was eliminated, and common ground was occupied for a trifle."[24]

The St. Louis guidebook was only half right. From the perspective of the fair's organizers, all of them established and prosperous citizens of their host cities, "caste and class distinctions" had indeed been eliminated. Nonetheless, the fifty-cent admission fee at the fairs served to filter out a significant proportion of the urban population. If the fair directors had set out to reach a larger and wider cross section of the urban public, they would not have kept their admission prices so high. Fifty cents was a considerable sum to pay for admission alone, especially considering that this fee granted visitors only the right to walk the fairgrounds and visit the official exhibits. Food, drink, midway shows and rides, and transportation within the fairgrounds cost extra.[25]

The guidebook photographs show groups of well-dressed fairgoers, the men with well-starched collars, in bowlers or top hats, never bareheaded; the women in shirtwaists, wearing bonnets, often with parasols in hand.* There were large numbers of native-born, churchgoing, proper middle-class city folk such as Mabel Barnes, a Buffalo schoolteacher and librarian, who visited the fairgrounds thirty-three times and kept a multivolume diary of her experiences. And there were gen-

---

*Many of these photographic albums were commissioned to promote the expositions and for this reason alone cannot be uncritically accepted as historical evidence. On the other hand, they contain so many photographs that are so remarkably similar that they cannot be ignored either.

uine American aristocrats like Henry Adams who visited the St. Louis exposition once and the Chicago fair twice, the second time with a large entourage including his two brothers. There were also, as the fair directors liked to point out, significant numbers of immigrant families who came to the midways to visit the friendly ethnic "villages."[26]

For many midway visitors, American-born and immigrant, the shows and rides constituted an introduction to the world of commercial amusements. These were women and men who patronized neither the first-class dollar theaters nor the vaudeville halls and popular-priced amusements, because they feared and distrusted amusements that were proffered entirely for their own sake. To make these visitors feel comfortable, the concessionaires cloaked their amusements in educational disguise. The amusement machines that sang through rubber tubes or exhibited moving pictures through a peephole were presented as "scientific" wonders, the roller coaster rides were reconfigured as scenic railways to distant lands, the "exotic villages" as anthropological replicas of life among the primitives. As one of the guidebooks to the St. Louis fair reassured visitors, the Pike was "not at all frivolous. Several of its attractions are of real scientific value and of deep human interest."[27]

Even the midway's haunted house exhibits and rides, soon to be replicated in amusement parks across the country, were overwhelmed with instructional allusions, in this case, biblical, literary, and scientific. In "Hereafter," in St. Louis, visitors were guided on a trip through Hades by a Monk who read from Dante's *Inferno*. "Creation" was entered through the front of an enormous blue dome in the center of which towered a bare-breasted sculpture of Eve (identical to the one that would later grace the entrance to Dreamland in Coney Island). Once inside, visitors glided by boat back twenty centuries to the Garden of Eden. In "Under and Over the Sea," one of the Pike's bigger attractions, visitors "traveled" by submarine to Paris (constructed, it was said, of 25,000 pieces of cardboard); rode an elevator to the top of the Eiffel Tower; and returned to St. Louis, via New York City, by airship.[28]

It is doubtful that fairgoers such as Henry Adams and his companions or the group of prize-winning St. Louis schoolteachers who were guided through the Chicago fair by the *St. Louis Republic*'s star reporter, Theodore Dreiser, learned much from these exhibits. But that was not the point. The educational allusions were not supposed to

The well-dressed women fairgoers in front of the entrance to "Creation" seem not at all perturbed by the presence of the enormous statue of the bare-breasted woman behind them. The photograph is from the St. Louis Pike, summer of 1904. (*Library of Congress, Prints and Photographs Division.*)

inform or edify, but to make customers feel at ease in a new type of setting where "fun" came first. And they succeeded. Dreiser's schoolteachers, to his delight, explored "even the risqué parts of the Midway." Henry Adams and his entourage also took in all the fair had to offer, including "what Henry called the 'lowest fakes' of the Midway. The group repeatedly rode the Ferris wheel and spent every evening in gondolas on the water." Charles Adams, the former president of the Union Pacific Railroad, was reported to have told his brother that "never had he enjoyed anything so much as seeing Chicago's exposition—although he still growled at the cost and the quality of the food."[29]

❖⇥◉⇤❖

Nowhere was this educational disguise more in evidence than in the foreign and historical villages that occupied a large part of every midway. In St. Louis alone, there were, in addition to the Jerusalem exhibit on its 11 acres, Tyrolean, Irish, Spanish, Moorish, Chinese, and Esquimau villages; "Mysterious Asia"; "Ancient Rome"; the "Old Plantation"; "Old Saint Louis"; the Bowery; the streets of Constantinople; "Fair Japan"; Paris; the streets of Cairo; and a "Cliff Dwellers" cave populated by "stone-age" Indians. It was not coincidental that the fairs devoted so much space to exhibits modeled on travelogues, nor that the showmen who organized them promoted their educational values. In the long decade between the opening of the Chicago and St. Louis world's fairs, the United States became an imperial power, augmenting its considerable overseas economic expansion with formal and informal colonies in the Caribbean, the Pacific, and the Philippine Islands, half a world away.

The world's fairs provided Americans with the opportunity to celebrate in public their nation's recent accomplishments in the international arena and learn more of the places, peoples, and battles they had read about in their newspapers. Among the most popular exhibits in Omaha and the fairs that succeeded it were reenactments of the Battle of Manila, the sinking of the *Maine*, and the bombardment of the Spanish forts in Cuba. In St. Louis, the "Battle of Santiago" was recreated by a fleet of 21-foot battleships on a 300- by 180-foot lake. In Buffalo, there were daily sham battles fought by the "wonderful collection of aborigines" that peopled the Indian Congress. Mabel Barnes, the schoolteacher and librarian, paid twenty-five cents to enter the "Darkest Africa" exhibit in Buffalo, because, as she wrote in her diary, she wanted to see the "presentation of real African life in a real African village."[30]

This ostensible and highly publicized "It's a Small World" theme provided the fair proper and its amusement areas with an additional patina of respectability. Fairgoers who would have been ashamed to spend a quarter to view sword swallowers, "dancing girls," or "Africans" in loin cloths in a dime museum or vaudeville hall were perfectly content to watch them perform their "authentic" rituals and dances in the ethnic village pavilions and theaters. Mabel Barnes recalled that the "finest exhibits of all [in "Darkest Africa" were] the natives themselves," most of them minimally clothed. In her diary, she noted that she and her friend, Mrs. Hale, were entranced by the "slender, strong and clean" African bodies and "especially interested" in one of the men who "had a skin so free from blemish, so clean and smooth that it almost tempted one to lay hands upon it." It is impossible to imagine that these women would have allowed themselves to experience and express such sentiments anywhere else but at a world's fair midway.[31]

Though such exhibits as "Darkest Africa" were promoted for their educational as well as their entertainment value, they were never intended to be ideologically neutral. As Robert Rydell has argued so persuasively, they functioned instead as festivals of racist imagery and ideology. In Chicago, the Dahomey village stood apart, geographically and conceptually, from every other national and ethnic village on the fairgrounds. The European, Middle-Eastern, and Asian villages included restaurants, bazaars, theaters, and a generally festive atmosphere; the Dahomey village consisted only of a museum and a series of crude huts at the far end of the midway. The isolation of the Africans from the rest of the fair was highlighted by the placard placed at the exhibit entrance requesting visitors not to ask villagers about cannibalism and by the exclusion of the Africans, alone among every nation and culture, from the parade celebrating Chicago Day at the fair's close.[32]

In St. Louis, the government-sponsored Philippine Exposition Board imported 1,200 Filipinos to inhabit several different native villages. To counter anti-imperialist arguments that the "savage" Filipinos were "inherently unfit to be members of the American body politic," the government experts carefully distinguished between the lighter-skinned Igorots, who it claimed were capable of progress, and the dark-skinned Negritos who were not. Visitors were continually reminded that, while all "primitive" peoples required the benevolent leadership and example of their white American brethren, only the lighter skinned could be civilized.[33]

While African-American visitors were not barred from any of the world's fairs or restricted to separate entrances, they were, as a "people," treated with consummate disdain. Fairgoers of European background were welcomed with festive "villages" commemorating a mythologized past and "ethnic" days and parades saluting their contri-

This photograph was labeled "Chief, Darkest Africa." It was taken at the 1901 Buffalo World's Fair. (*Library of Congress, Prints and Photographs Division.*)

butions to the present. African Americans were represented in exhibits that highlighted their racial "inferiority." As Frederick Douglass explained, "The Dahomians are here to exhibit the Negro as a repulsive savage."[34]

Because the Chicago fair was supposed to commemorate human progress, Frederic Douglass, among others, had argued for exhibits honoring the progress of black Americans since slavery.* But when the fair officials finally decided to hold a special "Colored People's Day," they made it into a cruel joke, with free watermelons for all African-American visitors. The *Indianapolis Freeman* demanded that blacks stay away. "The Board of Directors have furnished the day, some members of the race have pledged to furnish the 'niggers,' (in our presence Negroes), and if some thoughtful and philanthropic white man is willing to furnish watermelons, why should he be gibbeted?" Alone among the prominent African Americans in Chicago to participate in the "Day" was Frederick Douglass, who presided over the Haitian government's exhibit. When Douglass tried to read his prepared paper on "The Race Problem in America," he was "interrupted by 'jeers and catcalls' from white men in the rear of the crowd." As Paul Lawrence Dunbar remembers, Douglass responded to the hecklers by throwing down his prepared speech and roaring to the assembled crowd that there was "no Negro problem. The problem is whether the American people have loyalty enough, honor enough, patriotism enough, to live up to their own Constitution."[36]

As was the case in other amusement venues, on the world's fair midways, the African Americans who were barely tolerated as paying guests were prized as entertainers. Every fair had one or another variation of an "Old Plantation" village, managed by white showmen, where, as the misspelled advertisement for the Nashville fair proclaimed, "young bucks and thickliped African maidens 'happy as a big sunflower' dance the old-time breakdowns, joined in by 'all de niggahs' with wierd and gutteral sounds to the accompaniment of 'de scrapin' of de fiddle and 'de old bangjo.'" The "Plantation Village" at the 1897 Tennessee Centennial Exposition in Nashville was so successful that it was

---

*When fair officials refused to allow African Americans to mount their own exhibits commemorating their progress, Ida B. Wells, with Douglass's assistance, wrote, published, and distributed her own pamphlet about "the accomplishments of black Americans and their plight in a nation plagued by lynchings."[35]

shipped in its entirety to the Omaha Midway, where it was supplemented by a group of "thirty-five to seventy-five 'jolly, rollicking niggers' living in slave cabins transported from the south." The grandest plantation village of all was probably the one managed by Skip Dundy at the Buffalo fair directly across the street from "Darkest Africa." To make perfectly sure that his African-American performers acted as they should, Dundy sent them to a special "performance school in Charleston" to learn how to "act" like "darkies."[37]

The African and plantation villages were, of course, not the only ones that parodied the "natives" they represented. All non-European peoples were caricatured at the fairs, but none with the same dogged and brutal consistency as the Africans and African Americans. The lessons for fairgoers were indisputable. Unlike other peoples of the world who could, with appropriate training, be civilized or at least lifted up toward "white" standards, Africans and people of African descent were permanent outsiders, people to be feared or hated in their primitive African mode, ridiculed and humiliated in their African-American incarnations.

The villages' ideological lessons comported smoothly with their commercial purposes. The racist imagery and ideology they supported and elaborated made the exhibits even more attractive to fairgoers. The midway shows were group experiences; the crowd, an essential component in each one of them. As Neil Harris has written so perceptively, "Gregariousness was at the heart of [the midway] areas."[38]

In their portrayal of Africans and African Americans as the irrefutably inferior and indecent "other," the showmen provided an ideational and emotional ground for the crowd's otherwise ephemeral unity. Fairgoers of various ancestries and backgrounds, native-born, immigrant, and ethnic, were literally brought together as a white public to witness the spectacle of "black" inferiority and collectively celebrate their "whiteness."

-*-=⊃◯⊂=-*-

The international expositions, with their millions of visitors, were good for the cities and their businesses. The host cities basked in the glory refracted back upon them by the "White Cities," "Rainbow Cities," and "Ivory Cities." The metropolis was reconfigured not only as a tourist sight for visitors, but as a utopian vision of what the city could become.[39]

The cities of joy that arose at the world's fair sites crystallized visions of the harmonious relationship that could be established between commerce and amusements in urban settings. The fairs induced temporary fits of frivolity among ordinarily sober Americans, transforming them into sports and spenders. Culture and commerce joined together, with the support of the state, to proclaim the arrival of a new and better future where distinctions between work and play, day and night, education and amusement, fantasy and reality, beauty and excess, propriety and immodesty were delightfully blurred.[40]

After the schoolteachers, churchgoers, and sober citizens had had their fill of midway thrills, seen the sights, ridden the rides, listened to recorded music, witnessed the magic of pictures that moved, and returned home no less whole and wholesome than they had left it, they were better prepared to take the next step into the twentieth century and enjoy the city's abundant and expanding pleasure parks and palaces.

CHAPTER 7

"The Summer
Show"

ALTHOUGH MILLIONS OF AMERICANS VISITED
the world's fairs in the 1890s and 1900s, millions more stayed at
home, because they could not afford the excursion fare, the price of a
hotel room, or the admission charges at the fair site.[1] These less fortunate city folk were not, however, without the resources to have fun in
the summer. Because the nation's waterways had served as its main
transportation networks until the triumph of the railroad in the mid-
nineteenth century, almost every major and mid-size American city was
located on or near a waterfront that could, with minor adjustments, be
converted into a playland for excursionists. Those few cities without
beachfronts had nearby "picnic groves," where one could smell the
fresh air and forget momentarily the stone and concrete city a streetcar
ride away.

In the late 1880s, the resort areas at the outskirts of the city, once
the province of the wealthy, privileged, or politically connected, were
opened up to the city's working people as ferry boats, steamers, and
streetcar lines linked them to the central city. The traction companies,
having invested millions in electrical generators, rails, and rolling stock,
wanted full return for their capital. If city folk could be given a reason
to ride the trolleys seven days a week, instead of only five and a half,
the companies could put their "idle generating equipment" to use
"during slack periods" and noticeably increase ridership and profits.[2]

Decreased work hours, particularly for white-collar workers, increased wages, and summer slack times meant that more city folk had more money and time to play during the summer months. Consumer demand fed amusement supply. Small businessmen erected shacks and stands to keep the excursionists amused, fed, and smiling from the moment they stepped off their ferries and trolleys to the evening when they boarded them for the ride back to the city.

The trolley parks and summer resort areas welcomed an incredible variety of city types to their shores. Jimmy Durante, who played piano in Coney Island's honky tonks and barrooms, recalled that the island was a summertime haven for "young people—husky men and pretty girls in cheap finery; shipping clerks or truckmen or subway guards escorting their sweethearts [who] didn't have much to spend but [knew that at Coney one] could go a long way on a few dollars." There were also family groups who rode bumpy trolleys all the way to the beach, then paid additional nickels to ride the bumpier roller coasters; single working men and women who traveled in packs with their buddies looking for a good time and companions of the opposite sex; sportsmen who came to gamble at the race tracks and gambling dens; and the wealthy who "summered" in the expensive hotels.[3]

There was something for everyone at the summer resorts. In its 1899 *Visitor's Guide to the City of New York*, the *Brooklyn Daily Eagle* explained that the "great seaside playground for the people" at Coney Island "was divided equally amongst the rich and the poor," but urged those who stayed in the luxury hotels at the rich end of the island to spend time at "the great resort for the crowds" at the poor end. "There is no sight comparable to it in America. It is a happy-go-lucky place. . . . Walk through the streets, ascend the tower, see the crowds, the merry-go-rounds, listen to the frankfurter man, see the bathers—and perhaps take a dip yourself—and then go to Manhattan or Brighton Beach [on the rich side] so that you may leave the Island with pleasant, healthful memories."[4]

Julian Ralph, a consummate dandy and snob, had three years earlier offered the same advice to the readers of *Scribner's Magazine*. "There is not a thing (except the fireworks), in the higher-priced end of the island that cannot be obtained or witnessed at the cheaper end, but there are scores of attractions at the hurly-burly end that the more exclusive region does not hold forth." He strongly encouraged all visitors to the island, no matter where they stayed, to go to the Bowery (Coney's cheap amusement street) to listen to "the oom-pah bands of

rusted brass" and "have a luncheon of frankfurters and lager and a dinner of roasted clams and melted butter."[5]

The same sort of promiscuous intermingling that Julian Ralph
encouraged at Coney must have occurred at summer resorts such as
Lake Quinsigamond in Massachusetts, Euclid Beach and Cedar Point
in Ohio, and Meramec Falls outside St. Louis, which also had luxury
hotels and bungalows near strips of cheap amusement and concession
stands. Summer shows in the open air were more enticing to the
respectable classes than enclosed amusements in the city proper. There
was none of the discomfort or danger of congestion and contagion, no
compulsion to breathe the same air and expose oneself to the stale
odors of unwashed working people.[6]

At the summer resorts and amusement parks, visitors, having paid
their trolley fares and admission fees, were in control of their day's
entertainment. Instead of being seated in a fixed location and presented with a prefabricated show, they put together their own program
by walking from stand to stand, listening to the barkers, reading the
attraction boards, and deciding whether to enter or pass on by. The
beaches and amusement parks were not associated exclusively with any
one social group or class. Rather, they belonged to the abstract pleasure seeker, the refugee from everyday urban life and its mundane concerns. "What is peculiar to Coney Island," Julian Ralph explained, "is
that no one lives there." All were visitors encamped for the day or season, temporarily joined together in the pursuit of a good time.[7]

◆◈◐◑◈◆

By the early 1900s, summer resorts had become a big business. An editorial in the *Street Railway Journal* summarized the transformation
that had occurred so quickly few had taken notice. "The merry-go-
round with its single line of wooden horses has given place to the
three-row carrousel equipped with every kind of fantastic creature,
which will perform all sorts of rhythmic movements. The peanut stand
has been replaced by the restaurant. Scenic railways, roller coasters,
shoot the chutes, amusement palaces, skating rinks and shows of all
kinds have been added; in fact, every new amusement feature which
can be thought of is a drawing card and must be had. People have been
educated up to this sort of thing, they expect it and are ready to pay
for it."[8]

The first true amusement park had been erected on Coney Island when promoter George Tilyou in 1897 enclosed a number of unrelated rides and "shows" in what he called Steeplechase Park and charged admission at the gate. In 1901, Tilyou convinced Frederic Thompson and his partner, Skip Dundy, to move their sensational "Trip to the Moon" concession to Steeplechase at the close of the Buffalo world's fair. The "ride" proved to be as big a hit at Coney in 1902 as it had been on the Buffalo midway. The following summer, Thompson and Dundy left Steeplechase to build their own amusement park. With $200,000 of their own money and an additional half-million raised from outside investors, they bought the failing Sea Lion Park across the street from Steeplechase and reopened it the following season as Luna Park.[9]

According to Richard Snow, Thompson and Dundy at first advertised Luna as "another world's fair, but before long they realized it was something better, an 'electric Eden' unlike anything that had ever been built before." In constructing Luna, Frederic Thompson claimed that he had thrown all his architecture "books and plans on to the ash-heap and decided to start after something new. . . . I stuck to no style. . . . One result is Luna Park which is utterly unlike anything else of its kind. . . . An exposition is a form of festivity, and serious architecture should not enter into it if it will interfere with the carnival spirit."[10]

Like the rest of Coney Island, but more so, Luna was a "totally synthetic resort" where all was artifice, extravagance, and excess. It was, as Thompson himself put it, "bizarre and fantastic—crazier than the craziest part of Paris—gayer and more different from the everyday world." Thompson and Dundy filled their fantasyland with characters and animals as exotic as the architecture. There were camels to ride, diving horses, and elephants that slid down their own "Shoot the Chutes" ride. When journalist Albert Bigelow Paine entered Luna for the first time, he reported being filled with "profound amazement [at this] enchanted, story-book land of trelleses, columns, domes, minarets, lagoons, and lofty aerial flights. . . . It was a world removed—shut away from the sordid clatter and turmoil of the streets." At night this effect of being enclosed in a fairyland, a "world removed," was even more intense as 250,000 electric light bulbs—the largest number ever assembled on any one site—lit up the towers, arches, and minarets of the park in an exuberantly ornate, yet stately, skylight visible for miles.[11]

Luna was an instant and overwhelming success. The speed with which Thompson and Dundy not only repaid their investors but accu-

Coney Island's Luna Park was lit spectacularly at night by over a quarter of a million light bulbs. The photograph is from 1904. (*Museum of the City of New York.*)

mulated profits in the hundreds of thousands of dollars was sufficient incentive for others to enter the amusement park business. The following winter, a group of politicians and investors raised over three and one-half million dollars to build an even grander amusement park on the island. "Dreamland," as John Kasson has described it, "took Luna's formula and expanded it." It boasted two different Shoot the Chutes; a Doge's Palace with gondola rides; a Fall of Pompeii building; simulated submarine and airplane rides; a miniature railroad; "Lilliputia," a city peopled by 300 midgets and presided over by the former Mrs. General Tom Thumb; Bostock's animal show; Wormwood's Monkey Theater; a "Fighting the Flames" show with a burning six-story building and, reportedly, a cast of 4,000; a three-ring circus; and "an immense 25,000 square foot ballroom covered by a massive seashell."[12]

While no playgrounds in the world could match Coney Island's in capital investment, profits, and visitors (Luna Park in competition with Steeplechase and Dreamland in 1904 drew four million customers by itself), similarly spectacular amusement parks were constructed in cities across the country in the middle 1900s. In Cedar Point, Ohio, manager George Boeckling returned from the St. Louis world's fair of 1904 determined to upgrade Cedar Point into a full-fledged amusement park. To do so, he installed a powerhouse on the island and invited concessionaires to rent space on his new "midway." Outside Newark, where Electric Park had been established in 1903, the managers of Hilton Park added a full "midway" to their summer resort, thereby transforming it into Olympic Park, named after the 1904 Olympics in St. Louis. In Chicago, the Schmidt family opened Riverview Amusement Park on the grounds of what had been "the old German Sharpshooter Park."[13]

The amusement parks succeeded in attracting millions of visitors because they provided the city's residents with enclosed playgrounds, isolated and insulated from the demands of everyday life. In their promiscuous juxtaposition of sedate and seditious entertainments, the amusement parks were the self-conscious heirs of the world's fairs. Almost every park included among its offerings ribald attractions disguised as wholesome entertainment. Paragon Park had a "Streets of Cairo and Mysterious Asia" exhibit with no doubt one or more "Little Egypt" impersonators dancing the hootchi-kootchi. George Tilyou's Steeplechase Park on Coney Island was filled with "stunts" like the "Blowhole Theater," where hidden jets of air blew off men's hats and raised women's skirts, and dozens of rides—including the Steeplechase itself, the Funny Stairway, the Barrel of Fun, the Human Roulette Wheel, and the Razzle Dazzle—designed to upset the established order, throw strangers together, reveal petticoats, and literally shock (with electric prods wielded by midgets), disorient, and discombobulate visitors—to their own delight and that of nearby spectators. What made these "stunt" rides and shows acceptable was their context, their location in an enclosed "park" with luxuriously and formally landscaped Sunken Gardens, Venetian gondolas, a stately Ferris wheel, a decorous merry-go-round, pony rides for the children, and "serious" lecturers such as Carrie Nation speaking on temperance.[14]

⊷⇛⇚⊷

The amusement park was a "temporary world within the ordinary world," where "special rules" obtained, and visitors literally stepped out of their "real" lives into a world of play and make-believe.[15]

To accentuate the distance from the outside world and call attention to the wonders within, the parks built in the early 1900s were designed with monumental entrances. The first Coney Island amusement park, Steeplechase, channeled visitors inside "through entrances marked by triumphal arches of plaster accumulations of the iconography of laughter—clowns, pierrots, masks." Visitors to Dreamland, built in 1904, entered the park through a massive archway formed by the outspread wings of a bare-breasted sculpture entitled "Creation." The entrance to Olympic Park outside Newark, New Jersey, was described by a local German-language newspaper as "new and imposing" with "four huge pillars, entwined with electric lights," and the "word, 'Olympia,' in letters of fire . . . descending from the arch over the main gateway."[16]

The arches that bestrode the park gateways were more than ornamental. In accentuating the separation of the "play" world from the "real" one, the park entryways provided symbolic assurance to visitors that they would be secure within, that the amusement park, although it charged only five or ten cents for admission, was not an immigrant beer garden or picnic grove filled with surly, drunken crowds of manual workers. Every promotional brochure, press release, and souvenir bulletin published by the amusement parks assured visitors that "undesirables" had been effectively purged from their resorts. A 1904 full-page ad for Euclid Beach Park in the *Cleveland Plain Dealer* stated directly in bold type, "No Objectionable Persons Permitted on Grounds." A

Pittsburgh's Luna Park was entered through this enormous gateway set back from the street. The photograph is from 1905. (*Library of Congress, Prints and Photographs Division.*)

1909 brochure from Olympic Park promised, "if you come here you have no fear of contamination with the undesirable element usually found at summer amusement resorts. . . . Representatives of the rowdy element will not be tolerated."[17]

To discourage the wrong type of city dwellers, Edward Hulse had suggested in a 1907 article in the *Street Railway Journal* that traction companies locate their amusement parks "at a sufficient distance from the [city] to warrant the collection of two fares." Charging a double fare would, he predicted, deter the "cheaper class . . . who go out to hang around, to stand outside the entrances of the various concessions, to pass remarks on those who patronize them, to mix in with others' enjoyment, to see 'what's doing.' The word that expresses that class is 'mugs'—and they will kill any resort except one gaged [sic] especially to suit them." Hulse did not charge the "mugs" with crimes or disruptive behavior. They were discouraged from attending the park because they discomforted other visitors.[18]

On Coney Island, Frederic Thompson claimed that "the problem of handling the roughs . . . was solved very quickly and easily. The first rowdy I caught in Luna Park was soundly thrashed, and before he was thrown out of the grounds I told him the place was not run for him, but for his mother and sister."[19]

In Cleveland, the owners of Euclid Beach Park solved the "mug" problem by maintaining a "free gate" policy. Because they charged no admission, they claimed that all who entered were "guests upon private grounds" and could be ejected at any time for any reason. The gate-keepers carefully watched approaching visitors. Anyone coming out of a saloon was denied entrance.[20]

To keep out "undesirables" and reassure "desirable" visitors that they would be safe inside, amusement park managers hired, outfitted, and organized their own police forces. The 1904 Rand McNally *Handy Guide to Philadelphia* reassured potential visitors to Washington Park that, although "the patrons of this resort are largely of the less orderly class," there was little to fear, because "the police provisions here . . . are too strict for the really 'tough' element." The 1907 promotional brochures for Luna Park in Scranton, Pennsylvania, announced that the park was "patrolled by a specially drilled police force, to insure safety to the patrons." To further ensure civil behavior, liquor was banned from most of the parks.[21]

While discouraging misbehaving "mugs" from visiting their play-grounds, the amusement park owners went out of their way to attract the largest possible audience. Frederic Thompson publicly proclaimed that he had built his park for the "ninety-five percent of the American public [that] is pure and good." Even visitors without a lot of money to spend were welcome in the amusement parks. As the White City Amusement Company in Chicago announced in its magazine, "Once within the gates of *White City* everybody will be equally considered by the management. If a person chooses to spend the sum of 10 cents for a ticket at the gate and does not wish to spend any more there will be no possible opportunity for criticism."[22]

‹⊷⟩━○⊂━‹⊷›

Wherever they lived, amusement park patrons were attracted to the same sorts of amusements, in part because they wanted to ride the same rides and see the same shows as the folks at Coney or at the world's fairs, but also because, as city folk, they shared the same sorts of fears, which in the parks, were transmuted into thrills. Every park had its share of "disaster" exhibits. The most popular disaster shows were re-creations of actual events, such as the Johnstown and Galveston floods, the eruptions of Mt. Vesuvius and Mt. Pele, and the San Francisco earthquake, although crowds were also drawn to fictional apocalypses inspired by Dante's *Inferno* or "suggested by certain Biblical passages." The "Doomsday" exhibit at Luna Park in Scranton where "Professor C. Nelson Camp, the inventor, shows by electric scenic effect, the destruction of the world" was among the major attractions at that park.[23]

Park visitors were also captivated by reproductions of disasters closer to home. Luna and Dreamland on Coney, Cedar Point in Ohio, and many others had their own "Fighting the Flames" shows, with full-size buildings, thousands of extras dressed as "guttersnipes, factory girls, policemen, pawnbrokers, Chinese laundrymen, newsboys, and roisters," and performer/firemen fighting real flames with real equipment.*[24]

Every park also had its own complement of mechanized rides based on exaggerated, at times almost nightmarish, reproductions of real-life streetcars and railways. As Edwin Slosson noted in his 1904 article on "The Amusement Business," "In the popular amusements is most strikingly manifested that curious disposition of people to make their amusements so like their daily life. . . . The switchbacks, scenic railways and toy trains are merely trolley cars, a little more uneven in roadbed, jerky in motion and cramped in the seat than the ordinary means of transportation, but not much."[25]

One of the chief attractions of these pleasure rides—and their major advantage over the trolley one took to work every day—was the not so subtle way they induced couples to hold on to one another as the cars

---

*It was, ironically, the same sort of urban fire that the parks presented as entertainment that would, in the end, lay them waste. In 1907, Steeplechase, and in 1909, Dreamland, burned to the ground.

The "Sinking of the *Titanic*" exhibit at Chicago's Riverview was one of the park's leading attractions. (*Chicago Historical Society, Negative No. ICHi-16039.*)

careened around curves and down embankments. In an urban world that had not yet adjusted to new forms of courtship and girl-boy companionship, there were few places as comfortable as the park for meeting members of the opposite sex. "Hospitality and visiting in the country sense being impossible in city flats people must meet in public, and little trips by sea or land afford this opportunity. The reference to 'dear little Coney Isle' in the folk love songs show what a part it has played as a matchmaker."[26]

Boys and girls traveled together to the park or came in same-sex groups looking for someone to spend the day and, perhaps, part of the night with. Single working women, unable to afford a day's vacation on their meager wages, looked for men who could treat them—and not ask too much in return. Every park had dance halls, pavilions, and ballrooms where strangers could meet on the dance floor. At Cedar Point in Ohio, the "Coliseum," billed as the "Largest Dancing Pavilion on the Great Lakes," was divided in two, with half the floor reserved for couples, the other half for single men or women looking for partners.[27]

For those already paired off, there were "fun houses," mazes, and railway trips through caves and tunnels, where couples could become better acquainted. As the owner of a Coney Island fun house "unblushingly" informed the journalist Roland Hartt, "The men like it because it gives them a chance to hug the girls, the girls like it because it gives them a chance to get hugged."[28]

Although, as Sylvester Baxter wrote in *Harper's New Monthly* in the summer of 1898, "The American people—or at least a very large part of the American people—has become a pleasure-loving folk," not all of them, as we have seen in earlier chapters, were comfortable pursuing fun for its own sake. To attract the reluctant pleasure seekers to their grounds, the amusement park owners, like the midway entrepreneurs, scattered "educational" and "artistic" exhibits through their parks.[29]

The most important of these were the native villages imported or copied from the world's fairs. Paragon Park in Nantasket housed several "authentic" native villages, including "The Gypsy Camp"; "The Streets of Cairo and Mysterious Asia"; a Japanese village; the Klondike, and the Kennedy Brothers' "Wild West and Indian Congress," which, the Official Program explained, was especially "interesting and informative" because of the "rapid passing of the redmen."[30]

The native villages were not the only "educational" sideshows. Like the world's fairs and expositions, the amusement parks also presented their customers with the latest scientific and technological breakthroughs: roller coasters, Ferris wheels, halls of electricity, moving-picture shows, even incubators with premature infants. At Luna Park on Coney and the White City in Chicago, visitors, for a modest price of admission—never more than twenty cents—were admitted to an infant incubator ward and nursery presided over by a staff of trained doctors, attendants, and wet nurses clothed in white.[31]

Like other commercial entertainment sites, the amusement parks segregated or excluded African Americans from their grounds. Of the scores of photographs of pre–World War II amusement park visitors frolicking in the surf, eating hot dogs, or riding roller coasters, none that I have located presents a black face among the seas of white ones.[32]

Few amusement parks had written policies excluding Asian or African Americans. They didn't have to. Because there were almost universal proscriptions against interracial dancing, dining, and swimming in the early twentieth century, often enforced by the police, parks that featured these activities—and almost all of them did—had to be segregated.[33]

In a 1928 article on "Recreational Facilities for the Negro," Forrester Washington found that none of the twelve amusement parks he surveyed in the southern states "admitted whites and blacks at the same time," although in a few, blacks were admitted on "off days." In Atlanta, they were "given the use of Lakewood Park for an outing once a year. At Hot Spring, Ark., Negroes and whites use the largest amusement park on alternate days." In the North, two-thirds of the amusement parks surveyed were found to practice segregation.[34]

In most locations, North and South, African Americans avoided the amusement parks of their own volition and instead patronized public beaches that had been informally designated for their use. In a few cities with large African-American populations, such as Savannah, Georgia, traction companies operated separate "pleasure resorts . . . for colored patrons." After World War I, "when Negroes were earning larger wages," amusement parks were opened in southern and border cities, although few survived for long.[35]

The exclusion of non-Europeans from the summer places where whites played was never total. Most amusement parks had a large number of "natives" living on the grounds, but they were strictly quarantined in the "villages" where they were exhibited. Segregating nonwhites on the park grounds was a necessary element in the transmogrification of these "others" into alien objects, "spectacles" designed to evoke ridicule, contempt, or dread.

At Cedar Point in Ohio, where the "Igorrotes" from Luzon in the Philippines had been relocated after the St. Louis fair, the publicity director warned those who lived near the park to be on the lookout for Igorrote raiding parties looking for dogs to eat. The story, needless to say, brought scores of visitors to the park to see the dog-eating primitives in their native village. In advertising the new "Igorrote Village" to be erected at the White City Amusement Park in Chicago, the management stressed that the inhabitants were "an entirely new lot of genuine Dog-Eating Bontoc Igorrotes," never before seen in the United States, every one of them a complete "pagan, a barbarian in culture."[36]

To the gawking spectator who paid his dime to see the show, there was little difference between viewing the savages in their "native" villages and the fat lady in the "freak" show. In Coney Island's Dreamland, the entrepreneur who collected "human oddities" for the "Big Circus Side Show"—with Princess Wee and the Queen of Fatland: "She's So Fat That It Takes Seven Men to Hug Her"—also imported "aborigines" for the park's native villages. The villages were, like the "freak" shows and sideshows, designed to titillate, to frighten, and to encourage "normal" spectators to feel both superior and fortunate that they had been born and raised without "deformities."[37]

The amusement park crowd, gathered together to enjoy a public spectacle, was more than a benign instrument in the creation of its own pleasure. It was also capable of enormous brutality. Games of chance, where prizes were awarded for hitting the "coon" in the head with a rubber ball or dumping him into the water, were as commonplace in amusement parks across the country as Ferris wheels. They were so common, in fact, that Williams and Walker explicitly referred to them in their 1901 "Sons of Ham" show. In one of the show's most popular skits, Bert Williams, after being insulted, declares that unlike the amusement park "artful dodger," he knows how to take revenge. "'Let me tell you,' he says earnestly, 'he [the man who has insulted him] will never remember smoking the cigars he gets for hitting this coon.'"[38]

Each of Kansas City's three amusement parks had "Coontown Plunges." On Coney Island, according to Eddie Cantor, there was a "Hit the Nigger—Three Balls for Five" concession. Cantor was hired to lure customers to the exhibit by bouncing "a few soft balls on the negro's docile dome until a crowd gathered . . . The negro would make a slurring remark to irritate some likely sucker in the mob. This sensitive soul, observing the ease with which I struck the negro's shiny pate, would pay for three hard balls to vent his spleen. He missed because the negro was an expert dodger, but his pride would not let him quit before he struck a blow. The negro kept dodging and insulting him, and the heroic pitcher of wasted balls would spend as high as five dollars in the hope of hitting his tantalizing target." In Chicago's Riverview Park, concessions, known variously as the "African Dip," with the victim perched in a cage on a wooden bench above the water, and the "African Dodgers," where the victim plunged through "the wet mouth of a painted alligator" into the water, remained popular through the 1950s.[39]

Obviously, the "negroes" in these "shows" were not passive victims but performers paid to squeeze as much profit as they could from their marks. Still, it was the "suckers" who triumphed in the end. No matter how effective the black performers were in infuriating them, the show had to conclude with the "African dodgers" being thrown into the water, snarling or whining in pretended disgust, and thus acting out their racial inferiority to the white crowd assembled to celebrate their distress.

⊷⇒◖⊶

The crowd was a necessary constituent of the amusement park experience. The park was, in this regard at least, a twentieth-century adaptation of nineteenth-century festivals, fetes, and holiday celebrations, where revelers took over the streets, the parks, and the waterfronts to have a good time publicly and collectively. On entering the park, one surrendered one's individual standing in the outside world and merged into a temporary play community which coexisted with one's visit and dissolved immediately thereafter. Throwing balls at a "darky" perched over a tank of water, riding on a roller coaster, or visiting a fun house by oneself was inconceivable. One required companions to share the experience with, to laugh and scream with, to reflect back in recognizable form one's own heightened emotions. In a firsthand account of his trip to Coney, Elmer Blaney Harris, a New York journalist, described his ride with "Dora" on the Great Divide, a Luna Park roller coaster. "We reached bottom and immediately the strain relaxed as we shot heavenward and were pillowed on the air. 'Lordy, what a feeling!' [Dora] panted, weakly. A man in front turned round laughing and wiped his forehead." As they exited, an "old fox" who had ridden with them remarked, "'A long way from the husking bee!'" For a brief moment, Harris was fused with "Dora," the "man in front," and "the old fox"—people he had never met before and would never see again—into a group united for no other purpose than to have a good time together.[40]

Contained within the walls of the park was as large and as heterogeneous a crowd as could be found anywhere in the city. As the president of the White City Amusement Park Corporation stated in response to a question about "the advisability of charging an admission of only ten cents at the entrance," the amusement park had not been "built alone for the four hundred; it is for the entertainment of the four million."[41]

Every visitor, every commentator was impressed by the enormity of the amusement park crowds. The New York Times joked in an editorial in the spring of 1909 that no one ever went to Coney any more because it was too crowded. "Who ever goes to Coney Island nowadays except everyone.... Its fame is worldwide. It seems to represent, in its entirety, the nearest approach to festivalmaking of which the conglomerate American people are capable.... It is really worth visiting, if you can nerve yourself to it, if only to see the crowds." That October, in an article entitled "Balancing the Books of a Season at Coney Island," the *Times* concluded that "twenty million people had visited the island in the summer season just passed."* The figures for other amusement parks were almost as spectacular, even assuming that the numbers disclosed to the press and the public were wildly exaggerated. The reported attendance at Willow Grove Park in Philadelphia for 1903 was three million, and 600,000 people visited the Olentangy Park in Columbus, Ohio. Three million were admitted to the two parks outside Los Angeles. Over 2.25 million visited the White City Amusement Park in Chicago in 1905 when it opened. Kansas City's daily newspapers reported in 1911 that the city's three amusement parks had admitted over 1.6 million people.[43]

What was as remarkable as the size and heterogeneity of the crowds was their behavior. "Your pocketbook is not safe there yet," remarked Edwin E. Slosson of Coney Island, "but it is not likely to be opened by another than yourself." Even critic James Huneker, who had described Coney as "a disturbed ant-heap [with] human ants ferocious in their efforts to . . . heap up horrors of sound and of sight," could not help but be impressed by the thousands who camped out on the beach one impossibly hot August evening. "The entire beach was thick with humanity. At close range it resolved itself in groups, sweethearts in pairs, families of three or four, six or seven, planted close together. With care, hesitation, and difficulty I navigated around these islets of flesh and blood. . . . It was impossible for such a large body of people to be more orderly, more decent."[44]

---

*To put this number into perspective, let us recall that the entire population of the United States in 1910 was 92 million, which translates into 22 visits to Coney for every 100 Americans. In 1989, with a population approaching 250 million, the combined attendance at Disneyland in California and Disney World and Epcot Center in Florida totaled 44.5 million, or 18 for every 100 Americans.[42]

CHAPTER 8

The National Game

THE BASEBALL PARK WAS A CONTEMPORARY OF the vaudeville hall, world's fair midway, and amusement park. But it differed from them in one critical aspect. The availability of alcohol and gambling at the ballpark preserved the type of old-fashioned, male-only ambience that was disappearing from other commercial amusement sites. Even with such special promotions as Ladies' Days, women made up only about 10 percent of the baseball crowd.[1]

━◦═◦◐◖═◦━

While baseball as a game reached back to the early nineteenth century, the first all-professional club, the Cincinnati Red Stockings, was established in 1869; the first professional league in 1876. Only in the 1880s and 1890s did baseball become as much a "commercialized amusement business," to use the baseball historian Harold Seymour's term, as a sport played by boys in vacant lots.[2]

The traction company executives who owned trolley parks at the end of the lines were among the first businessmen to understand baseball's drawing power as a spectator sport. In 1885, Erastus Wiman, who controlled a ferry running between Staten Island and Manhattan and an amusement park on the Island, bought an entire baseball team, the Metropolitans or Mets, to boost attendance at his park and ridership on his ferry. Frank DeHaas Robison, the owner of a Cleveland traction company, purchased the National League Spiders in the late 1880s and made his businesses work for one another by building a new ballpark at the intersection of his two trolley lines. Spider "fans could purchase tickets covering round-trip transportation and admission to the game for sixty cents right on the trolley cars, without the inconvenience of waiting at the box office." In New Orleans, the trolley park which had offered opera as its main attraction switched to baseball and drew 400,000 visitors for the 1903 season.[3]

Baseball, as a spectator sport, took off in the early 1900s as major league clubs built new stadia just outside the central business districts at locations served by as many trolley, subway, and railroad lines as possible. Though only the Brooklyn club was nicknamed the "trolley dodgers," players and fans in every city had to "dodge" cars on intersecting trolley lines to get into the parks. Shibe Park, located in Philadelphia's North City, twenty to thirty blocks north of City Hall, was accessible by trolley and three different railroad lines. Forbes Field in Pittsburgh was fed by sixteen different streetcar lines. Ebbets Field in Brooklyn was served by nine trolley lines that transferred to thirty-two more. The park was twenty minutes from Wall Street and "within thirty to forty-five minutes' reach of three or four million people in the metropolitan area via trolley, subway or elevated railway."[4]

Big-league admissions doubled between 1903 and 1908. By 1908, attendance was "not only higher than ever before but . . . as a percentage of the population of the areas served by big-league clubs . . . higher than it would ever be in the future." "As an amusement enterprise," a book on the subject claimed in 1910, "baseball today is scarcely second to the theater."[5]

What was most remarkable about this sudden growth in attendance was that it was not supported by low ticket prices. While the National League requirement (written into its 1880 constitution) that no tickets be sold for less than fifty cents had been officially abandoned by the mid-1890s, the clubs continued to charge—and fans dutifully pay—prices that were higher than those charged by other commercial amusements. In Kansas City, where amusement park patrons paid ten cents for admission in 1911, baseball fans spent an average of forty-five cents on tickets to minor league games and a dollar to a dollar and a half for box seats in the big-league parks.[6]

Not only were prices higher at the ballparks, but at a time when other commercial amusement centers were beginning to eliminate distinctions between customers (heading in the direction of the one-price

This is Ebbets Field in 1920. Although some customers came by automobile, most of the men walking toward the entrance had traveled to the park on the subway. Note the number of well-dressed businessmen and white-collar workers wearing straw hats. (*Courtesy of the New-York Historical Society, New York, N.Y.*)

movie-theater policy), the baseball club owners were emphasizing them by segregating the cheap from the expensive seats. The best seats in the parks were in the enclosed stands and pavilions behind home plate and along the baselines. Much farther away, and entirely separated from the grandstands, were the uncovered bleachers, so named because without protection from the sun, fans in these cheap seats got "bleached."

Though the baseball clubs could have boosted admissions and profits as the vaudeville halls and "ten-twenty-thirties" had by increasing

the number of cheap seats, they did not. By 1910, more than 75 percent of the seats in big-league parks cost twenty-five cents or more.
Forbes Field was built in 1909 with only 3,500 fifty-cent bleacher seats
out of a total of 25,000. In Braves' Field built in Boston in 1915, there
were 18,000 seats in the grandstand, 20,000 in the pavilions, but only
2,000 in the outfield bleachers.[7]

The limited number of inexpensive seats, all of them far from the
action, uncovered, and uncomfortable, and the placement of the games
on weekday afternoons guaranteed that the bulk of the spectators
would be professionals, white-collar workers, and self-employed businessmen. Baseball was a long and leisurely game, played in "parks" a
trolley ride out of town. Only men who controlled their own hours
could afford to spend a weekday afternoon at the stadium.[8]

The baseball crowd was, in this respect, not unlike the vaudeville
audience, which, as we saw in chapter 3, was also predominantly white
collar. In fact, as the vaudeville managers in the Keith-Albee circuit
reported every spring, the opening of the season put a decided dent in
attendance. "Today [April 30, 1906] witnessed the opening of the baseball season in Cleveland. The sun shone, and the theater starved to
death. At one time I thought of asking our audience if he would go out
and have a cigar, but as he seemed to laugh at something I resisted the
temptation."[9]

In Chicago, downtown businessmen made up such a large part of
the stadium crowd that A. G. Spalding, the principal owner of the
Chicago White Stockings in 1884, lobbied the superintendent of the
local trolley company to provide extra cars on game days for businessmen traveling from the central business district to the ballpark. Politicians and government officials, who like the businessmen set their own
hours, were also well represented at the ballpark. Even before William
Howard Taft in 1910 began the tradition of the president throwing out
the ball to start the season, politicians, congressmen, and cabinet members regularly attended baseball games in Griffith Stadium in Washington. Baseball was, in fact, so popular an amusement with politicians
that the *Where to Go and How* guide published for the delegates to the
Republican National Convention in Chicago in 1908 included the ballpark in its theater and entertainment listings.[10]

To protect their high-price customers from unwelcome contact with
those in the inexpensive seats, the clubs hired squads of ushers and private police and made whatever deals they had to with city officials, who
deployed policemen to maintain order inside and outside the parks.

Baseball and its fans had a well-earned reputation for rowdyism, much of it fueled by free-flowing beer. The sale of alcohol constituted a considerable source of revenue for the owners, many of whom were in some branch of the liquor business. The American Association had in the 1880s been referred to as the "Beer Ball League," because four of the six team directors were brewers. In St. Louis, the owner of the Browns was a local grocer who sponsored the team because it was a way to boost his beer sales: "If it sells beer, then I'm all for it."[11]

In almost every park, there were handy barrooms on the premises. In many, including Cincinnati, infamous for its consumption of alcohol, peddlers hawked beer in the stands. At Crosley Field, in the downfront section of the park known as Rooter's Row, beer was sold, twelve glasses for a dollar.[12]

The division of the park into separately priced sections resulted in de facto ethnic segregation, with the Irish and German Americans in the bleachers, and the rest of the crowd in the more expensive grandstand, pavilion, and box seats. White Sox Park in Chicago had the largest twenty-five-cent section in the big leagues to accommodate Irish Americans from the South Side and Bridgeport, a nearby Irish community. In St. Louis the cheap section of the ballpark was called "Kerry Patch"; in the Polo Grounds, the bleachers were known as "Burkeville," testimony to the Irish Americans who came to the park to cheer for their boys.[13]

While most Irish- and German-American fans gathered in the bleachers because they could not afford better seats in the park's enclosed stands and boxes, African Americans of every income group and occupation were restricted to "segregated sections . . . usually in the less favorable locations" because of their race. Even in ballparks where "Negro" teams played against one another or against barnstorming white teams, seating was segregated, with the park's most "desirable" locations reserved for "white" spectators. The vast majority of black baseball fans, and there were many of them, stayed away from the major and minor leagues, not simply because of the segregated seating, but also because there were no black ballplayers in "organized" baseball.[14]

While, as we saw in chapter 5, white vaudevillians tried but failed to remove black entertainers from the stage, white baseball players succeeded in preventing black ballplayers from playing by intimidating them on the field and threatening boycotts against owners who employed them. As Jules Tygiel has written, "Racial and ethnic exclusion often constituted a means to define the distinctiveness of a given profession. . . . By designating some people as unworthy of admission, the baseball community elevated the status of those accepted into the profession." From the mid-1880s to the 1940s, no black ballplayers, other than those who "passed" for Indian or Cuban, played in the major or minor leagues.[15]

Though barred as players from the field and segregated as fans in the stands, African Americans remained a part of the "show." Originally hired to perform menial chores for the players in the locker room, a number were "adopted" as team "mascots . . . crowd pleasers and good-luck charms." Performing in their accustomed roles as "pickaninnies," "nigs," and "coons," these African-American "mascots" cavorted like carefree idiot children on the fields between innings, encouraging the white crowd in the stands to revel in their supposed superiority. In Cincinnati, according to the local paper, "Whenever anything goes wrong, it is only necessary to rub Clarence's wooly head to save the situation, and one of his celebrated 'double shuffles' to dispel all traces of care, even on the gloomiest occasion." Clarence Duval, the Cincinnati mascot, was apparently so valuable an entertainer he was invited on the Red Stockings' round-the-world exhibition tour in 1889–1890.[16]

⟶⟹⟸⟵

The baseball parks prospered in the early years of the new century for many reasons, not least of which was that they were able to offer men and boys a male-only alternative to the "mixed" entertainments that were proliferating on the streets of the city. In the absence of the ladies, the men at the ballpark were allowed, even encouraged, to act in ways that were prohibited in the vaudeville halls, theaters, and amusement parks. They could gamble, smoke, drink, spit, shout, curse, even hurl abuse at the umpire, the only available authority figure.

Although the city's saloons, tenderloin dives, and burlesque houses were also frequented by sporting men and boys, they were regarded as places of disrepute, if only because of the presence and availability of prostitutes. The baseball parks not only were free of prostitutes, they were situated entirely outside the boundaries of urban nightlife. And though most of the parks, squeezed into city blocks, were hardly the pastoral retreats their promoters claimed, they did offer spectators an afternoon of fresh air and sunshine.[17]

The ballpark's ambiguous standing, somewhere between the male-only saloon culture of the nineteenth century and the respectable, mixed assemblies of the twentieth, was represented appropriately in the confused editorial coverage provided by the *New York Times* in 1907. On May 23, 1907, after 10,000 fans had surged onto the field to try to rough up the umpires at the Polo Grounds, the *Times* excoriated baseball spectators as "a dull and ruffianly lot," claiming that they were in no way "representative" of the urban population. "This is a big city, but it contains no legitimately leisured class large enough to supply the multitude who devote a whole weekday afternoon to unproductive idleness." Had the ballpark been filled entirely with English aristocrats with no need to work, the *Times* was implying, it would have been above condemnation. But it was inhabited instead by men and boys who should have been working. "What [the riot] proves is that the baseball grounds should be closed by the police as places of disorderly resort unless the owners of the grounds see to it that the ruffians whom they attract are kept in subjection." The message was clear—baseball had no place in the modern city because it supported "unproductive idleness" and "ruffianly" male behavior.[18]

Four months later, the *Times* editorial writers returned to the subject of baseball. Although in September, as in May, the ballpark was filled with men and boys who should have been working, the *Times* now celebrated its beneficent integrative effects. "The one ever-dominating topic of conversation in this broad country from May to October is baseball. . . . The National interest in baseball is wholesome. . . . There is every reason why Americans should be proud of their National game."[19]

While baseball was never, as a spectator sport, the "democratic game" A. G. Spalding and other owners, promoters, and publicists declared it to be, it did breed a sort of social democracy in the ballpark. Twenty-five cents for admission was too high a price for most blue-collar workers to pay, but within range for white-collar clerks and salesmen, shopkeepers, factory foremen, and the skilled artisans who kept their own hours. Though the crowd was segregated, with the Irish- and German-American workingmen most likely in the bleachers and the businessmen in the stands, an afternoon at the park evoked a male bonding that transcended age, neighborhood, ethnicity, and most social divisions. Inside the stadium, crowds of strangers coalesced into a community of "fans." No matter where they had come from, who their favorite players were, or where they sat, the men had come out to root together for their "home" teams. Their identification as "fans" overrode all others, at least for the few hours "their" team was on the field.[20]

One didn't have to go out to the ballpark to be a fan. Scores of young, immigrant boys who rarely, if ever, visited the ballpark were part of the brotherhood of males. They joined it by reading the box scores in the newspapers, studying the sporting magazines and annual guides, and arguing feverishly about the game and the relative merit of its teams and stars.[21]

In *The Spirit of Youth and the City Streets,* first published in 1909, Jane Addams, certainly no shill for the baseball owners, described how baseball worked its magic every Saturday afternoon as "the entire male population of the city betakes itself to the baseball field. . . . The enormous crowd of cheering men and boys are talkative, good-natured, full of the holiday spirit, and absolutely released from the grind of life. They are lifted out of their individual affairs and so fused together that a man cannot tell whether it is his own shout or another's that fills his ears; whether it is his own coat or another's that he is wildly waving to celebrate a victory. He does not call the stranger who sits next to him his 'brother' but he unconsciously embraces him in an overwhelming outburst of kindly feeling when the favorite player makes a home run. Does not this contain a suggestion of the undoubted power of public recreation to bring together all classes of a community in the modern city unhappily so full of devices for keeping men apart?"[22]

CHAPTER 9

"Laughter and Liberty Galore": Early Twentieth-Century Dance Halls, Ballrooms, and Cabarets

"THE TOWN IS DANCE MAD," WROTE SOCIAL worker and journalist Belle Lindner Israels of New York City in the summer of 1909. "Everybody's Doin' It Now," Irving Berlin declared in his 1911 song. The turkey trot, bunny hug, and grizzly bear, *Life* magazine reported in February of 1912, have "spread up and down and far and wide through our metropolitan society. Little Italians dance them in Harlem, polite cotillions at Sherry's have been diversified by them, and they flourish above, below and between. The dancing set in our town must be half a million strong."[1]

While it might be somewhat of a stretch to characterize the "dance craze" of the early twentieth century as entirely female-driven, there was no doubt among contemporary observers that the "girls" were the carriers of the madness. When Michael Davis undertook his massive amusement survey of New York City in 1911, he found a surprising discrepancy between the boys and girls he interviewed on the question of dancing. While only one-third of the boys admitted to knowing how to dance, 88 percent of the girls said they knew how to dance, and 96 percent said they enjoyed it. Ruth True, the social worker and author of *The Neglected Girl*, reported that on Manhattan's West Side, young working girls were spending "several nights a week at dance halls where [they] stayed until one or two o'clock," even though they had to get up early for work six days a week. In Chicago, Elias Tobenkin found that Polish and Slavic girls recently arrived in the country preferred "scrubbing in restaurants for five or six dollars a week" to domestic work, because domestic work curtailed "the number of balls and dances" they could attend.[2]

It was not only poor and working girls who had been bitten by the dancing bug. The madness cut across every social division in every city, infecting seamstresses who patronized the nickel dance halls in the poorer neighborhoods and debutantes who spent the early-morning hours in cabarets where only champagne was served. Julian Street, in his 1913 book on New York nightlife, reported that the dancing craze had created "a social mixture such as was never before dreamed of in this country—a hodge-podge of people in which respectable young married and unmarried women, and even debutantes, dance, not only under the same roof, but in the same room with women of the town. Liberté—Egalité—Fraternité."[3]

In its Christmas 1914 issue, *Variety* claimed that the very landscape of Broadway had been changed by the dance craze. North of Times Square, "both sides of the street are lined with cabarets, Jardins, Gardens, Palaises and what not." "At last a New Yorker can look a Parisian in the face," proclaimed *Vanity Fair.* "No more need he stand by and hear—with mingled emotions of envy, humiliation, and rapture—those old familiar stories of all night life in Paris. . . . Now a New York man can dance until six A.M. . . . as a gentlemen [sic] should."[4]

While *Vanity Fair* celebrated the new night life, social reformers and settlement-house workers complained that the new leisure class was setting a dangerous precedent for the city's working girls. The *New York Times* in an editorial warned the city's social elites to begin policing their behavior on the dance floor. "Their own daughters may be quite safe from evil influence. Their pretty adaptations of the wigglings and posings of the taverns on the road to Gehenna may be considered quite harmless and too exquisitely droll for words. But their influence is far reaching." The working girls of the city, the *Times* claimed, had learned the turkey trot and the grizzly bear "from good society. . . . Because it was noised abroad that at a 'coming out' party of a daughter of good society, the 'slow rag' or the 'tango argentino' were danced, these grotesque posturings must, perforce, be imitated in the Saturday night dances of the poor girls, whose lives are not so well guarded and are ever subject to innumerable temptations."[5]

The reformers were relentless in their attack on "society" for its abnegation of responsibility. In January 1912, the Committee on

Amusements and Vacation Resources for Working Girls announced that it was going to send its dance investigators—who usually visited only the public dancé halls—into the Fifth Avenue hotels. The *New York Times* reported the announcement in a front-page story: "Movement Begins to Bar 'Turkey Trot' and 'Grizzly Bear' from Fifth Avenue. JUNIOR COTILLION WARNING. Dancers Told There Must Be No 'Antics'—Plan to Expose the New Dances to All Grades of Society."[6]

The response was immediate. Social leaders in New York, Philadelphia, and everywhere else, deeply embarrassed by the disclosure that their children were gyrating and embracing on the dance floor with the same abandon as the denizens of "tenderloin" dives and public dance halls, took immediate action. The *New York Times* announced the very next day, "PHILADELPHIA BANS THE TROT. Grizzly Bear Also to Be Eliminated from Society Dances." A few weeks later, the president of the International Art Society informed the 200 couples at its annual ball in the Hotel Astor that anyone doing the grizzly bear or the turkey trot or "an exaggerated form of the 'Boston dip'" would be "escorted from the hall."[7]

To make sure that the problem did not resurface, the better half took steps to teach itself and its children to dance with the grace and style that the "other half" lacked. "The smartest stratum of New York Society adopted" Englishman Vernon Castle and his demure, well-bred, quintessentially "WASP" wife, Irene, as their special dance instructors, because, as *Theatre Magazine* explained, they "spiritualized the dances thought to be hopelessly fleshly."[8]

The Castles and their sponsors modified and renamed the "tough" dances. The turkey trot, grizzly bear, and bunny hug were replaced by the one-step, the long Boston, and the fox trot. New rules were promulgated to govern dancing in the city's more expensive restaurants, cabarets, and nightclubs—and distinguish it from what went on in the cheap dance halls. "Do not wiggle the shoulders. Do not shake the hips. Do not twist the body. Do not flounce the elbows. Do not pump the arms. Do not hop—glide instead. Avoid low, fantastic and acrobatic dips."[9]

While the Castles removed the shimmy and the shake from the barnyard dance steps, they did not attempt to slow down or smooth out the syncopated ragtime beat that propelled the couples across the floor. As Vernon himself admitted, "When a good orchestra plays a 'rag' one has simply *got* to move. The One Step is the dance for rag-time music."[10]

This drawing by John Sloan was published in *The Masses* in 1914. The caption read, "An Editor: 'I think that this is a reactionary picture. The tango is all right.' An Artist: 'Yes, the *tango* is all right—this is the orango-tango.'"

The musicians, performers, and publishers who were profiting from the dance craze had to walk a fine line here. If they went too far in cleaning up the dances, they would destroy their appeal. The key to the new dances was ragtime music, and there was no way to disguise the fact that it had come from and was best performed by African-American musicians.

The fashion in dance music, up until about 1910, had been the so-called gypsy orchestras that virtually monopolized the hotel trade. The first "whites" to hire black musicians for their dances were members of New York's social elite. In August of 1913, society's favorite African-American conductor, James Reese Europe, played engagements for the Astors and the Vanderbilts at their summer homes. The Castles also "preferred to be accompanied by James Reese Europe's Negro band with drummer Buddy Gilmore, the admitted source of much of their inspiration."[11]

With the imprimatur of the Castles added to that of the Astors and Vanderbilts, black conductors and musicians became an essential component of the dance craze. "Most people felt they had to have a Jim Europe orchestra to play the new dance music for them, and he was only too happy to supply them with musicians." On the West Coast, the Oakland *Western Outlook* noted in 1914 that "the white-light districts simply clamor[ed] for colored manipulators of the rag-time muse."[12]

Ragtime and the new dances were, indeed, so closely associated with African Americans that one of the most popular dance steps was, in ironic tribute, called the "Nigger." And although "Alexander's Ragtime Band," which sold more sheet music than any other rag, was written by Irving Berlin, an immigrant Jew from the Lower East Side of Manhattan, the songwriter spent years dispelling rumors that he had stolen the song from an unnamed "Negro." Few believed that anyone but a "Negro" could have written a successful rag.[13]

-•-⇒◎⇐•-

Uptown and downtown, the social elites and the city's working people danced the same steps to the same kinds of music. And the urban reformers who looked after the moral health of future generations worried about them both. While the threat of adverse publicity had prompted the social elites to police their cotillions and "ban the trot," such tactics did not work with the "other half." To protect the innocent from animal dances and ragtime music, reformers sought and secured legislation mandating the regulation and licensing of public dance

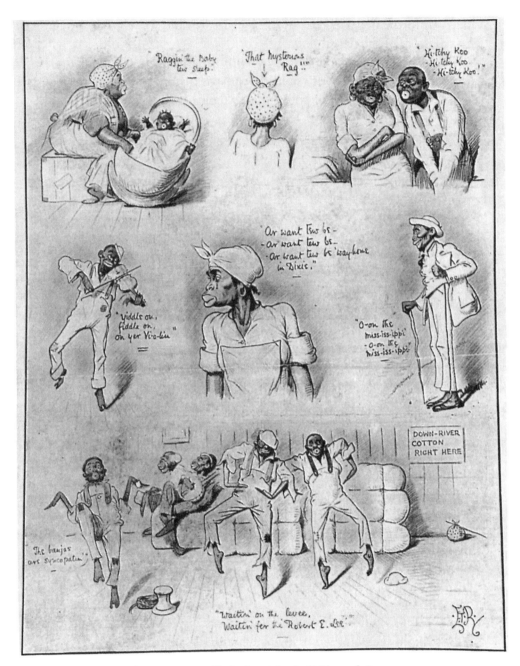

The caption for this cartoon, published in March 1913, read, "GOO-OOD-BYE, RA-A-AG-TIME! It seems almost too good to be true that the Rag-Time Fever is dying out, and that these syncopated and hypnotic sentimentalists will shortly return to their barbaric haunts." (*Photographs and Prints Division; Schomburg Center for Research in Black Culture; The New York Public Library; Astor, Lenox, and Tilden Foundations.*)

halls. Unfortunately, success in the legislatures did not easily translate into mastery of the dance floor.

There was never enough money appropriated to police the public dance floors properly. Nor could there have been. How many inspectors would it have taken to police the 49 dance halls in Kansas City and watch over the shoulders of 16,500 dancers, 80 percent of them under 25 years old, who patronized them weekly? Or to supervise the 12,000 to 13,000 dancers who spent Saturday nights in Milwaukee's dance halls and academies? Or the 86,000 young people, who, according to the Juvenile Protective Association of Chicago, danced nightly in that city's public halls and dancing academies?[14]

In Cleveland and Kansas City, where special legislation empowered deputy policemen to moonlight as inspectors, some warnings were given, a few rowdy offenders ejected, and a handful of halls temporarily closed, usually for building-code violations. The vast majority of boys and girls continued, however, to dance as they pleased. When the Cleveland social reformers and inspectors tried to outlaw the tango, which they considered the most sexually explicit of the new dances, even the court ruled against them, declaring that the inspectors had no right to "forbid a certain dance by *name.*" The tango was promptly reinstated.[15]

The simple truth was that there was no way of curbing or policing the dance craze short of closing down the cabarets, nightclubs, and dance halls, which no reformer dared suggest—and no politician dared consider. As long as these establishments remained open, the city's young people would patronize them in large numbers—and dance the steps they wanted to dance.

Outside the public dance halls, there were few spaces in the city where young working men and women could spend time together. As Ruth True reported from Manhattan's West Side, "The girls' homes are not very advantageous places for entertainment and fun. They are too cramped and often too forlorn. . . . Visits from gentlemen friends are frowned upon and not desired. The parents, especially of the younger girls, look askance on the boys who come to see them."[16]

Going out for dinner or to see a show with a member of the opposite sex with whom you were not engaged—or about to become engaged—was still something of a rarity. Young men and women went to the movies or the vaudeville hall with their same-sex friends and left with them. Occasionally, boys and girls would pair off in the street outside the theater but only with individuals they already knew. The amusement park was a great place to meet boys or girls, but it was a trolley ride away and closed nine or ten months a year. The dance hall alone was within walking distance and open all year long. And it offered opportunities available nowhere else to spend time with the opposite sex. For the women especially, there was safety in the anonymity of the dance floor. They could flirt, hug, even hold hands, if they chose, without parents, teachers, employers, or family friends looking over their shoulders.[17]

The best information we have on the dance halls comes from investigators paid by vice commissions and reformer agencies. Although they were hired to look for and find "dirt," in their unedited reports, they reveal a great deal about the ways the city's young men and women interacted in the dance halls. Mr. and Mrs. Hastings, investigators for the New York Committee of Fourteen, in the report of their September 1911 visit to the Terrace Garden described how the dancers paired off on the dance floor. "We observed that a large majority of the girls came by themselves and the young men by themselves, each finding partners at the hall. Few introductions were seen; two girls dance together and two young men whose fancy they suit pick them out and dance with them. Some fellows chat with them after the dance, and some do not. The crush around the edge of the floor when a dance starts is very great, the young men crowding half way into the middle of the floor to pick out partners. . . . The girls generally speaking, were bright and happy fun-loving girls, judging from their appearance. They did not seem to care, however, what manner of young men they met."[18]

If the partners enjoyed one another's company—and dancing—they might stay together for the evening. If they did not, they parted at the end of the number, and the entire process began again with the next dance. The girls who had come together to the hall kept a careful watch on each other, even after they had been "picked up." At the end of the evening, most left with their girlfriends. A smaller number went off with boys, some to walk home, others to nearby hotel rooms or illicit rendezvous.[19]

The reformers were, of course, more interested in the minority of boys and girls who left the dance halls together than in the majority who went home by themselves or with their same-sex friends. In almost pornographic detail, published reports such as those of Chicago's Juvenile Protective Association recounted the stories of young girls (and occasionally boys) led astray by vicious men and liquor. "In one case the investigator saw a young girl held while four boys poured whiskey from a flask down her throat, she protesting half-laughingly all the time that she had never had anything to drink before. A half hour later, her resistance gone, she was seen sitting on a boy's lap." In another case, "a young boy, evidently new to the city, was seen looking for a [dancing] partner. He found one, a prostitute, who, after drinking with him all the evening, persuaded him to give up his job. At the end of a week she induced him to go with her to St. Louis to act as cadet for a disorderly house."[20]

The testimony presented here is highly dramatic, but suspect. Why didn't the investigators who witnessed these events intervene to save the innocent? Why didn't they warn the young girl not to drink so much from the flask or tell the "young boy, evidently new to the city," that his dancing partner was a prostitute? Either the published stories were fictions invented by the reformers or the investigators were instructed to act as scientific observers and not intervene in the affairs of those they observed.

Reading the unedited reports of the individual inspectors, one is led to the conclusion that the reports published by the reformers were as much fiction as fact. Though the investigators, for example, tried their best, they were seldom able to interest the women they approached in leaving the hall with them, or in even dancing with them.* Although wherever they traveled, they inquired about "rooms" to take girls after the dance, they rarely found the "vicious situations" they were searching for.[22]

The vice commissioners and reformers who reported to the public on the city's dance halls were less interested in what actually occurred than in what might or could have happened. Even though there was little evidence that innocent young girls were being regularly seduced in the dance halls, the danger remained ever present in the license offered young people to act out their own rituals of interaction without the instruction or intervention of responsible adults.

It is easy to poke fun at the dance-hall reformers, investigators, and police. But it is wrong to dismiss their concerns as frivolous. While they

---

*See, for example, the report from the Pittsburgh investigator who visited a dance hall, where he claimed "intermingling was quite promiscuous" but admitted that he was "repeatedly 'turned down' and succeeded in dancing only one dance other than those with Miss X," his co-investigator.[21]

certainly underestimated the strengths of local mores and the boys' and girls' capacity to resist sexual harassment, they identified a danger that was implicit in the changing rules and rituals of heterosexual socializing.

Traditional courting rituals were breaking down with nothing to take their place. By the mid-1920s, certainly by the 1930s, the institution of "dating" would begin to structure the relationships of unmarried young people by limiting the range of acquaintances they might "go out" with, reducing the possibilities of indiscriminate assemblies, and, theoretically, providing parents with the opportunity to regulate or at least comment on the suitability of particular "dates." In the early years of the new century, however, "dating" was not yet institutionalized, certainly not for working youths who had left school.[23]

Week after week, working-class and immigrant youths came to the dance halls, some to dance with boys or girls from the neighborhood, others to throw themselves into the arms of strangers neither they nor their friends or families knew anything about. The new dance steps encouraged, almost mandated, physical intimacy with dancing partners. The dancers did not hold one another at arm's length as they had in the waltz or the polka, but pivoted and spun around the room, arms and legs entwined. In the turkey trot, the ladies' arms were placed around their partner's necks, not on their shoulders; their lower bodies, from waist to knee, were enclosed within the men's extended legs. In the grizzly bear, the partners wrapped their arms around one another, with the man embracing the woman as the grizzly bear embraced his mate or foe. In the bunny hug, couples hugged like bunnies. The Harvard *Lampoon* in 1912 had jokingly explained the raison d'être of the new dances:

HE: Shall we bunny?
SHE: No: let us just sit down and hug.[24]

Most dance-hall operators not only allowed but encouraged such behavior by permitting the free flow of liquor inside their establishments. Dancers, overheated on the dance floor, sought refuge and refreshment in the barrooms. Had water or soft drinks been available, customers might have opted for them. But in the commercial dance halls, as in many of the cabarets and nightclubs, it was usually easier, often cheaper, and always more stylish to drink alcoholic beverages. At the Terrace Garden, according to the investigator for the New York

Committee of Fourteen, "soda" cost ten cents, while beer cost only
five. While many of the young women were probably acquainted with
the deleterious effects of alcoholic beverages after strenuous physical
activity, some were not. Investigators in San Francisco reported that
"the warmth caused by dancing and the close atmosphere of the hall
induce them to accept invitations to drink. They see other girls drinking beer and whiskey, and they are ashamed to order anything else."[25]

The dangers of accepting drinks from strange men were twofold.
Young women might get drunk and be taken advantage of sexually. Or,
more commonly, as Kathy Peiss has written, lacking the money to buy
the men drinks in return, they would have to instead offer "sexual
favors of varying degrees. Most commonly, capitalizing on their attractiveness and personality, women volunteered only flirtatious companionship. . . . Not all working-class women simply played the coquette,
however." Those the vice commissions called "charity girls" were prepared to "go the 'Limit'" with men who paid their way through an
evening of dancing and refreshments.[26]

While the "public" nature of the dancing protected women from
most uninvited intimacies on the dance floor, there was no such protection off the floor. Many of the cabarets and after-hour lobster palaces
had private rooms where businessmen and sporting men could entertain and be entertained by their lady friends. In the public dance halls,
there were balconies or galleries above the dance floor and open
rooftops, backyards, courtyards, and lodging houses nearby. Off the
dance floor and away from the uniformed guards and the glare of the
"public," the boys, reinforced by the comaraderie and competition of
their peers, felt no compunction about acting rough with the girls who
accompanied them to the balconies. Still, while date and gang rapes
were probably not uncommon, there was surprisingly little record of
them in the investigators' reports. Most of the sexual activity they
reported was consensual.[27]

The reformers wanted to desexualize the dance halls, to remove the
liquor, the spaces for sexual liaisons, the prostitutes and sporting men
who were not there to dance, and the steps that they believed were little more than excuses for simulated sex. What they refused to understand was that it was impossible to remove sex from the dance halls and
the dance steps. One of the pleasures of dancing was dipping, gliding,
swirling, hugging, and wrapping your arms around your partner. Young
men and women came to the halls not only to dance but also to flirt, to
hold their partners close, perhaps even to kiss and embrace.[28]

-+-⟹ ⟸-+-

While young "whites" danced happily in the dance halls and night-clubs to ragtime played, composed, or adapted from African-American musicians, that was the full extent of racial integration. As long as the blacks performed on the bandstand or in the front of the hall or cabaret, geographically separated from the dancers, they were welcome. They were not, however, permitted to cross the invisible line that divided audience and performers any more than the black vaudeville stars could have stepped off the stage to sit with their white audiences.

The "dangers" of interracial socialization were compounded by the physical contact and sexual nature of the dancing. Not only could blacks and whites not dance together in couples, but also it was impermissible for black couples to dance alongside white couples. In the posh cabarets, neighborhood dance halls, even in the municipal parks, wherever whites gathered to dance in public, blacks were barred from the dance floor. In Chicago, according to the Commission on Race Relations established after the 1919 riots, African Americans, while permitted to use every other facility at the Municipal Pier, were strongly discouraged (though not legally prohibited) from entering the dance floor. "One of the floor managers . . . speaks courteously to the couple. He expresses regret that he must mention the matter of their dancing to them, but that they are not dancing properly, and he invites them to come to a corner of the dance floor where he will instruct them in the proper way to dance. This usually occupies the remainder of the particular dance, and results in the Negroes not coming on the floor again."[29]

Though excluded from the cabarets, nightclubs, and neighborhood dance halls patronized by whites, African Americans who wanted to dance or listen to ragtime music had plenty of places to do it. There were dozens of dancing-saloons, honky-tonks, and night spots in or adjacent to the vice districts coterminous with black neighborhoods. Through the 1920s, these "joints" expanded in number and prosperity, in part because during Prohibition it was easier to operate a "drinking" establishment beyond the regular theater district than within it. In Harlem in New York City, on South State Street in Chicago, on the Barbary Coast in San Francisco, on Decatur Street in Atlanta, on Beale Street in Memphis, along the Sixth Street corridor in Cincinnati, and in most other cities with sizable African-American populations, the streets after dark were transformed into carnivals of nightlife.[30]

Many of the smaller tenderloin establishments were patronized only by blacks, but the more expensive ones also catered to adventurous whites. While blacks were barred from white establishments, white "slummers" were welcomed in the black joints, clubs, and cabarets. The slummers, in fact, constituted such a sizable—and prosperous—audience that some club owners resegregated their establishments to make their white customers feel more at home. As the sociologist Katrina Hazzard-Gordon has written, in Cleveland's "black and tan" club, Cedar Gardens, located "on the outer edges of the still-burgeoning black community . . . reservation signs were routinely placed on all tables from Thursday through Saturday to restrict African Americans from the cabaret section of the club." Neighborhood residents were, however, allowed to sit wherever they wanted for Sunday matinees and Monday through Wednesday evenings. In Harlem, according to the jazz historians Samuel Charters and Leonard Kunstadt, such exclusive resorts as the Cotton Club, which opened in 1922, stationed "guards at the door [who] restricted admission to white patrons." After sustained protests from the Harlem community, the club agreed to "admit colored patrons" but raised prices so high few neighborhood residents could afford to attend.[31]

Except for the notorious "black and tan" resorts where blacks and whites socialized, drank, and danced together, segregation on the dance floor was an essential constituent of the entertainment experience. The African-American music on the bandstand combined with the exclusion of black dancers from the floor to accentuate and celebrate the "whiteness" of the audience. In dancing to animal dances accompanied by ragtime music, the white audience was ritually acting out its "whiteness" by playing black. When the music stopped, the play-acting also did.

As in other public amusement sites, the crowd in the dance halls was as essential an ingredient in the entertainment experience as the music. One "went out" not simply to dance but to dance "in public," surrounded by strangers. Businessmen, many already invested in the amusement industry, capitalized on what social worker and investigator Maria Lambin referred to as the "gregarious instinct" of urban pleasure seekers by building "spacious and handsome" dance palaces in the

1920s and filling them with "bright lights, jazz music, and continuous novelty [to] attract by the thousands young people who [were] seeking relief from monotony."[32]

Admission charges of fifty cents to a dollar attracted a wide range of dancers. A 1924 article in *Survey* magazine reported that while the patrons of the Broadway dance palaces were "in general, lower in social rank than the patrons of good cabarets and restaurants . . . one finds a rather high type of business man and business woman there [as well as] youngsters, out for a lark . . . the sightseer, alone or in parties, [and an occasional prostitute]. The typical patron, however, is a factory or clerical worker . . . who craves a little diversion from the tragic narrowness of the daily routine." A Pittsburgh survey from 1924 found the same mixed clientele in that city's dance halls. "The patrons generally represent all sections of the city" and almost every variety of wage earner: "mill and factory workers, clerks, mechanics, tailors, stenographers, domestics and so on."[33]

The public of pleasure seekers was not restricted to those who danced in the city's palaces and ballrooms. By the middle 1920s, no social group in the city was untouched by the dance "madness" that had surfaced ten years earlier. When, in 1924, investigators for the Women's City Club and the City Recreation Committee surveyed the dance scene in New York City, they visited "a benefit dance by a Hebrew relief society of the lower East Side"; "a costume ball by a group of young East Siders"; "a respectable lodge party where everyone is in formal evening clothes"; "the annual ball of one of the political parties"; "a Bohemian benefit dance to raise money for one of the numerous Bohemian charities"; "the annual ball of the Pullman porters"; "a society [ball] of negro cigar makers from the West Indies"; "the annual ball of a big Catholic society"; "Spanish, Italian, Ukrainian dances—and many more." What was even more remarkable than the variety of groups dancing was the uniformity of styles and music. The same music was being played and the same steps danced uptown and downtown. "Once in a while we see native folk-dance steps, but as a rule the dancing is the same as that found in the Broadway dance palaces, which seem to set the pace for all."[34]

Even in ethnically segregated immigrant neighborhoods, such as those in Chicago's stockyard district, the jazz and jazz dancing popular in the downtown nightclubs and ballrooms had displaced the once popular "Polish hop." As settlement-house founder Mary McDowell noted with evident distaste, within only a few years of their arrival in Chicago, young immigrants had abandoned "their old country dances and folk songs. . . . All was changed—American shoes, American clothes, American jazz with its saxophone were the rage. The Polish accordion with its folk music, folk dances and folk clothing had been completely displaced by what our young neighbors called 'American dances and music.' When I urged for the old-country dances I was told haughtily by these modernized young people, as I fancy their old-fashioned parents were told, 'Why, Miss McDowell, nobody dances those dances any more.' With a superior gesture and a look of 100% American they ordered the saxophone 'On with the jazz!' This type of Americanization by the dance hall and the movies goes on apace."[35]

In Pittsburgh, when investigators for the Girls' Conference visited a neighborhood hall "in hopes of seeing some of the Russian native dances," they found instead "a four piece, unharmonious, squeaking orchestra whin[ing] out what was supposed to be the latest American jazz while a few couples bounced over a rough floor à l'américain."[36]

Social dancing had, in Maria Lambin's phrase, become "as standardized as a patent breakfast food or a Ford automobile." What the devotees of the barnyard dances in the nightclubs, the downtown palaces, and the rented neighborhood halls appeared to share in common was their desire to distance themselves, if only temporarily on a Saturday night, from class and ethnic cultural forms. It was not only the Polish immigrants in Chicago or the Russians in Pittsburgh who in adopting the new dances abandoned the old ones. The debutantes and "smart set" in New York and Philadelphia also forswore their traditional waltzes, polkas, lancers, quadrilles, and the two-step for barnyard steps and jazz.

The dance halls and palaces provided their patrons with the sense that they were part of a larger social whole, a new public of pleasure seekers that cut across all social divisions. In traveling downtown to the larger dance halls and palaces, to Roseland and the Grand Central Palace in New York City or the Aragon, the Trianon, Dreamland, and the White City Ballroom in Chicago, dancers left behind their particular neighborhood and ethnic communities to join a new "American" public dancing to a new "American" music, jazz.[37]

On the dance floor, there was no reminder of the mundane world left behind. Dancing was pure pleasure, an activity indulged in because it was fun and might be a prelude to romance or sexual intimacy. In other amusement centers, most clearly at the world's fair and on the lyceum circuit, but in the theaters and amusement parks as well, an attempt was made to intertwine the amusing with the educational for those who still feared the corrupting influence of pleasure for its own sake. But not on the dance floor.

In going dancing, well-to-do and poor, the smart set and working folk entered a third sphere of everyday life, separated intentionally and irrevocably from the worlds of home and family, work and workplace. On returning home or leaving for work the next morning, the dancers would rejoin a world defined and divided by categories of class, income, neighborhood, and ethnicity. But, for the moment, for that evening, those identifications—and those social worlds—were left behind, as the dancers, in close embrace, whirled across the floor to a ragtime beat.

CHAPTER 10

Talking and Singing Machines, Parlors, and Peep Shows

T HE FIRST OF THE AUTOMATIC AMUSEMENT machines, the phonograph or "talking machine," was patented by Thomas Alva Edison in 1877. Edison, who early in his career had determined "not to undertake inventions unless there was a definite market demand for them," believed that his phonograph could have multiple uses as a business machine. It would, he predicted in an 1878 article for the *North American Review*, be the perfect dictation machine and record-keeper. It could also be used to record phonographic books for blind people; teach elocution; record the "last words" of aged family members; preserve dying languages; teach rote lessons to schoolchildren; transmit and preserve "permanent and invaluable" business records; and, when perfected, "be liberally devoted to music" and used in "music boxes, toys," and talking dolls.[1]

Although the first machines were quite primitive and able to record and play back less than a minute of barely audible sounds, Edison was impatient to see a return on his investment. His plant produced about 500 phonographs that were exhibited by trained lecturers on the lyceum circuit to whet the public's appetite and attract investors and capital. When, after only a few months, the novelty of hearing thirty seconds of scratchy sound wore off for audiences and investors alike, Edison turned his attention to inventions with more practical and immediate applications, like the incandescent light bulb.[2]

In 1886, Edison returned to his phonograph. Alexander Graham

Bell, who with associates had been working on his own dictating machine cleverly named the graphophone (reversing the syllables of Edison's machine), suggested that the two inventors combine their talents and organizations. Edison, angered by what he considered to be Bell's theft of his invention but stimulated by the competition (Bell's machine apparently worked better than his), turned down the offer and returned to the laboratory to improve his phonograph.[3]

By the spring of 1888, Edison and his assistants were ready to display their new dictating machine to investors and the public. When the initial demonstrations, however, failed to attract investment capital, Edison, again short of funds, sold the rights to market his machine to Jesse Lippincott, a venture capitalist who had already bought the rights to Bell's graphophone. With Edison's imprimatur, Lippincott enlisted investors across the country to buy state franchises to exploit the Wizard's latest discovery. The first phonographs and graphophones were designed as business instruments for taking dictation. Unfortunately, the machines were too complicated to run without extensive training and did not talk at all, but produced instead what one user described as "but a parody of the human voice." Court reporters, a potentially lucrative market, found the machines unworkable, stenographers lobbied against them, and the business firms that had been expected to lease them were discouraged by the poor sound reproduction and the constant maintenance required.[4]

Only as it became obvious that the phonograph was a failure as a "talking" machine did a few adventurous (and probably desperate) investors begin to reconfigure it as a "singing" machine. Louis Glass of San Francisco sounded one of the only bright notes at the 1890 inaugural convention of the phonograph company executives when, on the last day of the meeting, he addressed the group on the subject of "public exhibitions." Glass began his talk with the simple, yet powerful, statement that "all the money" the San Francisco company had "made in the phonograph business" came from what he called "the-nickel-in-the-slot machine." He explained how he had fitted his phonographs with four listening tubes attached to four slots for coins and placed them in local saloons. Customers deposited nickels in the slots to start the machines, put the tubes to their ears, and heard the muffled but recognizable sound of music accompanied by scratches, clicks, and strange whirring noises. Glass's company had, he claimed, already made almost $2,000 from the two machines it had placed in the Palais Royal Saloon in San Francisco.

MR. CHADBOURNE: Two machines in the same saloon?

MR. GLASS: Yes.

MR. CHADBOURNE: Did they do as well?

MR. GLASS: Yes, and I will state right here, that we seem to have the same patrons all the time. We change the cylinders every two days, and if a man puts a nickel in one and hears a piece of band music, he almost invariably goes over and hears a second one.

Additional machines had been placed in the waiting room of the Oakland–San Francisco ferry and in other saloons—and all, Glass asserted, had made money. "We have fifteen machines out. . . . We have taken in altogether from those machines, eight of which were placed in April and May $4,019.00; figure out the details yourself."[5]

The executives from the other companies questioned Glass about patents, operating expenses, and where and for how much they could purchase the rights to coin-operated phonographs. Although all appeared to be astonished by the amount of money the San Francisco company was taking in, none was completely surprised by the ease with which the business instrument had been turned into an entertainment machine. Each local company had already had some experience with what the director of the Georgia and Florida companies called "the social uses and amusement part of the instruments." Edison, always the wizard at attracting publicity for his inventions, had recorded a number of musical cylinders to demonstrate how the phonograph worked. For a modest price, local companies bought copies of these demonstration cylinders with opera singers, classical musicians (including the piano prodigy Josef Hoffman), brass bands, and "darky" songs whistled by a man Edison claimed to have met on a ferry ride into New York City, but who was in fact, George W. Johnson, a fairly well-known African-American minstrel.[6]

Everywhere they were played, the demonstration musical cylinders attracted crowds. In Atlanta, Georgia, the director of the local company found that the demonstration phonographs were "daily amusing great numbers of people, the majority of whom never had an idea of using the instrument practically or otherwise." The same thing had happened in Texas, where dozens of businessmen had visited the phonograph company offices not to lease dictating machines but to listen to "a very nice musical exhibition."[7]

Instead of capitalizing on the phonograph's ability to amuse customers by singing, as Glass had in San Francisco, most company executives banned the demonstration cylinders from their offices, fearful that customers, having been entertained by the machines, would regard them as toys instead of serious business tools. As the opening editorial in the *Phonogram*, the industry's trade journal, warned company executives, "The exhibition of the phonograph for amusement purposes [is] liable to create a wrong impression in the minds of the public as to its actual merits for other purposes."[8]

The advocates of the phonograph as a business machine were fighting a losing battle. Before their first business year was out, most of the phonograph companies had bowed to the inevitable and converted their dictating machines into nickel-in-the-slot amusement machines. The Texas Phonograph Company opened a separate office in Dallas where customers who wanted to hear recorded music could do so—for a fee. The Spokane company abandoned its attempt to lease business machines and concentrated entirely on placing nickel-in-the-slot phonographs "in the most popular resorts in the city."[9]

Salesmen on commission and independent exhibitors carried their phonographs into public spaces looking for crowds of passersby in a festive mood. The New England company put out machines at "all the summer resorts and beaches" in the Boston area. The New York Phonograph Company "placed a large number of these instruments at Saratoga." Machines were also exhibited at state, county, and world's fairs.[10]

Wherever the phonographs were displayed—on fair midways, in train stations, in hotel lobbies, and at summer resorts—they were greeted with enthusiasm by first-time users who thrilled to the novelty of hearing machines sing or play music. Recorded music appealed, as a *Phonogram* writer insisted in late 1891, "to all classes and conditions of the human race, from the millionaire in his opera box to the bootblack with his grimy hands and his harmonica—all love music."[11]

The demand of exhibitors for new recordings pushed the phonograph companies to expand their inventories. Because band music was popular with almost every type of audience, the larger companies entered into exclusive recording contracts with the better-known bands. The New York Phonograph Company recorded and distributed cylinders of Cappa's Seventh Regiment Band; the Columbia Phonograph Company entered into an exclusive contract with the United States Marine Band, which it proudly advertised as "in many respects, the most celebrated band in the world. It can play, without notes, more than five hundred different selections." (Exhibitors who chose to pur-

This 1893 photograph is of a train terminal where nickel-in-the-slot phonographs had been installed in a waiting room. The signs over the machines and in the rear of the room read, "ATTENDANT IN CHARGE WILL FURNISH CHANGE." (*U.S. Department of the Interior, National Park Service, Edison National Historic Site.*)

chase Marine Band cylinders were given display photographs of "the band in full uniform, as it appears when playing for the President of the United States at the White House, on state occasions, or in the grounds of the White House in pleasant weather.") Next in popularity to the bands were an assorted group of musicians, including artistic whistlers, the most famous of which was Mr. John Y. AtLee of Washington, D.C., cornet and clarinet soloists, and singers accompanied by orchestra in "Sentimental," "Topical," "Comic," "Negro," and "Irish" renditions. An increasing number of talking records, recitations, and humorous monologues, many in dialect, were also being produced.[12]

Although most of the cylinders were distributed by the larger firms, the local companies continued to record, exhibit, and sell their own versions of the big hits of the day, such as "After the Ball" and "Daisy Bell." The Ohio company made money with cylinders of Dan Kelly, who recited mock Irish vaudeville monologues in the name of Pat Brady. In New York City, an independent record producer, Gianni Bettini, produced and marketed classical music, including many of the best-known opera stars of the 1890s.[13]

Strangely enough given the fact that one of Edison's first musical cylinders had been of black performer George W. Johnson, African Americans were kept out of the early recording studios, although they were, as we have seen, featured performers in vaudeville, musical comedy, and on the world's fair midways. The "darky" cylinders that were produced and widely circulated in the early 1890s were, for the most part, recorded by white impersonators. Before World War I, the Edison, Victor, and Columbia companies put out hundreds of "coon" songs and parodies. The Ohio company boasted in 1891 that it had made up to $4.75 a day, more than it got from "some of the Marine Band" cylinders by hiring "a gentleman from an adjoining territory to sing a number of banjo songs" and advertising his cylinder as "an-old-time-before-the-war banjo song sung by a plantation darkey." The Louisiana Phonograph Company produced an entire "line of negro specialties . . . consisting of old plantation songs, darkey melodies, etc. Probably the most successful specialty is the work of 'Brudder Rasmus,' whose sermons, such as 'Charity ob de Heart,' 'Adam and Eve and de Winter Apple,' 'Sinners, Chicken Stealers, Etc.,' and 'De Lottrey,' with the characteristic participation of his congregation are wonderfully realistic and attractive."[14]

In addition to these officially recorded cylinders, there was a developing underground market for cylinders that indulged the amusement fantasies of the rougher elements of the male-only sporting crowd. To the dismay of phonograph company executives, "unscrupulous" exhibitors had begun to record, collect, and exchange recordings of "jim-jam songs," profanities, vulgar conversations, and simulated sexual encounters. "A lively trade developed . . . in pornographic and obscene material, as for example the purportedly secret recording of a husband's dalliances with the maid." One exhibitor made a small fortune with such recordings at a Rhode Island state fair until a competing "lady exhibitor" who had "heretofore . . . always done an excellent business" with "clean" material complained about the unfair competition and had the scoundrel run "out of town."[15]

⊷⟾⊙⟾⊷

While the traveling exhibitors were exhibiting phonographs during the warm weather on fair midways, at summer resorts, and in hotel lobbies, the parent companies had stumbled on what appeared to be an ideal—

and permanent—exhibition site in the central business districts. They had found that by grouping several machines together in a downtown "parlor," with full-time attendants to service the machines and make change, they could attract large numbers of customers from the streams of pedestrians who passed by day and night.

These first phonograph parlors were unlike any other amusement sites or exhibition spaces. From the outside, they looked like retail stores, except for their full-size show windows that were lit and decorated not with items for sale but with framed posters and photographs of Edison, the current program of selections, and a sign inviting passersby to "walk in," admission free. Inside, the decor was somewhere between that of a fancy saloon and a hotel or theater lobby, with potted palms, ceiling fans, and quasi-Oriental rugs. The lighting was theatrical, with a separate "incandescent electric light [over each machine] bringing out plainly the likeness of Edison and the name of the selection to be heard." The phonographs themselves were encased in "handsome oak automatic cabinets." As the Ohio Phonograph Company explained, "a magnificent piece of mechanism like the phonograph deserves a fine setting." More to the point, the oak cabinets, "specimens of the finest woodwork that can be secured," upgraded the image of what were still slot machines only recently transported from barrooms and ferry terminals.[16]

The show windows and lighting within signaled that these were establishments with nothing to hide. No one could be intimidated or frightened by the setting. No reputations would be risked by entering. Those who could not afford even a nickel or two of music were invited to "go partners" and share a listening tube with a friend. Those for whom money was no object could bring the whole family or spend a dollar or more listening once or twice to the selections on a dozen different machines. The parlors appealed, in particular, as the *Phonogram* suggested, to the large "number of travelers and visitors [who] come and go on business and pleasure" in the "great manufacturing and commercial centers." Customers did not have to plan in advance to visit the phonograph parlor. They merely "dropped in" on the way to or from lunch or appointments, or on their way home or to the theater.[17]

Because the stream of pedestrians from whom the parlors drew their customers included a wide range of city folk, the parlor managers had to provide something for almost every taste: popular songs and perennial classics, military bands and comic whistlers, monologues such as "Brady's Election Speech," and special effects recordings such as "'Night Alarm,' a band record descriptive of a fire, with calls of the firemen, ringing of the bells, the clattering of horses' hoofs and the unwinding of the hose carriage reel." Mr. Ott of the Kansas company, asked to describe his parlor at the fourth annual convention of the phonograph companies, emphasized the need to "keep a general assortment of good music" on hand. "All of them are more or less called for. There are some people who call for the talks, [like Shakespeare's] 'Seven Ages of Man' . . . and others call for sentimental songs, but I believe that the greatest number of calls . . . is for such songs as 'After the Ball,' or 'After the Fair.' . . . They don't last like 'Down on the Farm,' or 'Home, Sweet Home,' but for the time that they are popular they are extremely so, and our experience has been that that class of songs has made the most money per cylinder for the exhibitor."[18]

To bolster their receipts, the parlor owners surrounded their graphophones and phonographs with other "automatic" amusement novelties, machines that dispensed gum, candy, fruit, and miracle medicinals such as "Roy's Positive Remedy Curing Headache and Neuralgia in 15 Minutes—10¢ Per Package," and X-ray machines and fluoroscopes that displayed the bones in your hands and were all the rage until experimenters, including one of Edison's assistants, discovered that repeated exposure caused flesh to ulcerate, hair to fall out, and eventual death. The automatic dispensing machine industry had, the *Phonogram* reported in January of 1892, become "so valuable that companies are forming all over the country to cultivate it. . . . 'A penny in the slot.' This doesn't look like a heavy investment, but its earning capacity is great. . . . Few people realize the result of an accumulation of pennies or nickels."[19]

⊷⟾◯⟾⊷

The parlor owners were turning a profit by exhibiting the new amusement machines to a larger, more "respectable" slice of the urban population than had encountered them in the saloons or on the fair midways. Outside the larger cities, another group of amusement entrepreneurs were attempting to assemble similar audiences of "respectable" folk in small-town lecture halls and church auditoria. By the 1890s, the lecture-hall—or lyceum—circuit had grown in size and profitability until it had become a viable alternative to the vaudeville and live theater circuits. In almost every city and town with a vaudeville theater, there were church and school auditoria, libraries, lecture rooms, and rented halls where local religious, civic, charitable, educational, and fraternal associations sponsored special evening events for those who continued to regard the theater and commercial amusements as sinful at worst, indecent at best.[20]

The phonograph, properly exhibited, was an ideal "attraction" on the lecture-hall circuit because it was as entertaining as it was educational. Lyman Howe, the most prominent and successful of the phonograph exhibitors to travel the circuit, had in the 1880s, made his living exhibiting a model coal mine, complete with a coal breaker, as an "educational" exhibit in small towns and cities in Pennsylvania, Maryland, and Ohio. In 1890, he exchanged his coal mine for a phonograph. The phonograph not only was easier to transport from town to town but also had much greater drawing power.[21]

Howe billed his new attraction as Edison's latest scientific marvel, "the miracle of the nineteenth century," a photographer of sound that could break through the barriers of time and space, bring back the dead, and convey messages from thousands of miles away. While other traveling exhibitors ballyhooed their machines like sideshow barkers introducing dog-faced boys, Howe adopted the persona of the "professor" or "lecturer." As he explained in his advertising, "*his* entertainment would be 'Clean, Scientific, Amusing and Elevating—nothing like the Ordinary Phonograph that is seen on the Streets, in Hotels and at the Fairs.'" Howe mixed popular songs by quartets with banjo and cornet solos, comic parodies, recitations, sounds of babies crying, and lots of band music. His concerts also included demonstrations of music recorded live on stage and then played back for the audience. In large part as a result of Howe's commentary and his live demonstrations, audiences left his "concerts" entertained but feeling that they had learned something about science and mechanics as well.[22]

Although Howe was the first and most successful, he was not the only exhibitor on the lyceum circuit to offer his audiences full-length phonograph "concerts." Technical improvements, including huge new "concert horns" several feet in diameter, had by early 1893 liberated the singing machine from its coin-slots and listening tubes. A remaining problem was solved in the middle 1890s when phonographs with spring motors instead of cumbersome, leaky batteries appeared on the market, meeting—in the words of the D. E. Boswell catalog—"the long expressed demand for a single, light, inexpensive, compact, portable,

This catalog advertisement for a "concert horn" suggests that the traveling exhibitor who invested in such a machine would be able to fill concert halls with refined gentlemen and ladies. (*U.S. Department of the Interior, National Park Service, Edison National Historic Site.*)

talking machine for exhibition." With the new traveling kits, lecturers and showmen could put together their own entertainments, skillfully combining brief talks on the "science" of the phonograph, live demonstrations, and musical selections. The most successful "concerts" were those that presented a wide variety of recordings. "As to selections," a *Phonogram* article advised, "a mixture of both serious and humorous should be made, the latter predominating, as the phonograph adapts itself to the humorous more readily than to the serious. . . . Monotony is the bugbear of the phonograph. In order to escape it, tact must be exercised, and all the inventive powers of which the exhibitor is possessed should be used to vary the selections as they follow one another. The entire exhibition should be an animated, shifting kaleidoscope, presenting new features at every turn."[23]

⊷⟲⟳⊷

Arrayed in tastefully decorated parlors or presented in lecture halls with "concert horn" attachments, the phonograph's chief attraction remained its novelty. Exhibitors such as Howe, who traveled from city to city, seldom appearing in the same place more than once a year, had less trouble with this than the parlor owners who were tied to fixed locations. When, in the middle 1890s, word came out of Menlo Park that the Wizard was experimenting with a device that would record visual images as the phonograph had sound, parlor owners across the country lined up to secure these machines for their storefronts.

Thomas Lombard, the president of the North American Phonograph Company, was in early 1893 among the first civilians admitted to a private exhibition of the new moving-picture machine, the kinetoscope.* Through a peephole, he saw tiny, yet distinct, moving pictures of John Ott, one of Edison's assistants, doing an impromptu "skirt dance" and "going through all the phases of a prolonged sneeze." Entranced by the commercial possibilities of the peephole machines, Lombard formed a syndicate to exhibit them at the upcoming Chicago World's Fair, where he had already arranged to exhibit his phonographs.[25]

In April of 1894, over a year late, the first shipment of kinetoscopes was delivered to Lombard's syndicate, which, the world's fair having long since closed, installed them in a vacated shoe store remodeled as an amusement parlor on 27th Street and Broadway in the heart of New York's entertainment district.[26]

The first kinetoscope parlor looked and functioned much like the phonograph parlors, with one important exception. In the phonograph parlors, admission had been free and the minimum price of entertainment had been five cents for two minutes of song. In the kinetoscope parlors, customers were required to buy twenty-five-cent tickets at the door, which entitled them to peer into the peepholes of five different machines. For a second twenty-five cents they could see five more films in the remaining five kinetoscopes.[27]

In setting the minimum price at a quarter rather than a nickel, the owners signaled their intention to attract a comparatively upscale audience, one that could afford to spend fifty cents for two and half minutes of flickering images. An early drawing of the parlor shows a room tastefully decorated with potted palms on the perimeter, incandescent lamps shaped like dragons on either side, a life-size bronzed bust of

---

*Edison, borrowing from the Greek terms *kinet* or *kineto* for "movement," *graph* for "writing," and *scopos* for "watching," named his camera the kinetograph and his peep-show machine the kinetoscope.[24]

Edison in front, carpets and waxed floors, and the type of audience the owners hoped to attract: three elegantly dressed ladies and three men, one of whom was obviously a "gentleman" outfitted in top hat and cane.[28]

The *Phonoscope*, the voice of the new industry, reproduced this drawing in its first issue as it offered advice to prospective parlor owners. "In all exhibitions, the neater and the more attractive the show, the greater is also the financial success. . . . The above cut represents an exhibition parlor which it would be well to study in order to use it as a model, wherever practicable. . . . Nobody would ever hesitate to enter such a parlor; it invites and attracts all."[29]

Almost all of the early kinetoscope parlors were situated in downtown locations (State Street and Wabash Avenue in Chicago, Canal Street in New Orleans, Market Street in San Francisco, Tremont Street in Boston), where the business and entertainment districts intersected. In Chicago, a parlor was opened "in the Masonic Temple building, then Chicago's prided skyscraper." In San Francisco, Peter Bacigalupi, one of the more successful owner/operators of phonograph parlors, opened a kinetoscope parlor in the Chronicle Building on Market Street.[30]

Everywhere they were exhibited, the kinetoscopes drew crowds at once—and did so without much advertising. Edison's name and word of mouth were sufficient to lure customers inside. By the summer of 1895, new kinetoscope parlors had been opened in the nation's larger cities and in smaller cities—from Binghamton, New York, and Riverside, Rhode Island, in the Northeast, to Nashville, Tennessee, and Augusta, Georgia, in the South, to Olympia, Washington, and Cyrene, Wyoming, in the West. The new amusement machines appeared to have so much commercial potential that the New York Security and Trust Company in January of 1896 issued $200,000 in mortgage bonds to an upstate New York company to manufacture and sell an improved version of the moving-picture camera and peep-show machine. The only security the company offered in return for the bonds were the patent rights to its machines.* [31]

---

*The new company, the American Mutoscope Company, which included W. K. L. Dickson, Edison's former assistant among its principals, would within a few years be producing a successful peep-show machine and a marketable camera and projector. Under the Biograph corporate name, it would become one of the more successful early production companies.

We don't know much about the audience at these early parlors, although we do know that it was large enough to provide the owners with a profit and new investors with the incentive to buy into the business. A glimpse at the content of the early films suggests that the parlors probably attracted more sporting men than family groups or the well-dressed ladies in bustles pictured in the *Phonoscope* drawing of the well-run amusement parlor. According to the film historian Gordon Hendricks, the films distributed to the parlors included moving pictures of *Sandow* (the strongman stripped to the waist flexing his muscles); *Horse Shoeing; Barber Shop* (a slapstick skit); *Wrestling; Blacksmiths; Highland Dance; Trapeze* (probably with a lady acrobat in tights); *Roosters* (a cockfight); *Organ Grinder; Trained Bears;* and two turns by a contortionist, Mme. Bertholdi, intriguingly entitled *Mouth Support* and *Table Contortion.*[32]

The major problem with these early films was not the content, which, though heavy on exotic dancers, was still varied enough to appeal to many tastes. It was the lack of new films. Raff and Gammon, the sole authorized distributors for Edison's moving pictures and machines, complained continually to Edison and his subordinates about the lack of decent films for their kinetoscopes. Those that were available were, as often as not, defective, faded, fuzzy, or flickering beyond repair.[33]

The parlor owners and investors who had placed individual machines in drugstores, hotel lobbies, and in and around the summer resorts had little trouble getting them to peek in the peepholes. The difficulty was enticing them to return for a second look. Within a year of the opening of the first kinetoscope parlor, Raff and Gammon reported to their board of directors that business was "rather quiet." By the fall, the demand for new machines had fallen to a trickle. Raff and Gammon tried to sell the company but found no takers.[34]

There were by this time more than 900 machines and thousands of films already in distribution and enough parlor owners to support a new trade journal, the *Phonoscope*. But it had become apparent that the downtown amusement parlors were not going to survive on ladies and gentlemen customers alone. The future of the business appeared to be the sporting men and boys who had initially come to the parlors to see the boxing matches and the hootchi-kootchi dancers.

No matter how brightly lit or tastefully decorated, the kinetoscope parlors operated as "drop in" centers that, like saloons, offered amusements in five- to ten-minute packages and, not surprisingly, drew a large portion of their customers from the sporting crowd. The parlor owners' decision to concentrate on cultivating a male-only crowd was reinforced by the invention and marketing of the mutoscope by the Biograph Company in 1897. Like the first automatic amusement machine, the phonograph, the mutoscope had been designed as a business machine for traveling salesmen to exhibit their wares. It was reconfigured as an amusement machine when company executives recognized that by substituting moving pictures of "Little Egypt" for pictures of loom-weaving machines, they could increase sales and profits. "*Little Egypt* . . . the first Mutoscope success . . . was followed by *Serpentine Dancers, How Girls Go to Bed, How Girls Undress,* and similar tidbits," including the first commercial film to exhibit partial nudity, "*The Birth of the Pearl,* showing a girl in white tights and bare arms crouching in an oversized oyster shell."[35]

What made the mutoscope the perfect instrument for viewing such subjects was its mechanical crank. Unlike the kinetoscope that ran automatically when the switch was turned on or a coin dropped in the slot, the mutoscope was operated by hand. As an 1897 advertising brochure explained, "In the operation of the Mutoscope, the spectator has the performance entirely under his own control by the turning of the crank. He may make the operation as quick or as slow as fancy dictates . . . and if he so elects, the entertainment can be stopped by him at any point in the series and each separate picture inspected at leisure; thus every step, motion, act or expression can be analyzed, presenting effects at once instructive, interesting, attractive, amusing and startling."[36]

✦◦═◉ ◉═◦✦

By the time the mutoscopes reached the market in 1897, most of the phonograph and kinetoscope parlors had closed their doors and sold their machines secondhand to "tenderloin" arcades and shooting galleries. Although their rise and fall had been telescoped into only a few years, the parlors had opened a new phase in the history of urban amusements. Located in the heart of the city's business districts and offering entertainment in compact packages measured in minutes, not hours, they stretched the map of the entertainment world in new directions. They entertained customers—if only for a few minutes at a time—in drugstores, theater lobbies, railway and ferry terminals, department and general stores, resort hotels, boardwalks and midways, tents erected on vacant lots, small-town and city lecture halls, and parlors in the central business districts. Everywhere they were exhibited, they attracted an enthusiastic crowd of onlookers and customers willing to take a chance and buy a concert ticket or deposit a nickel in the slot for a few minutes of automatic entertainment.

Part of the attraction of the machines was their newness. They entered the public arena without a knowable past. They belonged neither to Fifth Avenue nor to the Bowery. They could present opera singers, vaudeville clowns, ballet dancers, or prize fighters. They were large enough to accommodate every taste and appeal to every audience.

The show businessmen were so enchanted by the amusement machines' potentially universal drawing power that they began to articulate their own psychology of amusements. Human beings, they were now convinced, were born with an inherent, inalienable need to be amused. As *Billboard* magazine explained in the spring of 1895, "Everybody knows that there is always an aching longing for diversion in the human heart. The public must, and will be amused." Or as the *Phonoscope* proclaimed in its inaugural editorial in 1896, "There is one great desire which animates all mankind, from the cradle to the grave, encompassing all:—the desire for amusement and entertainment."[37]

While individual projects might fail and fail again, the show businessman's faith was ever renewed by the crowds each machine attracted before the novelty wore off. The public had demonstrated its hunger for cheap amusements. The showmen would find a way to satisfy it, even if it meant carrying the new amusement machines on their backs from place to place.

CHAPTER 11

"The Surest Immediate Money-Maker Ever Known"

A S WE SAW IN CHAPTER 10, THE ARRIVAL OF Edison's kinetoscopes had boosted business in the amusement parlors, but not enough to guarantee their long-term commercial viability. Like the coin-in-the-slot phonograph, the peep-show machine had proved to be just another "novelty" entertainment with an abbreviated life span.

That neither his talking nor his peep-show machine had made much of a profit did not discourage Edison from assigning an assistant to work on an improved moving-picture machine that would take the images out of their cabinet and project them onto a screen. The search for such a machine had been going on since the 1880s. Now, in the mid-1890s, Edison, his associates, and independent inventors, mechanics, and showmen on two continents, their enthusiasm kindled by the crowds drawn to the kinetoscope exhibitions, reapplied themselves to the task.

In the spring of 1895, the Latham brothers, the proprietors of a kinetoscope parlor in New York City, announced that they had succeeded in devising a screen machine to exhibit boxing films. Edison claimed that the Lathams' projector was a poor copy of his kinetoscope (which it was), that he would sue them if they tried to market it (which he did), and that he would soon have a superior screen machine.

Within a year, "Edison's vitascope" was ready for exhibition, but ironically given Edison's public complaints about the Lathams, the new projector had not been invented by the Wizard or any of his associates. It was the product of a collaboration between C. Francis Jenkins, a government stenographer, and Thomas Armat, a real estate entrepreneur. Armat and Jenkins had originally named their projector the "phantascope" and exhibited it at the Atlanta Cotton States exposition in the fall of 1895. Although it failed to make much money in Atlanta, the "phantascope" did indeed project moving pictures onto a screen. Raff and Gammon, desperate to find a substitute for their failing kinetoscopes, offered Armat, now estranged from his partner, a contract to "exploit" his new machine. There was one catch to the proposal: They wanted to bring Edison into the partnership—"In order to secure the largest profit in the shortest time it is necessary that we attach Mr. Edison's great name to this new machine." Edison agreed to the proposal. His reputation provided the machine with instant legitimacy; his manufacturing plant mass-produced it; and a share of the profits discouraged him from claiming that the projector infringed on his kinetoscope patents.[1]

To make sure that their new machine got the appropriate send off, Raff and Gammon planned to exhibit it first at Koster & Bial's vaudeville house in New York City. As they wrote to Armat in Washington, D.C., "The reports through the [New York City] news-papers go out through the country, and we shall do a lot of advertising in the shape of news-paper articles which will excite the curiosity of parties interested in such things, and which will lead to more sales and larger profits than if we were to exhibit throughout the country at the same time." Even before the debut Raff and Gammon began informing parlor owners that the "Edison vitascope" was, at long last, "ready for negotiation [having] reached a wonderful state of perfection." They urged their customers to enter quickly into lease agreements. As they warned Peter Bacigalupi in San Francisco, they were ready to grant him exclusive California rights for $2,500, but he had to hurry as they had already received "several applications from your state." Identical letters were sent to other parlor owners.[2]

In April of 1896, Raff and Gammon followed up their initial letters with an elaborate sixteen-page pamphlet. "The Latest Marvel: The 'Vitascope'" was, they claimed, the perfect amusement machine. It was "simple in construction and easy of operation"; could be placed "from fifty to seventy-five feet distant from the canvas or screen" with the space in between occupied by "a large audience"; could project "a sub-

THE LATEST MARVEL

❧❧❧

"Vitascope"

❧❧❧

A NEW MACHINE is now ready to be exhibited to the public, which is probably the most remarkable and startling in its results of any that the world has ever seen ❧ Several marvels of inventive genius have, in past years, gone forth from the Edison Works, located at Orange, New Jersey ❧ "The Wizard of Menlo Park" has conceived and in due course perfected the Phonograph, the Kinetoscope and the Kinetophone, each of which in turn, has excited the wonder and amazement of the public and, from a practical standpoint, opened up opportunities for exhibition enterprises, many of which are paying handsomely to this day ❧ ❧

This is the cover of the brochure that Raff and Gammon mailed to potential "Vitascope" investors. (*U.S. Department of the Interior, National Park Service, Edison National Historic Site.*)

ject . . . for ten or fifteen minutes if desired, although four or five minutes is better"; used standard electric current; was protected by patents
"applied for through high-class patent attorneys"; and promised a
"large profit to those who control" its exhibition. The arithmetic of
exhibition was simply calculated. Raff and Gammon suggested that
customers be charged twenty-five or fifty cents for shows of "three to
six subjects, each lasting four or five minutes. . . . Thus, many exhibitions can be given in a day and evening, each at stated periods or hours,
and the audience on each occasion need only be limited by the size
of the room or hall. . . . No machine has ever been invented which
can compare with the 'Vitascope' in its large possibilities of money-
making."[3]

When A. Caswell of Jamestown, Rhode Island, who had apparently
not been convinced by their pamphlet, complained about the high
price they were asking for the rights to his small state, Raff and Gammon emphasized the difference between earlier entertainment
machines that could entertain only a few customers at a time and the
vitascope: "You should be able to reimburse yourself for the entire
amount we ask for the state by exhibition in Providence alone; for the
Vitascope can be shown to a very large audience at once."[4]

⤞⟹⟸⤝

After the successful debut of the vitascope at Koster & Bial's in New
York City—and the enthusiastic press response orchestrated by Raff
and Gammon—exhibitors and parlor owners from dozens of cities
lined up to purchase or lease state's rights to exploit the new amusement machine. By the summer of 1896, "Edison's vitascope" was starring on vaudeville bills at Keith's theaters in Boston and Philadelphia,
at the Orpheum houses in San Francisco and Los Angeles, in Hopkins'
South Side Theater in Chicago, New Haven's Grand Opera House,
Milwaukee's Academy of Music, and in smaller halls in Louisville,
Cleveland, and Wilkes-Barre. Audiences everywhere thrilled to the
magic of moving images enlarged and projected onto sheets or screens.
They hollered with delight as the speeding trains careened in their
direction and laughed and cheered as comedians, acrobats, and vaudevillians flickered onto the frame for two minutes at a time.[5]

The parlor owners who leased the new machines set aside space in
the rear of their storefronts to project the pictures onto a sheet and
took out newspaper ads to promote their new attraction. As an adver-

tisement in the *Providence Journal* exclaimed, "ALL THE TOWN IS TALK-ING! EDISON'S ASTONISHING VITASCOPE. . . . Your Life is Incomplete Without! Bring your wives, sweethearts, and aunts. . . . ADMISSION ONLY 25¢." In Los Angeles, the vitascope opened at the Orpheum Theater and toured nearby vaudeville theaters before it was permanently installed in Thomas Tally's phonograph parlor. Unfortunately, as Tally quickly discovered, customers were reluctant to enter darkened, unventilated back rooms to stare at pictures projected on a wall or sheet. Tally's solution was to punch holes in the partition separating the parlor from the vitascope room and allow customers to "peer in at the screen while standing in the comfortable security of the well lighted phonograph parlor. . . . Three peep holes were at chair level for seated spectators, and four somewhat higher for standees."[6]

One of the most ambitious of the early parlor owners was Mitchell H. Mark, the sales agent for Edison's machines and supplies in Buffalo, New York. Mark had earlier rented a narrow 12- by 50-foot storefront in the basement of the Ellicott Building, Buffalo's newest and most prestigious office building, for a phonograph and kinetoscope parlor. He now cleared out the back of his parlor to show vitascope pictures on a screen. As his full-page advertisement in the October 17, 1896, Star Theater program informed potential customers, "Vitascope Hall" would be open from 10 A.M. until 11:30 P.M., convenient for downtown businessmen, shoppers, and theatergoers, with "CONTINUOUS DAILY EXHIBITIONS of Edison's Wonderful Inventions ✳ ✳ ✳ THE VITASCOPE, KINETOSCOPE, PHONOGRAPH and X-RAYS." In the center of the ad was the engraving Raff and Gammon had sent their customers: a benevolent Edison (posed like God in His heaven) looking down upon a large theater while a projector in the second gallery beamed a larger-than-life moving picture onto a gilded screen in the rear of the stage. To make the connection between the vitascope and Edison even clearer, Mark, in subsequent advertisements, referred to his "Hall" as an "Edisonia Parlor."[7]

Unfortunately, even with Edison's name attached, and in spite of the fulsome praise bestowed by promoters and publicists, the first vitascopes could not entertain an audience for very long. The pictures—of waves pounding a beach, of boxers flailing at one another, of "pickaninnies" jumping up and down, even of skirt dancers and *The Kiss*, a sixteen-second close-up of two actors kissing—were fun to see the first time but did not offer enough excitement to bring customers back.

There were also continuing problems with the projectors that were difficult to run and impossible to repair and the electrical current or batteries that seldom worked as they should. The worst problem of all was the shortage of decent films. Edison and his associates had still not solved the production and distribution bottlenecks that had plagued their peep-show business. Films remained expensive, of poor quality, and in short supply.

Like its predecessors, the phonograph and kinetoscope, the vitascope projector, for all its promise, was proving to be only the latest in a succession of novelty amusement machines that attracted customers for a time and then receded from view. As an exhibitor reported from Oswego, New York, in June of 1897, the vitascope had, when first shown in that city, drawn "crowded houses on account of its novelty. Now everybody has seen it, and, to use the vernacular of the 'foyer,' it does not 'draw flies.'"[8]

Fortunately, for the traveling exhibitors who, unlike the parlor owners, could pack up their screen machines and leave town when they ran out of customers, the country was huge and laced with railroads and streetcar lines. With a little bit of planning, a railroad timetable, and a large suitcase, exhibitors could travel to new locations week after week showing their moving pictures to customers who had never seen them before.

There was no end to the variety of "attractions" that rode the rails. In Providence, Rhode Island, where in the mid-1890s there were already four downtown theaters offering melodramas, musicals, and vaudeville every night of the week, a never-ending succession of "store front impresarios [rented] empty shops where they set up whatever it was they had to exhibit and remained as long as they could make a profit." Among the major attractions for the 1895–1896 season were "The Crystal Maze," a portable fun house, and "Nana," a "portrait of a beautiful lady reclining on a couch." In May of 1896, a new "attraction" was brought to town by three itinerant showmen who rented an empty store opposite Lothrup's Opera House, hung a white cloth screen at one end, installed a projector at the other, placed chairs in the middle, papered the town with posters, and waited for the crowds to arrive to view "a series of pictures marvelous in the extreme" for twenty-five cents a show.[9]

Exhibitors who kept moving never ran out of customers willing to pay a dime to see pictures move for the very first time. In the summer

and autumn of 1896 alone, William Rock, one of the original purchasers of vitascope state's rights (he owned Louisiana), set up shop in
a New Orleans summer resort in West End Park, in a storefront on
Canal Street, and in a downtown theater. As the tourist season came to
a close, he packed his bags, his projector, his films, and his profits and
"moved out into the smaller cities of the state showing the same films
he had exhibited in New Orleans."[10]

Early vitascope investors, like Rock, had spent thousands of dollars
on licenses to exploit the screen machine because they had been
assured that they would have a monopoly in their territories. Unfortunately, business was too good and the technology too primitive to
enforce any sort of monopoly. For inventors, mechanics, and tinkerers
already familiar with electrical machines, it was a relatively simple matter to take apart an Edison kinetoscope, make a few minor improvements, and reassemble a new "projector" with a new name, skirting all
copyright infringements. In Wilkes-Barre, Pennsylvania, Lyman Howe,
with prior experience in the phonograph business and the help of an
electrician, built his own "animotiscope." William Paley, a trained electrician and "x-ray exhibitor who had suffered adverse effects from
excessive radiation," converted the vitascope into a kalatechnoscope,
which he then claimed as his own invention.[11]

Howe and Paley at least gave their projectors new names. Most of
the exhibitors who pirated machines didn't even do that much. In New
Orleans, Rock discovered a competitor within shouting distance of his
storefront, "crying out come in and see Edison's Vitascope ... with
large sighns [sic] up with Edison's name and pictures. Cannot something be done about this to stop it?" he wrote Raff and Gammon.
"When we paid you our money it was for Edison's name and nothing
else exclusive for the state of Louisiana." The Brown Electric and
Machine Company of Little Rock complained to Raff and Gammon in
September 1896 that they were faced with competition wherever they
traveled with their vitascopes.[12]

Terry Ramsaye characterizes these first years of screened moving
pictures as "The Lawless Film Frontier." Even Edison entered the fray,
"inventing" a new machine, the "Projecting Kinetoscope," which he
advertised as "an improvement over the Vitascope" and began selling
independently. Edison's jump into the marketplace with a second
machine bearing his name was, Ramsaye tells us, the signal that set off
the final free-for-all. The purchasers who had been promised an exclu-

sive monopoly over Edison's screen machine were suddenly deprived of their chief asset, Edison's name and endorsement. Their contract with Raff and Gammon, having been effectively abrogated, they "jumped their boundaries and went pell mell after business, wherever and whenever they thought they could find it. And on their heels ran the infringers with their make-shift, copied, and pirated machines. The gold rush had begun—the Devil take the hindmost."[13]

In the November 1896 *Phonoscope,* the editors listed, among the machines that had been exhibited in the past month, old vitascopes and new projectoscopes, motorgraphs, animotoscopes, kinematographs, cinemetroscopes, cinematographes, veriscopes, magniscopes, biographs, rayoscopes, eidoloscopes, viveoscopes, cinagraphoscopes, and animatographs. By November 1897, an exhibitor in Portland, Oregon, reported to the *Phonoscope* that even in that city, "projecting machines [had become] as plentiful as flies in Egypt."[14]

The best evidence for the accelerating growth of the exhibition business is the film equipment catalogs from the late 1890s with their pages of advertisements for lighter-weight, portable projectors designed for traveling showmen, lecturers, and exhibitors. The "projectoscope," which Edison began to sell independently in early 1897, was advertised as an improvement over the older vitascope, because it was "Compact! Well Made! Simple! Portable! . . . Operated by Hand Power [and] Light. Weighs Less Than 50 Pounds." F. M. Prescott, a former dealer for Edison, went the Wizard one step better by marketing a $235 cineograph that weighed just 25 pounds and was so compact it "can be easily placed in an ordinary trunk." Maguire & Baucus sold a complete "Projecting Kinetoscope" outfit for $300, with films, mender, and cement; blank film (for spacing); extra lamp carbons; safety fuse blocks; and 20 feet of double lamp cords.[15]

The moving-picture equipment companies tailored their sales pitch to the "young and ambitious man" who sought financial success *and* independence. "If you own a Phantoscope," C. Francis Jenkins explained to potential investors, "all the money you take in, over and above your expenses, IS YOURS." The Sears, Roebuck catalog explained over and over again that the moving-picture exhibition business was "profitable" and "pleasant because you are independent, you are not subject to any individual, company, corporation or community. You have no boss or bosses, you conduct the business to suit yourself."[16]

In an economy in which self-employment, though still prized as an ideal, was becoming more and more of an anachronism, the notion of being one's own boss had grown as attractive as it was elusive. As Daniel Rodgers has written, there "set in around the turn of the century a need to rebut the suspicion that the immensely increased scale of business had closed off opportunities. 'Are Young Men's Chances Less?' the articles began to ask." The moving-picture business answered with a resounding "No." Here was a field of endeavor with an opening for every man "who is ambitious and anxious to get on in the world, who desires to be independent, to throw off the day laborer's shackles, make a financial standing for himself, a position among business men and to earn a title of being a self-made man."[17]

It didn't matter in the slightest whether the aspiring exhibitor had any show business expertise or experience. Sears, Roebuck, and Company announced in bold letters that its moving-picture equipment catalog was targeted "to the Teacher, the Mechanic, the Clerk or the Clergyman; To the Partially Successful; To the Unfortunate, and even to the Unsuccessful Business man; To all of those who are not satisfied with their present occupation, to those whose income is perhaps less than $1,000 a year. . . . We address you with the greatest poor man's proposition . . . and the surest immediate money-maker ever known. . . . NEVER IN THE HISTORY OF BUSINESS HAVE PROSPECTS BEEN SO GOOD," proclaimed the company in bold uppercase letters, underlined for added emphasis. The bad times of the late 1890s had now passed. "EVERYBODY IS EMPLOYED ON FULL TIME AT BETTER WAGES THAN EVER BEFORE. MEN HAVE MONEY AND THE INCLINATION TO SPEND IT. THIS IS YOUR OPPORTUNITY. TAKE ADVANTAGE OF IT."[18]

The inestimable advantage of screened entertainments over live shows was their minimal costs. "A theatrical performance is a costly affair. The salaries of performers coupled with the cost of transportation eat heavily into the door receipts. . . . It follows that any art or device that will at once decrease the heavy expense alluded to, and at the same time maintain the door receipts, has almost fabulous earning power." The exhibitors' low overhead would enable them to keep ticket prices cheap enough to attract the whole city to their shows. Traveling exhibitors didn't even have to pay rent in the warm weather months. As the Chicago Projecting Company suggested, they could "carry with them a black canvas tent, which is made especially for motion picture exhibitions" and set it up on a vacant lot. There were indeed so many "tent" shows traveling the country in the early 1900s that Sigmund Lubin published a separate "Tents" catalog to showcase his equipment.[19]

✦⊷═◉◯═⊶✦

Among the earliest and most proficient employers of the new screen machines were performers on the lecture-hall circuit. Burton Holmes, who had toured since 1893 with assorted travelogues accompanied by slides, added moving pictures to his presentation in 1897. With the moving images to illustrate his talk—and no doubt add to its "novelty" and entertainment value—Holmes was able to build an even larger audience and book himself into theaters as well as lecture halls. In 1897, he "made his Manhattan debut with a series of 'Lenten lectures' at Daly's Theatre." The crowds that followed Holmes into Daly's Theatre were not regular theatergoers and certainly not vaudeville fans. As the *New-York Tribune* reporter commented, the moving pictures that accompanied Holmes's lecture appeared to have been "an entire novelty to a large part" of Holmes's audience, although they had "been on constant exhibition for the last year and a half in the music halls and continuous-performance theatres."[20]

Moving pictures quickly became not only a major part of Holmes's presentation but also one of its chief attractions. When he announced his engagement at the Boston Music Hall for the 1898–1899 season, he laboriously described the pictures he planned to show the following season and the technicians and consultants he had hired to take and project them. He neglected, however, to even mention the topic he would be lecturing on.[21]

Like Holmes, Lyman Howe profited enormously from adding moving pictures to his "concert" performances. With his new animotoscope pictures, he could fill the largest theaters and opera houses in almost every city he visited. As with his earlier phonograph concerts, Howe carefully constructed programs that combined the educational and the amusing. His first film programs, sponsored largely by church-affiliated associations, included such crowd favorites as *The Kiss, Watermelon Contest* (African Americans eating watermelon), and *The Morning Bath* (a "mammy" giving her "pickaninny" a bath), preceded and followed by educational "views" of city streets, country landscapes, and a sequence of three fire rescue shorts. His fall 1900 program featured educational films and travelogue views of European subjects but concluded with two popular slapstick comedies, *Weary Willie Takes His*

On the cover of the program for his 1897–1898 lecture series at the Music Hall in Boston, Burton Holmes highlighted his "Unique & Original MOTION PICTURES." (*Billy Rose Theatre Collection; The New York Public Library; Astor, Lenox, and Tilden Foundations.*)

Annual Bath and *Weary Willie Causes a Sensation.* Audiences no doubt left the theater, as he wished them to, satisfied that they had learned something from the travelogues, but with smiles on their faces from the comedies.[22]

The audience for lectures and travelogues continued to expand through the 1890s and early 1900s, fed by the growing appeal of the moving pictures that "illustrated" the talks. The "illustrated" lecture was being reconceived as a picture show with commentary. The film equipment companies anticipating this shift marketed packaged views and scripted lectures for use by exhibitors. As the Stereopticon and Film Exchange asserted, exhibitors could, with the use of their products, make a substantial living on the circuit without being good public speakers or preparing lectures. "Printed lectures on almost all subjects can be obtained. . . . Many of the most successful exhibitors have never spoken in public before."[23]

There were picture show/lecture packages on the evils of drink and gambling. Exhibitors who preferred current political and military events could, if they chose, buy or rent combination slide and moving-picture sets on *The Life of McKinley,* the Boer War, or *Land and Naval Battles at Santiago.* There were even picture shows with lectures for the devout who considered the theater, in particular, and secular amusements, in general, a threat to individual piety and community morality. As the Chicago Projecting Company informed potential purchasers, there was a great deal of money to be made showing films in churches "on a percentage basis, giving a percentage of the receipts, ranging from twenty-five to forty per cent, for the use of the church." Not only did the churches appreciate the opportunity to share "enjoyable and high class form[s] of amusement" with their parishioners, but picture shows had become an "important feature in . . . the replenishing of the usually depleted treasury. . . . When it is considered that there are . . . more than 200,000 churches in the United States, one begins to get some idea of the endless possibilities, and the vast field there is to cover in this line."[24]

Every moving-picture equipment company sold its own set of religious films. In cities where blue laws forced theater owners and other amusement entrepreneurs to close down on Sundays, the possibility of making money seven days a week by exhibiting religious pictures on Sundays was no small advantage. Selig promoted his *Parable of The Prodigal Son' in Five Tableaux* as "highly commended for Sunday school lectures church meetings and similar purposes."[25]

Almost everywhere they appeared the traveling exhibitors were broadening the public for commercial amusements by presenting moving pictures to audiences who would never have deigned to enter a vaudeville hall or amusement parlor. Like the world's fair customers who had ventured onto the midways, the audience that experienced the joy of watching pictures move across the screen left the lecture halls, theaters, lyceums, and church meetings convinced that moving pictures were neither intrinsically sinful nor necessarily frivolous. If presented under the right circumstances by the right person, they could be as educational and uplifting as they were entertaining.

-+≈◯⇐+-

While the movie men were converting lecture-hall audiences into picture-show fans, the same process was occurring in the nation's vaudeville theaters. Screened films, projected by vitascopes, eidoloscopes, cinematographes, and biographs, fit perfectly into the vaudeville program. "Dumb" acts (animals; puppets; pantomimists; magic lantern slides; and "living pictures," or *tableaux vivants*) had traditionally opened and closed the show, because, being silent, they would not be disturbed by late arrivals or early departures. The movies, the managers now discovered, were ideal dumb acts: they cost less than live performers, didn't talk back or complain about the accommodations, and could be replaced weekly.[26]

The early projectors held only fifty feet or sixteen seconds of film that, if looped and repeated five or six times, could be stretched out to almost two minutes. Seven or eight films, displayed one after another in this fashion, lasted fifteen to twenty minutes, the perfect length for a vaudeville "turn." As there was seldom any connection between the acts in the live shows, so was there none between the films in the moving-picture "act." In Providence, Rhode Island, where movies were first presented theatrically in B. F. Keith's vaudeville theater in September 1896, "The Living Photograph show was made up of short, totally unrelated segments with titles like, *A Childish Quarrel, A Dip in the Sea, London Street Dancers, The Charge of the Seventh Cavalry,* and others."[27]

The first moving pictures, shot in Edison's Black Maria studio in New Jersey, had been of vaudeville, musical theater, and circus acts. Had the producers continued to turn out similar films, the moving pictures would not have lasted long on the vaudeville bill. The studio images were dark, grainy, static—and depicted acts customers could see live and in person on the vaudeville stage. Audiences preferred pictures that moved across the frame: waves crashing onto a beach, trains barreling down their tracks, soldiers parading, horses racing. At the vitascope's debut performance at Koster & Bial's vaudeville theater in New York City, the crowd cheered loudest on seeing *Rough Sea at Dover*, the one picture shot outside the studio.[28]

When the biograph projector made its debut in Oscar Hammerstein's massive Olympia Theater in October 1896, the audience, "papered" with Republicans (probably by Hammerstein himself, who had an eye for publicity), wildly cheered the "living pictures" of a speeding train and then outdid itself when their candidate for president appeared on screen from his home in Canton, Ohio, talking to his son, reading a telegram, and then walking in the direction of the audience. "Seldom is such a demonstration seen in a theatre," reported the *Dramatic Mirror*. "The entire audience rose to their feet, shouting and waving American flags, and it was several minutes before they settled down quietly to enjoy the rest of the performance."[29]

Actualities and topical films such as these quickly became the dominant moving-picture form in vaudeville. Audiences everywhere were entranced not only by images of speeding trains and presidential candidates but also by life-size moving pictures of daily life in their cities. In Atlantic City, audiences cheered moving pictures of their fire department answering a mock alarm. At Keith's theater in Philadelphia, they watched pictures of a steam shovel digging a subway tunnel in nearby Reading. In Harrisburg, the managers of the Grand Opera House and the Bijou battled for the right to exhibit street scenes shot by an Edison company cameraman. As the *Harrisburg Patriot* reported on January 13, 1897, "The sudden announcement that the much talked of Harrisburg views will be shown at the Grand Opera House . . . to-day has aroused the greatest interest and despite the short notice a large crowd promises to see the very first of the local pictures. It will be a strange and novel sight for our townsmen to see themselves pictured the same as in everyday life and many a well-known personage will be easily recognized in the crowds that line the sidewalks and that participate in the various views which will be presented."[30]

Men, women, and children who might not ordinarily have patronized the vaudeville theater packed the house to see themselves and their neighbors on the big sheet and to compare the moving-picture images with the real thing. No other type of film had the same sort of visceral appeal to audiences newly acquainted with the magic of moving pictures. For the week of October 26, 1900, Keith's New Theater in Providence heavily advertised its biograph pictures of a fire drill sounded by Principal George E. Church at the Peace Street grammar school. This film was so popular—and drew such a large audience—that it was carried over for the next two weeks, a rare event at this theater.[31]

The producers did everything possible to keep up the "novelty" of their product. They sent cameramen around the world to film "views" never before seen by American audiences. While "local views" remained popular in local theaters, there was also a large market for pictures of the sights and scenes that had been popular on stereographs and would soon become even more popular on picture postcards.* Audiences welcomed these pictures as long as they were new, recognizable, and in sharp focus. The early film catalogs emphasized this last point, repeatedly punctuating their descriptions of the film subjects with praise of the film's quality. The International Film Company, which listed only nine films in its 1897–1898 catalog, used the terms "sharp and clear" to advertise four of them.[33]

While moving pictures that were produced with particular audiences in mind, such as travelogues, boxing films, and *Passion Plays,* continued to do well, general-interest comedies and actualities did not retain their attraction for vaudeville audiences who tired of seeing the same sorts of images, week after week. By the fall of 1897, a little more than a year after their debut, moving pictures had disappeared from Chicago's theaters. And, although they continued to be shown in New York City vaudeville halls, "they were not considered a permanent attraction."[34]

The industry was rescued from its doldrums by the Spanish-American War. The daily newspapers had been building circulation for months with written descriptions, cartoons, editorials, and grainy black-and-white illustrations of bloodthirsty Spaniards mauling innocent Cubans. When a mysterious explosion sank the battleship *Maine* and took 266 American lives in mid-February 1898, the moving pictures leapt out of the realm of cheap novelty amusements to assume a new and relatively exalted role as visual newspapers and patriotic

---

*Although the first American picture postcards appeared at the 1893 Chicago World's Fair, the cards did not begin to become commonplace until May 1898 when the price of privately printed cards was reduced from two cents to a penny, the price of government-issued postal cards.[32]

cheerleaders. Old and new pictures of battleships, sailors, soldiers, and flags were relabeled, advertised, and rushed into the vaudeville theaters. Audiences who had earlier watched pictures of troops idly marching on parade grounds now cheered images of the boys on the way to battle. As Albert Smith, one of the founders of Vitagraph, remembers, "The people were on fire and eager for every line of news." He and his partner took the ferry to Hoboken where they filmed a National Guard regiment on its way to Tampa, the assembly point for American troops bound for Cuba. That night the film was shown to a full house at Tony Pastor's vaudeville theater.[35]

Vaudeville impresarios, including some who had stopped showing moving pictures on their bills, quickly contracted with suppliers who promised to deliver "war films." The Vitagraph Company manufactured its own battle scenes on its rooftop studio with cutout pictures of battleships floating in one inch of water ringed by cigarette smoke. The Biograph and Edison companies, with the help of William Randolph Hearst, sent cameramen to Cuba to photograph American troops and ships. Edison renamed his projector the "Wargraph" and put out a special catalog supplement, the "War Extra," advertising new moving pictures guaranteed to "satisfy the craving of the general public for absolutely true and accurate details regarding the movements of the United States Army getting ready for the invasion of Cuba." Included among these films were scenes of the 9th U.S. cavalry watering its horses and the 10th U.S. Infantry, 2nd Battalion, in Tampa, Florida: "Hurrah—here they come! Hot, dusty, grim and determined! Real soldiers, every inch of them!"[36]

The new films not only provided images of soldiers, ships, and reenacted battles but also gave customers a forum to express concern for their "boys," their love of country, and their unrequited hatred of the enemy. As the *New-York Tribune* reported on February 25, 1898, ten days after the *Maine* explosion, "There is no other place where it is so easy to get the people of New York together as in a theatre. . . . So it is naturally to the theatres that one turns to find public sentiment expressed." (In chapter 15 on World War I, we will return to this subject.)[37]

Theater owners and managers made the most of their war films. They draped their theaters in flags, hired announcers to read newspaper headlines from the stage, accompanied the films with special sound effects and martial music, and arranged them in sequence, often concluding with pictures of the American flag flying high or the Spanish flag torn down by "the hand of righteous destiny." The audience was encouraged to join in the show, wave flags, sing patriotic songs, cheer the troops, and hiss any appearance of the enemy.[38]

The extended hysteria and the abbreviated war that followed enlarged the film audience by attracting to the vaudeville halls individuals who came to see the war pictures, not the dancing bears or Dutch comedians. In the big cities, where the dailies and vaudeville competed with one another to get the latest news and views to the public, it was possible to read newspaper reports about the war in the morning and view "living pictures" in the evening. While the newspapers covered the same events as the "living pictures"—and did so with graphic prose and inch-high headlines—they could not evoke the enthusiasms generated in the vaudeville halls, as crowds assembled each evening to watch the latest war pictures. Is it any wonder that publisher William Randolph Hearst, as early as 1898, was entering into cooperative arrangements with cameramen and producers to film and exhibit moving pictures of the stories his papers were reporting?[39]

Although immediately following the cessation of hostilities a few of the theaters that had featured war films abandoned them, the success of the pictures as a visual newspaper convinced most of the vaudeville managers to enter into regular arrangements with film companies to supply a weekly set of "views." No theater manager wanted to be caught short without films should another war or disaster hit the front pages. During slow news weeks, the moving pictures might be parked at the bottom of the vaudeville bill, but when big stories broke—when Admiral Dewey returned from Manila to be feted in New York City, when Galveston was destroyed by hurricane and flood, when President McKinley was assassinated at the Buffalo world's fair, when an earthquake destroyed San Francisco—they were returned to their headliner position as audiences filled the theaters to see moving images of the events they had read about.[40]

The film companies celebrated and promoted their new role as chroniclers of contemporary events and history. Edison's March 1900 film catalog devoted nine of its forty-eight pages to old Spanish-American and new Boer War films. The 1901 catalog featured new pictures of "The Boxer Massacres in Pekin. . . . Public interest is now intensely aroused, and people will eagerly appreciate any pictures that relate to localities in which the war in China was prosecuted." Selig thought so much of the commercial potential of his Russo-Japanese War films that he produced a special four-page catalog to promote them. "These films will be the money earners of the century. You cannot afford to be without them." The *Keith News,* a publicity sheet advertising Keith's Providence theater, claimed that there was "surely no better way to keep posted upon current events than through the moving picture machine. A large corps of men are kept constantly busy in all parts of the world photographing matters of interest."[41]

◦⊶⊷◦⊶⊷◦

While moving pictures were enlarging their audience in lecture halls and vaudeville theaters, they had not established an independent standing as an entertainment medium. The moving-picture business remained as yet an undifferentiated subset of a larger "show" business. There were, at the turn of the century, no national or regional trade associations of film exhibitors or equipment manufacturers, nor were there any journals, except the parlor-oriented *Phonoscope* that expired in June 1900. The notion that moving pictures could entertain an audience entirely by themselves would not have occurred to entrepreneurs or audiences in the early 1900s. Nor, as Miriam Hansen has argued, would the notion of the "film spectator" as a distinct genre of pleasure seeker or amusement consumer "come into existence until more than a decade later."[42]

The audience for moving pictures was composed not of dedicated "spectators" but of individuals whose attention had, for the moment, been directed to one set of moving images and would, a moment later, be diverted to other "attractions." In the "cinema of attractions," as Tom Gunning has referred to early moving pictures, the attractions were so numerous and diverse that it was virtually impossible for viewers to immerse themselves in the illusional world represented on the screen. Short followed short, interrupted by lecturers, exhibitors, and sometimes live acts as well. How could spectators enter the "self-enclosed fictional world" of the film when that world within a minute or two of its appearance would vanish into nothingness?[43]

Unlike later film spectators who were encouraged to suspend disbelief and emotionally enter the world represented on the screen, early viewers remained firmly affixed to their seats. Unlike Uncle Josh, the character in Edwin Porter's 1903 short who tried to dance with the Parisian dancer on the screen, the first film audiences knew that they were watching a picture of a scene they could not enter. But they could stare at it, laugh at it, shout at it, be reassured or frightened by it, perhaps even learn something from it. There were a multiplicity of possible reactions to the "curiosities" exhibited on the screen. Part of the magic of early cinema might well have been this chaotic, overabundant heterogeneity: of viewer reactions, film genres, subjects, sites, and audiences.[44]

By the turn of the century, moving pictures had survived their infancy and outgrown their "novelty" stage. They were no longer a plaything or a cheap novelty to be seen once and abandoned. Their permanent installation as part of the vaudeville bill and their expanding role on the lecture-hall circuit had expanded their audience to include hundreds of thousands of city folk who patronized these performances. Moving pictures had not yet assembled their own audience, but they were beginning to draw on every other kind of entertainment audience, accelerating the promiscuous mixing of disparate social groupings that would come to characterize commercial amusements in the early twentieth century.

CHAPTER 12

The First Picture Shows

T HE AMUSEMENT PARLORS THAT HAD OPENED
with such promise in the late 1880s and 1890s had by the turn of
the century been reconfigured as penny arcades;* their audiences of
refined ladies and gentlemen replaced by the young men and boys who
gathered at the peephole machines to watch *How Girls Undress*. As a
visitor to Samuel Swartz's arcade on S. Clark Street in Chicago observed, the sign reading "'For men only' attracts the small boy like a
magnet." Because so many of the boys who gathered around the mutoscopes were not tall enough to reach the eyehole, arcade managers had
to supply them with stools to stand on.[1]

In one arcade in Chicago, the boys who paused before depositing
their coins were encouraged by the attendant, "'You mustn't miss this
one,' he says, 'It's the hottest yet. She takes off everything from the top
of her head to the soles of her feet.'" Such was the come-on, punctuated by the films' suggestive titles and lurid lithographs (most of them
borrowed from the cheap melodrama houses). The pictures themselves
were much tamer.[2]

*The *Oxford English Dictionary* locates the first use of the term *penny arcade* in 1908 and
the *Unabridged Random House Dictionary,* between 1905 and 1910. By 1906, and certainly
by 1907, urban reformers around the country were using the term to refer to what they considered to be the latest and most virulent of the cheap amusements preying on the morals of
city residents, especially children.

As a New York City investigator reported in 1906, "The signs on nine out of ten picture machines are deceptive—the effort in every instance being to make the customer believe that the exhibition within is most vulgar. It is a trick which serves the double purpose of catching extra pennies and impressing the casual observer [as well as the police and antivice crusaders] that there is nothing real bad about the place." In only two of the twenty arcades he visited did this investigator find "thoroughly indecent pictures," not enough, he reported, to interest Anthony Comstock, secretary of the Society for the Suppression of Vice, in undertaking a more thorough investigation. Elsewhere, in Boston, Buffalo, Philadelphia, Washington, D.C., Baltimore, Cleveland, Cincinnati, and Providence, Rhode Island, reformers reported in 1906 and 1907 that the arcade owners were staying well within the spirit of the law, as defined by the cop on the beat. The pictures, as a Boston investigator reported in 1907, "come very near the line of obscenity, but, as a rule, are not such as can be reached by the law."[3]

-*-⟫⟪-*-

While most of the arcade owners were content to cater to the boys who crowded around the peep-show machines, a few visionaries foresaw a different—and even more prosperous—future for the automatic vaudeville machines. In 1903, Mitchell Mark, who, as we saw in chapter 11, had opened one of the first amusement parlors in a Buffalo office building in 1896, moved to New York City to establish a penny arcade. He chose, however, to locate his arcade not on the Bowery or any of the city's cheap entertainment districts, but on 125th Street in Harlem, a prosperous Jewish neighborhood soon to be connected by subway to the rest of the city. When his first New York City arcade proved successful, Mark raised capital to build arcades in similar locations throughout the city. Through an acquaintance whom he had met at the Pan-American Exposition in Buffalo, Mark approached Adolph Zukor, who was so impressed by the crowds of customers and coins collected at the 125th Street arcade that he and his partner in the fur business, Morris Kohn, invested their money in the "Automatic Vaudeville Company," capitalized at $300,000. For their first arcade, they rented a vacant dairy kitchen and restaurant on 14th Street at Union Square, two blocks from the New York offices of their fur company.[4]

Although the Union Square area no longer housed as many first-class legitimate theaters as it once had, it was still an important shop-

This is the interior of Zukor's 14th Street arcade. To attract the broadest possible crowd, Zukor and his associates stocked a wide variety of moving pictures. The first four machines on the left contain pictures with titles like *Peeping Jimmies, A Ride with the Motorman on the L, French High Kickers,* and *Fish That Swim in the Sea.* The sign in the middle of the room explains, "A Penny operates any machine." (*Museum of the City of New York.*)

ping and entertainment district. Day and night, the street in front of Zukor and Kohn's arcade was crowded with a steady stream of potential customers: blue-collar workers on their way to and from their factory lofts and workshops; English-speaking sons and daughters of the Lower East Side who worked in nearby office buildings and stores; visitors from the suburbs who shopped in the area's department stores; tourists, traveling businessmen, and pleasure seekers who patronized its theaters and restaurants.[5]

Zukor and Kohn, flush with capital from their fur business, spent a great deal outfitting their arcade. The entrance on 14th Street was recessed and decorated with an extravagantly inlaid dome roof. Extending a story above the entrance was a huge electric sign inviting passersby into the "Automatic One Cent Vaudeville" emporium.

Inside, the long narrow arcade extended a block south to 13th Street. It was lit with chandeliers and hundreds of large white-frosted bulbs; the floor jammed with the latest and most luxurious collection of automatic coin-in-the-slot machines available anywhere. For the sporting crowd, there were punching bags to compare your punch with Corbett's, Jeffries', Fitzsimmons', or Terry McGovern's; shooting-gallery rifles; weights to pull; hammers to pound; stationary bicycles and hobby-horses. There were also automatic amusement machines that dispensed cards with your fortune, your horoscope, or your future wife's picture; metal embossers that spit out "Your Name in Aluminum"; "automatic" gum, candy, and peanut machines; coin-in-the-slot phonographs with the Floradora Sextet, Sousa's Band, and comic monologues; and more than 100 peep-show machines.[6]

The peep-show machines were the main attraction and the largest money-maker in the arcade. A custom-designed miniature electric train ran on a track underneath them. When a customer dropped a coin into a machine, it was stored there until the train came by, at which point a trap door opened and the coins were dumped onto the train. At the end of its journey, the car unloaded its coins into a funnel "from the other end of which they emerged, all counted and wrapped and ready for deposit in the bank." Here was the perfect business, one that was so well automated it literally ran itself.[7]

The "Automat" on 14th Street quickly became "one of the sights of the town." William Fox, the future film mogul who had made his fortune in the ready-to-wear clothing business as a "shrinker" and cloth inspector, was so entranced by the sight of the coins dropping into the toy train that he tried to buy his own arcade. Unsuccessful in Manhattan, he opened one in Brooklyn.[8]

Penny arcades were, indeed, so profitable that Kohn and Zukor liquidated their fur business to devote themselves full-time to the Automatic Vaudeville Company and open new arcades in Newark, Boston, and Philadelphia. Fellow furrier Marcus Loew, an early investor, established his own "People's Vaudeville Company," capitalized at $100,000, with actor David Warfield as a partner. Following Zukor's example, Loew located his first arcade on one of the city's densest shopping and entertainment streets, at 172 West 23rd Street, just west of Proctor's 23rd Street Music Hall. He reinvested his profits in four more arcades in New York City and a fifth in downtown Fountain Square in Cincinnati.[9]

Entrepreneurs opened arcades in the Loop in Chicago, on Main

Street in Worcester, on Baltimore Street in Baltimore, and on the major shopping streets of other cities. The first arcades located on major downtown shopping streets proved to be gold—or, at least, penny and nickel—mines for their investors. As one local manager told a Chicago investigator, "the man who has a Penny Arcade on a main thoroughfare in any city above 15,000 inhabitants has a fortune." Herbert Mills, the proud proprietor of twenty-five arcades in cities across the country, encouraged prospective owners not to shy away from, but seek out congested, high-rent districts. Arcades on the city's "most populous streets," he suggested, could stay open from 8 A.M. until 11 P.M. or midnight. During daylight hours, they would be patronized by nearby office workers, traveling salesmen, tourists, vacationers, and shoppers from the suburbs. After dark, their blinking colored lights would entice theatergoers, restaurant patrons, couples out for a stroll, and assorted pleasure seekers. On Sundays, they might be visited by out-of-towners who spent their day off taking in the sights of the city.[10]

Mills warned prospective arcade owners to establish and enforce strict rules of decorum. "Loafing, flirting, or boisterous crowds" could not be tolerated. Arcades had to be "well lighted," especially "at the front," and "possess an inviting air of respectability. . . . The cashier selected should be preferably a woman whose appearance indicates refinement, for many of the patrons of an arcade are women and children."[11]

The penny arcades were new types of amusement sites. For only a nickel, sometimes a penny, city folk enjoyed mechanical wonders that until recently had been locked away in the laboratories of electrical wizards. The show businessmen spared no energy in identifying their amusements with the new machine age. The appeal appeared to work, judging from the scores of amusement sites that advertised the word "automatic" in their title. Visiting an arcade was almost like window shopping, a temporary pause or respite in one's everyday life. The arcades were casual institutions that required (and indeed sold) no advance tickets, had no assigned seats, and, as importantly, required no cultural capital of their audience. All viewers, regardless of social background or educational level, had equal access to the "meaning" of the images viewed through the peephole or on the larger screen. One didn't even have to speak English to understand the story.

Customers put their pennies in the slot and stared into the eyepiece. If ever there were a potentially "one-dimensional" amusement, one that offered no glimpse of a transcendent world but was firmly anchored in the here and now, it was the entertainment squeezed into the coin-in-the-slot machines. Here was the perfect diversion for busy city folk, a momentary break from routine that was so unobtrusive it could be seamlessly interwoven into the fabric of daily life.

In every other setting, the pictures had been a part of or an adjunct to a larger show. In the arcades they were the featured attraction. Unfortunately, the number of customers who could view them at any one time was limited by the number of machines in the arcade. To build a larger customer base, the proprietors had to find a way to liberate the moving pictures from their peep-show machines and broadcast them to larger audiences. Mitchell Mark had tried to do this in his Buffalo parlor, but without much success. Thomas Tally had attempted it in Los Angeles, but failed as well. Now around 1904, arcade owners across the country, flush with profits, yet fearful that the "novelty" was wearing off, tried again to interest their customers in projected moving pictures. This time, with better films, better projectors, and customers who were more familiar with moving pictures, having seen them countless times in vaudeville halls, they succeeded.[12]

In April of 1904, Harry Davis, Pittsburgh's most prosperous show businessman, opened an amusement arcade near his Grand Opera House. When a fire burned it down, he rented a larger storefront, but instead of outfitting it as an arcade, he filled the room with opera chairs, gaily decorated the exterior, and advertised the opening of a "nickelodeon." Davis's nickel theater was an instant success, drawing crowds almost from the day it opened. He built additional picture theaters in Pittsburgh, and, within the year, in Philadelphia and Rochester, New York, as well.[13]

Although Davis was the first exhibitor to use the name "nickelodeon," similar experiments were taking place in other parts of the country. Marcus Loew on a visit to his Cincinnati arcade in 1905 learned from his manager that an arcade owner across the river in Covington, Kentucky, had come up with a marvelous new "idea in entertainment. . . . I went over with my general manager—it was on Sunday . . . and I never got such a thrill in my life. The show was given in an old-fashioned brownstone house, and the proprietor had the hallways partitioned off with dry goods cases. He used to go to the window and sell the tickets to the children, then he went to the door and took the tickets, and after he did that he locked the door and went up and operated the machine. He also used to lecture while he was operating the machine. I said to my companion, 'This is the most remarkable thing I have ever seen.' The place was packed to suffocation." Loew returned to Cincinnati and opened his own picture show the following Sunday. "The first day we played I believe there were seven or eight people short of five thousand and we did not advertise at all. The people simply poured into the arcade. That showed me the great possibilities of this new form of entertainment." Back in New York City, Loew rented space for picture-show theaters adjacent to his arcades.[14]

Adolph Zukor, not to be outdone, added a screen show on the second floor of his arcade and built a spectacular glass staircase to focus attention on it. In Baltimore, Philip Scheck and Marion Pearce, a machinist and an electrician who had been booking moving-picture shows in churches, lodges, and rented halls, refitted the back of a burned-out arcade as a store-theater with moving pictures and vaudeville. According to a Baltimore historian, additional "minute movie parlors [were opened] by grocers, saloon keepers, and haberdashers, most of whom did not know beans about the movie business. . . . Saloon keepers in particular opened many of the tiny theaters of this era."[15]

In cities across the country, arcade owners shut off the back of their storefronts or rented additional space upstairs or next door for picture shows, and vaudeville managers, traveling exhibitors, and show businessmen left their jobs to open nickel picture theaters. *Billboard* suggested in October 1906 that "summer show people . . . without definite plans" for the fall go into the picture-show business which, it claimed, offered "excellent opportunities . . . for the investment of small capital for the winter. There is an abundance of new territory to be opened up for the five-cent theater, or nickelodeon, and the vogue of this institution promises a great future." In Niles, Ohio, the Warner brothers, their parents, and their sister Rose pooled their savings and with a converted kinetoscope and an old print of *The Great Train Robbery* opened a storefront theater on the main street in town.[16]

In New York City, nickel theaters were opened on 14th, 23rd, and 125th streets; in Boston, they "were stretched out in a long line along Tremont Row and Washington Street"; in Chicago, they were clustered throughout the Loop; in Philadelphia, they were located up and down Market Street; in Dallas, "more than a dozen—nearly a score, in fact . . . literally line[d] Main and Elm Streets from one boundary of the business district to the other."[17]

For men who wanted to run their own business, opening a nickel show presented the opportunity of a lifetime. The Chicago Projecting

Company claimed in its 1907 catalog that only $200 would cover the "price of the necessary machines, remodeling, and decorating the interior of the theatre and the entrance, which must be made attractive, and the cost of seating—every expense ready to open the place. No other business on earth paying as large a return can be started for so little money." Once a location had been chosen and leased, the owner had only to clear the storefront, fill it with folding chairs, paper over the windows, and rent or buy a projector and a piece of canvas for a screen. Because store-shows required no props, scenery, or stage lighting and were too small to be legally classified as theaters, owners did not have to pay heavy license fees, meet strict building codes, or, in many cities, close down on Sundays. There were no actors, stage hands, electricians, or ushers to pay.[18]

Immigrant small businessmen, without a great deal of capital to invest, opened nickelodeons on the secondary shopping streets adjoining the city's working-class residential districts. In Gary, Indiana, the first nickelodeon was built by Ingwald Moe, a Norwegian-born contractor. In New York City, a report on nickelodeons issued by the Bureau of Licenses in 1908 included the names not only of successful show businessmen like Zukor, Loew, and Fox who owned several downtown nickel theaters but also of individuals like Michael St. Angelo, James McMiddleton, Giuseppi Brunelli, Bernard Kiernan, J. E. Costello, and Streneman, Gottlieb, Weisenburg, and Samwick of the Lower East Side, all of whom owned one or two storefront theaters. The *New-York Daily Tribune* reporting on the first meeting of the Moving Picture Association in December of 1908 commented that "Every section of the city was represented—the Bowery, Grand street, Essex Market, Park Row, Canal street, the numerous avenues, 14th street, West Broadway, the upper West Side, Brooklyn and The Bronx. Chubby-faced Irishmen with clay pipes between their teeth were there, as well as Hungarians, Italians, Greeks, and just a handful of Germans, but the greater portion of the assembly were Jewish-Americans, who practically control the enterprise."[19]

The moving-picture business was, in these early years, almost too good to be true. Contemporary commentators used terms like "madness," "frenzy," "fever," and "craze" to describe the rapidity with which nickel theaters were being built. The first nickel show on a street was almost guaranteed to draw a full house wherever it opened. Passersby could simply not resist the call of the barkers out front, the gaudy blinking lights, and the opportunity to see a moving-picture show for only a nickel. By November of 1907, a little more than two years after the opening of the Pittsburgh nickelodeon, there were already, according to Joseph Medill Patterson of the *Saturday Evening Post*, between "four and five thousand [nickel shows] running and solvent, and the number is still increasing rapidly. This is the boom time in the moving-picture business. Everybody is making money . . . as one press-agent said enthusiastically, 'this line is a Klondike.'"[20]

The rapid and unregulated proliferation of nickelodeons turned the city's shopping streets into bawdy amusement districts, as theater owners hired live barkers or played phonograph recordings to focus the pedestrians' attention on the show inside. "'It is only five cents!' coaxes the barker. 'See the moving-picture show, see the wonders of Port Said tonight, and a shrieking comedy from real life, all for five cents. Step in this way and learn to laugh!'"[21]

On the immigrant and working-class shopping streets, the call of the barker blended in with the cacophony of street life and peddlers' chants. In the central business districts, however, where peddlers were already banned, the barkers' megaphones and phonograph recordings were so omnipresent and obtrusive that they disturbed the orderly bustle of downtown shopping. In Paterson, New Jersey, the Board of Aldermen outlawed "phonographic barkers" after complaints from local storekeepers, including M. L. Rogowski, a millinery dealer, who claimed that the "rasping music, ground out for hours at a time annoyed his milliners until they became nervous." In Philadelphia, where the city's largest nickel theater was "within a stone's throw of the Wanamaker store, on the principal side of Market Street," the commotion was so great and so constant that the Market Street merchants banded together to seek legislation banning the barkers. "For fifteen years, Market Street has been developing from a wholesale street to the leading retail thoroughfare of the city. . . . Nickel shows threaten to check this progress."[22]

While many showmen resisted the pressure to quiet their barkers and remove their phonographs from the street, a large number voluntarily shut down their "outside" shows, fearful that brassy, rude pitchmen were creating the impression that the nickel shows were only for the poor and uncultured workingman. The theater owners in the central business districts hoped to attract tourists and shoppers in town for the day as well as the thousands of workers in white collars on their lunch breaks or their way to and from work or home.[23]

In Providence, the *Sunday Journal* reported on the phenomenon of "nooning," the "noon-hour-picture-seeing propensity on the part of business men and clerks." Several Providence businessmen were quoted, including the manager of a seed company and a hotel official who confessed, quite good-naturedly, that they had developed the habit of spending their lunch hours watching the picture shows at the "business mens house." The theater owners didn't mind in the least that the audience was using their establishment as a lunchroom because, as one manager asserted, "the lunchers never leave boxes or papers on the floor."[24]

The downtown nickel theater owners also tried to attract the "ladies," especially those in town from the suburbs for a day of shopping. When Keith and Albee opened their "Nickel Theater" in downtown Providence in April 1906, they took out a large advertisement in the *Journal* announcing that their new theater would cater "to families, especially ladies and children." To make the ladies feel especially welcome, they announced that they had designed a "Ladies Retiring Room [with] all the comforts of home. Come in on your way to lunch," the *Journal* ad proclaimed, "come in when tired from shopping—come in any time between 10 a.m. and 10:30 p.m." A *Moving Picture World* writer suggested in May 1907 that lady shoppers who had previously been forced to ride the streetcar to rest their feet could now do so in the nickel theaters. "They are great places for the foot-sore shopper, who is not used to cement sidewalks, to rest."[25]

Though some of the downtown nickel theaters, especially those managed by established show businessmen like Keith and Albee, might have been successful in wooing "the ladies," it is hard to imagine many "lady shoppers" from the suburbs visiting darkened, airless storefronts to see a fifteen-minute picture show. The smell inside the nickel shows that were housed in storefronts must have been overpowering. The ceilings were low, and any opening that might have let in air or light was sealed off or papered over. Larger vaudeville halls, with high ceilings, windows, balconies, and lobbies, provided for at least minimal air circulation. Enclosed storefronts did not.

The picture show's one-price, no-reserved-seats policy would have been a further deterrent for the lady shoppers. In the vaudeville theaters, they could, if they chose, sit safe from the rabble in the more expensive box and orchestra seats. There were no such sanctuaries in the nickel and dime theaters. Any "white" person with the price of admission could sit anywhere he or she pleased.

For these reasons alone, the lady shoppers would have stayed away from the picture shows. The women who patronized them were more likely from the lower ranks of the white-collar work force. A March 1909 article in the *Film Index* reported that "In St. Louis every working day there are hundreds of young women employed downtown who forego their noonday luncheon that they may be able to visit the moving-picture shows. Instead of filling up on canned beans and the like, they fill up with canned drama. They laugh at the comedy scenes enacted on the screen, applaud the cracked-voiced singer at the conclusion of his illustrated song, and go back to the counter and the typewriter, stomach hungry, but mentally fed."[26]

Although the "canned beans" crowd must also have cringed on inhaling that first breath of stale auditorium air, they put up with it because the price was right. Despite the fetid atmosphere, "nooning" at the nickel theater must have been an exhilarating—and slightly scandalous—break from routine. The trip to the nickel theater was an act of almost pure hedonism—in the middle of the workday, where it most certainly did not belong.

The nickelodeons' gaudily ornamented facades, radiating with visual delight, advertised the distance between the gaiety within and the drab routine on the outside. The penny arcades had opened their fronts to encourage passersby to "drop in." The nickel and dime theaters reenclosed their fronts by pulling back their entrances about six feet from the sidewalk, in effect extending the distance between the theater and the street. This recessed, sheltered entrance functioned as a buffer or filter between the inside of the theater and the tumult outside. Framing this recessed entrance were massive entry arches or oversized columns that jutted out onto the sidewalk. The Bijou, which opened its doors in March 1908 in Providence, Rhode Island, was housed in a converted storefront that had been covered over by a huge false front, decorated with 2,000 light bulbs. Glittering facades like these were essential advertisements for the thousands of nickel theaters that were too small to afford newspaper notices.[27]

To attract an audience large enough to fill and refill their theaters twenty to thirty times a day, nickelodeon owners had to meld into one institutional space the openness of the saloon and the selectivity of the hotel. They had to welcome all who sought entrance to their amusements, while simultaneously "appearing" to screen their customers. Even the lowest-level, lowest-paid white-collar workers needed to feel that, on entering the nickel theater, they were not placing themselves or their reputations in jeopardy. As the journalist Roland Hartt wrote in 1909, "To get an audience hour by hour all day and all through the evening, the M.P. [moving-picture theater owner] must offend no one. The best taste of his patrons rules. There prevails a uniform decency which would ruin the patrician playhouse but is here the 'sine qua non' of big profits. . . . The wise M.P. strives by all means to vindicate his gold-lettered device, 'For Man, Woman, and Child.' He makes his establishment so interesting, so delightful, so altogether irresistible, that he attracts people who look askance at the traditional theatre, as well as people who adore the Arcade; in short, he attracts every-body except our moral and social snobs, who make it a part of their religion to think evil of each new contrivance for affording pleasure to the humble."[28]

⟞⟞⟝⟝

The nickelodeon boom appeared to be—and was indeed—too good to be true. While the first and second nickel shows to open on a street had no trouble filling their houses, by the time the third and fourth appeared, business began to fall off. Increased accessibility meant decreased magic. Adolph Zukor recalled years later that by 1907–1908 the public was already beginning "to lose interest" in the nickelodeon and its standard fare. "The novelty had worn off and the picture-makers remained in a rut. . . . We found ourselves where we could not carry on the business profitably. There were plenty of pictures made but they were so much alike that there was no more public interest in them."[29]

Most of the nickel theater owners, well aware that they had to com-pete not only with one another but also with the continuous vaudeville theaters that offered customers a full show of live acts and moving pic-tures for a quarter, hired live singers to supplement their picture shows. The "singers" led the audience in a rendition of popular songs whose lyrics were flashed on the screen while the reels were being changed. They varied enormously in age and talent. Jack Warner and his sister Rose sang the illustrated songs in the Warner brothers second theater in Newcastle, Pennsylvania. Rose may have sounded good, but Jack's voice was changing and "every couple of bars it would sound like the ice cracking on the Mahoning River." Sophie Tucker claimed that she began her show business career singing in a storefront theater owned by Marcus Loew and Adolph Zukor at 116th Street and Lenox

Avenue in Harlem. "All they showed was a one-reel slapstick comedy and me in blackface for the ten afternoon shows, and whiteface for the ten night shows."[30]

Though the illustrated songs were an indispensable part of the show (no matter how bad the singer, the audience would have felt cheated without a song or two), the moving pictures were the reason one attended the nickelodeons. By 1907, one-reel story films had become the standard in the industry. The vast majority were comedies, condensed melodramas, and, after 1907, westerns, although a considerable number of classics, including fifteen-minute adaptations of Shakespeare, Dickens, and Sophocles, and a variety of historical films were also produced. Most of the dramas took their plots, as well as their costumes and conventions, from the staged melodramas that had been mainstays of the cheap repertoire theaters in the 1890s and early years of the new century. Some adopted contemporary themes, such as Porter's *The Kleptomaniac* or *The Eviction;* others condensed familiar old stories, such as *Uncle Tom's Cabin,* or borrowed from the stage. Several of the most popular were taken directly from yesterday's headlines, like *The Unwritten Law,* based on the trial of millionaire Harry K. Thaw for murdering architect Stanford White. No matter what the source, the filmed melodramas had innocent heroes and dastardly villains, chases, visual climaxes or sensation scenes (that could be advertised on the lithographed posters out front), and usually a happy ending.[31]

The crime films and westerns also borrowed widely for their stories. The success of *The Great Train Robbery,* the industry's first "blockbuster," spawned dozens of criminal-chasing imitations; many, like their progenitor, "posed and acted in faithful duplication of the 'Hold Ups' made famous by various outlaw bands in the far West." Other westerns, like *Daniel Boone* and *The Pony Express,* borrowed loosely from history. And still others, like *Hooligans of the West,* combined "actualities" or staged documentaries of actual cowboys or Wild West shows with fiction.[32]

The one-reel comedies that tried to tell a story managed only to string together a series of comic incidents or chases, held together by what John Fell calls "motivated links." The *Energizer,* described as a "Comic Satire on the Breakfast Food Craze," demonstrated the effects of the cereal on a collection of individuals who were shown eating it. In *The Suburbanite's Ingenious Alarm,* produced by Edison Films for distribution in January 1908, the "story" is of Mr. Early's attempts to get to work on time and the catastrophes that befall him.[33]

Most of the early comedies borrowed their characters, if not their plots, from vaudeville skits. As in vaudeville, ethnic and racial parodies were prevalent, with dim-witted Irish servants blowing themselves up trying to light the stove or taking off their clothes when asked to serve the salad "undressed"; unscrupulous Jewish merchants in full beards and long black coats cheating their customers; and blacks behaving like children—cakewalking, grinning, shooting craps, stealing chickens, and eating watermelon. The comic representations of white ethnics were seldom subtle or gentle. They poked fun at old-world "greenies" in such a way as to permit cosmopolitan, assimilated ethnics to laugh at the figures on the screen. Producers and exhibitors, many of them European-born or the children of immigrants, had little desire to make or show films that might offend their families or large portions of their audiences. When *Murphy's Wake*, a comedy about a drinking party so riotous even the corpse awakes to join the fun, opened at the Lyric Theater in Providence, "a party of loyal Irishmen from Pawtucket" threatened to "create a riot" if it were not withdrawn. Mayor McCarthy, on viewing the picture, ordered the theater to cease showing it. The owners agreed at once.[34]

Because African Americans were seldom permitted in the nickel theaters, and because there were as yet no black producers, exhibitors, or mayors, there was little restraint when it came to representing them on the screen. Occasionally, blacks were presented with dignity, as in the Jack Johnson boxing films, or with humanity, as in some of the *Uncle Tom* adaptations. For the most part, however, they were portrayed, often by whites in blackface, as the nadir of human intelligence and beauty. In Edwin Porter's 1903 film, *What Happened in the Tunnel*, a "masher" tries to kiss a pretty young girl as the train they are riding enters a tunnel. When they reemerge into the light, the masher discovers to his horror that his lips are firmly planted on the black maid's face. Early versions of the same tunnel film had used a baby's bottom, but Porter had substituted the African-American face because it made for a bigger contrast—and bigger laughs. In other films African Americans were pictured, often in plantation settings, dancing, cavorting, stealing, and gleefully overeating in movies with such titles as *The Pickaninnies*, *Dancing Nig*, and *How Rastus Got His Pork Chops*. In Biograph's 1907 *The Fights of Nations*, different "national" types are

shown using their characteristic weapons: the Latins have knives, the
Jews "guile and gesture," the Scots, swords, while the "blacks in 'Sunny
Africa, Eighth Avenue' slash each other with razors over a woman." In
its final scene, this film epitomizes the screen treatment of blacks. All
the national groups, including the Indians, parade together in harmony
"under a flag-festooned proscenium." Only the blacks are missing because they alone did not belong in the American parade.°[35]

⊹⊱⩪◖═⊰⊹

Although the first nickel theaters had been established in the central
business districts, the vast majority were built on secondary shopping
streets adjoining immigrant and working-class residential districts. In
Milwaukee, the *Sentinel* in 1907, defending the nickel shows from
attack, reported that there was a "demand for them among people who
have not much money to spend on their amusements. Those who cannot afford champagne must put up with beer. Those who cannot afford
$5 for grand opera must take their pleasure at . . . the humble five-cent
picture show."[36]

While *Variety* in 1908 marveled at the number of nickelodeons
springing up, it reassured vaudeville performers and impresarios that
they had nothing to fear from the new theaters, because moving pictures were "poor men's entertainment" and could not compete with
vaudeville. "The movies," Milton Berle remembered in his autobiography, "were something for the lower classes and immigrants." Barton
Currie in a widely quoted article in *Harper's Weekly* in 1907 ridiculed
those who, from a distance, warned that the cheap theaters were little
more than dark dens for pickpockets and their victims. No thief in his
right mind, Currie claimed, would have spent time among an audience
of "workingmen . . . tired drudging mothers of bawling infants [and]
the little children of the streets, newsboys, bootblacks, and smudgy
urchins. . . . Why, there isn't an ounce of plunder in sight."[37]

Price alone marked the nickelodeons off from other commercial
entertainments as suitable for the entire family. Where else could a
workingman take his family or a mother her children to see a show for
five cents a ticket. As numerous commentators remarked—it became
almost a standard item in the early articles—the afternoon matinees

---

°There are strange echoes here of the actual "Chicago Day" parade at the close of the
Chicago World's Fair, which, as we saw in chapter 5, included the inhabitants of all the ethnic villages except the Dahomeans.

were filled with neighborhood women laden with groceries, perambu-
lators, and children who had "dropped in" to see the show.[38]

In the early evening and on weekends, the mothers were joined
by single women, who, according to Kathy Peiss, found in the moving-
picture theaters "convenient places for meeting men, courting, and
enjoying an inexpensive evening's entertainment." Working women
who lived at home had little spare time or money for leisure-time activities. Chores, tight budgets, and parental restrictions tied most of them
to their homes when they were not at work. "Filomena Ognibene, an
Italian garment worker brought up by strict parents, claimed that 'the
one place I was allowed to go by myself was the movies. . . . My parents
wouldn't let me go out anywhere else, even when I was twenty-four. I
didn't care. I wasn't used to going out, going anywhere outside of going
to the movies. I used to enjoy going to the movies two or three times a
week. But I would always be home by nine o'clock.'"[39]

Not all parents were quite this strict—and not all working women
lived at home. Still, the nickelodeon was the preferred amusement
space for young single women, because it was cleaner, cheaper, more
accessible, and posed less of a risk to one's reputation than the dance
halls, cheap cafés, and amusement parks. Even the "settlement girl,"
a model of propriety who shunned other commercial amusements,
"nevertheless went frequently to the movies."[40]

The nickelodeons were also extremely popular among the city's children. Dozens of reports, in city after city, breathlessly counted the
number of children in the nickel theaters. A 1909 Chicago report estimated the percentage of children daily attending the picture shows at
more than one-third the total audience. A Boston investigation of the
same year concluded that "nearly all the children between ten and
fourteen years of age attend some sort of theatre occasionally."[41]

The moving-picture theaters' low price and the increasing availability of money for children who worked on the streets as newsies, hustlers, scavengers, bootblacks, and peddlers made the nickel theaters as
accessible as the vacant lot on the corner. "Never before," wrote Jane
Addams in 1909, "have such numbers of young boys earned money
independently of the family life, and felt themselves free to spend it as
they choose in the midst of vice deliberately disguised as pleasure."
When Ina Taylor interviewed over 500 newsboys in St. Louis in 1910,
she found that 87 percent regularly attended the cheap theaters. "In
Chicago, William Hard, a journalist, claimed [in a 1908 article] to have
found a group of children who sold papers every afternoon for the sole

purpose of raising money for movie tickets. They worked until they had their nickels for admission, quit to see the show, and then returned to 'work again until they [had] another nickel to be spent for the same purpose at another 'theatorium.' "[42]

For young girls, ready cash was a bit more difficult to come by, but only a bit. Those already working had no trouble hiding a few nickels a week from the pay envelopes they delivered each Friday afternoon to their mothers; those still at home had more difficulty getting their nickels, but they too had their means of earning, teasing, or stealing it from their elders. "It is so easy for a girl, when sent to the corner grocery for 15 cents worth of coal oil, to get a dime's worth and save a nickel for the show," reported a social worker from Birmingham, Alabama, in 1911.[43]

Once inside the cheap theaters, the children took over, especially during the afternoon and early evening performances, which they were most likely to attend with their friends, not their parents. As I have written elsewhere, "The Bijous, Pictoriums, Theatoriums, Jewels, Electrics, and Dreamlands became the children's 'general social center and club house.' 'Young people,' Jane Addams reported from Chicago, 'attend the five cent theaters in groups, with something of the "gang" instinct, boasting of the films and stunts in "our theater."' When the lights went down, they were free—as they were free nowhere else indoors—to behave like children: to shout, scream, howl, laugh aloud, and jump up and down in their seats. 'They were called silent pictures,' Sam Levenson remembers. 'Maybe the pictures were silent, but the audience certainly wasn't.' "[44]

The children made the best possible use of their clubhouse/theaters. The younger ones played together through the afternoon matinees, singing along with the illustrated songs, eating candy and peanuts, throwing wrappers and shells at one another, booing the villains, cheering the heroes, and generally making as much noise as they could. In the larger theaters, many of them recently converted from vaudeville, the older children could, if they chose, retreat to the balconies. While the reformers in many cities had succeeded in forcing the theater owners to turn up the lights, the balconies remained in shadows. For couples looking for a place to be alone or exchange sexual favors, there were no better seats in the city.

Women and children were a significant part of the early nickelodeon audiences, but workingmen—by themselves or, on weekend evenings and afternoons, with their families—also regularly attended the nickel shows. As Roy Rosenzweig has written, "Journalists and other commentators penned such phrases as 'the academy of the workingman,' the 'drama of the multitude,' 'the workingman's college,' and the 'true theater of the people' to dramatize the new development." For immigrant men who had arrived in the new world without their families, the movies offered not just entertainment but "their first nonwork contact with the larger American society." Here was an entertainment that was not only amusing, accessible to those who spoke no English, and enlightening on the ways of Americans, but also one that was cheap enough for the most impecunious workingman to indulge in.[45]

When the social researcher George Bevans studied *How Workingmen Spend Their Spare Time* in late 1912 and early 1913, he discovered that, no matter what their jobs, they spent more of their spare time at the picture show than anywhere else. In fact, as Bevans and other commentators noted, the city's workingmen appeared to be spending more time at the movies than at the saloon. William Fox claimed that the saloons in the vicinity of his theaters "found the business so unprofitable that they closed their doors. . . . If we had never had prohibition," he would later tell Upton Sinclair, "the motion pictures would have wiped out the saloon."[46]

There were, indeed, many similarities between the motion-picture house and the saloon that led to competition between them. The nickelodeons, like the saloons, were located on almost every major shopping street, were wondrously cheap, required no advance tickets or planning, and provided instant amusement to those with little time to spare. It was by no means accidental that a great many of the early nickel theater owners, among them Tom Saxe in Milwaukee, moved into the exhibition business after having successfully owned and operated neighborhood saloons.[47]

-◦-≈⊙⊂≈-◦-

Only the African-American population of the cities was purposely excluded from the expanding nickelodeon audience. Because the storefront theaters had no balconies or galleries, there was no efficient way to segregate blacks from the rest of the audience. They either had to be excluded entirely or permitted to sit wherever they pleased. The latter alternative being unthinkable, the former was adopted, although in most states and cities outside the South, it was expressly illegal. In Detroit, Springfield, Illinois, Perth Amboy, Newark, New York City, and Los Angeles, black moviegoers, often with the help of local National Association for the Advancement of Colored People chapters, sued theater owners who had denied them entrance. Even when fines were levied, however, they did not result in changed admission policies.[48]

Not one of the dozens of articles in the daily press and the trade journals that described the motley crowds in nickel theaters mentioned blacks as among them. The almost-intimate setting inside the nickel shows demanded their exclusion. Had the nickel theaters been better lit and more spacious, there might have been "room" inside to accommodate black patrons in separate sections. But mixing blacks and whites in the cramped, darkened storefronts was beyond the bounds of possibility.

Occasionally, white or black entrepreneurs tried to accommodate African Americans in separate storefront theaters or segregated sections of the white theaters. The March 5, 1910, "Operator's Column" of the *Moving Picture World* reported receiving a letter from "an exhibitor from a town in Louisiana [who] is confronted with the problem of separating the white and black patrons of his show." The exhibitor wanted to divide the theater in half and project his pictures through a transparent screen in the middle of the storefront. In this way, he could not only segregate the audience, but make sure that black patrons were seated in the rear. The *World* writer responded that the scheme could not work and suggested instead that reserving "one side for each race would be sufficient segregation."[49]

In Dallas, a theater owner starving for patrons tried to expand his audience by cutting a second door in his front entrance and, in the words of the *Moving Picture World* reporter, turning "over . . . one side of the house . . . to the simple-minded darkey." Most such attempts to attract black moviegoers to segregated theaters failed, perhaps, as one theater manager suggested, because African Americans preferred to patronize amusements where they could be sure of seeing "black faces in the performance."[50]

When show businessmen in southern cities attempted to establish moving-picture theaters for African Americans, they were dissuaded from doing so by law or vigilante violence. In Montgomery, Alabama, "city authorities" forbade a white man to open a moving-picture show for "colored people" because it was to be located on one of the city's "main streets." A crowd in Jackson, Mississippi, destroyed the moving-picture house for "colored people" in that city. "They ran the ticket seller out of the office, cut the wires, disconnected the moving picture apparatus, and locked the doors."[51]

--»═)═«--

For the bulk of the city's population, the sudden emergence of not one but five or ten nickel shows within walking distance of work or home must have been nothing short of extraordinary. The previous expansion of commercial entertainments—the rapid proliferation of cheap stock theaters, ten-twenty-thirties, vaudeville and lecture halls, phonograph parlors and penny arcades, amusement parks and summertime fairs— had led up to, yet hardly prepared anyone for, this sudden explosion. Imagine for a moment what it must have meant to be able to attend a "show" for a nickel in your neighborhood. And not just any show, but a moving-picture show with live entertainment. City folk who had never been able to afford the theater or, indeed, any commercial amusement could now, on their way home from work or shopping or on a Saturday evening or Sunday afternoon, enter the darkened auditorium, take a seat (not in the gallery or balcony, but wherever they chose), and witness the latest technological wonders, all for five or ten cents.

One understands the passion of the early commentators as they described in the purplest of prose what the moving-picture theater meant to the city's working people. There was a heavy dose of condescension in their voices, but that did not invalidate their impressions of the "modern-day miracle" that enveloped the toilers, the tenement dwellers, and the dirty children of the ghettoes, who were now, for the first time, admitted to the "house of dreams," their horizons instantly broadened to the world outside their simple, stunted lives. Mary Heaton Vorse concluded her June 1911 article in *Outlook* by referring directly to the picture-show audiences she had observed on Bleeker Street and the Bowery in New York City, "You see what it means to them; it means Opportunity—a chance to glimpse the beautiful and strange things in the world that you haven't in your life; the gratification of the higher side of your nature; opportunity which, except for the big moving picture book, would be forever closed to you."[52]

CHAPTER 13

"The Pernicious 'Moving Picture' Abomination"

F OR THE CRITICS OF COMMERCIALIZED POPULAR
culture who had for a century complained about—and organized
against—the evils of saloons, bawdy houses, honky-tonks, variety theaters, cheap vaudeville, prize fights, dime novels, and story papers, the
nickel shows presented an unparalleled danger to civic morality. Never
before had so many innocent children and working people been placed
in such immediate danger by unscrupulous (often immigrant) purvey-
ors of commercial filth.[1]

Although the theater had once, wrote John Collier of the People's
Institute and the National Board of Censorship, served as a "moral
agent of religion" and "a patriotic agent of the state," it had in twentieth-century America become an entirely "commercialized institution
. . . ministered to at this day almost wholly by irresponsible, money-
making agencies. . . . Commercialized recreation means dissipation. . . .
It means the theater dominated by financial speculation and the moving picture reduced to the general level of yellow journalism."[2]

What made the discourse on the moving pictures cataclysmic in tone
was the changed nature of the audience. Vaudeville and live theater
had deadened the taste, moral sensibilities, and intellectual capacities
of relatively prosperous, English-speaking audiences; moving pictures
"demoralized" working people, immigrants, and children who lacked
the intellectual, educational, and cultural resources to resist or coun-

LADIES AND CHILDREN
ARE CORDIALLY INVITED
TO THIS THEATRE
NO OFFENSIVE PICTURES
ARE EVER SHOWN HERE

Slides were flashed on the screen before and after the show and during intermission to encourage audience members to behave themselves in the darkened theaters. (*Library of Congress, Prints and Photographs Division.*)

terbalance their effects. Edward Chandler of Boston likened moving pictures to a "disease" that was poisoning "beyond recovery . . . the very life blood of the city." The Ohio Humane Society, which viewed 250 films in early 1910, found 40 percent of them "unfit for children's eyes." Working-class and immigrant children whose family backgrounds and lack of educational and financial capital condemned them to unskilled, probably manual labor, were identified as being particularly susceptible to the temptations exhibited in such pictures. They would learn from viewing them not only that crime paid but also that it paid handsomely and required much less toil than labor in factory, mine, or mill.[3]

While dedicated to protecting children from the moral dangers of the moving-picture show, the antivice crusaders were not above also using them as a Trojan Horse to invade the theaters and censor the

With gallery seats priced at only ten cents for matinees, boys like the one pictured here gazing at the poster could easily save enough money from their earnings as newsboys or bootblacks to attend the vaudeville or picture show a couple of times a week. (*Library of Congress, Prints and Photographs Division.*)

moving pictures seen by adult working people. In 1907, Chicago passed a censorship ordinance requiring police permits for films shown in nickel and dime theaters. Jake Block, a Chicago theater owner, and his colleagues challenged the law in the Illinois Supreme Court, arguing that legislation requiring only nickel theater owners to secure prior approval of their shows was discriminatory and unconstitutional. The Court denied their contentions: "The ordinance applies to five and ten cent theaters . . . which, on account of the low price of admission, are frequented and patronized by a large number of children, as well as by those of limited means who do not attend the productions of plays and dramas given in the regular theaters. The audiences include those classes whose age, education, and situation in life specially entitle them to protection against the evil influence of obscene and immoral representations. The welfare of society demands that every effort of municipal authorities to afford such protection shall be sustained." The cheap theaters, in other words, had to be regulated and the moving pictures censored because they were patronized by children and childlike adults who required the special protection of the law.[4]

The fact that a good number of nickelodeon owners were, like Jake Block, Jewish or Catholic, and of working-class and immigrant backgrounds, made it easier for civic-minded reformers and public officials to castigate them for their foul deeds, interfere with their rights as businessmen, and threaten their property. In May 1908, the *Moving Picture World* reported that a special bill was going to be introduced at the 1909 session of the New York State Assembly mandating that moving-picture theater licenses be issued only to citizens. "It is . . . aimed . . . at the horde of foreigners who operate the moving picture shows in New York and the other large cities in the State." The bill, if introduced, was never passed, but the threat remained.[5]

The ethnicity of the exhibitors, although seldom attacked this blatantly, remained an underlying subtext in the critique of the new medium. At a public hearing on the nickelodeons held by Mayor McClellan in December of 1908, former Assemblyman Cyrus W. Gale, now an exhibitor and because of his ethnic background and political standing, able to speak more freely in public, addressed the mayor directly on the question of discrimination. Why, he wanted to know, were the "clergymen" objecting only to the moving-picture shows, when there were many other theaters and concert halls that also stayed open on Sundays?* "Would you be so unjust as to close one portion of amusement in this city and not close the rest? I say the poor have just as much right as the rich. If you are going to close the moving picture shows which are good and conducted right and have a tendency to

---

*Legitimate theaters, concert halls, and even vaudeville halls flouted the blue laws by presenting educational programs or "sacred concerts" on Sundays.

raise and not to corrupt the morals, I am going to ask you isn't it just as fair . . . that you close the Metropolitan Opera House on Sunday or the theaters that show picture shows and the Y.M.C.A. which does the same thing."[6]

⊷⊷⊜⊜⊷⊷

While the antivice crusaders railed against the immoral content of the films and demanded that the picture shows be closed down on Sundays, more moderate progressive reformers and politicians worried more about the unsafe conditions inside the theaters. They feared, and rightly, that overcrowded theaters with blocked exits would one day result in a tragedy comparable to the 1903 Iroquois Theater fire in Chicago that had taken 600 lives in fifteen minutes. When in December of 1908, in response to the antivice crusaders' complaints about immoral films, Mayor George B. McClellan, Jr., and Chief Oliver of the Bureau of Licenses personally inspected dozens of theaters, they found the most deplorable conditions. "The exit facilities of almost all of the places . . . examined are inadequate to safeguard human life. Passageways are unlighted, exit doors are locked or blocked, and are not large enough for the large number of people who, in an emergency, would be compelled to use them." Had a fire broken out or even a spark appeared, hundreds would have been burned alive or trampled to death trying to escape.[7]

On December 24, 1908, Mayor McClellan issued executive orders revoking the licenses of the city's nickel theaters until they had been inspected and their owners had stipulated "in writing" that they would not open on Sundays. Although the theater owners eventually won an injunction against the mayor's action, the city had served notice on the nickel show proprietors that they would be held accountable for adhering to minimum fire-safety regulations. In the months that followed, many of the worst fire traps were closed down and new legislation was written enforcing minimal fire-safety standards and prohibiting nickel shows from opening in tenement buildings.[8]

On January 12, 1909, with the theaters reopened but the debate on immoral films, unsafe theaters, and Sunday closings still current, the People's Institute, a progressive reform group that had earlier investigated the nickel shows and found the theaters dirty but the pictures "rarely, almost never, indecent," tried to inject a note of moderation into the controversy. In a letter to the editor of the *New York Times*, the Institute affirmed the right of the government to exercise its "police powers" to safeguard the public from overt physical or moral endangerment but emphasized that the nickel theaters fulfilled a singular and important purpose. "There is no other form of amusement at prices sufficiently low which meets the amusement needs of the workingmen's or immigrant's entire family. The possibility of cheap, wholesome, dramatic amusement for the people is involved in the moving picture problem. Let us remember this in our efforts at reform."[9]

Such a sympathetic voice must have immediately appealed to the nickelodeon owners who had won the battle to stay open but could not be sure about the larger war. To protect themselves from the antivice crusaders, the owners, joined by the movie producers, signed an agreement with the People's Institute in March 1909 to establish a National Board of Censorship.[10]

The agreement did not satisfy those who wanted to protect the morals of the young by keeping them out of the movie theaters. In 1909, the City's Board of Aldermen and the New York State Legislature passed legislation banning children unaccompanied by parent or guardian from the picture shows. *The Nickelodeon*, commenting on the legislation, remarked caustically that with a censorship board already organized to keep the movies "clean," laws barring unaccompanied children had lost their utility. "Perhaps it has never occurred to the municipal lawmakers who seek to legislate the children out of one of their greatest enjoyments, how absurdly anomalous their position is. Why have we gone to the trouble and expense of censoring pictures for the sake of those who will not be permitted to see them?"[11]

What was as galling to the antivice crusaders as the proliferation of nickel theaters was their owners' blithe disregard of the blue laws that mandated theaters be closed on Sundays. Because the storefront shows were not licensed as "theaters," they did not fall under these laws. In Chicago, Jane Addams and her associates kept their experimental Hull House nickel show open on Sundays, without protest of any sort. In New York City, Adoph Zukor and Marcus Loew rented legitimate playhouses from the Shuberts for special Sunday film shows.[12]

The New York City antivice forces fought back with a citywide petition drive in 1911 demanding that all nickel theaters be closed on Sunday and all pictures be censored by a board administered by a city agency (the Board of Education was suggested). The Board of Aldermen, overwhelmed by petitions from civic and religious groups, voted almost unanimously for the censorship and Sunday-closing ordinance.

Mayor Gaynor, a former judge, staunch First Amendment supporter, and astute politician who knew that there were more movie fans than censorship advocates, vetoed the ordinance. While never directly taking issue with the clergymen's claims that they were acting "in behalf of the children," he exposed the censorship measure for what it was, "class" legislation aimed at the working people and immigrants who owned, operated, and patronized the nickel theaters. "These moving picture shows are attended by the great bulk of the people, many of whom cannot afford to pay the prices charged by the theaters. They are a solace and an education to them. Why are we singling out these people as subjects necessary to be protected by a censorship? Are they any more in need of protection by censorship than the rest of the community?"[13]

⁃⋗⫝̸⬤⫇⋖⋆⁃

While the antivice crusaders failed to close the movie theaters on Sunday or establish mandatory government censorship, moderate progressive reformers fared better in their attempts to pass legislation establishing fire-safety and health standards. They were supported in this effort by the trade journals, whose editors were convinced that dirty, dangerous theaters threatened the future of the picture industry. As the *Moving Picture World* warned in early 1911, "The justified criticism of the health authorities may prove disastrous one of these days. Should a malignant epidemic strike New York City, and these conditions prevail, the result might be a wholesale closing down of these germ factories."[14]

The massing of individuals in the store shows was unlike that in any other public space, greater than in the most congested sweatshops, flophouses, and multifamily tenement flats. Worse yet, in the storefront theaters there were no lobbies, vestibules, entryways, or staircases to ease congestion; no windows, skylights, or doorways to provide light or air. In March of 1911, Commissioner of Accounts Raymond Fosdick, at Mayor Gaynor's request, sent investigators into fifty picture shows chosen at random in Brooklyn, the Bronx, and Manhattan. Over two-thirds of the theaters visited were found to be dangerously overcrowded, "in some instances, indeed, with the aisles completely blocked by standing spectators, so that it was impossible for our inspectors to force their way into the hall." On Fulton Street, in Brooklyn, all the seats were "filled and standing in the rear were 61 persons completely blocking the aisles. As a matter of fact, including the persons standing, there were 373 people in attendance at the time of inspection and a panic or fire could not but have resulted disastrously."[15]

Even had fire not broken out, antivice crusaders and progressives alike feared that congestion of this sort would endanger the health and morals of assembled audience members. In his marvelous essay on nineteenth-century utopian fiction, Neil Harris has described the "consciousness of crowding which invaded the late nineteenth-century mind." Urban reformers, housing experts, public health authorities, child savers, journalists, and novelists were worried about the effects of overcrowding in urban dwellings, on the streets, and in public spaces. "Continual contiguity led to aggression, loss of control, and social decline. 'Contact breeds contagion and decay,' wrote Captain Nathan Davis in *Beulah*. Dense 'populations which are in constant contact breed moral contagion and deadly corruption.'"[16]

As the Chicago Vice Commission reported in 1911, the young and innocent were likely to be "influenced for evil by the *conditions surrounding* [the nickel shows]. . . . Many liberties are taken with young girls within the theater during the performance when the place is in total or semi-darkness. Boys and men slyly embrace the girls near them and offer certain indignities." The New York Society for the Prevention of Cruelty to Children, in its annual reports, press releases, and lobbying efforts before governmental bodies, presented case after case of such depravities. "This new form of entertainment," it claimed in its 1909 *Annual Report,* "has gone far to blast maidenhood. . . . Depraved adults with candies and pennies beguile children with the inevitable result. The Society has prosecuted many for leading girls astray through these picture shows, but GOD alone knows how many are leading dissolute lives begun at the 'moving pictures.'"[17]

The moral dangers of overcrowding, though severe, paled in comparison to the health hazards. Even in the darkness, audience members could protect themselves from mashers, perverts, and their own temptations. Not even the strongest resolve, however, could save them from the dangers that floated unseen through the air. Decades of urban epidemics and the pronouncements of public health reformers and journalists had, by the turn of the century, begun to convince the public (or at least that portion of it that went to public school, had contact with the settlement houses, or read the daily newspapers or general interest magazines) that, as Harris puts it, "dangerous microbes—insidious, omnipotent, invisible enemies of humanity, able to attack anyone and anywhere" flourished in overcrowded, unventilated spaces. And

This is another of the slides flashed on the screen during intermission. It does not appear from this image that the young women in the balcony were terribly troubled or "annoyed" by the attention of the young men who sat next to them. The slide is a subtle reminder that the balconies provided privacy for young couples who wanted to enjoy an hour together in the dark. (*Library of Congress, Prints and Photographs Division.*)

nowhere in the city were there more congested spaces with staler air than in the nickel theaters. As the *Independent* reported in early 1910, the city's "moving picture places [had] become foci for the dissemination of tubercle bacilli."[18]

Robert Bartholomew, inspecting the movie houses in Cleveland in 1913, was appalled by the "condition of the air." In some of the larger theaters, attendants using "large atomizers squirted a solution around the room to allay the odor of the foul air." In others, fans were supposed to provide fresh air but did little more than circulate the foul air already accumulated. Bartholomew concluded, in what was otherwise an extremely favorable report, that "probably 35,000 people are daily subjected to the dangers of contracting disease from the foul air laden with death-dealing germs. In ten theaters the air was found to be so foul that the investigators could not stay more than a few moments and even this short stay resulted in sneezing, coughing and the contraction of serious colds. One theater was visited at the opening of an evening performance after having been closed one and one-half hours succeeding the afternoon performance. The air was then so bad that three patrons left within a few moments complaining of faintness and headache."[19]

In many cities, progressive reform groups called for government intervention to protect the health and safety of moving-picture audiences. Legislation passed in New York State in 1911 required that all new "public entertainments or exhibitions by cinematograph or any other apparatus for projecting moving pictures," no matter how large or small, enclose their projectors in "fireproof booths." An additional state law, also from 1911, established a special licensing procedure for the operators of these projectors. In Chicago, a special ordinance forbid moving-picture theaters, no matter how safely constructed, from being built above the first floor of non-fireproof buildings.[20]

The effect of these laws on the exhibitors cannot be underestimated. The fire-safety laws passed by the Pennsylvania state legislature were so stringent, *Film Index* reported in July 1909, that a large number of the smaller theaters in the state, unable to meet them, were closing down. In Chicago, the Juvenile Protective Association reported in 1911 that, as a result of better laws and cooperation between the reformers and the police, "there has been a great improvement in the physical conditions of the theatres. The exits are now much better and the ventilation has been much improved."[21]

Unfortunately for the reform community, it was easier to pass laws than to get them enforced. The reformers were particularly stymied when it came to enforcing the laws barring underage, unaccompanied children from the nickel shows. As a confidential investigator for the Kehillah, a Jewish reform agency, reported of the Lower East Side movie houses in 1913, "Minors go in here with anyone who act as their guardian and once they get inside they take care of themselves."[22]

The exhibitors paid the law no attention at all. The New York City Commissioner of Accounts reported in March of 1911 that it had become "a common practice in most of the shows to admit children under sixteen years of age unaccompanied by a guardian or parents in spite of the provisions of section 484 of the Penal Code. Indeed, one important official of the Moving Picture Exhibitors Association stated in his testimony before us that 75 per cent of the moving picture shows of this city would be driven out of business if this law were strictly enforced." The problem was, of course, not confined to New York City. A 1913 survey in Cleveland found that more than one-half of the children attending the moving-picture theaters were unaccompanied by adults. For the evening performances, the percentage exceeded two-thirds.[23]

Not only did the reformers fail to keep the children out of the nickel shows, but their attempts to improve the pictures they saw were only minimally successful. When Jane Addams and her associates—under the impression that the children would patronize any moving-picture show provided the price was right—opened their Hull House theater, the first in what was supposed to have been a "settlement-house circuit" of wholesome nickelodeons, they were surprised to find only thirty-seven children in the audience. (The experiment was soon terminated.) When questioned about the "clean" show they had seen at Hull House, the children responded that they had enjoyed watching *Cinderella* and travel scenes of Japan and Java, but their tastes ran in other directions. According to Jimmy Flaherty, twelve years old (his words recorded by the reformers who did all they could to make them sound cute and tough), "Things has got ter have some hustle. I don't say it's right, but people likes to see fights, 'n' fellows getting hurt, 'n' love makin', 'n' robbers, and all that stuff. I like to myself, even. This here show ain't even funny, unless those big lizards from Java was funny." Had the choice been between *Cinderella* and nothing, the children would have paid their nickels to see *Cinderella*. But, with dozens of local nickelodeons anxious to attract their nickels, the children could, for the same price, see *The Pirates, The Defrauding Banker, The Adventures of an American Cowboy, An Attack on the Agent,* and *The Car Man's Danger,* all playing within a few blocks of Hull House.[24]

The reformers struggled valiantly to convince the producers to produce and the exhibitors to exhibit "educational" and "uplifting" pictures for the children. But their powers of persuasion were never sufficient to supersede the logic of the marketplace. Because the children bought more tickets than the reformers, the pictures that they wanted to see were produced and exhibited more regularly than the educational fare.

Even the crime pictures that had earlier been banned because of their supposed evil influence on the impressionable young soon returned to the theaters, as producers and exhibitors found ways to reintroduce them without violating censorship board restrictions. By 1910, according to John Collier, 20 percent of all the movies being produced presented characters who were "tempted to commit crimes, and sometimes do commit crimes," though none of these films, Collier proudly reported, portrayed crime "for its own sake" or allowed a criminal to go unpunished. In fact, crimes committed on the moving-picture screen were "invariably dealt with by a stern justice which is far more certain and terrible with its lightnings than is human justice in real life."[25]

Despite the reformers' attempts to protect them, the children remained an important segment of the moving-picture audience. The calculus of commercial amusements dictated that the show business-men—with their cheap prices and abbreviated shows—empty and refill their houses several times a day. The children were an essential part of their audience, because they filled the theaters during fallow periods in the late afternoons, in early evenings, and for weekend matinees. The producers and owners consequently did all that was necessary to hold on to them. To disarm their critics, they followed the advice of the National Board of Censorship and cooperated with the local state and municipal censorship boards that were organized in the early 1910s. But they continued to sidestep the laws barring underage, unaccompanied children from their theaters and ignored the reformers' pleas that they substitute educational films for trashy crime melodramas and slapstick comedies.[26]

The nickelodeon's critics in the long run, achieved both more and less than they had bargained for. While the antivice crusaders never succeeded in instituting mandatory government censorship, Sunday closing, or age restrictions, their continual attack on "the pernicious 'moving picture' abomination" provided more moderate reformers with leverage to push for industry self-censorship and regulatory legislation. And that legislation, according to the film historian Charlotte Herzog, "hastened the demise of the nickelodeon" as new building codes and fire-safety ordinances made it more costly and less efficient to operate movie theaters in tiny, airless storefront theaters.[27]

CHAPTER 14

Combination Shows, Stars, and Features

WHILE THE REFORMERS WOULD TAKE CREDIT for the demise of the nickelodeon, they were only half right. As long as there was no alternative to the nickel theaters, customers were content to squeeze themselves into darkened, airless storefronts to watch fifteen- to twenty-minute shows, with seven- or eight-minute "features." With increased competition, however, came the bigger theaters and better shows that would put the nickelodeons out of business.

The early exhibitors were entertainment retailers with no commitment to film as such. One of the earliest—and the most successful—was Marcus Loew. Loew, in later years, confessed to an audience of Harvard University graduate business students that the idea to combine vaudeville with pictures into a combination show "all came about through an accident." An unemployed actor applied for a position as doorkeeper at one of Loew's nickel shows. Loew "felt kind of sorry" for him and asked him if he could recite. The actor could, so Loew "had him recite 'Gunga Din' twenty times a day. That was the beginning of vaudeville as an adjunct to motion pictures."[1]

Exhibitors who, like Loew, opened combination vaudeville and picture-show theaters were creating a new entertainment tier between the poor man's nickelodeon and the vaudeville theater. While the city's regular vaudeville theaters continued to charge a minimum of twenty-five cents for gallery seats and up to two dollars for box seats, the combination houses, or small-time vaudeville theaters, as they also were called, charged twenty-five cents for their best seats and ten cents for all the others.[2]

The trade journals, which from their inception had urged the exhibitors to upgrade their theaters and shows to attract a more prosperous audience, were outraged by the combination shows. "Vaudeville Vitiates the Pictures," argued a *Moving Picture World* writer in June of 1910. "You are disgusting, you are repelling a large section of the public who would be firm and consistent patrons of moving picture theaters by interjecting vaudeville of such ridiculous nature that I have heard audiences openly jeer at it." Cheap vaudeville, another writer complained, was attracting the wrong kind of customers to the picture show. "Where the management feeds the patrons with cheap vaudeville in addition to pictures a spirit of roughness grows up with the swiftness of weeds. These are the theaters, where scorbutic-looking youths with atrophied brain cells are hanging about the lobbies. The sight of them alone is a distinct threat to a normal man's appetite and digestion, and women avoid such places, as if they were infested with the plague."[3]

Despite such criticism, the combination shows were enormously successful. By 1910, there were combination theaters on the downtown and secondary shopping streets of most large and medium-size cities. Loew operated a chain of hundreds; William Fox owned fourteen in Greater New York alone. On Chicago's South State Street where Robert Motts had opened the Pekin Theatre in 1904, there were by the early 1910s, as Mary Carbine has written, "combination" houses like the "Grand, the Monogram and the States adverti[sing] 'Light Vaudeville and Photo-Plays,' 'Big Musical Program—Pictures That Move,' or 'Vaudeville de Luxe and Best Motion Pictures.'" Although most of these houses were owned and operated by white entrepreneurs, they were patronized almost exclusively by Chicago's black residents.[4]

The expansion of the small-time vaudeville theaters brought millions of dollars to the show businessmen and cheap amusements to millions of city folk, some of whom had dared not enter the nickelodeons. Pleasure seekers on a budget could for a dime get two hours of live entertainment and moving pictures at Fox's Dewey in New York, six live acts and film at Lubin's "Palace of Delight" in Philadelphia, and similar full-length shows in combination theaters across the country.[5]

The exhibitors who were moving their films into larger theaters and supplementing them with live vaudeville were convinced that moving

pictures had as yet attracted only a small portion of their potential audience. If the moving-picture show were to become a permanent part of
the city's respectable nightlife, it would have to tap into that portion of
the population for whom live theater was too expensive, the vaudeville
theater too crude, and the nickelodeons too dark, dirty, and cheap.

To attract these kinds of customers, moving-picture exhibitors had to
keep prices low, but not too low. Raising the price of the picture show
from five to ten cents, they believed, would not only increase revenues
but also raise the reputation of the house. As *The Nickelodeon* editori-
alized in January of 1910, "It is a mistake to suppose the people will not
pay [a dime instead of a nickel]. They will. Not only would there be little protest, but it might even be found that the dimes came easier than
the nickels. There is a psychological side to the question which will
bear investigating. In the first place, a dime is a respectable coin, while
a nickel is not. For the very reason that we value a nickel lightly, we are
apt to value lightly whatever we buy with that nickel. . . . Prices too low
demoralize any business. . . . Almost everything in the world has
advanced in price in the last few years except the 'nickel show.' Let's
not lag behind."[6]

While it is difficult to put full credence in this editorial, it does touch
on an important point. The enormous success of the nickelodeon was
paradoxically blocking future growth of the moving-picture business.
In building a clientele that included "millions of people who had next
to no disposable income or recreation time," the storefront picture
show had, in the film historian Miriam Hansen's words, acquired an
audience that "displayed a . . . distinct class profile." Potential customers who preferred not to mingle with the lower orders stayed
away.[7]

It was not simply the presence of poorer people in the audience that
gave the nickelodeon a less than stellar reputation. In price, content,
and ambience, the nickel show was still much closer to the saloon and
the penny arcade than to the legitimate playhouses. As Adolph Zukor
would later put it, the nickelodeon attracted "the casual passers-by, but
[not] people leaving their homes, going out in search of amusement."[8]

If the new, full-size moving-picture theaters were going to draw the
audience they were looking for, they had to sharply distinguish themselves from the nickel show. As Roxy explained to fellow exhibitors in
one of a series of articles he wrote for the *Moving Picture World* in
early 1910, "The secret of the successful moving picture theatre of the
future will be the ability of the management to make the people forget

that they are witnessing a moving picture, to make them forget that they only paid you five or ten cents to witness the performance." Homer W. Sibley of the *Moving Picture World* was even blunter in his assessment, "The 'dump' is doomed, and the sooner the cheap, ill-smelling, poorly ventilated, badly managed rendezvous for the masher and tough makes way for the better class of popular family theater the better it will be for the business and all concerned."[9]

The new full-size picture shows, though not nearly as large, glamorous, or spectacularly ornamented as the picture palaces would later be, were built and operated according to Roxy's and Sibley's specifications. They resembled legitimate playhouses more than storefront nickelodeons, with lobbies lit by chandeliers, floors covered in inlaid tile, aisles patrolled by uniformed ushers, restrooms—a necessity now that the show had been extended to an hour or more—and live orchestras or pipe organs to introduce and accompany the pictures. One planned in advance to take in the show in these theaters, dressed accordingly,

The interior of this 1909 moving-picture theater resembled in size and ornamentation a legitimate playhouse rather than a storefront nickelodeon. (*Library of Congress, Prints and Photographs Division.*)

and spent an evening "out" rather than half an hour "dropping in" on the way somewhere else. Where the nickel shows had been dark, dirty, congested, and reeking, the new theaters installed expensive ventilation systems that, they claimed, removed not only bad odors but germs as well. The Chicago Orpheum boasted of an "air-washing device that insures the audience an atmosphere actually purer than outside the building." The Swanson Theater in Chicago claimed that "the air in the theater is changed completely every three minutes." The management of the National Theater in Cleveland stated unequivocally that it was "the best ventilated theater in the city—warm in winter and cool in summer."[10]

The openings of these full-size moving-picture theaters were celebrated with written endorsements from the local gentry, businessmen, and politicians, all of whom had been assiduously courted by the exhibitors. The Saxes opened their Princess Theater in 1909 with a gala invitation-only premiere. "A Saxe brother was quoted that night saying, 'this invitation affair was given in the effort to secure the patronage of a better class of people.' In attendance were city officials, theater managers, and members of Milwaukee society. [Special invitations had also been sent to members of Milwaukee's Merchants and Manufacturing League and Citizen's League.] Mayor David S. Rose delivered the dedicatory address."[11]

Such endorsements, scattered through the pages of the local papers, punctuated the point the theater owners were trying to make: that those who disdained the nickelodeon should not, on that account, boycott picture shows exhibited in respectable theaters. Just as Barnum had propelled Tom Thumb into the rank of first-class attractions by arranging and widely publicizing an audience for him with the Queen of England, and Keith and Albee, as we saw in chapter 3, had consecrated their "New Theatre" by inducing Mrs. Jack Gardner of Boston society to hire a box, so did the exhibitors cloak themselves in mantles of respectability borrowed from the crowned heads of their communities.[12]

⧖⧖⧖

The first moving-picture and combination theaters had been built on the downtown shopping and entertainment streets alongside the established vaudeville theaters and legitimate playhouses. They were quickly followed by a ring of theaters built in urban fringe and suburban neighborhoods to reach the white-collar workers who had begun to settle there. The picture-show exhibitors were the first show businessmen to focus their attention—and their capital—outside the central city. While there were scores of nickel theaters on the shopping streets adjacent to the immigrant and working-class residential districts in the central city, few had been built in the "better" neighborhoods, in part because of restrictive zoning and licensing ordinances. After 1910, as the lobbying power of the movie industry grew stronger and fears of fire were ameliorated by new laws mandating safer theaters, these zoning restrictions were lifted.

The new neighborhood theaters did quite well. Not only were they cheaper than the downtown playhouses and vaudeville palaces, but also they were only minutes away from home. White-collar workers, middle managers, and small proprietors who lived in the urban periphery but worked in the central business districts found the theaters particularly convenient. As the *Moving Picture World* reported in July 1911, "To persons residing at any distance from the theater district of a large city the trouble occasioned in rushing home from business to dress for the theater outweighs the anticipated pleasure. Throw upon one side of the scales the nearby picture theater where one may with little physical exertion and small cost, pass the evening pleasantly and in comfort and you have the answer to the diminishing attendance at the legitimate house."[13]

The theater-building spree that had begun with the nickelodeon "craze" of the middle 1900s would accelerate through the 1910s and reach far beyond the central cities. In Boston, where the "theater district [had in 1910 been limited] to two downtown thoroughfares," there were by the end of 1913 new moving-picture theaters on the main streets of Dorchester, Roxbury, Cambridge, Somerville, Newton, Belmont, and Watertown. In August of 1914, G. B. Crain, Jr., in an article for the *Moving Picture World,* contended that "the suburban theater" had become "probably the most interesting development of recent years. . . . There are thriving suburbs in all of the larger cities which are almost clamoring for picture shows. They have demonstrated time without number their ability to provide the necessary volume of patronage and to keep the theaters going constantly, and not merely a few nights a week. . . . New subdivisions where the population consists largely of young married couples make good locations, because as a rule the newlyweds are trying to save money to pay for a home and

This is the exterior of Detroit's Majestic Theatre, a first-class "combination" house. (*Library of Congress, Prints and Photographs Division.*)

consequently prefer cheap amusements. They can go to the movies for the carfare they would need to take them downtown."[14]

⊷⇒◠⇐⊶

The picture-show industry had expanded its audience by upgrading its exhibition sites. But to attract a higher-paying audience, "better" pictures were also necessary. By continually emphasizing the quality of their product, industry spokesmen sought to counter the arguments of the antivice crusaders and to broaden their audience to encompass those who were disinterested in chase films and crude comedies but might be lured into the theater to see a "filmed" version of Shakespeare, the Bible, or the latest Broadway drama. In this, as in other matters, the industry proceeded by fits and starts. While a scattered minority of producers and exhibitors were committed, at least rhetorically, to making and exhibiting "quality" story films, most were satisfied with the audience they already had. As long as there were customers for a daily diet of chases and melodramas, the producers would continue to make them, the exchanges distribute them, and the nickel theaters exhibit them. Much of the talk about "quality" films was just that.

The major manufacturers spent more time and energy in the late 1900s trying to regulate competition than to improve their pictures. In early 1909, after months of negotiation, the Motion Picture Patents Company was formed, combining the major producers into one huge "Trust." From this point on, exhibitors who wanted to show Trust pictures had to pay a two-dollar-a-week licensing fee *and* agree to show only films made by the Trust producers. While most of the exhibitors signed on with the Trust, fearful that without its films they would be frozen out of the business, a sizable number refused. These unlicensed exhibitors and the exchangemen who could no longer show or distribute Trust films constituted a sizable market for the "independent" producers who supplied the renegades with a daily change of film.[15]

The Trust companies found themselves in the situation they had been trying to avoid. Instead of stifling competition, they had provoked even more. They now had to compete not only with one another but with the independent producers as well. In this intensified competitive situation, the manufacturer's reputation for turning out decent pictures was critical. Because the exhibitors changed their programs daily, neither "word of mouth" nor reviews brought customers to the theater to see particular pictures. Distributors, exhibitors, and audience members had, in fact, precious little information to go on in deciding whether or not to spend money on a film. What counted most—far more than the advertising copy, the lithograph on the poster, or the title of the film— was the "brand name" attached to it. Before audience members knew who D. W. Griffith or any of his actors and actresses were, they patronized pictures with the "Biograph" name because they associated it with quality. According to a *Moving Picture World* review from the spring of 1909, the Biograph Company had achieved a "unique position among American manufacturers. Within the last few months its reputation among exhibitors and the general public has increased by leaps and bounds." In Easton, Pennsylvania, the Casino called itself "The Home of the Biographs," and advertised in the daily paper, "Every Day a Biograph Feature." Elsewhere audiences pestered exhibitors who pestered their exchangemen to supply them with as many Biograph subjects as possible.[16]

The Edison Company, which had been the prime mover in forming a "Trust" to regulate competition, suffered the most from it. While the company continued to promote its "brand" by emphasizing the name and moral character of its founder, its reputation was damaged by the release of films audiences found difficult to follow. By late 1908, according to Charles Musser, "Edison films were frequently and stridently criticized for their failure to present clear, enjoyable, and effective narratives." *The Tale the Ticker Told,* released in December 1908, was disparaged as "a confused, unintelligible series of scenes. . . . The story is in an unknown picture language and if one can't understand the story what is the use of all the acting? The tale that this ticker told needs translation."[17]

This had not been a problem for the Edison Company or its competitors in the early days when pictures told stories audiences already knew (*Uncle Tom's Cabin, Goldilocks, The Night before Christmas*) or had plots so simple-minded they could be encapsulated in the film's title (*How a French Nobleman Got a Wife through the* New York Herald *Personal Columns, Rescued from an Eagle's Nest, Saved by Love*). Unfortunately for producers in general and Edison in particular, the rapid growth of exhibition sites and the consequent need for new pictures had exhausted the supply of familiar stories.[18]

From 1909 on, more and more pictures had to be made from stories audiences did not know. To narrate an unfamiliar story without sound required new techniques in lighting, editing, staging, camera work, screenwriting, directing, and acting. Much of the burden fell on the actors and actresses who had to convey more subtle and diverse emotions and the directors who had to teach them how to do it.

Actors and actresses in the early films had borrowed their gestures, poses, grins, and grimaces from melodrama and pantomime. They gesticulated broadly, waved their arms, and exaggerated every movement. There was little individuation in expression or posture. The action on the sheet was seen at a distance as if performed on a far-away theatrical stage. Because the film actors followed established conventions, there was no need for a closer view. Any child in the audience could tell who the villain was (the man in the long, black coat), why he acted as he did (he was evil), and what he was going to do next. By 1909 or so, critics and audiences alike appeared to be growing weary of what Roberta Pearson has called this "histrionic" performance style. In the theater and on the screen, actors and actresses adopted instead a "more natural" or "slower" style of acting. As cameras moved in closer to capture their more subtle and personalized expressions, audiences began to distinguish individual performers from one another. Fans who went regularly to the picture show took specific likes or dislikes to particular players. As the manufacturers never divulged their actors' given names, the fans referred to their favorites by their brand names, as the Vitagraph or the Biograph Girl.°[19]

The producers, more interested in publicizing the names of their studios than of players who might or might not stay with them, saw no benefit to be gained from "featuring" their actors or even naming them. But the picture fans demanded to know more about them. "Dear Stranger," wrote a Mister Leland Ayers in December of 1909 to Florence Lawrence, at the time the anonymous Biograph Girl, "Will you please answer this letter, a postal will do, just telling me your name, your name not a stage one?" Similar letters were handed to exhibitors and mailed to production companies.[20]

It didn't take long for the manufacturers to recognize the benefits that might be gained from exploiting their audience's curiosity. Kalem was the first to identify its actors and actresses by name in a group photograph published as an advertisement in the January 15, 1909, *Moving Picture World* and made available to exhibitors for posting in their lobbies. In that same year, Carl Laemmle, a distributor who was preparing to manufacture his own films, hired Florence Lawrence to star in them for the then-exorbitant salary of $15,000 a year. To make sure the public knew that the Biograph Girl would now be appearing exclusively in IMP pictures, Laemmle engineered the first publicity coup. In March of 1910, he leaked the rumor that Miss Lawrence had been killed in a streetcar accident in St. Louis and then took out a huge ad in the *Mov-*

°The only picture players to receive individual billing were imported theatrical stars or celebrities, such as the swimmer Annette Kellerman, who had assembled their reputations outside the picture show and might, for that reason alone, bring new customers inside.

ing Picture World to announce that the story of Miss Lawrence's demise was the "blackest and at the same time the silliest lie yet circulated by enemies of the 'Imp.'" Within weeks, Laemmle produced Miss Lawrence in person in St. Louis to promote her latest film and reassure her fans that she was indeed alive.[21]

Promoting stars not only sold films to audiences but also upgraded the image of the industry. With the appearance of stars in its dramas, the industry could separate itself further from its peep-show past (there had been no "stars" in the penny arcades) and connect itself with the legitimate theater (which gloried in them). Like the stars of the live theater, the movie stars were larger than life. But they were innocent, accessible, and on a first-name basis with their fans. Monstrous close-ups brought audience members into intimate contact with the stars. Fans could not help but feel "close" to those whose smiles and frowns they knew by heart.

It took only a few years for the picture players to ascend from anonymity to omnipresence and their own kind of notoriety. A new institution, the fan magazine, was created to better acquaint audiences with their favorite stars. Mary Pickford became "Little Mary" to her fans; Florence Turner was so "accessible" she got thousands of letters proposing marriage. By 1911, movie stars were touring local theaters to promote their films, granting regular interviews, writing their own articles in newspapers and fan magazines, and distributing photographs to their admirers. Their pictures or names could be seen on picture postcards, lobby posters, calendars, pillow tops, radiator caps, sheet music, and massage cream. Their words could be read everywhere. Their images were ubiquitous.[22]

The best evidence we have of the stars' newfound importance is the huge salaries the producers were willing to pay them. On Broadway, Mary Pickford had been paid $25 a week to appear in David Belasco's production of *The Warrens of Virginia*. In 1910, Carl Laemmle lured her away from Biograph, her first movie home, with an offer of $175 a week. Her starting annual salary with Zukor at Famous Players in 1914 was $20,000, soon raised to $1,000 a week, and then in January of 1915, to $2,000 a week and half the profits from her pictures. In June of 1916, another contract increased her compensation to 50 percent of the profits of her films against a guaranteed $1,040,000 a year, payable at the rate of $10,000 a week, with a bonus of $300,000 for signing the contract and an additional $40,000 for the time she had spent reading scripts during contract negotiations. And this was only the beginning. Subsequent contracts with other producers would be even more lucrative.[23]

The stars were worth the money because their appearance in films boosted receipts and added a degree of predictability to the business, a predictability that was welcomed by the banks and financiers who in the 1920s would assume a larger role in the industry. The most reliable, perhaps the only predictor of success for any given film was the presence of an established star. As the investment house of Halsey, Stuart and Co. explained to potential investors in 1927, "'stars' are today an economic necessity to the motion picture industry." They guaranteed that the features they "starred" in would be seen—at least by their fans.[24]

The stars not only were bringing new customers into the theaters, they were incorporating a movie audience scattered over thousands of different sites into a unified public, a public that not only saw its favorite pictures but talked about them, read about them, collected their pictures and posters, and bought fan magazines to learn more about their personal lives and loves. Stars were, by definition, actors or actresses whose appeal transcended every social category, with the possible exception of gender. The first Hollywood stars were a remarkably diverse lot: there were European Jews, such as Charlie Chaplin and Theda Bera; ethnic exotics, such as Pola Negri and Rudolph Valentino; clean-cut Anglo-Saxon heroes, such as Wallace Reid, Earle Williams, Francis X. Bushman; and their counterparts, the girls next door, Pearl White, Norma Talmadge, Lillian Gish, and, of course, Mary Pickford. Although they came from every corner of the country and overseas, their transformation into stars made them the property of all. As theater and now film critic Walter Prichard Eaton explained in 1915, "The smallest town ... sees the same motion-picture players as the largest. . . . John Bunny and Mary Pickford 'star' in a hundred towns at once."[25]

--⋆--⟞⟝--⋆--

While the earliest fan magazines had been designed to give moviegoers information about the stories the movies told and their stars, it quickly became apparent that the fans were much more interested in the latter than the former. Part of the reason for this was that the movie manufacturers were, through the early 1910s, continuing to turn out the same tired one-reel chases, melodramas, and comedies. Only a handful of producers, like Vitagraph, were experimenting with longer, multiple-reel story films. Vitagraph, smaller than Edison, and less highly regarded than Biograph, promoted its "quality" multiple-reel films to distinguish its "brand" name from the larger manufacturers. It also expected that its versions of classics like *Vanity Fair* and *Elektra* would appeal to educated theatergoers who were familiar with the original versions as well as ordinary picture fans who appreciated a good story, spectacularly filmed. *Elektra* was promoted as a "film that will stand 'billing like a circus.' . . . You want big audiences; you want big returns. 'Elektra' is the biggest thing yet in moving pictures. It catches them big." The five-reel, seventy-five-minute *Life of Moses* was similarly sold to the Sunday school audience as an authentic representation of biblical truths and to the picture-show crowd as the most expensive, most spectacular moving picture ever made.[26]

In publicizing the cost, size, and spectacular nature of its "quality" films, Vitagraph was following standard amusement industry practices. In every other form of commercial entertainment, audiences were beginning to equate "bigger" with "better." The more spectacular and the more expensive the stage show, midway exhibit, or amusement park ride, the better it drew. The moviemakers followed suit, spending vast sums of money on extravagant sets and stupendous effects. The producers of the Italian epic, *Homer's Odyssey*, claimed that they had built and peopled an entire ancient city to make their movie. Vitagraph boasted that it had spent $50,000 to produce *The Life of Moses*, $10,000 alone on the "Miracle of the Red Sea."[27]

Vitagraph tried to exhibit its longer, quality films in the theaters that handled its shorter comedies. But the exhibitors, with few exceptions, refused to book the multireel films. They preferred short films to long ones because they cost less to rent and because shorter films meant shorter shows and more rapid audience turnover. Albert Smith, one of the Vitagraph owners, recalled in his autobiography that when the company tried to distribute its multiple-reel *Life of Moses*, "The exhibitors told us the public wouldn't sit through a film lasting more than a full hour. We sent them reams of material telling our idea of how to put a feature picture over, how to bring patrons into their houses in greater number than ever before . . . but their theaters were small, seating a few hundred persons. The returns did not justify the rental they paid Vitagraph for the longer films."[28]

Spurned by the majority of exhibitors and locked out of the regular distribution network, Vitagraph and the importers who distributed foreign-made spectaculars were forced to book legitimate playhouses to exhibit their films. Phineas P. Craft, a former publicist for the Buffalo Bill Wild West Show, secured American rights to an Italian multireel feature, *Dante's Inferno,* in 1911 and exhibited it as if it were a live theatrical troupe instead of a film in a can. To help audiences follow the plot and to signify that this was no ordinary moving-picture show, Craft accompanied the film with "specially chosen and rehearsed music" and hired a lecturer to explain the action on the screen. The film played well in New York, Boston, Washington, and other eastern cities. In Providence, it was exhibited at fifty cents a ticket "to crowds who came out in the pouring rain" to see it. In Baltimore, it was held over a second week at Shubert's Auditorium Theater at prices of fifteen to seventy-five cents, much higher than the nickelodeons' but below the first-class legitimate theaters' usual price scale.[29]

Encouraged by his success, Craft in 1912 imported a second Italian spectacular, *Homer's Odyssey,* which he claimed, in an eight-page spread in *Moving Picture World,* had cost $200,000 to produce. Like its predecessor, *Homer's Odyssey* was heavily promoted and exhibited only in legitimate theaters. Ticket prices, however, were raised to two dollars top, the price theatergoers paid for live spectaculars with imported stars. Even at this price, the show sold out wherever it played. According to Terry Ramsaye, "a considerable percentage of [Craft's] patrons demanded to know if Mr. Homer was travelling with the show to make personal appearances." He was not, but those who were interested in learning more about him were invited to purchase the "plaster busts . . . postcards, and souvenir programs" Craft hawked in the lobby. Obviously, the film was drawing large numbers of spectators who had little or no familiarity with the classics.[30]

The "features," as the multiple-reel films came to be known, were building new audiences for moving pictures. City folk who would not have spent a nickel to see a chase film at a nickelodeon were spending twenty-five cents to two dollars to view full-length historical dramas in a first-class playhouse. The *Moving Picture World* asserted without reservation in August of 1911 that the new films had "destroyed the absurd idea, that people will not pay high prices for a moving picture entertainment, regardless of its high character." *Moving Picture News* gloated in July of 1912 that "people who looked with scorn upon the moving picture five or six years ago are now constantly seen among its most consistent and earnest patrons."[31]

One of the first American producers to actively compete for this audience was Adolph Zukor. Hearing that Sarah Bernhardt had agreed to film her stage performance of *Queen Elizabeth*, Zukor in 1912 arranged to purchase American rights to the picture for what he later claimed was the exorbitant price of $35,000. Zukor billed the filmed *Queen Elizabeth* as a "special presentation" designed exclusively for theatergoers, used the name of his partner, Broadway producer Daniel Frohman in the publicity—the film was promoted as "Presented by Daniel Frohman"—and leased the "sacrosanct Lyceum Theatre for a special invitation matinee performance. This setting alone gave it the seal of dramatic respectability," wrote Zukor's admiring biographer, Will Irwin.[32]

The following year, the American distributor George Kleine imported the Italian spectacular, *Quo Vadis?* and exhibited it in the same manner. Booked into the Astor Theater, "presented" by theatrical impresarios Cohan and Harris, priced at a dollar a ticket, and presented like live theater with three intermissions between acts, *Quo Vadis?* did even better than Bernhardt's *Queen Elizabeth,* playing to full houses on Broadway for an unprecedented twenty-two weeks. After its Broadway run, the film was toured to first-class playhouses across the country, including McVickers Theater in Chicago, the Academy of Music in Baltimore, Teller's Broadway in Denver, and the Tremont in Boston. In Worcester, the film attracted a larger audience "in three days than had its live version in an entire week." Kleine made so much money on *Quo Vadis?* and the Italian films he imported and toured in its wake that he was able to build his own picture theater on Broadway in New York City.[33]

--*===)(===*--

Theater owners and managers across the country watched, at first with apprehension, then with delight, as "feature" films drew capacity crowds to the better playhouses. Instead of fighting the tide, many allowed themselves to be swept up in it. Robert Grau predicted that the 1912 theater season would "be a noteworthy one, in that the leading theatrical managers who were wont to decry the motion picture industry are nearly all interested heavily in what are called special releases, and it is a fair statement to proclaim that one-third of the nation's playhouses will revert to the silent drama." The *New York Dra-*

matic Mirror suggested in May of 1913 that the small playhouses that closed their doors during the summer stay open and book the new "features" instead.[34]

The box-office potential of feature-length moving pictures exhibited in legitimate theaters was greater than anyone had imagined. While the Italian historical dramas had done excellent business at a dollar a ticket, films aimed at a broader audience and priced lower did even better. When Universal in November 1913 opened its white-slavery feature, *Traffic in Souls,* at Joe Weber's theater for twenty-five cents for every seat in the house, more than "a thousand fans had to be turned away the first night. Thirty thousand saw the film the first week, many of them girls of between sixteen and eighteen."[35]

The Inside of the White Slave Traffic, the four-reel feature that opened at the Park Theatre in December 1913, also at twenty-five cents a ticket, turned away 2,000 customers on the second night; the producers had to book a second theater to accommodate the overflow. In December, *Variety* reported that "The 'white slave pictures' have again this week occupied the whole attention of the show business. There has been no end to the talk, comment and arguments over them. . . . Meanwhile, also the regular movie house exhibitor of New York's three [sic] boroughs is yelling his head off. The slavers are cutting into his receipts."[36]

Many of the customers who saw these films for twenty-five cents in legitimate playhouses were no doubt white-collar workers employed in nearby offices, stores, and shops. Had the potential audience been more prosperous, the exhibitors would have raised their prices; had it been less prosperous, they would have kept them at a dime for all but the better orchestra seats. That they chose instead to price all seats at a quarter tells us that they were seeking—and finding—a "middling" audience for their features.

The white-slavery films, appropriately advertised and booked into the city's better theaters, drew large crowds wherever they played. One of the ingredients in their success was their moralistic treatment of a sensational subject. Like newspaper articles, stage plays, and dime novels about white slavery, the moving pictures simultaneously attracted young men and boys whose interests were voyeuristic, if not prurient; young women who identified, if somewhat precariously, with the victims; and middle-class matrons and gentlemen who attended the films, they said, to "learn" more about the menace that stalked their cities. The success of the white-slavery features testified to the moving picture's newfound reputation as a respectable entertainment for a broad range of city folk. The presence of large numbers of women willing and able to pay a quarter to see a feature was proof indeed that the medium was no longer a "poor man's entertainment."[37]

Variety reported in early January of 1914 that the three biggest theaters in Boston, the Tremont, Park, and Boston, were considering converting to feature films before the theatrical season came to an end. For the summer of 1914, according to a story in *Motography*, six of Chicago's premier theaters were changing over to moving pictures. "Chicago photoplay fans have a gay and glorious summer before them, as one loop theater after another is installing pictures for the summer months and offering de luxe attractions six, seven, eight, and even nine reels in length, at bargain prices of twenty-five and fifty cents."[38]

The ultimate triumph of the "feature" film came the following winter when *The Birth of a Nation*, directed by D. W. Griffith from Thomas Dixon's novel *The Clansman*, opened to critical acclaim and immense crowds, first in Los Angeles at Clune's Auditorium and then, in March 1915, at the Liberty Theater in New York, a first-class Broadway playhouse leased from the Klaw and Erlanger chain. As just about everybody who saw the film agreed, there had never been a picture like it. The audience response was unprecedented. *The Birth of a Nation* would eventually make more money than any film of its time and be seen by an audience that extended from President Wilson and his cabinet to prosperous theatergoers who paid two dollars to see it in the first-class legitimate theaters and the women, children, and men who viewed it at regular prices in their neighborhood moving-picture houses. As the critic from *Variety* explained, assessing the film's commercial potential in an early review, Griffith "knew just what kind of a picture would please all white classes."[39]

While reviewers and audiences, with few exceptions, ignored the malicious caricatures of blacks on the screen, local NAACP branches protested strenuously against Griffith's uncritical, almost celebratory acceptance of what the Boston NAACP chapter referred to as Thomas Dixon's "foul and loathsome misrepresentations of colored people and the glorification of the hideous and murderous band of the Ku Klux Klan."[*] Assisted by black newspapers, protest organizers massed hun-

---

[*]According to reports in the NAACP's *Crisis*, there were organized protests in Los Angeles, New York, Boston, San Francisco, Pittsburgh, Chicago, Oakland, Tacoma, Portland, and Atlantic City.[40]

dreds, at times, thousands of African Americans to demonstrate against the film, enlisted the support of such prominent citizens as Jane Addams and President Eliot of Harvard, and secured face-to-face meetings with the mayors of New York City, Boston, and Chicago to explain their objections to the picture.[41]

In similar situations, as we saw in chapter 12, European-American ethnic groups had been able to exert sufficient pressure to get theater owners to withdraw or censor offensive material. Unfortunately, African Americans had no such leverage. They could not threaten to boycott theaters they were not allowed to enter, and, as reporter and commentator Lester Walton complained in the *New York Age,* a black weekly, the Negro community was not yet organized enough to raise money for court battles or convince local politicians to pay attention to its demands. "Had the picture defamed the Irish or the Jews how different things would be! But the Irish and Jewish citizens of New York are organized and are always ready to effectively fight any attempt to publicly libel and humiliate them. The colored man in New York is long on talk, but short on the ammunition necessary to fight to a successful issue."[42]

Although the NAACP and its allies were not able to convince city officials or theater owners to ban the picture entirely, they caused a great deal of trouble for its producers and distributors. By 1915, when *The Birth of a Nation* opened, there were multiple censorship boards in cities and states across the country, each reserving for itself the right to order "cuts" in individual films. The largest and most influential of these was the National Board of Censorship in New York City, but there were separate state boards in Ohio, Pennsylvania, and Kansas, municipal boards in a large number of cities, and legislation pending to establish additional state boards and a federal motion picture commission in Washington.[43]

The protesters concentrated their attention on these censorship boards and, through perseverance, organization, and with the assistance of their "white" allies, succeeded in convincing most of them to make cuts in Griffith's film. As *Crisis,* the journal of the NAACP, concluded in October 1915, the film's opponents had not been able to close down *The Birth of a Nation,* but they had "succeeded in wounding it." The widespread agitation "in almost every major northern center," the film historian Richard Schickel has written, forced "the film's proprietors and exhibitors . . . to endure what became an almost ritual process of protest and quasi-judicial proceedings, generally resulting in small cuts and large publicity."[44]

The Mutual Corporation, which distributed *The Birth of a Nation* in Ohio, tried to circumvent the censors in that state by asking the courts to declare the censorship board unconstitutional. The case went to the Supreme Court, which ruled, in a decision that would stand until the 1950s, that contrary to the producers' and distributors' claims, local governments had every right to censor films. "The exhibition of moving pictures is a business pure and simple, originated and conducted for profit, like other spectacles, not to be regarded, nor intended to be regarded . . . as part of the press of the country or as organs of public opinion. [Moving pictures] are mere representations of events, or ideas and sentiments published or known; vivid, useful, and entertaining, no doubt, but . . . capable of evil, having power for it, the greater because of their attractiveness and manner of exhibition."[45]

The 1915 Supreme Court decision invalidated what had been the industry's chief argument against censorship, that the moving pictures were a form of free speech, protected by the Constitution. It also served as a sharp reminder that, while the picture industry had moved a long way toward respectability, it was still not safe from government interference. Over the next few years, the industry would succeed in defeating many attempts to establish new federal, state, and municipal censorship boards. But these small victories did not silence the censorship advocates. Moving-picture producers and exhibitors remained on the defensive, forced, as the distributors of *The Birth of a Nation* had been, to battle censors in dozens of locations and to rebut the argument, now supported by a Supreme Court decision, that moving pictures, unlike other entertainment forms, were a potential public menace requiring government licensing, regulation, and censorship.[46]

CHAPTER 15

Waving the Flag

BUSINESS COULD NOT HAVE BEEN BETTER FOR the movie men in early 1914. As *Motography,* the trade journal that had changed its name from *The Nickelodeon,* signifying the industry's leap into respectability, reported in January, "People who never before dreamed of entering the portals of a motion picture theater . . . are gazing with surprise upon the miracles unfolding before them and going away astonished at their own narrowmindedness in the past. . . . Thousands of these people are being converted to the pictures, and will, in the future, be found among the 'regulars.'"[1]

While the industry congratulated itself on its newfound "respectability," its critics were renewing their efforts to secure mandatory government censorship of all moving pictures. By the mid-1910s, bills authorizing federal censorship were making their way through Congress, and exhibitors everywhere were struggling on an almost weekly basis with local censors who were cutting their films. In the August 22, 1914, issue of *Motion Picture News* alone, there were news items on battles with censors in Omaha, Nashville, Philadelphia, Dallas, Milwaukee, and the state of Pennsylvania. Fortunately for the industry, the public and the politicians would soon have more pressing concerns before them than whether or not to tighten movie censorship.[2]

-→-≡=○◖═══-→-

When war broke out in Europe in 1914, the moviemakers, as they always did with a big story, rushed new films into production and reached into the vaults to reedit and recycle old ones. What they didn't recognize at the time was that the war would, in the long run, prove to be a godsend for the entire industry. During the course of the war in Europe, producers and exhibitors alike would discover that the best defense against their critics was to shift the discourse about moving pictures to another plane. Instead of simply rebutting the charges that their pictures were immoral, they would demonstrate to the nation that they fulfilled a positive public purpose. Instead of treating the government as a potential enemy, they would embrace it as a comrade in arms.[3]

President Wilson's immediate response to the outbreak of hostilities in Europe was to call on the nation to exercise neutrality "in thought as well as action." The moving-picture producers and exhibitors interpreted the president's request as meaning that as long as they did not take sides, they could do pretty much as they pleased.

The Great War was too large, too spectacular, and too dramatic an event not to be exploited by American filmmakers. Less than two weeks after Germany declared war on France, independent producers were already advertising their "neutralist" war pictures. "War, War, War. Ramo Films, Inc., Announce *The War of Wars* or *The Franco-German Invasion of 1914.* 400 Stupendous Scenes Taken on the Actual Battlefields of France will be released within a week. The First Authentic Events of the Reigning Sensation of the World. Wire for Territory or Bookings." Like the "neutralist" war films that would follow it, *The War of Wars* was intentionally, sometimes ridiculously, even-handed. *Motion Picture News* described it as "a triumph of neutrality. During its course, fortune smiles alternately on the contending parties, and their German and French principals are seen as heroes in a regular sequence. As a final victory of nonpartisanship the film closes with an impending Franco-German alliance between an officer from the Fatherland and a fair maid of la belle France." In *With Serb and Austrian,* another "neutralist" film that enjoyed a moment of popularity in the summer of 1914, an Austrian prince fell in love with a Serbian girl and turned his back on war.[4]

As the war proceeded without pause, the advocates of intervention on both sides raised their voices to sway American public opinion to their side. By 1915, the supporters of Britain and France were speaking loudest of all and demanding that President Wilson, if not yet ready to lead the nation into war against Germany, at least "prepare" it for that possibility. Filmmakers, while still paying lip service to the president's call for "neutrality," took up the "preparedness" theme in their features, producing slightly disguised portraits of German treachery and barbarism.

The Battle Cry of Peace, the most spectacular and commercially successful of the anti-German preparedness films, was based on *Defenseless America*, a book by Hudson Maxim, brother of the inventor of the Maxim machine gun. The hero of the picture was a young banker who advocated immediate and massive American armament. He was engaged to the daughter of a millionaire pacifist. The villain, a close friend of the millionaire, was a spy from an unnamed foreign nation whose agents had infiltrated America, taken over the peace movement, and effectively lobbied the government against military appropriations. While the millionaire was addressing a huge peace rally, the nation was invaded by land, air, and sea. All the major characters were killed and downtown New York City was devastated by off-shore shelling and aerial bombardment.

There could be little doubt that this was a propaganda film, supported and probably financed by advocates of immediate intervention on the side of the British.* According to the *New York Times,* J. Stuart Blackton, the producer, who had until August 1915 been a British citizen, advanced "his argument by bludgeon strokes. There is nothing in the least bit subtle about 'The Battle Cry for [sic] Peace.'" As the *Photoplay* critic concluded, "The horrors attending the descent of a hostile force upon a defenseless land are shown with a ruthlessness that makes the message 'register.' . . . But the question now remains, whether or not argument can be regarded as entertainment. . . . Will the public pay for propaganda, even if the propaganda is popular? . . . If the answer is 'Yes,' motion photography has reached another stage in its evolution."[5]

---

*The picture was endorsed by every "preparedness" advocate Blackton could find, including the National Security League, the Army League, the Navy League, the American Red Cross, the American Legion, General Leonard Wood, Admiral George Dewey, Secretary of War Garrison, Secretary of State Lansing, the Reverend Lyman Abbott, and Theodore Roosevelt whose words of praise were read to the audience at the film's New York City premiere.

The box-office success of *The Battle Cry of Peace* answered these questions in the affirmative. The feature film had established itself as a source of propaganda as well as entertainment. Blackton's commercial triumph spurred other producers to make similar "preparedness" spectaculars. Thomas Dixon, author of *The Clansman,* the novel and play that Griffith had adapted for *The Birth of a Nation,* wrote and produced his own "preparedness" epic, *The Fall of a Nation.* Like Blackton, Dixon ridiculed pacifists in his film with vivid images of America being invaded, this time through Long Island, by an army of black-mustached brutes, backed by 20,000 immigrant traitors. The film, with an original score by Victor Herbert, did well across the country.[6]

The commercial success of *The Battle Cry of Peace, The Fall of a Nation,* and similar films such as Thomas Ince's *Civilization* demonstrated that audiences were attracted to pictures that aroused their patriotic ardor. As important, the producers learned that, while waving the flag, they could splatter the screen with images of rape, murder, and pillage. Critics and censors who might have objected to such images in other contexts appeared to be disarmed by the producers' claims that they had inserted pictures of sex and violence not to boost box-office receipts but to alert the nation to the need to prepare for war.

⋅→⊨◎⊫←⋅

The declaration of war against Germany, when it came, allowed the industry to drop its "neutrality" and "preparedness" disguises and produce unvarnished war pictures.

The exhibitors greeted the war by decorating their theaters with flags, displaying recruiting posters in their lobbies, and projecting slides on their screens with patriotic messages and reminders. "Official" Allied newsreels quickly became hot items. As the exhibitors discovered, it was possible to be patriotic and make a sizable profit at the same time. The *Motion Picture News* advertisement for the French newsreel film, *In the Wake of the Huns,* made this point explicitly, "These pictures . . . will stir the blood of every beholder and raise it to fighting pitch. Through miles of wanton destruction, villages pillaged, orchards fiendishly cut down, nothing untouched—everything burned, dynamited or defiled—you see the conquering armies of France, our allies, hot on the trail of the perpetrators of unmentionable deeds! This is History indeed. It will outdraw any two reel picture ever filmed."[7]

While the fighting in Europe had not harmed, and in some in-

This recruiting poster was produced, distributed, and displayed by the Associated Motion Picture Advertisers in theaters across the country. Like the war pictures, the poster tells the story of a woman in distress awaiting rescue from American soldiers—and their supporters on the homefront. (*Library of Congress, Prints and Photographs Division.*)

stances, had even been good for the picture business, the industry was worried that America's entry into the war would change all that. There would be less time and money for amusements in wartime. And, should the fighting continue through the winter, the movie men could expect to have their stars drafted, their lights turned out, and raw materials, such as cellulose, requisitioned. Worse yet, it was inevitable that the debate on federal censorship, still unresolved, would be rekindled, this time in a context far from favorable for the industry. Within days of the declaration of war, Secretary of the Navy Josephus M. Daniels had already laid the groundwork for federal censorship by requesting that the newsreel companies cease showing pictures "of American naval vessels, preparations and naval activities, and pictures of American merchant ships, unless the same have been properly passed upon by the authorities at the Navy Department. It is only by the co-operation of 'all hands' that information can be prevented from reaching possible enemies of the United States or their agents in this country."[8]

As the *Exhibitors Trade Review* warned the producers in April 1917, with war came new responsibilities and new dangers of censorship. "Unless producers take the utmost care concerning the contents of their pictures . . . there is every indication that the Federal authorities will suppress such pictures without hesitation. . . . Public welfare takes precedence over any private right, especially in time of war, and it is upon that principle that the Federal Government will proceed against any influence intentionally or unintentionally hostile to the public welfare."[9]

Producers and exhibitors had to worry about both future films and old ones that might, under present circumstances, be construed as obstructing the war effort. Especially vulnerable were the pacifist films and preparedness epics that had graphically displayed the horrors of the battlefield. In times of peace, such images had been acceptable and warmly received by the military. Now, however, with war declared, images of blood and guts on the battlefield might discourage recruitment. To forestall any possible problems with the federal government or local censors, J. Stuart Blackton retitled his preparedness film and reedited it to eliminate the most violent battlefield scenes. *The Battle Cry of Peace* reappeared in May of 1917 as *The Battle Cry of War.* "If there is a single foot of film in that picture or a single word in any title that might, even in the remotest way, suggest to any person that he should not enlist, we want that doubtful part removed. We are with the

Government, body and soul. We want to assist the Government in every way. While the changing of all the prints will be costly, we consider it our patriotic duty to make the change."[10]

The threats to producers and exhibitors who did not move as quickly as Blackton were real. The Espionage Act of 1917 made it illegal to "willfully obstruct the recruiting or enlistment service of the United States" or to "cause insubordination, disloyalty, mutiny, and refusal of duty in the military and naval forces of the United States during war." Any doubts as to whether the government would use this law against moving-picture producers were quickly put to rest when *The Spirit of '76*, a film about the revolutionary war, was removed from distribution and its producer and writer, Robert Goldstein, arrested, found guilty, and sentenced to a fine of $5,000 and twelve years in the federal penitentiary at McNeil's Island.*[11]

What was Goldstein's crime? Like other producers in 1916 and 1917, he had set out to make a historical epic like *The Birth of a Nation*. Unfortunately, he had chosen the wrong subject with the wrong villain, the British in 1776. (It didn't help that Goldstein was a German Jew, thus automatically suspect of harboring anti-British sentiments.) The scenes of British brutality in his film were unsparing, with graphic images of soldiers shooting innocent women, dragging off young American girls, "sometimes by the hair of the head," even bayoneting babies. Such images, wrote Judge Benjamin Bledsoe of the southern California federal court that heard the case, might have been historically accurate and "in ordinary times . . . clearly permissible, or even commendable, [but] in this hour of national emergency [they were] subject to review and repression. The constitutional guaranty of 'free speech' carries with it no right to subvert the purposes and destiny of the nation." Goldstein had broken the espionage law by causing "dissension among our people [and] creating animosity or want of confidence between us and our allies."[12]

Goldstein's case was an extreme one. It was possible to argue that he had brought his fate on himself by agreeing to censor the film before it opened in Los Angeles and then reneging on the agreement. Still, the punishment was harsh and had a substantial influence on the industry.

---

*Goldstein's sentence was ultimately commuted by President Wilson, but only after he had spent almost two years in jail.

From this point forward, only films that were unambiguously patriotic, pro-English, and anti-German would be produced and distributed.

-•-=◉⊂=-•-

Because it was hoped that the war might soon be over, and because moving pictures were in 1917 still perceived as crude, uncertain, and untested instruments for molding public opinion, the federal government did not, at first, attempt to utilize them to influence public opinion. The Committee on Public Information (CPI), charged with overseeing the government's propaganda efforts, did not even establish a Division of Films "until more than five months after the U.S. entered the war. Even then, another six months passed before the Division of Films began full-scale operations."[13]

Although the government did not require its assistance in making moving pictures, the industry pushed itself into the spotlight by volunteering its most valuable resources: its stars and its theaters. Mary Pickford refereed a prize fight for the French Emergency Hospital Fund, led a marine band down Market Street in San Francisco, marched in the Allied War Exposition in Los Angeles, raised money for Liberty bonds in a tour of New England cities, and contributed $100,000 of her own funds to a southern California bond drive. Douglas Fairbanks emceed benefit concerts and rodeos, gave his name to a Red Cross chapter, led a parade through Los Angeles, and raised over $8 million for Liberty Bonds in a tour of the Middle West.[14]

The government was pleased with the studios' loan of its stars to raise money, but it was even more grateful for the assistance of the theater owners in raising and maintaining morale. The Great War, as President Wilson knew only too well, had to be sold to the public. Within a week after the declaration of war, Wilson formed the Committee on Public Information to spearhead the government's propaganda efforts and hired George Creel, a former journalist, to head it. Creel's committee employed every medium it could to get its messages to the people. It inserted stories, cartoons, and photographs in newspapers, produced a ton of pamphlets on "How the War Came to America," published a newspaper for the nation's teachers, and even used the Boy Scouts to deliver five million copies of the President's Flag Day Address. Unfortunately, there were no guarantees that any of this material would ever be read. As Bertram Nelson, a CPI executive, explained in 1918, there were "a surprisingly large number in every community who do not read; there are others who read no English; and a still larger number

who read nothing but the headlines. . . . How can we reach them?"
There was, fortunately, a simple answer to this question. Many of those
who did not or could not read were picture fans. "Every night eight to
ten million people of all classes, all degrees of intelligence, black
and white, young and old, rich and poor, meet in the moving picture houses of this country."* It was here that the government could
deliver its messages.[15]

The idea for using the picture theaters for propaganda purposes was
suggested to Creel by Donald Ryerson, a Chicago businessman who
had before the declaration of war sent speakers into Chicago theaters
to argue for universal military training. Within days of his own appointment, Creel enlisted Ryerson to put together a national "organization
of volunteer speakers for the purpose of making patriotic talks in
motion-picture theaters." The speakers would be called the "Four
Minute Men" to recall the heroes of the revolutionary war and reassure
theater owners and audiences that the entertainment portion of the
program would be interrupted for only four minutes at a time.[16]

In mid-May 1917, only weeks after the declaration of war, the Four
Minute Men began appearing in movie theaters across the country. To
make absolutely certain that they delivered the proper messages, the
Four Minute Man Division was established at the Committee on Public Information in Washington to supply them with weekly topics of discussion and sample speeches. The speech prepared in Washington for
the week of March 31, 1918, for example, instructed speakers to ask
audiences to contribute old spyglasses, binoculars, and telescopes to
the war effort. "This is a warm, comfortable theater to-night. We are
enjoying a good show. What time is it—let's see. (Speaker looks at his
watch and gives time.) So it's now dark night (state time) on the
Atlantic near France. Our ships are over there. Steering along as quietly as possible. Lights out. No cigarettes. Watchfulness everywhere on
deck. Why? You know why! The murderous submarines are lurking
somewhere—the pirates of our time. They attack not only the battleships, but all vessels, even little innocent fishing crafts. And when they
attack, they kill." At the conclusion of the speech the Four Minute
Men were instructed to ask audience members to send their used
"glasses" to Franklin Roosevelt, Assistant Secretary of the Navy, who

---

*Contrary to Nelson's assertion, "black and white" did *not* meet in the nation's "moving picture houses." World War I neither signaled nor effectuated any change in the exhibitors'
policy of segregating or excluding blacks from their theaters.

would pay one dollar in rent if they were usable. If unusable, Roosevelt would return them immediately, with the Navy's thanks.[17]

By 1918, the moving-picture industry was also aiding the war effort by exhibiting newsreel shorts and features shot by Army Signal Corps cameramen and produced by the CPI's Division of Film. Although some of the government footage was quite dull, Roxy, the nation's most renowned theater manager, explained in a series of articles in the *Motion Picture News* that, if advertised properly, placed in the right position in the program, and accompanied by suitable music, the newsreel pictures could be turned into big hits. He warned exhibitors, however, not to overplay the national anthem as the audience always rose to its feet when the music played, destroying the rhythm and "psychology" of the presentation.[18]

The exhibitors profited as much as the government from sponsoring the Four Minute Men and exhibiting "official" newsreels. From its earliest days, the picture industry had been fighting off charges of immoral opportunism. Moving-picture exhibitors had been routinely compared to dirty-picture peddlers or peep-show proprietors who profited by pandering to the public's lowest instincts. By participating in the war effort, the movie men sought to demonstrate that they had been unfairly maligned and that the moving-picture industry was as vital a national resource as the churches and schools and, as a dispenser of propaganda, much more effective.

The federal government acknowledged as much, repeatedly and publicly thanking the industry for its assistance in the war effort. In early April 1918, the president wrote an open letter to the nation's moviegoers that was read on stage by the Four Minute Men. He declared that he had chosen to send government speakers into the moving-picture theater because it was a "great democratic meeting place of the people, where within twenty-four hours it is possible to reach eight million citizens of all classes." There was nothing wrong with taking in a picture show at a neighborhood movie house, the president reassured moviegoers. "The Government recognizes that a reasonable amount of amusement, *especially* in war time, is not a luxury but a necessity."[19]

-◆-▰◉◖-◆-

The film industry not only welcomed Washington's spokesmen and "official" newsreels into its theaters, but assisted the propaganda campaign by churning out dozens of war films. Recognizing full well that women made up a large and growing segment of their audience, producers found ingenious ways to fuse romance and war by telling stories of innocent young women entangled with nefarious alien agents and soldiers. In 1918 alone, American screens were graced with such films as *Daughter of Destiny, A Daughter of Uncle Sam, The Gown of Destiny, Mrs. Slacker, The Woman in the Web, Joan of Plattsburg, Daughter Angela, In Pursuit of Polly, The Girl of Today, Her Country First, Bonnie Annie Laurie, Johanna Enlists, Battling Jane, Every Mother's Son,* and *Wife or Country.*[20]

There were also a large number of pure "Hate the Hun" films, where any hint of romance or feminine heroism was submerged beneath a visual avalanche of German villainies. Led by Fox, every major studio rushed into production films like *The Claws of the Hun, The Kaiser's Shadow, To Hell with the Kaiser, Huns without Our Gates, The Hun Within, The Prussian Cur, Wolves of Kulture,* and *The Kaiser's Finish. The Kaiser, the Beast of Berlin,* one of the most vicious, "catalogued every conceivable German atrocity from the sinking of the *Lusitania* to the rape of Belgium. Advertisements and posters for the picture urged American film audiences to 'hiss the Kaiser' every time he appeared on the screen." "'The Kaiser,'" wrote the *Motion Picture News* reviewer, "dramatizes patriotism more intensely than any other picture the writer has seen. . . . Its appeal to red blooded Americans is boundless."[21]

My Four Years in Germany, adapted from the memoirs of James Gerard, the former American ambassador to Germany, was, if anything, even more violent. In the final scene, as an American soldier triumphantly bayonets "one German after another, he cries exultantly, 'I promised Dad I'd get six!'" The press campaign highlighted what Kevin Brownlow refers to as the "casual viciousness" of the film itself. "In Cleveland a press show of *My Four Years in Germany* was enlivened by hanging the Kaiser in effigy."[22]

As the movie theaters became arenas for staging patriotic rallies in support of the war, they gained in legitimacy and added new layers to their prewar audience. The movie theater became not only a place to go out to have fun but also a staging ground for the city's respectable people to demonstrate their commitment to the war effort. The trade journal advertisements for *My Four Years in Germany* advised exhibitors that "The Mayor of your town will be proud to support the the-

ater which shows 'My Four Years in Germany.' The best people in town
will pat you on the back for showing it. It will give your theater more
prestige and you more profits than anything you have ever booked. . . .
And here's your chance to win that highbrow [newspaper] editor who
has always refused to take the 'movies' seriously."[23]

While the theaters welcomed parents, politicians, businessmen, and
religious leaders, patriots all, antiwar activists and sympathizers stayed
away or kept their mouths shut. Those who did not were treated appropriately. A theater manager in Oklahoma who refused to allow flags or
patriotic songs in his theater was forced by the local sheriff to kiss the
flag in front of the audience. "There was great applause." Elsewhere,
movie audiences were enlisted to fight the domestic war against spies
and slackers. Dozens of films were produced about enemy agents who
had infiltrated the nation. When Universal released one of these, *Yellow Dog*, based on a *Saturday Evening Post* story subsequently
released in book form, it was promoted with special newspaper ads that
attacked "food hoarders," "lounge lizards," and the "vilifier of America,
the slacker, the fellow who fails to buy Liberty Bonds."[24]

Only the local censors stopped short of total admiration for the war
movies. While reviewers and politicians praised the films for their realism and value as propaganda, state and municipal censors continued,
as they had in peacetime, to cut titles and scenes of sexual violence
and graphic bloodletting. In Chicago, Major Metellus Lucullus Cicero
Funkhouser, the police official who served as municipal censor, removed a few scenes and titles from *My Four Years in Germany*, almost
all of them dealing with sexual violence and abuse or dripping blood.
Ambassador Gerard on whose book the film had been based complained directly to George Creel, the director of the Committee on
Public Information, in Washington. Creel refused to interfere with the
Chicago censor but suggested that the governor of Illinois be con-
tacted. The attack on Funkhouser continued to build until he was suspended as censor, brought up on charges, and dismissed from the
police force. The first act of his replacement was to restore the thirty-
two feet he had cut from *My Four Years in Germany*.[25]

The industry, enjoying unaccustomed acclaim for its good deeds,
fought back as never before against censors who dared to interfere with
its films. In a truly stunning counterattack, the industry claimed that
the moviemakers, not the censors, were the true guardians of the public welfare. In May of 1918, the *Exhibitor's Trade Review*, expressing

This poster was for D. W. Griffith's *Hearts of the World,* a moving picture filled with so much violence, violation, and blood-letting that the Chicago censor cut thirty feet, including images of blood flowing from a bayonet wound and girls harassed by German officers who had trapped them in an underground dugout. (*Library of Congress, Prints and Photographs Division.*)

the moviemakers' newfound confidence, warned the censors in remarkably blunt language, "KEEP YOUR HANDS OFF WAR PICTURES. THESE PICTURES ARE A PART OF THE FIGHTING FORCES OF THE UNITED STATES. . . . SUPPRESS ANY PART OF ANY ONE OF THESE PICTURE MESSAGES AND—WHETHER YOU ADMIT IT OR NOT—YOU ARE PLAYING THE GAME OF GERMANY AS LOYALLY AS IF YOU WERE A PAID HIRELING OF THE WIL-HELMSTRASSE. . . . If you adapt and persist in a policy of interference, you will be dealt with accordingly—and you will speedily cease to interfere. Your patriotism, your Americanism, is on trial. See to it that it is and remains above suspicion."[26]

In the course of the war, the industry had learned that waving the flag was not only good for business; it was the best possible protection against government regulation and censorship. As long as the industry presented itself as a fourth branch of government, Washington would leave it alone. When, for example, in the spring of 1918, the War Industries Board ruled that motion pictures were a "non-essential" industry and could thus be closed down to conserve the nation's resources, William Brady of the National Association of the Motion Picture Industry (NAMPI) telegrammed George Creel, who, in turn, telegrammed "Treasury Secretary William McAdoo, Herbert Hoover of the Food Administration, and Harry Garfield of the Fuel Administration, asking them to comment on the movies' importance. 'As you know,' Creel added, 'the fifty thousand Four Minute Men use the motion picture theatres, the film plays a big part in every one of our drives, and . . . constitutes one of our most effective aids in the matter of publicity.'" To buttress the case that the moving-picture industry was "essential" to the war effort, NAMPI assembled a twenty-six-page brief, complete with letters of recommendation from numerous federal officials and "a detailed outline of the many services the industry had performed for the CPI, Treasury Department, Army, Navy, Red Cross, YMCA, and the Food and Fuel Administrations." In late August, after a meeting with Brady and NAMPI officials, Bernard Baruch, chairman of the War Industries Board, reversed himself and officially recognized the movies as an "essential industry."[27]

What higher accolade could the moviemakers have possibly wished for? And at so insignificant a price. In return for its seal of approval, Brady promised the War Industries Board that exhibitors and producers would conserve raw materials, including film containers, film, projectors, and fuel, and make "wholesome pictures."[28]

⁌⟹⟸⁍

The movie industry having found comfort in the warm embrace of Washington during the war was not willing to abandon it in peacetime. It would continue to fight the nation's enemies, as identified by the federal government. As early as November of 1918, according to the historian Steven Ross, David Niles, the chairman of the government's "Joint Committee on Motion Picture Activities dispatched a letter to all major studios . . . asking that they confer with him 'prior to starting productions based on Socialism, labor problems, etc.' . . . Failure to cooperate, Niles warned in subtle but clear terms, might lead to federal censorship of films." As the *Motion Picture News* warned on December 7, 1918, the moviemakers had to resolve at once never to "aid the production, distribution, or exhibition of a picture that directly or indirectly gives strength to the venom of the bolshevik."[29]

The overt censorship hinted at by Niles did not have to be invoked in the postwar period, because the industry did precisely as Washington wished. The Washington-Hollywood partnership formed in wartime was extended into the postwar period, the only difference being that German soldiers, spies, and enemy agents were now replaced by Russians abroad and their supposed agents at home: Bolsheviks, Socialists, radicals, and labor leaders. While before the war films with overt socialist messages had been booked into local movie houses, after the war such films virtually disappeared from the screens. Labor activists continued to make independent films but found it more and more difficult to exhibit them in regular picture theaters.[30]

A tacit agreement had been reached with the federal government. The industry would voluntarily remove all alternative or oppositional political content from its films and deny exhibition space to independent films with such messages. The government would, in turn, allow the industry to police itself without explicit federal controls.

The producers and exhibitors, by displaying their patriotism and subservience to Washington during the war and immediately afterward, had demonstrated that the picture show was much more than a drop-in amusement or a poor man's entertainment. Adolph Zukor, the head of Paramount Pictures, was not exaggerating when, in summarizing the events of 1918, he wrote that, while the world had previously "accepted the motion picture as the foremost agency of entertainment and amusement extant . . . it remained for the activities of the past year to register indisputably the fact that as an avenue of propaganda, as a channel for conveying thought and opinion the movies are unequalled by any form of communication."[31]

From this point forward, producers and exhibitors alike would wave the flag with regularity. The industry had discovered that patriotism paid and paid well. During the Great War, audiences had gravitated to theaters, where, in addition to being entertained for two hours, they could rally in support and celebration of the nation. In going to the movies, they affirmed their inclusion in a great American public now united as never before against its foreign and domestic enemies.

The feeling of solidarity and inclusion that was becoming a significant dimension of the moviegoers' experience required, as we have seen, the existence of an excluded other. Prior to 1917, that excluded other had been defined entirely in terms of race and behavioral characteristics. With the outbreak of war, lack of patriotism became an additional defining characteristic. Those who were not at all times and for all reasons ready to stand in attention to salute the flag, sing the national anthem, and cheer the troops, wherever they might be, were no longer welcomed in the movie theater.

CHAPTER 16

Palaces for the
People

W HILE THE PUBLIC FOR MOVING PICTURES HAD expanded in the early 1910s to include everyone from seamstresses to socialites, seldom, if ever, were they entertained under the same roof at the same time. As *Motography* declared in May 1914, "It is no new prediction that the motion picture exhibiting business is bound to divide automatically into two classes: the big feature show which has already invaded the former legitimate theater, and the regular five and ten cent program made up of single reel subjects displayed in neighborhood and other small theaters. That condition, in fact, is almost established now."[1]

Only with the emergence of the picture palaces in the late 1910s and 1920s would this "condition" be challenged and the disparate audiences for moving pictures assembled on one site.

To expand the audience for its multiple-reel feature films, the Vitagraph Company in late 1913 bought the Criterion Theater on Broadway and refurbished it as a movie theater. The Vitagraph, as the new theater was called, was the first of the Broadway palaces to attempt to bridge the gap between the legitimate playhouses that charged a dollar or more for multireel feature films and the nickel and dime theaters that showed only one- and two-reel shorts.

As the film historian Eileen Bowser has written, the Vitagraph "was no ordinary movie theater." Its exterior was ornamented with a $10,000 electrically lit marquee, its lobby hung with oil paintings of the Vitagraph stars, its musical accompaniment provided by a $30,000 Wurlitzer. Seats were "sold on a reserved basis, for twenty-five cents up to a dollar," more than in the nickelodeon but less than in the legitimate playhouses.[2]

The Vitagraph's reign as the premier Broadway movie palace lasted only until the March 1914 opening of the Strand on Broadway and 47th Street. The site had been purchased the year before by Mitchell Mark, the show businessman who had entered the exhibition business in the 1890s with an Edisonia amusement parlor in Buffalo, and gone on to successfully own and operate kinetoscope parlors, arcades, nickelodeons, and movie theaters through the Northeast. In the months following the site purchase, rumors had it that the palatial Strand would open as a fifty-cent vaudeville house, a poor man's Hippodrome with spectacular stage shows at ten and twenty cents a ticket, a legitimate playhouse at popular prices, an opera house, and a musical comedy theater. In early 1914, as the theater neared completion, Mark, taking his cue from the sellout crowds at the legitimate theaters where *Quo Vadis?* and *Traffic in Souls* were playing, announced that the Strand would open with feature films at popular prices.[3]

To manage his picture palace, Mark hired Samuel Rothapfel or Roxy, the most famous—and successful—exhibitor in the industry. To design it, he hired Thomas Lamb, the architect who had built the magnificent Regent Theater on 116th Street. Spending money prodigiously, Roxy and Lamb designed a theater and a "show" so stupendous that audience members forgot they were sitting in a popular-priced picture house.

The opening-night show at the Strand began with three gun blasts, followed by total darkness, and then the playing of "The Star-Spangled Banner" and several classical and almost-classical musical selections by the fifty-piece Strand orchestra. After the musical prelude came the "Strand Topical Review," featuring moving pictures shot that morning of baseball in Brooklyn; a "'scenic' one-reeler made in Italy called *A Neapolitan Incident* and accompanied by a tenor singing 'O Sole Mio' behind the screen"; a one-reel Keystone comedy; the live Strand quartet singing from *Rigoletto;* and a nine-reel feature, *The Spoilers,* played without pause and accompanied by the Strand orchestra. The theater historian Ben Hall quotes Mitchell Mark as telling a newspaper reviewer that he had intended the Strand to be a "'national institution' which would stand for all time as the model of Moving Picture Palaces." Whether that was or was not his initial intention, the Strand succeeded in redefining the public image of the movie theater—and its audience. As Victor Watson, a New York drama critic, reported of the opening, "Going to the new Strand Theatre last night was very much like going to a Presidential reception, a first night at the opera or the opening of the horse show. . . . I have always tried to keep abreast of the times and be able to look ahead a little way, but I must confess that when I saw the wonderful audience last night in all its costly togs, the one thought that came to my mind was that if anyone had told me two years ago that the time would come when the finest-looking people in town would be going to the biggest and newest theatre on Broadway for the purpose of seeing motion pictures I would have sent them down to visit my friend, Dr. Minas Gregory at Bellevue Hospital. The doctor runs the city's bughouse, you know."[4]

⊷⇌⫤⊶

Although large and luxurious combination theaters had been built in cities and suburbs since 1910, palaces such as the Strand and those that would follow in the 1920s were different. They were larger, more spectacular in design and ornamentation, and were often owned and operated not by independent exhibitors but by production companies. When in the mid 1910s, the exhibitors had attempted to combat the growing power of the producers by forming their own company to make films, Adolph Zukor of Paramount retaliated by building his own theaters. His plan was identical to that adopted by John D. Rockefeller, who, on achieving dominance in oil production, set out to control the retail branch of the industry. Zukor's agents in the field, like Rockefeller's, let it be known that local exhibitors who did not join his theater chain not only would be denied the right to show Paramount features but also could expect to wake up one morning and find "de luxe" theaters being constructed across the street from their own. To put teeth in his threats, Zukor raised $10 million in 1919 from a stock issue underwritten by Kuhn, Loeb. With First National (the production company formed by the exhibitors) and Zukor having integrated production, distribution, and exhibition, the rest of the industry had no choice but to follow suit. Exhibitors like Loew and Fox began to produce their own films; producers such as United Artists and Warner Brothers followed Zukor's example and acquired their own theaters.

The result was a building boom of palaces and neighborhood theaters bearing the names or booked and controlled by Fox, Loew, Paramount, United Artists, and Warner's.[5]

By the early 1920s, a "pre-release" or premiere in a palace had become a necessity in showcasing a big movie, because the palaces, with their thousands of seats, generated more admissions and more revenue than other outlets, and because a palace opening certified that the picture was first-class. The moving-picture industry had, in this regard, adopted the same strategy as the legitimate theater, which opened plays on Broadway, and then, after securing maximum publicity, toured them to the hinterlands. "The advertising and publicity of a first run in a key city," Benjamin Hampton explained in 1931, "create a demand for the picture in the surrounding district. Theaters in Long Island or New Jersey, for example, learned that a photoplay first shown at the Strand or the Rialto, in New York, would draw large audiences, while a film with no first run in the metropolis would attract little attention. Soon exhibitors everywhere in the United States followed the line of least resistance, giving preference to pictures with the prestige of key-city first runs, ignoring all others or renting them only at very low rates. Within a few years photoplays without first runs were not regarded by theatergoers as first class, and unless a producer could obtain first runs his chance of making money grew very slim."[6]

⊹⊷═◑ ◐═⊶⊹

By the mid-1920s there were more than 20,000 moving-picture theaters in the country. A surprisingly large number of them continued to present live entertainment with their feature films. At the pinnacle of the exhibition pyramid, according to Harold Franklin, president of a West Coast theater chain and author of *Motion Picture Theater Management*, were the handful of "Super" palaces that presented the best live stage shows money could buy. But there were also hundreds of "De Luxe First Run" and "Neighborhood Theaters" with live shows and musicians to accompany the films.[7]

While the larger chains were already in the 1920s standardizing their stage shows and touring them from theater to theater, the "neighborhood" houses designed their live performances to suit the particular tastes of local audiences. As Lizabeth Cohen has written of Chicago in the early 1920s, "When one entered a movie theater in a working-class neighborhood of Chicago, the ethnic character of the community quickly became evident.... In Back of the Yards, near the packinghouses, viewers often saw a Polish play along with the silent. . . . Everywhere, amateur nights offered 'local talent' a moment in the limelight. At the Butler Theater in Little Sicily, which the community had rechristened the 'Garlic Opera House,' Italian music shared the stage with American films."[8]

Along the "Stroll," Chicago's African-American entertainment district, recent migrants from the South could simultaneously immerse themselves in the cosmopolitan culture of the Hollywood feature and reaffirm "their ties to the South . . . by attending the picture show in the same venue that showcased blues artists, the Georgia Minstrels or a 'Jubilee Week of Sunshine in Music,' featuring the 'Music Born in Our Own Southlands.'" According to Mary Carbine, while black-patronized movie theaters only occasionally presented black-produced films, they provided local jazz and blues performers with steady employment. African-American moviegoers, barred from the "palaces" and "de luxe" theaters along the Loop, flocked to South State Street, where for the price of admission they saw a Hollywood picture; watched a stage show with stars like Louis Armstrong, Bert Williams, and Ethel Waters; and heard the equivalent of a full jazz concert by the orchestras that accompanied the film on the screen. The musicians in the pit were as much a part of the show as the feature film. Unlike the "palace" orchestras and orchestrations that "matched" the action on the screen, the jazz musicians in the black theaters frequently went "over the top" and, to the consternation of the *Chicago Defender's* movie critics, called attention to themselves by "ranting and shimmying in the pit." The audiences accepted the "discordance" between the pictures and the music more readily than the critics. They "responded to jazz with enthusiasm" even when it was "inappropriate" to the images on the screen.[9]

Nothing was too good for the patrons of the movie palaces, de luxe theaters, and better neighborhood houses. They paid their money not just to see a film, but to be immersed in a total and transcending experience. The film was not the "show," only a part of it—and not always the most exciting part. A quarter of the managers surveyed in an exhibitors' poll conducted in 1922 reported "that it made absolutely no difference at the box office whether the feature attraction was any good or not." As Paul Morand recalled from his visit to New York City in 1930, it was "surprising how small a place is held by the actual film in these diversified entertainments."[10]

Each week brought new films and a new stage show and musical feature. Customers at the Chicago theater for the week of August 6, 1928, watched *Foreign Legion* and a serial, a short, and newsreels on the screen; heard an organ solo and "Neapolitana" played by the Chicago Theatre Orchestra featuring E. Concialdi—Tenor; and saw an original stage show, "Kat Kabaret" starring Eddie Perry and his band. In April of 1928, the Four Marx Brothers appeared in succeeding weeks at the Chicago, the Uptown, and the Tivoli theaters.[11]

As the palaces grew in size and magnificence, so did the musical portions of their shows. By 1925, each of Baltimore's nine "de luxe" theaters had its own orchestra. When the Roxy opened in 1927, live music was provided by a 110-person symphony orchestra, four conductors, an organ so mammoth it required three organists to play it, the Deagan Chimes with twenty bells, fourteen Steinway pianos, and a music library that was reportedly the largest in the world, most of it purchased from Victor Herbert's widow.[12]

Why such enormous expense and attention focused on live music? Because it was necessary to create the magical environment the palaces and de luxe theaters offered their patrons. The music didn't simply accompany the pictures; it preceded, followed, surrounded, and engulfed them. Private conversations that fragmented the audience into smaller groups and distracted attention from the show were impossible in theaters where the music was continuous and so thundering that it overwhelmed all attempts at extraneous communication.

Although in the smaller neighborhood theaters and the black-patronized ones, like those along the "Stroll" in Chicago, the musicians were totally on their own, in the palaces and de luxe theaters they were provided with scores or cue sheets to play from. The "movie music" that resulted was *sui generis,* an overorchestrated jumble of classical and quasi-classical selections, hymns, ragtime, folk music, and popular tunes. Hugo Reisenfeld's score for *King of Kings,* which opened Sid Grauman's Chinese Theatre in Hollywood in 1927, borrowed liberally from Tchaikovsky's *Pathétique* symphony, Wagner's *Parsifal,* Beethoven's *Hallelujah Chorus,* and such popular hymns as "Lead, Kindly Light" and "There Is a Green Hill Far Away." Although Roxy and a few others eschewed jazz and ragtime as too plebeian for their palaces, it too was thrown into the musical assemblage. The Balaban & Katz theaters specially advertised that their live shows combined "the various arts into one grand finale; blending the opera to the fastest tempo of jazz."[13]

While some of the showmen, including Roxy, claimed that they were uplifting their audiences by presenting them with a potpourri of orchestral music, the picture palace was not a rival or a substitute for the concert hall—and this was one of its drawing cards. As Lawrence Levine has argued in *Highbrow/Lowbrow*, the late nineteenth- and early twentieth-century symphony hall had broken with the "traditional practice of mixing musical genres and presenting audiences with an eclectic feast." It had become a "sacralized" ground for the presentation of a "sacralized" classical music instead. Those without the cultural capital to "appreciate" the music or the financial capital to pay premium prices were excluded. The picture palace, on the contrary, desacralized the classical music it presented. Movie music had no class, ethnic, or educational labels attached. It was intended to be enjoyed by all who enjoyed the movies, no matter what they had paid or where they had come from.[14]

⋅→⇒◉⇐←⋅

In building their palaces, the producers were not only constructing gaudy advertisements for their companies and their features, they were creating monuments of ostentation so stupendous that customers willingly paid the price of admission to get a peak inside. While the first "de luxe" theaters had, like the Strand, resembled banks or office buildings, the mature palaces glowed and glittered, their neoclassical facades strung with garlands of electrical lights. Vertical marquees climbed the facade, projecting their light far beyond the theaters and drawing the gaze of residents and visitors; horizontal marquees colonized the sidewalk directly outside the theater, covering it with a ceiling of light bulbs and providing shelter for pedestrians to examine the posters and billboards.[15]

Once inside the theater, customers were ushered through a complex series of entrance halls, atria, and lobby spaces. In Loew's State Theatre in St. Louis, they began their journey toward the auditorium in a ticket lobby that opened onto an oval room with fountains on either wall and a white marble staircase in front. After ascending the staircase, customers entered another lobby. Turning left, they were led down a slanting corridor that opened into a hemispherical-shaped room, the mezzanine lounge. From here, they descended a staircase to the orchestra lobby. This complicated maze of corridors, promenades, staircases, lobbies, and lounges served many purposes. Had the thousands of customers waiting for the next show been herded into one huge room or made to stand in one line, their wait would have seemed interminable. The carefully arranged traffic pattern made the wait less onerous, gave the customers the sense that they were steadily moving toward the auditorium, and overwhelmed them with the splendor of the palace.[16]

No expense was spared in furnishing the theaters' lobbies, foyers, reception halls, and rest rooms with antiques, paintings, and plush furniture. The architects worked closely with decorators who covered every inch of floor, wall, and ceiling with elaborate bas-relief designs, expensive fabrics, and boughs of gold leaf. Loew's Midland in Kansas City, Missouri, was, according to the historian David Naylor, "thoroughly filled with royal splendors. . . . The Oriental room of W. K. Vanderbilt's demolished Manhattan townhouse was brought to Kansas City and reassembled in the Midland as a women's lounge. . . . The building plus furnishings cost over $3 million. Six-and-a-half million square inches of gold and silver leaf were used on the walls and ceilings." The Roxy rotunda with its twelve green marble columns, its dome topped by a twenty-foot chandelier, and its marble floor covered by "the largest oval rug in the world" was so transcendently glorious that the *The New Yorker* in 1929 ran a cartoon that pictured a child gazing upward and asking, "Mama: does God live here?"[17]

The moviegoer's final destination was the palace's inner sanctum, the auditorium. If the lights outside were meant to attract and the lobbies to amaze, the auditoria were designed to enthrall the audiences who entered. In the auditoria, the architects abandoned all restraint and forged their own models. Occasionally, the interior decor was in keeping with the regional architecture: Spanish models were popular in Texas, Florida, and California; Aztec and Mayan ruins inspired architects and designers in the Southwest. More often, however, there was neither rhyme nor reason in the choices the architects made and the owners supported. In Loew's State Theater in Syracuse, the auditorium was "permeated by the Orient." Architect Thomas Lamb's design for the Loew's Ohio in Columbus was characterized by his office as "a faithfully carried-out Mexican baroque." Loew's 72nd Street Theater in Manhattan had an auditorium "inspired by the great tower of the pagoda of Wat Ching in Cambodia."[18]

What counted more than the source of the inspiration was the elaboration of that inspiration—and the extravagance with which it was carried through. The Marshall Field and Company monthly magazine, reporting on the opening of the Chicago Theater in the fall of 1921, explained that it had "been built and decorated" with perhaps more extravagance than taste, because "the great mass of people are hungry

Movie palaces were built throughout the country in large and many medium-size cities. This photograph is of the outer lobby and promenade of the Joliet Rialto, in Joliet, Illinois, a 2,800-seat movie palace designed by the architectural firm of Rapp and Rapp. At the front of the promenade are staircases leading to the first balcony. (*Billy Rose Theatre Collection; The New York Public Library; Astor, Lenox, and Tilden Foundations.*)

for beauty, for color, in a form that they can assimilate and comprehend. The more elaborate schools of decoration and architecture provide the means to administer to this hunger."[19]

Like the amusement parks, the palaces were totally synthetic environments cut off from the world outside. The wildly exotic decors, even those tangentially related to European architectural or design models, bore no resemblance whatsoever to models closer at hand in the city or in the memories of those who resided there. There were Hispano-Persian lobbies, Mexican Baroque auditoria, Mayan, Moorish, Oriental, Egyptian, and Italian Renaissance palaces galore but none based on old New England, Eastern European, or Russian-Jewish motifs.[20]

The heterogeneous crowd assembled in the movie palaces required its own fantastic environments, its own stylized amusement spaces. Nothing that smacked of the class-bound, ethnically divided, gender-stratified everyday world would do. The owners, designers, and builders deliberately set out to create new types of public spaces, "shrine[s] to democracy," as the architect George Rapp called them, "where there are no privileged patrons, [where] the wealthy rub elbows with the poor—and are better for this contact. Do not wonder, then, at the touches of Italian Renaissance, executed in glazed polychrome terra-cotta, or at the lobbies and foyers adorned with replicas of precious masterpieces of another world, or at the imported marble wainscoting or the richly ornamented ceilings with motifs copied from master touches of Germany, France and Italy, or at the carved niches, the cloistered arcades, the depthless mirrors, and the great sweeping staircases. These are not impractical attempts at showing off. These are part of a celestial city—a cavern of many-colored jewels, where iridescent lights and luxurious fittings heighten the expectation of pleasure. It is richness unabashed, but richness with a reason."[21]

All felt equally welcome inside the picture palaces because all were equally out of place. The gentry and established middle-class property owners and professionals could not have been comfortable in neoclassical edifices strung with garlands of twinkling light bulbs. Nor could blue- or white-collar workers have been at ease in sumptuous reception halls decorated with terra-cotta, gold-leafed statues of Aztec sun gods. The modern movie palace, Balaban & Katz asserted in their magazine/program, was built not for the "few who want to appear as more aristocratic than the rest [but] for 'all the people all the time.'" There were no reserved seats, no privileged tiers. The balcony was

The lobby of Chicago's Oriental Theater was designed by Rapp and Rapp for Balaban & Katz, who opened it in 1926. (*Billy Rose Theatre Collection; The New York
Public Library; Astor, Lenox, and Tilden Foundations.*)

"just as desirable [as] the main floor [with] the same architectural beauty, the same comfortable chairs, the same ventilation, the same rich carpeting, and furnishings as characterized the main floor." As Balaban & Katz declared with pride, they had not "attempted to establish financial class distinctions, or to divide our auditoriums by means of reserved sections which seem to be more desirable and exclusive [because] *the American people don't like this distinction.*" To make absolutely sure that their one-price, no reserved-seat policy was not violated by customers who paid ushers to save seats for them, tipping was strictly forbidden.[22]

⋅✦⋙◉⋘✦⋅

While many working women and men continued to patronize their local movie theaters, where prices were lower and transportation costs nil, a large number traveled or remained "downtown" after work to see first-run features in the movie palaces. In Worcester, Massachusetts, according to Roy Rosenzweig, after about 1917, "the ethnic working class increasingly patronized the first-class theaters" outside their neighborhoods. Fred Fedeli, the proprietor of the Bijou Theater in the heart of Worcester's immigrant district, recalled in later years that while the downtown movie-palace patrons never visited the neighborhood theaters, his working-class, immigrant customers often left the neighborhood to "visit the first-class theaters."[23]

The working people who patronized the downtown theaters were most likely those who wore white collars and could afford the time and extra money it cost to be entertained in luxury. Ernest Dench, a columnist for *Motion Picture Magazine,* characterized them in 1916 as "the well-to-do working classes" and claimed that they patronized the "de luxe" theaters not because they refused "to associate with their poor brothers and sisters," but because the downtown palaces gave them so much more for their money. "Quality is the deciding factor. For five or ten cents more they see a longer and better program, amid more comfortable surroundings."[24]

The palaces were visited as well by the women who worked in the central business district's offices, retail shops, and department stores. At the Strand, "there was a cafeteria for 'working girls' serving lunch to crowds of young women, as many as 1,500 each day during the first year." To further attract a female audience, the industry produced and promoted features with such stars as Lillian Gish and

Mary Pickford and serials like *The Hazards of Helen* and *The Perils of Pauline*.[25]

The extra attention apparently paid off. Though the percentage of women in the commercial amusement audience had grown steadily from the 1890s on, only in the 1920s picture theaters and palaces did the women constitute a majority of the moviegoing audience. Stephen Bush estimated in 1920 that 60 percent of the film audience were women; a 1927 *Moving Picture World* investigation put the figure at 83 percent. A 1925 letter to the editor of the Balaban & Katz magazine headed "WANTS TO GET AWAY FROM WIMMIN" requested that a new theater be built for men only, because women dominated all the existing palaces. Balaban & Katz responded to the request with a simple "No, it wouldn't pay."[26]

Lloyd Lewis, surveying the "de luxe" theaters in Chicago for the *New Republic,* reported that the palaces, in the afternoons, belonged to the women. "In the dim auditorium which seems to float in a world of dream and where the people brushing elbows on either side are safely remote, an American woman may spend her afternoon alone. . . . In the isolation of this twilit palace, she abandons herself to these adventures with a freedom that is impossible in the legitimate theater, where the lights are brighter and the neighboring seat-holders always on the edge of her vision; the blue dusk of the 'de luxe' house has dissolved the Puritan strictures she has absorbed as a child."[27]

An additional layer of the movie-palace audience came from tourists and traveling businessmen in town for the week or the weekend. With their lights blazing a welcome onto the street and their cheap ticket prices, the palaces became tourist attractions as popular and, for many, a lot more exciting than the city's legitimate playhouses. No longer did tourists have to spend dollars to take a chance on a Broadway show. Now for a quarter they could see a picture-palace extravaganza. The picture palace, claimed J. Victor Wilson, the director of publicity for the Strand in New York City, had "removed dull evenings from that visit to the metropolis. The new motto of the traveller is, I would say: 'Be sure you're right—or go to the movies.'"[28]

The movie palaces were bringing together groups of picture-show fans that had formerly been divided among several sites. Assembled in the palace audience were patrons of the legitimate theater who had until recently paid two dollars a ticket to see moving pictures in the first-class playhouses, vaudeville customers who had enjoyed the pictures in the vaudeville halls, and nickelodeon and neighborhood theater regulars who were accustomed to paying a nickel or a dime for thirty minutes to an hour of short films and a few illustrated songs.

To assemble an audience from these disparate groups was no simple task. The palace managers had to keep their prices low enough to attract the nickelodeon crowd and assure prosperous theatergoers that they would not in any way be contaminated by contact with the "other half." The problem with the "masses," as perceived by the "classes," was that they were prone to rowdiness, smelled poorly, and were laden with germs. While there was no danger of being affronted by bad smells or attacked by germs outdoors in the amusement parks, precautions had to be taken indoors, especially in the aftermath of the 1919 influenza outbreak, which had reached such epidemic proportions that government officials in some cities were requiring theater owners to separate customers by an empty seat.[29]

The palace owners went out of their way to convince customers that the air in their theaters was not only odorless but perfectly hygienic. A. L. Shakman, owner of the 81st Street Theater on Broadway, proudly proclaimed in *The Triangle,* a promotional brochure distributed to moviegoers, that there were "no clothing or body odors noticeable even during the capacity hours of the 81st Street Theater, for the simple reason that the air is changed by dome ventilators every twenty minutes. The air is just as sweet and pure in the balcony as it is downstairs." The Butterfly Theater in Milwaukee advertised that its "Perfect Ventilation" system provided customers with a "Complete Change of Air Every Three Minutes." Balaban & Katz claimed that in their movie palaces, "You breathe fresh, new air with every breath you draw."[30]

The guarantee that there would be clean air to breathe while watching the show was a necessary—although not a sufficient condition—for winning the allegiance of theatergoers who were not compelled by price considerations to patronize the city's picture shows. More was required to convince them they would be safe and secure in the lobby, the rest rooms, and the cavernous movie-palace auditoria they shared with the "humble worker" and his wife and children.

Erving Goffman has described in great detail the conditions under which "engagements of the unacquainted" take place in public spaces. "Normal" folk enter into face-to-face, direct encounters only with those with whom they are already acquainted. There is one general exception to this rule. In certain well-defined "open regions," such as cocktail lounges and resort hotels, strangers are permitted to engage one another without risk or opprobrium, because "the assumption of mutual regard and good will built into open regions guarantees a rationale for discounting the potential nefariousness of contact among the unacquainted."[31]

It was this "assumption of mutual regard and good will" that the palace owners had to "build into" their theaters. Their task was made easier by their customers, almost all of whom had come to the theater prepared to merge unobtrusively into the crowd. In the movie palace, there existed a spirit of accommodation, an implicit compact among customers to have a good time together without intruding on one another's private space. Audience members might not feel free conversing with the strangers on either side of them, but they did feel comfortable laughing, crying, and cheering with them.

To enforce and embody this compact, the palaces hired small armies of ushers and uniformed attendants. We have, in earlier chapters, touched on the importance of the ushers in maintaining the appearance of order in commercial amusement centers. In the movie palaces, with low admission charges and enormous audiences, the presence of a well-drilled platoon of ushers was an absolute necessity. The movie palaces paraded their ushers, advertised them, and bragged about them whenever they had the chance. Balaban & Katz in Chicago claimed that most of their ushers were University of Chicago students, picked with as much care as West Point cadets. Josef Israels II, writing in *Liberty* magazine, insisted that all the movie palaces employed the same criteria in choosing their ushers: they wanted them tall and handsome. The palace ushers were indeed so tall, dark, dignified, and handsome that they became the subject of *New Yorker* magazine jokes and were even mentioned in Cole Porter songs: "You're the Top . . . you're the steppes of Russia. You're the pants on a Roxy usher."[32]

The ushers were the embodiment of the class, beauty, dignity, and other-world gentility the palaces tried to represent. But they were at the same time a visible police force, a drilled army with uniforms, ranks, and military commanders prepared for any eventuality. Each one of the ushers at the Rialto on 42nd Street and Broadway carried "a swagger stick with mother-of-pearl tips that lit up in the dark. The Head Usher carried a bugle." At the Avalon in Chicago, the ushers were dressed in French Foreign Legion uniforms. Balaban & Katz hired West Point graduates to drill their ushers; Roxy hired ex-marines, although he also employed other military men on occasion. His drillmaster at the Capitol, he proudly told a reporter from the *Brooklyn Daily Times,* had served as Teddy Roosevelt's bugler.[33]

To further enhance the stature of their ushers and free them for ceremonial guard duty, the movie palaces hired African-American women, men, and children to perform the menial tasks in the theaters. Balaban & Katz's *Fundamental Principles of Theater Management* was quite specific on this point. Only white males, seventeen to twenty-one years of age, could serve as ushers; the footman had to "be a colored man, about six feet in height, medium heavy, erect, about fifty years of age, preferably with some gray hair, approaching the old southern coachman type . . . service boys and messengers [had to be] not over five feet four, of slight or slender build, well formed and in good proportion, not markedly of negro type with heavy features"; "colored girls about twenty-five or thirty years of age, well past the frivolous and playful age" could be hired as maids; and "colored [men] of about thirty to forty years of age" as porters. While the white attendants were dressed in military garb, befitting their honored position, the blacks were dressed in "livery" appropriate to their servant status.[34]

As important as the ushers in undergirding the "assumption of mutual regard and good will" in the movie palaces was the unwritten promise management offered that it would refuse admission to those who did not meet minimal standards of respectability and self-control. Prostitutes, drunks, and African Americans had to be barred at the box office, because, it was assumed, they were neither respectable nor capable of controlling their behavior in public.

The exclusion or segregation of blacks was critical in this regard. While for more than a century, the "black image in the white mind" had oscillated between the carefree but improvable darky and the rapist "nigger beast," it was the latter image that had become dominant in early twentieth-century popular culture. By the mid-1910s, the happy-go-lucky vaudeville "darky" had been displaced in popular song by the razor-wielding "coon," and the lazy, ghost-fearing, watermelon-eating "niggers" of early film had been supplanted by the leering rapists, sadists, and brutes so vividly portrayed in *The Birth of a Nation*. It was imperative that palace managers guard their white patrons against possible insult or injury from black customers, who, no matter how refined they might appear to be, it was now assumed, were genetically prone to violence and incapable of restraint.[35]

While it had been relatively easy to segregate African Americans in theaters with reserved seats, it was more difficult to do so in picture palaces where customers were free to sit wherever they chose. Palace ushers were instructed to steer Negroes away from the center aisles and seat them instead next to the wall or in the balconies. When "two intelligent, well-dressed, quiet-mannered Negro women" working for the Chicago Commission on Race entered a movie theater on State Street in Chicago, they were directed to the far left side of the theater. "Later, seeing two vacant seats further front in the center section which gave us a much better view we decided to take them and see what would happen. As we rose, the usher tried to block us by putting his hands on the back of the seat in front and saying, 'I am sorry that you can't take those seats.'" The women brushed past him and took the seats anyway. In another Chicago theater, black customers who had similarly been directed to the balcony complained to the manager after the show. He "told them that as they had seen the show, heard the music, and shared everything with other patrons, he did not see they had any real cause for complaint." He then directed their attention to the notice on the back of their ticket stubs that stated that management had the right to "revoke the license granted in the sale of the ticket, by refunding the money paid." As late as 1940, the sociologist Charles Johnson reported that in Dayton, Ohio, movie theaters changed their prices without notice when African Americans appeared at the ticket window. "If this fails to discourage their patronage, Negroes are ushered to an inconspicuous corner of the theater."[36]

African Americans and their allies did not, of course, accept segregation in the movie theaters, but fought against it as best they could, wherever they could. The *Moving Picture World* reported in October of 1913 on the case of a Rochester, New York, "colored woman" who had sued the theater that made her sit in the balcony. While in the South, "the colored brother" never complained about being seated in a separate section, "in the North the case is different and every now and then there seems to be an organized effort on the part of the negroes to make as much trouble as possible." The only effective way to counter such discriminatory practices was for African Americans to build and operate their own movie houses, which they did, but these were almost without exception smaller neighborhood theaters. There were no picture "palaces" opened by or for African Americans.[37]

-*≒◯⪡*-

The exclusion or segregation of people of color was as necessary a condition for the "democratization" of the palace audience as a visible usher/police presence. Unsegregated and unpoliced, the "crowd" was a potential menace. Segregated and policed, it became part of the attraction. In the picture palace as, to a lesser degree, in other commercial culture sites, a magical, though temporary, transmutation took place as disassociated individuals were gathered into a crowd that became a community. That community was ephemeral and would vanish as soon as the individuals who composed it left the amusement center, but the experience of belonging to it was an integral aspect of going out. As the psychologist Albert Mehrabian has written, "The presence of others permits the expression of heightened emotions. . . . The laughter of others at a comedy somehow adds to the general sense of enjoyment and amusements. At a tearjerker, the sobs and sniffles of a nearby person seem to remove all barriers for freely expressing one's emotions." Arthur Meloy, the author of a 1915 treatise on theater construction, advised prospective show businessmen to build their theaters as large as they could because moviegoers preferred theaters with larger audiences. "They will go where the crowd is."[38]

What transformed these disparate audience members into a community of pleasure seekers was not only the experience they shared in common but also the recognition that in sharing it, they were privileged and deserving of this privilege. The movie palaces demanded that their customers, especially the male ones, restrain their impulses: that they cease or at least disguise their predatory behavior regarding unescorted women, that they stop smoking and drinking, or, for that matter, eating, chatting, flirting, or in any way distracting those sitting alongside them. One's capacity for following these rules and behaving decently in public was regarded as a marker of one's moral worth.

Going out to the movie palace meant more than just having a good time; it meant having it in the company of a heterogeneous community of privileged strangers with whom one shared two integral and connected characteristics: "whiteness" and decency. In going out, one entered a third sphere of daily life (beyond work and home), defined by rules, rituals, and behavioral codes observed nowhere else. Once inside the palace auditorium, all audience members, female and male, young or old, in the cheap seats upstairs or the more expensive ones downstairs were expected to perform the same rituals and obey the same rules. Wherever they sat, whatever they paid, they were obliged to dress up for the show (but not too much and certainly not in formal wear), take off their hats on entering, quietly follow the usher to their seats, refrain from smoking, drinking, or walking the aisles while the show was in progress, and, when the lights went down, join their com-

panions in cheering the heroes and heroines, booing the villains, laughing, and weeping, but always in unison with the congregation, never
alone, and never too raucously.

⤙⭤⭤⤚

In his 1929 article in the *New Republic,* Lloyd Lewis tried to explain
why the picture palace was such an enormous success in cities across
the country. Part of the reason, he claimed, was that the palaces represented, indeed were, an alternative world, one richer, more romantic,
and far more democratic than the mundane worlds the picture-palace
customers inhabited on the outside.

"All of this splendor has been planned for her [the customer's]
delight, and with a luxuriance that she had imagined was enjoyed only
in Cleopatra's court, oriental harems, or Parisian and Viennese society.
She strolls voluptuously through lobbies and foyers that open into one
another like a maze; her feet sink in soft rugs, she is surrounded by
heavy Renaissance tables, oil paintings, and statues of nudes. She
enjoys the sense of leading a sophisticated, continental life with none of
the practical risks. For she sees church members and respectable
householders savoring the same delights about her.

"When she goes home that evening, she will perhaps clean spinach
and peel onions, but for a few hours, attendants bow to her, doormen
tip their hats, and a maid curtsies to her in the ladies' washroom. She
bathes in elegance and dignity; she satisfies her yearning for a 'cul-
tured' atmosphere. Even the hush that hangs over the lobbies means
refinement to her; voices that have been raucous on the street drop, as
they drop on entering a church.

"When she takes her seat, she is further flattered by the same color-
ful magnificence on the stage as in the lobby. . . . The royal favor of
democracy it is: for in the 'de luxe' house every man is a king and every
woman a queen."[39]

The key to this kingdom of democracy was the universal taste for
amusement that economic prosperity appeared to be unlocking. While
earlier amusement entrepreneurs had had to disguise their "diversions"
as inherently educational to attract the "refined" middle class and those
who aspired to it, that pretense had been almost entirely abandoned by
the 1920s. As Woodrow Wilson had assured the nation during the
Great War, "a reasonable amount of amusement" was not a "luxury but
a necessity."[40]

Harold Franklin, the president of a chain of West Coast theaters, would use almost the same words in 1928 to describe the new role of moving pictures—and moving-picture palaces—in American society. "The hundreds of thousands who congregate nightly under the exhibitor's roof are indulging in a luxury only in a secondary sense. Truly, they gather here as they go elsewhere for bread; because here, as nowhere else, is to be found the civilized man's great necessity—release from the day's routine—an alternation from perhaps tedious reality to liberating romance."[41]

Going to the movies had become the hallmark of a new American civilization. In myth, and to only a slightly lesser extent in reality, the picture palace represented the partial fulfillment of the American dream of an interethnic, cross-class, genderless, luxury-laden urban democracy. While that democracy was founded on the segregation of African Americans, it was nonetheless a remarkable achievement.

In the final analysis, we must perhaps forgive the movie-palace architects, owners, managers, and publicists for their hyperbolic descriptions of the "democracy" enshrined and daily celebrated in their theaters. For they had, as they claimed, created a new public space, one that was at least as "democratic" in form and function as the church and schoolhouse they compared it to. As Lloyd Lewis concluded in his *New Republic* article, "In this suave atmosphere, the differences of cunning, charm, and wealth, that determine our lives outside, are forgotten. All men enter these portals equal, and thus the movies are perhaps a symbol of democracy. Let us take heart from this, and not be downcast because our democratic nation prudently reserves its democracy for the temple of day dreams."[42]

CHAPTER 17

Decline and Fall

T HE 1920s WERE A PROFITABLE DECADE FOR THE public amusement business. Although more and more Americans were beginning to entertain themselves at home—with radio and phonograph—attendance at the movie theaters continued to increase. The sound pictures that followed rapidly on the box-office success of *The Jazz Singer* in 1927 kept the theaters full through 1930. Not even the coming of the Great Depression slowed this forward momentum for long. By 1935, moving pictures had recaptured much of their lost audience and, according to James Rorty in *Forum* magazine, were doing better than any other industry except food products.[1]

Live theater did not do as well. Vaudeville, decimated by moving pictures in the 1920s, did not survive the Depression. By 1932, the premier vaudeville theater in the nation, the Palace, had been converted to moving pictures, and all that remained of the Keith-Albee empire was the letter *K* in the RKO company, which had bought and converted the remaining vaudeville halls to moving-picture houses.[2]

The city's dance halls and ballrooms survived because they kept admission prices below a dollar and struck strategic alliances with local radio stations. In Chicago, Andrew Karsis, owner of the Trianon and Aragon ballrooms, broadcast his band music live through a telephone line to the WGN studios and, on Sunday afternoons, coast to coast over the Mutual Network. With the publicity provided by the radio, Karsis's ballrooms filled to capacity. In New York City, mammoth ballrooms that had been built in the 1920s flourished during the 1930s. Uptown at the Savoy in Harlem, and downtown at Roseland, owners kept prices low (the Savoy charged only thirty cents for dancers who arrived before 6 P.M.), employed the best big bands in the nation (often two at a time), showcased such new dances as the Lindy or, as it was better known, the Jitterbug, and made a great deal of money, especially from the "swing craze" that revitalized nightlife in the late 1930s.[3]

Organized baseball also outlasted the Depression, though in reduced circumstances. By 1931, eleven of the sixteen major league baseball teams were losing money. In Philadelphia, revenues declined to the point where owner Connie Mack sold off his star Athletics to competing clubs. As paid admissions continued to fall, Jack Shibe, the stadium owner, erected a "spite" fence to block the view of local fans, who had, since the early 1920s, watched the games from the roofs of North Twentieth Street apartment buildings.[4]

The amusement parks did better. The industry had undergone its own retrenchment during the 1920s, at which time many of the smaller trolley parks closed or were sold by the transit companies that owned them. Now, in the 1930s, park owners reduced their investments in new rides and facilities and advertised instead their beaches, picnic groves, lawns, and ballrooms. Olympic Park outside Newark staged dance marathons that drew participants and spectators from as far away as Philadelphia. Euclid Beach Park in Cleveland and Kennywood outside Pittsburgh survived the 1930s by hosting company picnics and "nationality days," where family and friends could spend the day in the sunshine, eating sausage and hot dogs, drinking home-made wine, and playing baseball or tug of war, all for the price of admission.[5]

The 1930s were, as the Coney Island historian Lucy Gilman has written, the era of the "dripper." Visitors on a budget unable to afford even the dime it cost to rent a bathhouse, traveled by subway to Coney with their bathing suits under their clothes and "dripped" their way back to the city. Like other amusement resorts short on capital, Coney's parks, rides, and concession stands grew seedier year after year. At Luna Park, pigs replaced elephants on the water slides; sugar, coffee, and crackers were substituted for kewpie dolls; and cockroach races were held. The crowds, which had increased almost geometrically with the extension of the subway in the 1920s, didn't seem to mind. The round-trip cost a dime, hot dogs and rides a nickel, the beach was free, and there was always plenty to gawk at.[6]

⊷⇒◉⇐⊶

With the end of World War II and the return of the veterans, the amusement business picked up immediately. On July 4, 1947, Coney Island registered its biggest day ever with a reported 1.3 million visitors, one-fifth the population of New York City. The *New York Times Magazine* was so taken with Coney's return to prosperity that for two years running it published glowing articles on the "packed" resorts and their new "atomic screamer" rides. Organized baseball also did remarkably well in the late 1940s. Attendance figures topped twenty million in 1948, the best year ever for the major leagues. Some of the boost in admissions came from the thousands of African-American fans who came to the major league parks for the first time to see black ballplayers like Jackie Robinson and Larry Doby. By integrating their ball clubs in the postwar years, Branch Rickey in Brooklyn and Bill Veeck in Cleveland tapped into a new source of customers, the former patrons of the Negro leagues. Brooklyn, with Jackie Robinson in 1947, drew almost two million customers, many of them former Newark Eagles fans. Cleveland in 1948 drew more than two and a half million, many of them Buckeye fans who had deserted the Negro Leagues to stand in the front of the outfield stands and watch Larry Doby play big-league baseball.[7]

While the baseball club owners welcomed black fans to their stadia, the amusement park owners discouraged their attendance—and suffered as a result. Maintaining segregated amusement sites was politically difficult in the late 1950s and early 1960s and economically self-defeating. As the percentage of blacks in the total population more than doubled in New York City, Chicago, Philadelphia, Los Angeles, Baltimore, Cleveland, St. Louis, Washington, and Pittsburgh between 1950 and 1970, and more than tripled in Detroit, Boston, Milwaukee, Buffalo, Minneapolis, and Newark, those facilities that continued to discourage black attendance found themselves drawing on a smaller and smaller pool of customers.[8]

Only when the pressure from civil rights activists and legal authorities became insurmountable did the amusement park owners open their gates to blacks. Olympic Park outside Newark began to admit African Americans in the late 1950s after a sustained campaign by the local NAACP. In Cleveland, according to the journalist Cyril A. Dostal, the Euclid Beach owners submitted to pressure to allow blacks on "the rides and other paid admission attractions," although they continued to bar them "from the dance floor, roller rink and the eating and swimming facilities." In Pittsburgh's Kennywood Park, management, forced to integrate its swimming pool, converted it instead into a huge water ride. In Baltimore, the owners of the Gwynn Oaks amusement park battled civil rights protestors outside their gates for an entire summer before reluctantly desegregating in August 1963.[9]

Although the show businessmen feared that desegregation would be bad for business because it would drive away white customers, the opposite case could also be made. Broadening the traditional customer base to include blacks could also increase attendance—and profits. That had certainly been the case at Ebbets Field in Brooklyn, Municipal Stadium in Cleveland, and County Stadium in Milwaukee, where the Braves and Henry Aaron played to huge crowds in the middle 1950s.[10]

Outside organized baseball, the first show businessmen to understand the potential profits in integrated amusements were rock and roll promoters like Alan Freed. Freed, the son of a Lithuanian-Jewish father and a Welsh-American mother, was born in Pennsylvania and grew up in Ohio. His first job in radio was announcing on a nightly classical music program in New Castle, Pennsylvania. After ten years of disk jockeying in big towns and small cities through Pennsylvania and Ohio, Freed landed a job on nighttime radio in Cleveland. Here, for the first time, he billed himself as the "Moondog," opened his program with the sounds of a dog howling, and played "rhythm and blues" records.

There was nothing particularly new about the music—it was already being played on several radio stations and sold in countless record stores. But Freed, like only a handful of disk jockeys in the country, played these "race" records on a white radio station patronized by white listeners. To make the "Negro" music more palatable to parents and sponsors, he called it "rock and roll." His uninhibited style and the music he played struck a chord with Cleveland's white and black teenagers who stayed up to hear him and came to the live rhythm and blues shows he sponsored and hosted at the Cleveland Arena. According to the rock historian Charlie Gillett, Freed's "success among white audiences with Negro music was widely reported in *Billboard,* and in 1954 he was signed by a New York station, WINS, which he quickly established as New York's leading popular music station."[11]

In New York, Freed continued to play rhythm and blues records on the radio. While some African-American disk jockeys and community leaders complained that he was taking away listeners from black radio stations and aping "Negroes in a jive talk manner that belittles them," Freed weathered the protests and managed to ingratiate himself with segments of the community by refusing to play "white copies of rhythm and blues songs," which he regarded as "anti-Negro."[12]

In 1955, his first year in New York, Freed not only increased his station's advertising revenues by almost 50 percent but began to host his own live rock and roll shows. The first of these, in St. Nicholas Arena, a boxing and wrestling hall, drew thousands of fans at two dollars apiece to hear the Drifters, the Clovers, the Harptones, Ruth Brown, Fats Domino, and other black rhythm and blues stars. What was most astounding about the show was the fact that the audience was half white.[13]

Having filled a boxing arena for two shows, Freed was now ready to move on to bigger and better theaters, crowds, and profits. The best available sites were the movie palaces, which still featured live performers as an integral part of their shows. It was here that the swing bands had reached their largest audiences in the 1930s and Frank Sinatra had drawn thousands of swooning teens in the 1940s.[14]

Freed tried at first to lease the Broadway Paramount for an Easter rock and roll show, but was turned away by the owners who worried about the "racial stigma" attached to the music. He booked the Brooklyn Paramount instead, and, with the help of continuous radio promotion, drew a crowd of almost 100,000 and a box-office gross of $107,000, surpassing the house record set by crooner Russ Columbo in 1932. Freed's 1955 Brooklyn Paramount show was the beginning of a string of sold-out engagements in movie palaces. In 1957, Freed moved his Easter show to the Broadway Paramount where he broke additional house records. The crowds were so huge the *New York Times* reported the opening on page one under the headline, "Rock 'n' Roll Teen-Agers Tie Up the Times Square Area." Although by 1957, with the twin dynamos of Elvis Presley and Dick Clark fully unleashed, rock and roll was growing whiter, Freed's shows still featured mostly black artists. For his 1957 Christmas show at the Paramount, he presented two white acts, the Everly Brothers and Jerry Lee Lewis, among a dozen black performers, including Fats Domino, Chuck Berry, the Cadillacs, the Moonglows, Frankie Lymon and the Teenagers, and

Screamin' Jay Hawkins, who, dressed entirely in a black satin bat-wing cape, began his performance by leaping out of a coffin placed in the center of the stage.[15]

There was little positive response to the rock and rollers' experiment with desegregation. Instead, the public commentary that greeted Freed and the disk jockeys who promoted live shows with integrated audiences focused entirely on the degraded state of the music and the rowdy behavior of the teenagers. Much of the opposition, as might have been expected, came from white southerners. In Birmingham, Alabama, the White Citizen's Council distributed pamphlets and held a press conference attacking rock and roll as immoral "Negro bop" imported by the NAACP as a form of "integration brainwash for Southern white teenagers." When Nat King Cole, who was not a rock and roller but a "Negro" singer with a large following of white teenage girls, arrived in Birmingham to give a concert in a segregated auditorium (even the stage was segregated with Cole separated by a curtain from the white members of his band), he was attacked on stage by four men who ran down the aisles, jumped onto the stage, and beat him as he began to sing "Little Girl." The following year, southern television stations protested so effectively after Frankie Lymon danced with a white girl on Alan Freed's "Big Beat" television show (Freed had been hired to host a network television show in the summer of 1957) that Freed was warned to hire only white performers. He refused. His television show was canceled the following week.[16]

While the White Citizen's Councils directly objected to the debilitating, "mongrelizing" effects of "Negro bop" on white teenagers, more "responsible" citizens, from Catholic church officials and the Board of Education in Boston to local politicians, congressmen, psychiatrists, recording executives, music critics, television commentators, and youth experts, attacked the music for inciting juvenile delinquency, claiming by indirection and innuendo that black music was inherently dangerous for white teenagers. A Dr. Francis J. Braceland, identified as "a noted psychiatrist" by the *New York Times*, in a veiled reference in 1956 to rock and roll's origins in the black community, called it a "cannibalistic and tribalistic" form of music that functioned much like a "communicable disease."[17]

The *New York Times Magazine* explained the effect of the music in much the same terms in January 1958, describing it as an extension of "Rhythm and Blues, a music . . . aimed primarily at the Negro market. . . . It is a tense, monotonous beat that often gives rock 'n' roll music a jungle-like persistence." No teenagers, white or black, could sit still once the "Big Beat" started. At Alan Freed's first Broadway Paramount show in February 1957, the dancing and feet stamping was so loud, the newspapers reported, that frightened firemen called out city inspectors to inspect the balconies for structural damage (there was none). In Atlanta, authorities took additional steps to control the teens, according to a *New York Daily News* article, issuing "a police order banning teenagers from dancing in public without the written consent of their parents."[18]

Freed continued on from city to city, unperturbed by the powerful enemies he was making. He met his downfall in Boston in May of 1958 when, according to police reports, the crowd exiting the theater erupted into violence and fifteen persons, including a Navy sailor, were injured. The police charged that Freed, who was emceeing the show, had incited the riot. Eyewitnesses and local television news footage placed the blame instead on the police who demanded that the teens stop dancing in the aisles, and, when they refused to do so, turned on the houselights.[19]

The next day, John B. Hynes, the mayor of Boston, banned future rock and roll concerts, and a grand jury indicted Freed under a nineteenth-century "anti-anarchy" statute for inciting "the unlawful destruction of property." Although local police officials had immediately after the disturbance discounted any racial motivation, a later unsubstantiated report claimed that all the victims had been white and their attackers, who had fled before they could be apprehended, black. Public officials across the country responded to the news from Boston by banning rock and roll shows from their jurisdictions; promoters canceled their tours; and even Dick Clark, whom no one had ever accused of inciting a riot, halted his "Cavalcade of Stars" tour. Freed was eventually acquitted of the Boston charges. But he never recovered the bookings he had lost and was fired from his New York City radio job. His career was effectively ended the following year when he was indicted in the "payola" scandals for taking bribes to play and promote records on his radio program.[20]

For a brief moment in the 1950s, the movie palaces and the downtown entertainment districts had recaptured a bit of the glamour and excitement they had enjoyed in their glory days. But the connection between rock and roll and juvenile delinquency, emphasized by journalists, congressional committees, and local politicians—and graphically portrayed in rock and roll "teenpics" such as *Blackboard Jungle*—

was too much for the movie industry to contend with, especially in the middle 1950s as it confronted renewed charges of communist influence and infiltration. Rather than risking negative publicity as abettors of juvenile delinquency and corrupters of white youths, the palace owners stopped booking rock and roll shows. By 1959, with Freed unemployed, the live rock and roll shows suspended, and Chuck Berry under arrest for a Mann Act violation in St. Louis, "for transporting a minor across state lines for immoral purposes," the era of cheap, live rock and roll at the movie palaces was effectively over.[21]

⟡⟶⟹⟸⟵⟡

With the loss of the overflow crowds that the rock and roll shows had attracted to the downtown palaces, the movie industry sank deeper into the decline that had begun after the war. Between 1948 and 1967 alone, annual admissions to indoor moving-picture theaters fell by 600 percent. To lure customers back to the movie theaters, the industry experimented with new types of features and technologies. Unfortunately, neither spectaculars, Technicolor, Cinerama, CinemaScope, nor 3-D movies brought back the "lost audience" of adults. Struggling to sustain falling revenues and perhaps worried about the image of the movie theater as a teenage hangout, exhibitors raised their prices after 1950 at twice the rate of the consumer price index. (If movie theater prices had risen at the same rate, the average ticket price in 1990 would have been under $2.50.) This too had an adverse effect on overall attendance.[22]

Television has been retroactively blamed for the decline in moviegoing, but the drop in attendance was greatest between 1948 and 1950, when fewer than 10 percent of American homes had televisions, and between 1965 and 1969, long after television had been installed in every American household. A larger percentage of the falloff was probably caused by the postwar suburbanization and the baby boom. Americans were marrying younger, having babies, and moving to the suburbs in record numbers in the 1950s, sped on their way by an expanded national highway system and federal mortgage funds. Had the movie industry been better prepared, it would have moved to the suburbs as well. Unfortunately, the industry was in the 1950s suffering its own postwar crisis, as it struggled to adjust to sagging attendance and the 1948 Supreme Court antitrust decision that forced the major studios to sell off their theaters.[23]

The industry's initial response to suburbanization was to build drive-ins that were less expensive to construct and operate than enclosed theaters and promote them as the ideal amusement site for young parents who could put their children to sleep in the back seats, while they watched a double feature in the front seats. By 1951, drive-ins made up 15 percent of the nation's movie theaters and 20 percent of its revenues. By 1958, there were almost 5,000 of them.[24]

Although television and suburbanization accounted for some of the decline in moviegoing, they cannot explain all of it. Millions of potential moviegoers remained in the cities, and they too had stopped going out at night. A "great fear" had invaded the cities, and, like the Great Fear of 1789 that spread through the French countryside and mobilized the rural masses for insurrection, it was founded in worsening material conditions and exacerbated by rumors of brigands roaming the land. After a half-century of steady improvement—at least in image—American cities were again perceived as awash in poverty, criminality, and violence. After 1920, as Kenneth Jackson has argued, "no one could deny that the cities were poor and that the suburbs were, relatively speaking rich." In the postwar period, this economic polarization was exacerbated by racial division, as the percentage of African Americans in the central cities increased dramatically. "After World War II, the racial and economic polarization of large American metropolitan areas," in Kenneth Jackson's words, "became so pronounced that downtown areas lost their commercial hold on the middle class. Cities became identified with fear and danger rather than with glamour and pleasure."[25]

It is impossible to ascertain the degree to which this "great fear" of the cities was imaginary or exaggerated. The statistics pointed to an increase in crime in the downtown districts and in the "black ghettoes" that encircled them. But these areas had always been plagued by high crime rates, no matter what the color or ethnicity of their inhabitants. Still, for the first half of the twentieth century, the excitement of going out at night more than compensated for the potential danger.[26]

In the end, it mattered little why people were afraid to go out and to what extent their fear was based on reality or rumor. The result was the same. As the numbers of pleasure seekers dwindled, the protective cover of the crowd diminished and the threat of danger increased. The downtown movie palaces so conspicuously located in the heart of the entertainment districts were doomed to extinction. They were too big for the reduced moviegoing audience, too expensive to operate and maintain, and too difficult to police. One after another, they were closed, partitioned, or demolished. The Broadway Roxy, which had been temporarily reduced in size and converted to a Cinemiracle large-screen theater in 1958, closed forever in 1960. In San Francisco, the State theater was razed in the summer of 1961, the Fox in 1963. In Kansas City, the Midlands theater, Marcus Loew's favorite, was turned into a bowling alley in 1961 with lanes built on top of the orchestra seats.* [27]

The end of the movie-palace era and, according to David Naylor, "the ultimate architectural insult" came in the early 1970s when Detroit's magnificent Michigan Theater was turned into a parking garage and the Brooklyn Paramount that had hosted Freed's rock and roll shows was sold to Long Island University, which converted the lobby into a student cafeteria, the balcony into classrooms, and the auditorium into a gym.[28]

◦•◦◦

The picture-show business was too large, too profitable, and too integrated into the everyday life of Americans to disappear entirely. After a brief period of reorganization and consolidation, the industry marshaled its profits and its considerable access to capital and relocated its theaters to suburban shopping centers, where costs were lower and parking plentiful. In the late 1960s and early 1970s, 70 percent of the moving-picture theaters built in the nation were constructed in suburban shopping malls. And none of them were palaces.[29]

There was no longer any need to impress potential customers with the grandeur of the picture show. Large enclosed public spaces—lobbies, atria, foyers, staircases, and lounges—signified danger rather than elegance. The new suburban theaters were designed instead like motels, with one box-shaped auditorium next to or on top of another. The huge "general interest" audience that had gathered in the prewar movie palaces was split up into distinct audience groups, divided by age, gender, education, and "race." In the suburban multiplexed theaters, each "niche" grouping could see its own film on its own screen, without having to suffer the inconvenience or discomfort of associating with the rest of the crowd.

The downtown movie palaces were the most conspicuous of the public amusement sites razed in the late 1950s and 1960s. But they

---

*Moving pictures would eventually return to the Midlands but only after it had been renovated and reduced in size from 3,800 to 1,300 seats.

In 1960, Gloria Swanson, wearing $170,000 in jewels, posed amid the detritus of New York's Roxy Theatre, where thirty-three years earlier she had starred in the film *The Love of Sunya*. (AP/Wide World Photos.)

were not the only ones. The central city baseball parks and amusement parks met a similar fate. Although integration had brought thousands of black fans to the ballparks in the late 1940s, overall attendance began to drop precipitously in the 1950s and 1960s. Television was responsible for keeping some fans at home, but so too were aging stadia with insufficient parking. The vast majority of urban baseball parks were located in residential neighborhoods a short distance from the central business districts. After 1950 and the influx of African Americans to the cities, the racial composition of many of these neighborhoods changed dramatically. The chief obstacle to getting fans back in the seats, club owners such as Walter O'Malley of the Dodgers and Bob Carpenter of the Philadelphia Phillies believed, was their ballparks' locations in such neighborhoods. Bob Carpenter, the owner of the Phillies who in 1970 moved the team out of Shibe Park, where major league baseball had been played since 1909, told the historian Bruce Kuklick that baseball was no longer "a paying proposition" in Shibe because of "the 'undesirable' neighborhood," "undesirable," according to Kuklick, serving as a code word "for 'black.'" Carpenter was convinced that white baseball fans "would not come to a black neighborhood" to see a baseball game.[30]

Through the 1950s and 1960s, major league baseball teams abandoned the neighborhoods they had grown up in. The first teams to leave were the Boston Braves, the St. Louis Browns, and the Philadelphia Athletics, the weaker franchises in cities that could no longer support two major league clubs. In 1958, they were followed by the Brooklyn Dodgers and the New York Giants. In 1963, the Washington Senators left Griffith Stadium in Washington, D.C., for suburban Bloomington, Minnesota. The stadia these teams settled in were far from their home neighborhoods, far, indeed, from any type of neighborhood. Baseball team owners had once actively sought locations accessible to mass transit; they now chose sites on major highways, surrounded by wide-open spaces that could be converted to parking lots.[31]

Developments in the amusement park industry paralleled those in professional baseball. The urban amusement parks of the 1950s and 1960s, like the ballparks, were a bit grimier than they had been, but probably no more dangerous. The amusement park had always been home to pickpockets, tough guys, short-change artists, and some very scary—and sometimes dangerous—roller-coaster rides. While some visitors, like Walt Disney, were disturbed by the "carney" atmosphere and the aura of danger and disorder, millions more continued to come and have a good time. The playwright David Mamet recalls that Riverview Park on Chicago's North Side, which he regularly visited in the mid-1950s, was "magnificent, dangerous and thrilling. . . . There was illicit gambling, one could die on the tracks, the place reeked of sex. A trip to Riverview was more than a thrill, it was a dangerous dream adventure for the children and for their parents." Unfortunately, Riverview was located in a neighborhood and a city that were falling victim to racial tensions. While it had withstood the effects of Depression, world wars, and the polio scare of the 1950s, it could not survive the anxieties and petty violences that accompanied the desegregation of the city's public spaces. According to Garry Cooper, a Chicago native, writing in the *Chicago Tribune Magazine*, Riverview for a long time "remained a haven," while the rest of the city seemed to descend into "increasing crime, fear, despair and violence. . . . But inexorably, its natural defenses began to crumble. Racial tension increased in Chicago and soon ran rampant inside the park. When the first riots flared in Chicago, Riverview closed for a few days, unannounced." When it reopened, park officials began to leave the lights on in "Aladdin's Castle." It was too late. Parents fearful that the acceptable level of danger, sexuality, and disorder would be surpassed with the addition of thousands of black teenagers, forbade their children to visit the park. Riverview closed its doors forever in 1967.[32]

Two years before, Olympic Park outside Newark had similarly shut down after a group of black teenagers reportedly went on a rampage in the park and the neighboring residential community. The Town Council in Irvington, where the park was located, voted immediately not to renew its license. Mrs. Mary Pilart, a member of the Council, announced that she had voted against renewal because "she felt property and life in the area around the park were in danger." Olympic Park was permitted to stay open for the remainder of the season. It was sold in the fall of 1965 to real estate developers.[33]

The last year for Steeplechase on Coney Island was also 1965. When asked by a *New York Times* reporter in June 1964 to explain the reasons for the decline in visitors to Coney after so many glorious years, concessionaires cited a variety of reasons, including "unsafe subways," "teen-age hoodlums," "bad weather," and "inadequate parking." First in the list, however, was the "growing influx of Negro visitors to the area. Once a small minority," reported the *New York Times*, "they now comprise half the weekend tourists, and the concessionaires believe that the presence of Negroes has discouraged some white persons from visiting the area."[34]

Even where there were no confrontations or only minimal and sporadic disruptions, some white patrons stayed away from the parks because they were now desegregated. As the marketing director of Cedar Point in Ohio explained, "Many traditional patrons of the country's amusement parks did not feel comfortable sharing their amusement park experience with minorities." By 1966, Bay Shore Park in Baltimore, Playland Park in Houston, and Glen Echo in Washington, D.C., closed down permanently. In 1969, Euclid Beach Park in Cleveland, which had only recently been desegregated, shut its doors.[35]

The amusement parks that survived were those like Kennywood outside Pittsburgh, Cedar Point in Sandusky, Ohio, and Conneaut Lake Park in western Pennsylvania that were not linked to the central city by mass transit. They were joined by an entirely new species of amusement resort, the suburban or exurban theme parks modeled on Disneyland in Anaheim, California. Unlike the older amusement parks, Disneyland and the theme parks were clean, secure, and orderly. Gone were the clutter, the unpredictability, the gap-toothed, slightly sinister-looking carnival workers, the aura of sensuality and of danger. Unlike the amusement parks that radiated excitement with their glittering lights shining for miles beyond their gates, the theme parks were situated off major highways, "surrounded by buffer zones of vegetation," or as in Anaheim, by a twenty-foot earthen wall. Their entrances were not simply inconspicuous. They were, like the entryways to the Bonaventura Hotel, which Frederick Jameson characterized as emblematic of the "postmodern" era, "backdoor affairs," almost deliberately obscured from public view as if announcing that the space within did "not wish to be a part of the city." According to Judith Adams, author of the most comprehensive history of American amusement parks, the decision to build the new theme parks outside the cities was far from coincidental. "Disneyland's location beyond the Los Angeles urban area, with no mass transit connections to the city, isolated it from the unruly and poorer elements of the urban population. Thus predominately middle- and upper-class clientele was ensured. . . . Later theme parks copied Disneyland's features, especially its location beyond the reach of urban transportation systems."[36]

To guard further against an influx of the wrong sort of revelers, the suburban amusement and theme parks, after experimenting with a variety of pricing strategies, adopted a one-price admission policy. Customers were charged a flat fee at the gate and nothing additional for rides and shows. The size of the admission fee, which, according to *Newsweek,* was already "fairly stiff" in 1973, continued to increase in the years that followed, until by 1993, Walt Disney World in Orlando was charging $35 for a one-day pass, $125 for four days. Teenagers and working people without the price of admission or cars to get to the park were shut out entirely. The result was a remarkably homogeneous— and safe—population of grandparents, parents, and children. Gone were the huge numbers of teenagers and young adults that had been such an important part of the amusement park crowd. According to Judith Adams, the latest available demographic breakdown on Disney World's visitors, which are not unlike those at other theme parks, reveals that 2 percent of its visitors are laborers, 3 percent black, and 2 percent Hispanic. "Unlike Coney Island, where almost every reveler was a laborer, location ensures that the subway crowd has no access to Disney's world."[37]

⊷⊷⇒◎⇐⊷⊷

So ended the era that began with such enormous promise when the city lights were turned on in the 1890s. We no longer "go out" as much as we once did. The newest, most technologically advanced amusement sites are our living rooms. There is less "need" to leave the home to be amused when telephone lines, cable boxes, computer terminals, videos, and compact discs can bring so much entertainment into our living rooms—at so little cost and inconvenience. As the public amusement realm is year by year impoverished, the domestic one is enriched.

The public amusement centers that survive and prosper are those that have been reconceived, repackaged, and transported out of town. The symbol of public sociability in the late twentieth century is not the picture palace or amusement park, but the enclosed shopping mall. Unlike the turn-of-the-century amusement sites, the mall exists not to assemble a public for collective amusement but to dissociate it into discrete consumers. Monuments of safety, guarded by private police and security systems, removed from the streets and inaccessible by mass transit, the malls are located outside the metropolis in a privatized space all their own. As Margaret Crawford has written, "Many malls now clarify the extent of their public role by posting signs that read:

'Areas in this mall used by the public are not public ways, but are for the use of the tenants and the public transacting business with them. Permission to use said areas may be revoked at any time.'"[38]

While the cities remain tourist attractions and places of fun, especially for foreigners who travel here to feast off a weakened dollar, they no longer sparkle as they once did. The lights are dimmer, the crowds thinner, less joyous, and more frightened-looking. "Downtown" appears to have disappeared entirely as a geographic and conceptual location, transmuted instead, as the sociologist Sharon Zukin has written, into a "fluid" space with no discernible boundaries. The "Loop" in Chicago has "multiplied fourfold in size" to the point where it has lost all geographic distinctness. According to *New York* magazine, "downtown" is no longer a place, but "a style, a sensibility, a state of mind."[39]

The displacement of "downtown" and the vanishing of its public entertainment sites has robbed the cities of more than revenues and tourists. It threatens to entomb them once again in the shadows that the electrically lit Great White Ways lifted at the turn of the century. The cities and their leaders have responded with bond issues, tax incentives, and all the moral and fiscal support they can muster to "revitalize" their downtowns by building ballparks, civic centers, and "festival marketplaces." New baseball stadia have been built in downtown Chicago, Baltimore, and Buffalo. Large and small cities have shining enclosed shopping-and-amusement centers such as Faneuil Hall and Quincy Market in Boston, or plans to build them. And there remain the thousands of dreamers and a few entrepreneurs with their own schemes to bring baseball back to Brooklyn and Steeplechase Park back to Coney.

No society can prosper without centers of civility and public sociability. This is the role that the cities and their amusement centers have always played. The turn-of-the-century theaters, parks, and palaces assembled the city's white people into a republic of pleasure seekers. What we require today is a new generation of spectacular and accessible public amusements to do the same for all the city's people, to bring us together once again into what the journalist Edwin Slosson in 1904 referred to as that "ordinary American crowd, the best natured, best dressed, best behaving and best smelling crowd in the world."[40]

LIST OF ABBREVIATIONS

The following sources are abbreviated throughout the notes:

BECHS	Buffalo and Erie County Historical Society, Buffalo, New York.
BRTC-NYPL	Billy Rose Theatre Collection, The New York Public Library at Lincoln Center, New York.
CCC-CHS	City Club of Chicago Records, Archives and Manuscripts Department, Chicago Historical Society, Chicago.
CF-NYPL	Records of the Committee of Fourteen, Rare Books and Manuscripts Division, The New York Public Library, New York.
CHS	Chicago Historical Society Library, Chicago.
CSS-CU	Community Service Society Papers, Rare Book and Manuscripts Library, Columbia University, New York.
GK-NYPL	George Kleine Papers, Rare Books and Manuscripts Division, The New York Public Library, New York.
JPA-UIC	Juvenile Protective Association of Chicago Papers, Manuscript Collections, University of Illinois at Chicago.
JR-NYPL	Jacob A. Riis Neighborhood Settlement Papers, Rare Books and Manuscripts Division, The New York Public Library, New York.

KA-UI   Keith/Albee Collection, Special Collections Department, University of Iowa Libraries, Iowa City.

LW-CU   Lillian Wald Papers, Rare Books and Manuscripts Library, Columbia University, New York.

MA-NYC   Municipal Archives, New York City.

MM-CHS   Mary McDowell Papers, Archives and Manuscripts Department, Chicago Historical Society, Chicago.

MP-HU   Magnes Papers, Hebrew University, Jerusalem, Israel.

MPC-TE   Thomas A. Edison Papers, *Motion Picture Catalogs: By American Producers and Distributors, 1884–1908: A Microfilm Edition,* Frederick, Maryland.

NBR-NYPL   National Board of Review of Motion Picture Papers, Rare Books and Manuscripts Division, The New York Public Library, New York.

NYHS   New-York Historical Society Library, New York.

OH-CU   Oral History Collection, Columbia University, New York.

RG-HU   Raff and Gammon Collection, Manuscripts and Archives Department, Baker Library, Harvard University, Cambridge, Massachusetts.

RHARS-NYPL   Rodgers and Hammerstein Archives of Recorded Sound, The New York Public Library at Lincoln Center, New York.

SC-NYPL   Schomburg Center for Research in Black Culture, Manuscripts, Archives, and Rare Books Division, The New York Public Library, New York.

NOTES

Chapter 1. Introduction

1. "Wideopenness," editorial, *New York Times,* January 28, 1899, 6.
2. The 1869 figure for New York City is found in, "Our Theatres," February 10, 1869, newspaper clipping in Robinson Locke Collection, vol. 78, Billy Rose Theatre Collection, The New York Public Library (hereafter abbreviated as BRTC-NYPL). On New York City theaters, see *The Theatre* I (July 1901), 8; and Michael M. Davis, *The Exploitation of Pleasure: A Study of Commercial Recreations in New York City* (New York, n.d.), 21, 25, 26, 36. On San Francisco in 1912, see Commonwealth Club of California, "Public Recreation," *Transactions* VIII, no. 5 (June 1913), 227; on San Francisco in 1870, see Edmond M. Gagey, *The San Francisco Stage: A History* (New York, 1950), 102–3, 107–8.
3. On world's fair attendance, see Robert W. Rydell, *All the World's a Fair: Visions of Empire at American International Expositions, 1876–1916* (Chicago, 1984), 40, 102, 124, 155; John Allwood, *The Great Exhibitions* (London, 1977), 179–85. For Coney Island, see the *New York Times,* May 17, 1909, 8; for the Disney parks, Judith A. Adams, *The Great Amusement Park Industry: A History of Technology and Thrills* (Boston, 1991), 134–35.
4. Sam Bass Warner, Jr., *The Urban Wilderness: A History of the American City* (New York, 1972), 70; Arthur Meier Schlesinger, *The Rise of the City: 1878–1898* (New York, 1933), 287–88; U.S. Department of Commerce, Bureau of the Census, *Historical Statistics of the United States: Colonial Times to 1970,* Part One (Washington, D.C., 1975), 165, 168, 211.

5. Roy Rosenzweig, *Eight Hours for What We Will: Workers and Leisure in an Industrial City, 1870–1920* (Cambridge, Eng., 1983), 1. See also Steven Ross, *Workers on the Edge: Work, Leisure, and Politics in Industrializing Cincinnati, 1788–1890* (New York, 1985); and Francis G. Couvares, *The Remaking of Pittsburgh: Class and Culture in an Industrializing City, 1877–1919* (Albany, N.Y., 1984).

6. On the changing conception of play in the late nineteenth century, see Daniel T. Rodgers, *The Work Ethic in Industrial America, 1850–1920* (Chicago, 1978), 94–124 (the citation is from 108). The final citation is from Andrew R. Heinze, *Adapting to Abundance: Jewish Immigrants, Mass Consumption, and the Search for American Identity* (New York, 1990), 130.

7. Alba M. Edwards, *Sixteenth Census Reports: Comparative Occupation Statistics for the United States, 1879–1940* (Washington, D.C., 1943), 91, 110, 112, 119, 121; U.S. Bureau of the Census, *Fourteenth Census, Vol. 4: Population* (Washington, D.C., 1922), 1068–71, 1076–80, 1099–1101, 1123–25, 1140–44, 1154–57, 1226–30. Comparable figures for New York City were 22 percent; Des Moines, 23 percent; San Francisco, 21 percent; Milwaukee, 20 percent; Buffalo, 19 percent; New Orleans, 17 percent; and Kansas City, 16 percent.

8. Stuart M. Blumin, *The Emergence of the Middle Class: Social Experience in the American City, 1760–1900* (Cambridge, Eng., 1989), 270–75, 283; Robert S. Lynd and Helen Merrell Lynd, *Middletown: A Study in Modern American Culture* (New York, 1929), 53.

9. George G. Foster, *New York by Gas-Light and Other Urban Sketches*, ed. Stuart M. Blumin (1850; Berkeley, 1990), 69. See also Michael Denning, *Mechanic Accents: Dime Novels and Working-Class Culture in America* (New York, 1987), 85–117.

10. Theodore Dreiser, *Sister Carrie* (1900; New York, 1981), 10, 90–91, 140.

11. Harold L. Platt, *The Electric City: Energy and the Growth of the Chicago Area, 1880–1930* (Chicago, 1991), 91; David E. Nye, *Electrifying America: Social Meanings of a New Technology, 1880–1940* (Cambridge, Mass., 1990), 49; Richard Rudolph and Scott Ridley, *Power Struggle: The One Hundred Year War over Electricity* (New York, 1986), 36; Jon C. Teaford, *The Unheralded Triumph: City Government in America, 1870–1900* (Baltimore, 1984), 230; Wolfgang Schivelbusch, *Disenchanted Night: The Industrialization of Light in the Nineteenth Century*, trans. Angela Davies (Berkeley, 1988), 73.

12. Schivelbusch, *Disenchanted Night*, 142, 148. I have rearranged his phrases in constructing the first quotation.

13. Richard Harding Davis, "Broadway," in *The Great Streets of the World* (New York, 1892), 26.

14. On nineteenth-century practices, see Mary Ryan, *Cradle of the Middle Class: The Family in Oneida County, New York, 1790–1865* (Cambridge, Eng., 1981), 116–32; for Providence, Rhode Island, see also John S. Gilkeson, Jr., *Middle-Class Providence, 1820–1940* (Princeton, N.J., 1986), 65–94; John Allen Corcoran, "The City Light and Beautiful," *The American City* VII (July 1912), 46–47.

15. Nye, *Electrifying America,* x, 50–51, 60.

16. *The Four-Track News* VI (February 1904), 121.

17. Charles W. Cheape, *Moving the Masses: Urban Public Transit in New York, Boston, and Philadelphia, 1880–1912* (Cambridge, Mass., 1980), 6, 7, 208, 213–14; Mark S. Foster, *From Streetcar to Superhighway: American City Planners and Urban Transportation 1900–1940* (Philadelphia, 1981), 14.

18. Nye, *Electrifying America,* 112; Warner, Jr., *Urban Wilderness,* 109–10.

19. Nye, *Electrifying America,* 119–120.

Chapter 2. Dollar Theaters, Concert Saloons, and Dime Museums

1. David Grimsted, *Melodrama Unveiled: American Theater and Culture 1800–1850* (Chicago, 1968), 53–54; George C. Foster, *New York by Gas-Light and Other Urban Sketches,* ed. Stuart M. Blumin (1850; Berkeley, 1990), 154–55; Walt Whitman, *November Boughs,* cited in Luc Sante, *Low Life: Lures and Snares of Old New York* (New York, 1991), 74.

2. Foster, *New York by Gas-Light,* 154. On prostitutes in the theater, see Ruth Rosen, *The Lost Sisterhood: Prostitution in America, 1900–1918* (Baltimore, 1982), 83–84; Claudia D. Johnson, "That Guilty Third Tier: Prostitutes in Nineteenth-Century American Theaters," *American Quarterly* XXVII (December 1975), 575–84; and, for a discussion of the place and role of prostitutes in the larger realm of nineteenth-century commercial amusements, Timothy J. Gilfoyle, *City of Eros: New York City, Prostitution, and the Commercialization of Sex, 1790–1920* (New York, 1992).

3. Grimsted, *Melodrama,* 53.

4. Lawrence W. Levine, *Highbrow/Lowbrow: The Emergence of Cultural Hierarchy in America* (Cambridge, Mass., 1988), 21–22.

5. Levine, *Highbrow,* 63–65. On the riot and nineteenth-century theater, see also Peter Buckley, "To the Opera House: Culture and Society in New York City, 1820–1860" (Ph.D. diss., State University of New York at Stony Brook, 1984).

6. Grimsted, *Melodrama,* 75.

7. Francis G. Couvares, "The Triumph of Commerce: Class Culture and Mass Culture in Pittsburgh," in *Working-Class America: Essays on Labor, Community, and American Society,* ed. Michael H. Frisch and Daniel Walkowitz (Urbana, Ill., 1983), 142–43. For a fuller discussion of the bifurcation of the theater audience in the 1880s, see Levine, *Highbrow,* 13–81.

8. For theater prices, I have consulted programs for assorted New York and Boston theaters, in clipping files, BRTC-NYPL; the Globe Theatre program, January 1886, is located in the Robinson Locke Collection, vol. 33, p. 15, BRTC-NYPL. Prices for minstrel theaters are from "Minstrels: U.S.: 1887," clipping file, BRTC-NYPL. The figures on average nonfarm daily earnings and hourly wages come from the United States Department of Commerce, Bureau of the Census, *Historical Statistics of the United States: Colonial Times to 1970,* Part One (Washington, D.C., 1975), 165, 168.

9. George C. D. Odell, *Annals of the New York Stage. Vol. VIII:. 1865–1870*

(New York, 1936), 586–650; Mary C. Henderson, *The City and the Theatre: New York Playhouses from Bowling Green to Times Square* (Clifton, N.J., 1973), 110–11.

10. Douglas Gilbert, *American Vaudeville: Its Life and Times* (New York, 1940), 113–14; Glenn Hughes, *A History of the American Theatre: 1700–1950* (New York, 1951), 199; Francis Couvares, *The Remaking of Pittsburgh: Class and Culture in an Industrializing City, 1877–1914* (Albany, N.Y., 1984), 39.

11. On concert saloons and variety theaters, see Joe Laurie, Jr., *Vaudeville: From the Honky-Tonks to the Palace* (New York, 1953), 10–11; Robert W. Snyder, *The Voice of the City: Vaudeville and Popular Culture in New York* (New York, 1989), 7–25; Gilbert, *American Vaudeville*, 10–100. The Spokane incident is from the *Spokane Falls Review,* March 5, 1891, cited in Eugene Clinton Elliott, "A History of Variety-Vaudeville in Seattle: From the Beginning to 1914," *University of Washington Publications in Drama,* no. 1 (Seattle, 1944), 23.

12. On English music halls, see Peter Bailey, *Leisure and Class in Victorian England: Rational Recreation and the Contest for Control, 1830–1885* (London, 1978), chap. 7 and conclusion; Gareth Stedman Jones, "Working-Class Culture and Working-Class Politics in London, 1870–1900: Notes on the Remaking of a Working Class," in *Languages of Class* (Cambridge, Eng., 1983), 204–8.

13. James D. McCabe, Jr., *New York by Sunlight and Gaslight* (New York, 1882), 614; *Stranger's Guide to the Garden City* (Chicago, 1883).

14. Mary Ryan, *Cradle of the Middle Class: The Family in Oneida County, New York, 1790–1865* (Cambridge, Eng., 1981), 147, 181. See also Stuart M. Blumin, *The Emergence of the Middle Class: Social Experience in the American City, 1760–1900* (Cambridge, Eng., 1989), 1–16, 258–97.

15. Paul Boyer, *Urban Masses and Moral Order in America: 1890–1920* (Cambridge, Mass., 1978), 156; on middle-class families and their children in residence, see Ryan, *Cradle,* 155–85; Richard Sennett, *Families against the City: Middle-Class Homes of Industrial Chicago, 1872–1890* (New York, 1974), 52–53, 224.

16. Brooks McNamara, "'A Congress of Wonders': The Rise and Fall of the Dime Museum," *Emerson Society Quarterly* 20 (Third Quarter 1974), 220–21.

17. Gilbert, *American Vaudeville*, 20–24; McNamara, "Congress," 228–29; Roland Lynde Hartt, *People at Play* (Boston, 1909), 87–112.

18. The quotation is from an 1850 American Museum program, cited by McNamara, "Congress," 218.

19. Roger Brett, *Temples of Illusion* (East Providence, R.I., 1976), 49; McNamara, "Congress," 222; Sante, *Low Life,* 97–100.

Chapter 3. "Something for Everybody" at the Vaudeville Theater

1. Albert F. McLean, Jr., "Genesis of Vaudeville: Two Letters from B. F. Keith," *Theatre Survey* I (1960), 90–91; Robert Snyder, *The Voice of the City: Vaudeville and Popular Culture in New York* (New York, 1989), 26–27; "The Profits in Clean Vaudeville," *The Literary Digest* (October 7,

1911), 603. For the July 6 program, see "Theatres: U.S.: Boston: Keith and Batchellor," clipping file, BRTC-NYPL.

2. Gunther Barth, *City People: The Rise of Modern City Culture in Nineteenth-Century America* (New York, 1980), 204–5; B. F. Keith, "The Vogue of Vaudeville" (1895), in *American Vaudeville as Seen by Its Contemporaries*, ed. Charles W. Stein (New York, 1984), 15–16.

3. Walter Prichard Eaton, "The Wizards of Vaudeville," *McClure's* (September 1918), 45.

4. Douglas Gilbert, *American Vaudeville: Its Life and Times* (New York, 1940), 200.

5. McClean, Jr., "Genesis," 84–85, 90, 94; Roger Brett, *Temples of Illusion* (East Providence, R.I., 1976), 56.

6. On Hollis Street Theatre and Globe Theatre prices, see Robinson Locke Collection, vols. 33 and 79, BRTC-NYPL.

7. Snyder, *Voice of the City*, 29–30; "Catalogue," Gaiety Musee and Bijou Theatre, 4, BRTC-NYPL.

8. Brett, *Temples*, 83. See clipping books, Pawtucket, R.I., Keith's Theatre and Scenic Music Hall, October 1903–May 1924, vol. 1, Keith/Albee Collection, Special Collections Department, University of Iowa Libraries, Iowa City, Iowa (hereafter abbreviated as KA-UI).

9. Clipping books, Pawtucket, R.I., Keith's Theatre and Scenic Music Hall, October 1903–May 1924, vol. 1, KA-UI.

10. Joe Laurie, Jr., *Vaudeville: From the Honky-Tonks to the Palace* (New York, 1953), 366. For more on Proctor, see William Mouton Marston and John Henry Feller, *F. F. Proctor: Vaudeville Pioneer* (New York, 1943).

11. Edward F. Albee, "Twenty Years of Vaudeville" (1923), in Stein, *American Vaudeville*, 215.

12. The descriptions of these acts are taken from the programs for Tony Pastor's Opera House, in Townsend Walsh Collection, BRTC–NYPL, and Morgan's Variety Theater in Tacoma, Washington, in Eugene Clinton Elliott, "A History of Variety-Vaudeville in Seattle from the Beginning to 1914," *University of Washington Publications in Drama*, no. 1 (Seattle, 1944), 23.

13. Snyder, *Voice of the City*, 131–32.

14. Edwin Milton Royle, "The Vaudeville Theatre," *Scribner's Magazine* 26 (October 1899), 487.

15. Kathy Peiss, *Cheap Amusements: Working Women and Leisure in Turn-of-the-Century New York* (Philadelphia, 1986), 8, 57.

16. Peiss, *Cheap Amusements*, 142; Parker Zellers, *Tony Pastor: Dean of the Vaudeville Stage* (Ypsilanti, Mich., 1971), 61; Gilbert, *American Vaudeville*, 112. On prostitutes in the theater, see Claudia D. Johnson, "That Guilty Third Tier: Prostitutes in Nineteenth-Century American Theaters," *American Quarterly* XXVII (December 1975), 575–84; and Timothy J. Gilfoyle, *City of Eros: New York City, Prostitution, and the Commercialization of Sex, 1790–1920* (New York, 1992), 107–11.

17. Felix Isman, *Weber and Fields: Their Tribulations, Triumphs and Their Associates* (New York, 1924), 207–8. On Tony Pastor, see Laurie, Jr., *Vaudeville*, 333–37, and Zellers, *Pastor*, 45–46.

18. Peiss, *Cheap Amusements*, 34, 57; Elizabeth Ewen, *Immigrant Women in*

the Land of Dollars: Life and Culture on the Lower East Side, 1890–1925 (New York, 1985), 94–109; Louise Montgomery, *The American Girl in the Stockyards District* (Chicago, 1913), 31–32.

19. Joanne J. Meyerowitz, *Women Adrift: Independent Wage Earners in Chicago, 1880–1930* (Chicago, 1988), 4, 5, 101–3.

20. Peiss, *Cheap Amusements,* 143; Commonwealth Club of California, "Public Recreation," in *Transactions* VIII, no. 5 (June 1913), 233, 239; City Club of Milwaukee, *Amusements and Recreation in Milwaukee* (Milwaukee, 1914), 26.

21. Report from Philadelphia, October 13, 1902, in "Report Books, 1902–1923," KA-UI. On ballplayers in vaudeville, see Laurie, Jr., *Vaudeville,* 118–32. On boxers, see William A. Brady, *Showman* (New York, 1937), 83. On women as boxing fans, see Charles Musser, *Before the Nickelodeon: Edwin S. Porter and the Edison Manufacturing Company* (Berkeley, 1991), 44.

22. On Nesbit and the "shooting stars," see Abel Green and Joe Laurie, Jr., *Show Biz: From Vaude to Video* (New York, 1951), 18, 20. On Pantages, see Theodore Saloutos, "Alexander Pantages, Theatre Magnate of the West," *Pacific Northwest Quarterly* 57 (October 1966), 145.

23. On Proctor, see Robert C. Allen, "Vaudeville and Film 1895–1915: A Study in Media Interaction" (Ph.D. diss., University of Iowa, 1977), 41–42, and Laurie, Jr., *Vaudeville,* 365–70. On "dignity acts" in general, see Laurie, Jr., *Vaudeville,* 404–5; B. F. Keith, "The Vogue of Vaudeville," in Stein, *American Vaudeville,* 18; Gilbert, *American Vaudeville,* 156–58.

24. *New York Dramatic Mirror* (April 24, 1897), 12; William Morris, "Vaudeville—Past and Present," *Billboard* (December 11, 1909), 24.

25. On the Boston palace, see "B. F. Keith's New Theatre Boston Mass," in "Theatres: U.S.: Boston: Keith," clipping file, BRTC-NYPL.

26. On the Philadelphia palace, see advertising circular, "Keith's New Theater," vol. 7 (1902), in "Theatres: U.S.: Philadelphia: Keith," clipping file, BRTC-NYPL.

27. Eaton, "Wizards of Vaudeville," 46–47.

28. Allen, "Vaudeville and Film," 202–6; Laurie, Jr., *Vaudeville,* 237–49; Snyder, *Voice of the City,* 82–103.

29. Albert F. McLean, Jr., *American Vaudeville as Ritual* (Lexington, Ky., 1965), 52; "1910 Survey for National Board of Censorship, of People's Institute," Jacob A. Riis Neighborhood Settlement Papers, Box 8: Miscellaneous Papers—Motion Picture and Vaudeville Shows, Rare Books and Manuscripts Division, The New York Public Library (hereafter abbreviated as JR-NYPL); Commonwealth Club of California, "Public Recreation," 234.

30. Ethel Waters, with Charles Samuels, *His Eye Is on the Sparrow* (New York, 1951), 124; see also John E. Di Meglio, *Vaudeville USA* (Bowling Green, Ohio, 1973), 116; E. Franklin Frazier, "Recreation and Amusement among American Negroes: A Research Memorandum" (New York, 1940), 51–52, in Carnegie Corporation of New York, *Carnegie-Myrdal Research Memoranda, 1935–1953,* Manuscripts, Archives, and Rare Books Division, Schomburg Center for Research in Black Culture, The

New York Public Library (hereafter abbreviated as SC-NYPL); Edward Renton, *The Vaudeville Theatre: Building, Operation, Management* (New York, 1915), 15.

31. Warren Susman, "'Personality' and Twentieth-Century Culture," in *Culture as History: The Transformation of American Society in the Twentieth Century* (New York, 1984), 280–81.

32. Henry James, *The American Scene* (1907; New York, 1968), 103.

33. Renton, *Vaudeville Theatre*, 134, 238–39. See also the 1890 program from Cordray's Theater in Seattle, in *The Story of Seattle's Early Theaters*, comp. Howard F. Grant (Seattle, 1934), 37.

34. Snyder, *Voice of the City*, 30; Richard Sennett, *The Fall of Public Man: On the Social Psychology of Capitalism* (New York, 1977), 206.

35. Royle, "Vaudeville Theater," 495.

Chapter 4. "The Best Smelling Crowd in the World"

1. Jack Poggi, *Theater in America: The Impact of Economic Forces: 1870–1967* (Ithaca, N.Y., 1968), 47; Robert Toll, *The Entertainment Machine: American Show Business in the Twentieth Century* (New York, 1982), 6; Glenn Hughes, *A History of the American Theater 1700–1900* (New York, 1951), 320. The numbers I have quoted are from Robert Toll who gets his figures from Hughes, 228. Poggi, 6, estimates the number of touring "combination" companies at about 100 in 1876–1877 and 420 in 1904.

2. *Theatre Magazine* 4 (April 1904), 90.

3. On this earlier period, see David Grimsted, *Melodrama Unveiled: American Theater and Culture: 1800–1850* (Chicago, 1968), 24–35; Robert A. M. Stern, Gregory Gilmartin, and John Massengale, *New York 1900: Metropolitan Architecture and Urbanism 1890–1915* (New York, 1984), 206; M. Christine Boyer, *Manhattan Manners: Architecture and Style: 1850–1900* (New York, 1985), 65–66; Frank H. Brooks, "Architecture in Its Relation to the Theater," *Dramatic Mirror* (December 22, 1917), 7, 9.

4. *New-York Tribune* (October 23, 1882), in William C. Young, *Documents of American Theater History. Vol. I. Famous American Playhouses, 1716–1899* (Chicago, 1973), 224.

5. Stern et al., *New York 1900*, 206.

6. William Wood Register, Jr., "New York's Gigantic Toy," in *Inventing Times Square: Commerce and Culture at the Crossroads of the World*, ed. William R. Taylor (New York, 1991), 247–49.

7. Marian Spitzer, "Ten-Twenty-Thirty: The Passing of the Popular Priced Circuit," *Saturday Evening Post* CXCVIII (August 22, 1925), 40–48.

8. Arthur Ruhl, "Ten-Twenty-Thirty," *Outlook* 98 (August 19, 1911), 887, 891; John L. Fell, *Film and the Narrative Tradition* (Berkeley, 1974), 17.

9. On San Francisco, see Northern California Writers Project, *Famous Playhouses of San Francisco, Part Two*, in Works Progress Administration, *Theatre Research Series* XVI (1940), 189–90; Edmond M. Gagey, *The San Francisco Stage: A History* (New York, 1950), 172–74; George W. Bush, Jr., "The Old Chatterton: A Brief History of a Famous Old Opera House," *Journal of the Illinois State Historical Society* XXXVI (1943), 14; G. Harri-

son Orians, "The History of the Burt Theatre in Toledo," *Northwest Ohio Quarterly* 33 (Spring 1961), 79.

10. Harry Mawson, "In Stock," *Theatre Magazine* 18 (July 1913), 27–28; Ward Morehouse, *Matinee Tomorrow: Fifty Years of Our Theater* (New York, 1949), 133–35. One of the most successful of the stock companies was the one resident in the Castle Square Theatre in Boston. On this, see P. M. Stone, "An Outline History of the Castle Square Theater, Boston, 1894–1932," unpublished typescript (n.p., n.d.), BRTC-NYPL; and Charles Elwell French, *Six Years of Drama at the Castle Square Theater: May 3, 1897–May 3, 1903* (Boston, 1903).

11. These figures are derived from *Julius Cahn's Official Theatrical Guide,* 1896–1897 and 1909–1910 editions. For Chicago, see 133–47 in 1896–1897 edition, 219–33 in 1909–1910; Denver, 173–75 in 1896–1897, 265–67 in 1909–1910; Baltimore in 1909–1910, 153–61; Philadelphia, 137–52 in 1909–1910.

12. Elston J. Melton, *The First One-Hundred Years* (Boonville, Miss., 1957), 20.

13. "Revival of the Stock Company," *Theatre Magazine* 3 (February 1903), 38; George Esdras Bevans, *How Workingmen Spend Their Spare Time* (New York, 1913), 23; Louise Marion Bosworth, *The Living Wage of Women Workers: A Study of Incomes and Expenditures of 450 Women in the City of Boston* (New York, 1911), 88; Louise Bolard More, *Wage-Earners' Budgets: A Study of Standards and Cost of Living in New York City* (New York, 1907), 167–71.

14. John Gillin, *Wholesome Citizens and Spare Time,* in Cleveland Foundation, *Cleveland Recreation Survey* (Cleveland, 1918). The story of D. is found on pages 62–68; of F. on 71–76.

15. Hughes, *American Theater,* 332–34.

16. Nahma Sandrow, *Vagabond Stars: A World History of Yiddish Theater* (New York, 1986), 109–31; Irving Howe, *World of Our Fathers: The Journey of the East European Jews to America and the Life They Found and Made* (New York, 1976), 479–85; F. H. McLean, "Bowery Amusements," University Settlement Society, *Annual Report* (1899), 18; Twentieth Century Club of Boston, *The Amusement Situation in the City of Boston* (Boston, 1910), 7.

17. Walter Prichard Eaton, *The American Stage of To-Day* (Boston, 1908), 274–75; "Theatrecitis," *The Theatre* 4 (August 1904), 224.

18. George Jean Nathan, *The Popular Theatre* (New York, 1923), 227–33.

19. *New York Dramatic Mirror,* editorial (September 13, 1902), 14. On vaudeville and musical revues, see Julian Mates, *America's Musical Stage: Two Hundred Years of Musical Theatre* (Westport, Conn., 1985), 146–63.

20. E. J. Hobsbawm, *The Age of Empire: 1875–1914* (New York, 1989), 171–72, 180.

21. On the concept of "contradictory locations," see Erik Olin Wright, *Classes* (London, 1985), 19–63; and Erik Olin Wright et al., *The Debate on Classes* (London, 1989), 24–31.

22. Ilene A. DeVault, *Sons and Daughters of Labor: Class and Clerical Work in Turn-of-the-Century Pittsburgh* (Ithaca, N.Y., 1990), 177.

23. E. P. Hutchinson, *Immigrants and Their Children: 1850–1950* (New York, 1956), 201–5; Roy Rosenzweig, *Eight Hours for What We Will: Workers and Leisure in an Industrial City, 1870–1920* (Cambridge, Eng., 1983), 28; James Gilbert, *Perfect Cities: Chicago's Utopias of 1893* (Chicago, 1991), 30. For department store workers, see also Susan Porter Benson, *Counter Cultures: Saleswomen, Managers, and Customers in American Department Stores: 1890–1940* (Urbana, Ill., 1988), 209, and for white-collar workers in general, Stuart M. Blumin, *The Emergence of the Middle Class: Social Experience in the American City, 1760–1900* (Cambridge, Eng., 1989), 295–96.

24. DeVault, *Sons and Daughters*, 21–23, 173; Blumin, *Emergence of the Middle Class*, 291.

25. David Nasaw, *Children of the City: At Work and at Play* (New York, 1985); Kathy Peiss, *Cheap Amusements: Working Women and Leisure in Turn-of-the-Century New York* (Philadelphia, 1986), 6; Lizabeth Cohen, *Making a New Deal: Industrial Workers in Chicago, 1919–1939* (Cambridge, Eng., 1990), 144–45. On immigrant women and theater attendance, see also Sue Ainslie Clark and Edith Wyatt, *Making Both Ends Meet: The Income and Outlay of New York Working Girls* (New York, 1911), 61.

26. Victor Turner, *From Ritual to Theatre: The Human Seriousness of Play* (New York, 1982), 51.

27. Edwin E. Slosson, "The Amusement Business," *Independent* 59 (July 21, 1904), 135.

Chapter 5. The "Indecent" Others

1. On the subject of Chinese cultural and residential insularity, see Ronald Takaki, *Strangers from a Different Shore: A History of Asian Americans* (New York, 1989), 112–31.

2. Henry James, *The American Scene* (1907; New York, 1968), 126–28.

3. Ray Stannard Baker, *Following the Color Line: American Negro Citizenship in the Progressive Era* (1908; New York, 1964), 147, 216, 297–98, 299–300.

4. Baker, *Color Line*, 120; Gilbert Osofsky, *Harlem: The Making of a Ghetto: Negro New York, 1890–1930* (New York, 1968), 41. Van Woodward, cited by Howard N. Rabinowitz, "More Than the Woodword Thesis: Assessing *The Strange Career of Jim Crow*," *Journal of American History* 75 (December 1988), 844; C. Van Woodward, "*Strange Career* Critics: Long May They Persevere," *Journal of American History* 75 (December 1988), 858. I have rearranged Woodward's quotation.

5. Mary Frances Berry and John W. Blassingame, *Long Memory: The Black Experience in America* (New York, 1982), 350; August Meier and Elliott Rudwick, *From Plantation to Ghetto*, 3d ed. (New York, 1976), 206; James R. Grossman, *Land of Hope: Chicago, Black Southerners, and the Great Migration* (Chicago, 1989), 118. On Chicago, see also Alan H. Spear, *Black Chicago: The Making of a Negro Ghetto: 1890–1920*

(Chicago, 1967), 41. On Detroit, see David M. Katzman, *Before the Ghetto: Black Detroit in the Nineteenth Century* (Urbana, Ill., 1973), 98–99.

6. Chicago Commission on Race Relations, *The Negro in Chicago: A Study of Race Relations and a Race Riot* (Chicago, 1922), 317–18.

7. Allen Woll, *Black Musical Theatre: From Coontown to Dreamgirls* (Baton Rouge, La., 1989), 40, 50–53.

8. *Crisis* II (May 1911), 6; IV (September 1912), 221; V (March 1913), 222; VII (January 1914), 116.

9. Grossman, *Land of Hope,* 117.

10. Henry T. Sampson, *The Ghost Walks: A Chronological History of Blacks in Show Business, 1865–1910* (Metuchen, N.J., 1988), 233; Spear, *Black Chicago,* 76. On the Pekin, see Sampson, *Ghost Walks,* 280–81, 383–84; and Henry T. Sampson, *Blacks in Blackface: A Source Book on Early Black Musical Shows* (Metuchen, N.J., 1980), 116.

11. Sampson, *Ghost Walks,* 348, 382.

12. *Indianapolis Freeman,* August 6, 1910, in Sampson, *Ghost Walks,* 523.

13. Mari Kathleen Fielder, "Wooing a Local Audience: The Irish-American Appeal of Philadelphia's Mae Desmond Players," in *Theatre History Studies* I (1981), 50–63. On the Yiddish theater, see Nahma Sandrow, *Vagabond Stars: A World History of Yiddish Theater* (New York, 1986), 80, 91–131, 251–54. On "national theaters" in New York City, see Michael Davis, *The Exploitation of Pleasure: A Study of Commercial Recreations in New York City* (New York, n.d.), 35–36.

14. Douglas Gilbert, *American Vaudeville: Its Life and Times* (New York, 1940), 61.

15. On "Makey and Stewart," see manager's report, New York, November 24, 1902, in Report Books, 1902–1923, KA-UI. For a good discussion of the "Jew comic" type in vaudeville and musical comedy, see Barbara W. Grossman, *Funny Girl: The Life and Times of Fanny Brice* (Bloomington, Ind., 1992), 22–23.

16. Robert W. Snyder, *The Voice of the City: Vaudeville and Popular Culture in New York, 1880–1930* (New York, 1989), 110; *New York Dramatic Mirror* LXIX (April 30, 1913), 8; Grossman, *Funny Girl,* 110–11.

17. Gilbert, *American Vandeville,* 251. On tramp acts, see Charles Musser, "Work, Ideology, and Chaplin's Tramp," in *Resisting Images: Essays on Cinema and History,* ed. Robert Sklar and Charles Musser (Philadelphia, 1990), 40. On Fields, see manager's report, New York, May 21, 1906, in Report Books, 1902–1923, KA-UI.

18. David R. Roediger, *The Wages of Whiteness: Race and the Making of the American Working Class* (London, 1991), 117–18.

19. George M. Walker, "The Real 'Coon' on the American Stage," *Theatre* VI (August 1906), 224–26. See also Sampson, *Ghost Walks,* 101; Sampson, *Blacks in Blackface,* 76–79; James Weldon Johnson, *Black Manhattan* (New York, 1930), 102–3, 108; Nathan Irvin Huggins, *Harlem Renaissance* (New York, 1971), 258–59.

20. Sam Dennison, *Scandalize My Name: Black Imagery in American Popular Music* (New York, 1982), 423; James H. Dormon, "Shaping the Popular Image of Post-Reconstruction American Blacks: The 'Coon Song' Phe-

nomenon of the Gilded Age," *American Quarterly* 40 (December 1988), 453.

21. J. Stanley Lemons, "Black Stereotypes as Reflected in Popular Culture, 1880–1920," *American Quarterly* 29 (Spring 1977), 104–5; Dennison, *Scandalize My Name*, 354. On the caricaturing of African Americans in material culture, see also Joseph Boskin, *Sambo: The Rise and Demise of an American Jester* (New York, 1986), 121–47.

22. On "violence" in the coon songs, see Ian Whitcomb, *Irving Berlin and Ragtime America* (New York, 1988), 109–15.

23. "I'm the Toughest, Toughest Coon" (1904), cited in Dennison, *Scandalize My Name*, 375.

24. Dormon, "Popular Image of American Blacks," 455; Andrew Sterling, "I've Got a White Man Working for Me" (1899), in Dormon, "Popular Image of American Blacks," 462.

25. Raymond Brown, "The Mormon Coon" (1905), in Dennison, *Scandalize My Name*, 357.

26. Sampson, *Ghost Walks*, 199, 230; for examples of black performers' comparisons of European and American audiences, see *Ghost Walks*, 123, 177.

27. Snyder, *Voice of the City*, 111; Sampson, *Blacks in Blackface*, 62–65; Sampson, *Ghost Walks*, 283–84, 403. For an example of a black performer playing a "Chinaman," see manager's report on the vaudeville team "Cook and Stevens," at the Colonial Theater, in Lawrence, Massachusetts, October 19, 1910, in Report books, 1902–1923, KA-UI.

28. Max Horkheimer and Theodor W. Adorno, *Dialectic of Enlightenment*, trans. John Cumming (New York, 1988), 141; Bert Williams, "The Comic Side of Trouble," *American Magazine* 85 (January 1918), 33–34.

29. The notion that "laughter is social" and requires the "human collective as the precondition" was also an important element in Renaissance theories of laughter. On this point, see Michael D. Bristol, *Carnival and Theater— Plebeian Culture and the Structure of Authority in Renaissance England* (New York, 1989), 125–39.

30. *Indianapolis Freeman*, April 2, 1904, cited in Sampson, *Ghost Walks*, 314–17.

31. Roediger, *Wages of Whiteness*, 97–100; "Coon Songs Must Go," cited in Dennison, *Scandalize My Name*, 448.

32. H. G. Wells, *The Future in America: A Search after Realities* (New York, 1906), 192–93.

33. Ibid., 186–87, 193–94.

Chapter 6. The City as Playground:
The World's Fair Midways

1. The term "vacation habit" is taken from Franklin Matthews, "Vacations for the Workers," *World's Work* 6 (June 1903), 3516–17. See also "Vacations for Everybody," *Outlook* 71 (May 1902), 303–4.

2. Edward Hungerford, "Our Summer Migration: A Social Study," *Century* 42 (August 1891), 569.

3. Robert S. Lynd and Helen Merrell Lynd, *Middletown: A Study in Modern American Culture* (New York, 1929), 262; *Facilities for the Use of Workers' Leisure during Holidays* (Geneva, 1939), 8–11, cited in Ivan Greenberg, "Class Culture and Generational Change: Immigrant Families in Two Connecticut Industrial Cities during the 1930's" (Ph.D. diss., City University of New York, 1990), 274.

4. "Vacations for Everybody," 304; Matthews, "Vacations," 3517–19; Roy Rosenzweig, *Eight Hours for What We Will: Workers and Leisure in an Industrial City, 1870–1920* (Cambridge, Eng., 1983), 68–69; Susan Porter Benson, *Counter Cultures: Saleswomen, Managers and Customers in American Department Stores, 1890–1940* (Urbana, Ill., 1986), 195.

5. Abraham Cahan, *The Rise of David Levinsky* (New York, 1917), 404; Theodore Dreiser, *The Color of a Great City* (New York, 1923), 120–21.

6. Mrs. George Archibald Palmer, "The Best Two Weeks' Vacation for a Family," *Ladies Home Journal* 21 (June 1904), 24; "The Best Two Weeks' Vacation for a Girl," *Ladies Home Journal* 21 (June 1904), 25.

7. On urban tourism in general, see John A. Jakle, *The Tourist: Travel in Twentieth-Century North America* (Lincoln, Nebr., 1985), 245–85. On the "boosting" of New York City, see Neil Harris, "Urban Tourism and the Commercial City," in *Inventing Times Square: Commerce and Culture at the Crossroads of the World*, ed. William R. Taylor (New York, 1991), 66–82. On the new literature of and about the city, see William R. Taylor, "The Launching of a Commercial Culture: New York City, 1860–1930," in *Power, Culture, and Place: Essays on New York City*, ed. John Hull Mollenkopf (New York, 1988), 107–33. On the weekly tourist guides, see, *The Amusement Bulletin* I (1889), BRTC-NYPL; and *Daily Attractions in New York* I (April 2–8, 1906).

8. John F. Sears, *Sacred Places: American Tourist Attractions in the Nineteenth Century* (New York, 1989), 10.

9. Taylor, "Launching of Commercial Culture," 117.

10. *The Four-Track News* VI (June 1904), 378–79; James Gilbert, *Perfect Cities: Chicago's Utopias of 1893* (Chicago, 1991), 58.

11. "A Vacation on Fifth Avenue," *Outlook* 83 (May 26, 1906), 203.

12. J. W. Buel, ed., *Louisiana and the Fair: An Exposition of the World, Its People, and Their Achievements*, vol. 10 (St. Louis, 1904), 3804. On the effects of the world's fairs, on tourism, see Harris, "Urban Tourism," 68–69.

13. On the Philadelphia "Centennial Exposition," see Robert W. Rydell, *All the World's a Fair: Visions of Empire at American International Expositions, 1876–1916* (Chicago, 1984), 9–37; and Thomas J. Schlereth, *Victorian America: Transformations in Everyday Life: 1876–1915* (New York, 1991), 1–5.

14. On the "Centennial City" shows, see Eno McCullough, *World's Fair Midways* (New York, 1966), 34–35; Rydell, *All the World's a Fair*, 33–35; Robert Bogdan, *Freak Show: Presenting Human Oddities for Amusement and Profit* (Chicago, 1988), 48.

15. Charles Rearick, *Pleasures of the Belle Epoque: Entertainment and Festivity in Turn-of-the-Century France* (New Haven, Conn., 1985), 89,

120–26, 134. The figures on Philadelphia attendance are from Rydell, *All the World's a Fair*, 10.

16. Rydell, *All the World's a Fair*, 38–71; Gilbert, *Perfect Cities*, 75–130; Alan Trachtenberg, *The Incorporation of America: Culture and Society in the Gilded Age* (New York, 1982), 208–34; John F. Kasson, *Amusing the Million: Coney Island at the Turn of the Century* (New York, 1978), 17–28; Neil Harris, *Cultural Excursions: Marketing Appetites and Cultural Tastes in Modern America* (Chicago, 1990), 111–31.

17. Buel, ed., *Louisiana and the Fair*, 3806; Mark Bennitt, *Bennitt Illustrated Souvenir Guide [to the] Pan American Exposition* (Buffalo, 1901), 18.

18. On the Chicago Midway, see McCullough, *World's Fair Midways*, 36–50; David F. Burg, *Chicago's White City of 1893* (Lexington, Ky., 1976), 216–25; Reid Badger, *The Great American Fair* (Chicago, 1979), 106–9; Gilbert, *Perfect Cities*, 109–21. The final quotations are from McCullough, *World's Fair Midways*, 48.

19. Terry Ramsaye, *A Million and One Nights: A History of the Motion Picture through 1925* (New York, 1926), 78–90; Gordon Hendricks, "The History of the Kinetoscope," in Tino Balio, ed., *The American Film Industry*, rev. ed. (Madison, 1985), 45–48; *Official Catalogue of Exhibits on the Midway Plaisance: World's Columbian Exposition Group 176* (Chicago, 1893), 10–11; Gene G. Kelkres, "A Forgotten First: The Armat-Jenkins Partnership and the Atlanta Projection," *Quarterly Review of Film Studies* 9 (Winter 1984), 50.

20. *Official Guide Book to Omaha, Trans-Mississippi and International Exposition* (Omaha, 1898), 32; Frederic Thompson, "The Making of Coney Island," *Bohemian* (June 1907), 783, in Robinson Locke Collection, envelope 2342A, BRTC-NYPL.

21. Bennitt, *Souvenir Guide*, 20; *Billboard* XIII (January 12, 1901), 100; *Billboard* XIII (March 2, 1901), 11; Rydell, *All the World's a Fair*, 144. For a description of Thompson's exhibit, see, "Midway Attractions for Good Roads Day," *Official Program of the Pan-American Exposition* (Buffalo, September 21, 1901); McCullough, *World's Fair Midway*, 54–56. See also Ralph Barton Diary, July 10 to July 14, 1901, 9–10, and Mabel E. Barnes Diaries, "Peeps at the Pan–American," vol. 3, pp. 152–53, in Buffalo and Erie County Historical Society, Buffalo, New York (hereafter abbreviated as BECHS).

22. See list of Pike concessionaires, in Thomas R. MacMechen, *The Pike* (St. Louis, 1904), 38–39. The official history was the one edited by J. W. Buel, *Louisiana and the Fair*. It was here that the figure of $10 million was quoted; other guidebooks, most published before the fair opened, reported that $5 million had been spent on the Pike concessions.

23. "Prospectus of the Jerusalem Exhibit Co.," 2, in uncataloged pamphlet collection on St. Louis World's Fair, Research Division, The New York Public Library; MacMechen, *The Pike*, 31–32.

24. Gilbert, *Perfect Cities*, 121. For attendance figures on the world's fairs, see Rydell, *All the World's a Fair*, 40, 124, 155; John Allwood, *The Great Exhibitions* (London, 1977), 179–85; Buel, ed., *Louisiana and the Fair*, 3809.

25. Rydell, *All the World's a Fair*, 192; Stanley Appelbaum, *The Chicago*

World's Fair of 1893: A Photographic Record with Text (New York, 1980), 5–6; Paul Nagel, "Twice to the Fair," *Chicago History* 14 (Spring 1985), 8, 12, 14.

26. On immigrant visitors and ethnic villages, see Gilbert, *Perfect Cities,* 77–78; Harris, *Cultural Excursions,* 51; MacMechen, *The Pike,* 1; McCullough, *World's Fair Midways,* 65.

27. *The Greatest of Expositions* (St. Louis, 1904), 248.

28. MacMechen, *The Pike,* 3, 11; *The Greatest of Expositions,* 242.

29. On Dreiser's visit to the fair, see Richard Lingeman, *Theodore Dreiser: At the Gates of the City: 1871–1907* (New York, 1986), 118–22; Gilbert, *Perfect Cities,* 76. On the Adams's entourage, see Nagel, "Twice to the Fair," 12; Henry Adams, *The Education of Henry Adams* (Boston, 1918), 339, 342.

30. Bennitt, *Souvenir Guide,* 3, 20; Rydell, *All the World's a Fair,* 148–49; Buel, ed., *Louisiana and the Fair,* 3810–11; Mabel Barnes Diaries, III, 71, BECHS.

31. Mabel Barnes Diaries, III, 84–85, BECHS.

32. Burg, *White City,* 219; Gilbert, *Perfect Cities,* 82, 115–17.

33. Rydell, *All the World's a Fair,* 174–76.

34. Quoted in Trachtenberg, *Incorporation of America,* 221.

35. William S. McFeely, *Frederick Douglass* (New York, 1991), 369.

36. McFeely, *Frederick Douglass,* 366–72; Trachtenberg, *Incorporation of America,* 220; Rydell, *All the World's a Fair,* 53.

37. Rydell, *All the World's a Fair,* 87, 119, 146–47.

38. Harris, *Cultural Excursions,* 123.

39. This is a central theme in James Gilbert's discussion of the Chicago World's Fair in *Perfect Cities,* which he appropriately subtitles, *Chicago's Utopias of 1893.*

40. On this point, see Trachtenberg, *Incorporation of America,* 217.

Chapter 7. "The Summer Show"

1. I take this chapter title from the article on Luna Park by Frederic Thompson, "The Summer Show," *The Independent* 62 (June 20, 1907), 1460–63.

2. On the first trolley parks, see David E. Nye, *Electrifying America: Social Meanings of a New Technology, 1880–1940* (Cambridge, Mass., 1990), 122–23; C. W. Waddell, "Park Attractions," *Street Railway Review* XIII (March 20, 1903), 142.

3. Jimmy Durante and Jack Kofoed, *Night Clubs* (New York, 1931), 48–49.

4. *Brooklyn Daily Eagle, A Visitor's Guide to the City of New York,* 2d ed. (New York, 1899), 29.

5. Julian Ralph, "Coney Island," *Scribner's Magazine* XX (July 1896), 16–17.

6. On Lake Quinsigamond, see Roy Rosenzweig, *Eight Hours for What We Will: Workers and Leisure in an Industrial City, 1870–1920* (Cambridge, Eng., 1983), 172–83; on Cedar Point, see David W. Francis and Diane DeMali Francis, *Cedar Point: The Queen of American Watering Places* (Canton, Ohio, 1988), 50.

7. Ralph, "Coney Island," 19.

8. "Parks and Pleasure Resorts," editorial, *Street Railway Journal* (February 23, 1907), 309–10.

9. Richard Snow, *Coney Island: A Postcard Journey to the City of Fire* (New York, 1984), 13–14, 77–78; Oliver Pilat and Jo Ranson, *Sodom by the Sea: An Affectionate History of Coney Island* (Garden City, N.Y., 1941), 146–47. According to Richard Snow, Thompson and Dundy claimed the park cost $2.5 million. Snow believes the true figure was much closer to $1 million. Pilat and Ranson put the figure at $700,000. In the discussion that follows on the mature Coney Island amusement parks, I have learned much from *Coney Island: A Documentary Film* (1991), produced by Ric Burns and written by Richard Snow.

10. Snow, *Coney Island*, 14; Frederic Thompson, "Amusing the Million," *Everybody's* XIX (September 1908), 385.

11. Rem Koolhaas, *Delirious New York: A Retroactive Manifesto for Manhattan* (New York, 1978), 29–30; Thompson, "The Summer Show," 1461; Albert Bigelow Paine, "The New Coney Island," *Scribner's Magazine* 68 (August 1904), 535; Robert E. Snow and David E. Wright, "Coney Island: A Case Study in Popular Culture and Technical Change," *Journal of Popular Culture* 9 (Spring 1976), 967.

12. Snow, *Coney Island*, 92–103; John F. Kasson, *Amusing the Million: Coney Island at the Turn of the Century* (New York, 1978), 82–86; Judith A. Adams, *The Great Amusement Park Industry: A History of Technology and Thrills* (Boston, 1991), 52.

13. Francis and Francis, *Cedar Point*, 41–51; Alan A. Siegel, *Smile, A Picture History of Olympic Park, 1887–1965* (Irvington, N.J., 1983), 13–15; Chuck Wlodarczyk, *Riverview: Gone but Not Forgotten: 1904–1967* (Chicago, 1977), 74.

14. Kasson, *Amusing the Million*, 59–61; Snow, *Coney Island*, 68–73; Lucy P. Gilman, "Coney Island," *New York History* 36 (July 1955), 274.

15. The language I have used to describe the amusement park is taken from the description of the "ideal" playground in Johan Huizinga, *Homo Ludens* (Boston, 1955), 8–10. The original German edition of the book was published in 1944.

16. Koolhaas, *Delirious New York*, 30; Francis and Francis, *Cedar Point*, 13.

17. Lee O. Bush, Edward C. Chukayne, Russell Allon Hehr, and Richard F. Hershey, *Euclid Beach Park Is Closed for the Season* (Fairview Park, Ohio, 1977), 39; *Cleveland Plain Dealer* ad cited in Bush et al., *Euclid Beach Park*, 39; Siegel, *Smile*, 21, 35.

18. Edward P. Hulse, "Laying Out an Ideal Inland Amusement Resort," *Street Railway Journal* XXIX (January 23, 1907), 317.

19. Thompson, "Amusing the Million," 385–86.

20. Cleveland Foundation, *Cleveland Recreation Survey: Commercial Recreation* (Cleveland, 1920), 113.

21. Rand McNally & Co., *Handy Guide to Philadelphia* (Chicago, 1904), 40; Promotional Brochure, 1907 season, and "Luna Park Souvenir & Guide Book," vol. 2 (1907), "Amusement Parks: U.S.: Scranton (PA): Luna Park," clipping file, BRTC-NYPL. For a picture of the Euclid Beach Park police force, see also Bush et al., *Euclid Beach Park*, 28. On liquor in the

parks, see Kathy Peiss, *Cheap Amusements: Working Women and Leisure in Turn-of-the-Century New York* (Philadelphia, 1986), 119; Adams, *Great Amusement Park Industry,* 59; *Street Railway Journal* XXXI (January 25, 1908), 104.

22. Thompson, "Amusing the Million," 380; "The Necessity for White City," *White City Magazine* I (March 1905), 11.

23. Kasson, *Amusing the Million,* 71–72; "Luna Park Souvenir Program" II (1907), "Amusement Parks: U.S.: Scranton (PA): Luna Park," clipping file, BRTC-NYPL.

24. Roland Lynde Hartt, *The People at Play* (New York, 1909), 67–68; Francis and Francis, *Cedar Point,* 51.

25. Edwin Slosson, "The Amusement Business," *The Independent* 59 (July 21, 1904), 135–36.

26. Slosson, "Amusement Business," 139; Hartt, *People at Play,* 78.

27. Joanne J. Meyerowitz, *Women Adrift: Independent Wage Earners in Chicago, 1880–1930* (Chicago, 1988), 102; Peiss, *Cheap Amusements,* 126–27; Francis and Francis, *Cedar Point,* 50. For a fuller discussion of "dating" and "treating," see chapter 9 on dance halls.

28. Hartt, *People at Play,* 81.

29. On the importance of catering to the "artistic" needs of amusement park patrons, see "The Necessity for White City," *White City Magazine* I (March 1905), 11.

30. "Official Program, Paragon Park, Nantasket Beach, June, 1905," n.p., in BRTC-NYPL.

31. Adams, *Great Amusement Park Industry,* 50–52; Pilat and Ranson, *Sodom by the Sea,* 191–200; "How Incubators Save Lives: Raising Infants Whose Existence Hangs by a Thread," *White City Magazine* I (March 1905), 20–23.

32. See, for example, the hundreds of photographs in Bush et al., *Euclid Beach Park.* Only the photographs on p. 72 from 1969 and p. 78 from 1968 show the presence of African Americans.

33. On the taboos against interracial dining, see Charles S. Johnson, *Patterns of Negro Segregation* (New York, 1943), 59–63, 143–45; on the segregation of swimming facilities, see Allan H. Spear, *Black Chicago: The Making of a Negro Ghetto: 1890–1920* (Chicago, 1967), 206.

34. Forrester B. Washington, "Recreational Facilities for the Negro," in American Academy of Political and Social Science, *Annals* CXXXX (November 1928), 276–77.

35. "Street Railway Parks in 1904," 177; Washington, "Recreational Facilities," 280–81.

36. Francis and Francis, *Cedar Point,* 51–52; *White City Magazine* III, (1907), 17.

37. Robert Bogdan, *Freak Show: Presenting Human Oddities for Amusement and Profit* (Chicago, 1988), 56–57; Kasson, *Amusing the Million,* 52; Pilat and Ranson, *Sodom by the Sea,* 175–79.

38. Henry T. Sampson, *The Ghost Walks: A Chronological History of Blacks in Show Business, 1865–1910* (Metuchen, N.J., 1988), 237.

39. Fred F. McClure, "Survey of Commercial Recreation of Kansas City,

Mo.," in *Second Annual Report of the Recreation Department of the Board of Public Welfare* (Kansas City, 1911–1912), 90, 93; Eddie Cantor, *My Life Is in Your Hands* (New York, 1928), 102–3; Wlodarczyk, *Riverview*, 53; Garry Cooper, "The World That Was at Belmont and Western," *Chicago Tribune Magazine* (May 16, 1976), 22; Joseph Sander, "Riverview: Wonderland on Western Avenue," *Chicago Magazine* (November 1983), 189; John Powers, "Requiem for Riverview," *Chicagoan* 1 (July 1974), 63–64.

40. Elmer Blaney Harris, "The Day of Rest at Coney Island," *Everybody's Magazine* XIX (July 1908), 28, 32–33.

41. *White City Magazine* I (February 1905), 13.

42. Adams, *Great Amusement Park Industry,* 134–35.

43. *New York Times,* May 17, 1909, 8; October 24, 1909, part 5, p. 7. The figures for Philadelphia, Columbus, and Los Angeles are found in "Street Railway Parks in 1904," *Street Railway Review* XIV (March 20, 1904), 178–80. For Chicago, Perry Duis and Glen E. Holt, "Bright Lights, Hard Times of White City," *Chicago Magazine* II (August 1978), 178; for Kansas City, McClure, "Commercial Recreation of Kansas City," 86.

44. James Huneker, *New Cosmopolis: A Book of Images* (New York, 1915), 159, 161, 168; Slosson, "Amusement Business," 135.

Chapter 8. The National Game

1. Steven A. Riess, *City Games: The Evolution of American Urban Society and the Rise of Sports* (Urbana, Ill., 1989), 223; Allen Guttmann, *Sports Spectators* (New York, 1986), 114–5.

2. Harold Seymour, *Baseball: The Early Years* (New York, 1960), 3, 56–58, 76–80.

3. Seymour, *Baseball: The Early Years,* 3, 203, 214; Walton H. Holmes, "To What Extent Should Street Railways Engage in the Amusement Business," *Street Railway Journal* XIV (October 1898), 642; *The Sporting News, Take Me Out to the Ball Park,* rev. 2d ed. (St. Louis, 1987), 94; "Street Railway Parks in 1904," *Street Railway Review* XIV (March 20, 1904), 177.

4. Bruce Kuklick, *To Every Thing a Season: Shibe Park and Urban Philadelphia, 1909–1976* (Princeton, N.J., 1991), 21–22; Harold Seymour, *Baseball: The Golden Age* (New York, 1971), 42, 53.

5. Riess, *City Games,* 197; Benjamin G. Rader, *American Sports: From the Age of Folk Games to the Age of Spectators* (Englewood Cliffs, N.J., 1983), 127 (I have rearranged the quotation from Rader); Johnnie Evers and Hugh S. Fullerton, *Baseball in the Big Leagues* (Chicago, 1910), 24, cited in Gunther Barth, *City People: The Rise of Modern City Culture in Nineteenth-Century America* (New York, 1980), 190.

6. Fred F. McClure, "Survey of Commercial Recreation of Kansas City, Mo.," in *Second Annual Report of the Recreation Department of the Board of Public Welfare* (Kansas City, 1911–1912), 84, 86.

7. Seymour, *Baseball: The Golden Age,* 68, 51; Cleveland Foundation, *Cleveland Recreation Survey: Commercial Recreation* (Cleveland, 1920),

128; Lawrence S. Ritter, *Lost Ballparks: A Celebration of Baseball's Legendary Fields* (New York, 1992), 20–21, 64, 93.

8. Seymour, *Baseball: The Early Years,* 326–27; Rader, *American Sports,* 121–22.

9. Report books, Cleveland, April 30, 1906, KA-UI.

10. Peter Levine, *A. G. Spalding and the Rise of Baseball: The Promise of American Sport* (New York, 1985), 45–46; Congress Hotel Company, *Where to Go and How* (June 1908), n.p., Chicago Historical Society Library (hereafter abbreviated as CHS).

11. George Lipsitz, *The Sidewalks of St. Louis: Places, People, and Politics in an American City* (Columbia, Mo., 1991), 58; Levine, *A. G. Spalding,* 51; Rader, *American Sports,* 116.

12. Seymour, *Baseball: The Early Years,* 198.

13. Riess, *City Games,* 103; Seymour, *Baseball: The Early Years,* 326–27.

14. Charles S. Johnson, *Patterns of Negro Segregation* (New York, 1943), 72.

15. Jules Tygiel, *Baseball's Great Experiment: Jackie Robinson and His Legacy* (New York, 1983), 14–15.

16. Levine, *A. G. Spalding,* 101–2; Robert Peterson, *Only the Ball Was White* (New York, 1992), 30; Marc Okkonen, *Baseball Memories: 1900–1909* (New York, 1992), 13.

17. On the location of the parks, see Ritter, *Lost Ballparks,* 34; and the street maps in Okkonen, *Baseball Memories,* 28–78.

18. *New York Times,* May 23, 1907, 8.

19. *New York Times,* September 15, 1907, 8.

20. Barth, *City People,* 191. On the importance of "localism" and "home" teams in baseball, see Warren Goldstein, *Playing for Keeps: A History of Early Baseball* (Ithaca, N.Y., 1989), 101–19.

21. Peter Levine, *Ellis Island to Ebbets Field: Sport and the American Jewish Experience* (New York, 1992), 87–91.

22. A. G. Spalding, *America's National Game* (New York, 1911), 6; Jane Addams, *The Spirit of Youth and the City Streets* (New York, 1909), 96.

Chapter 9. "Laughter and Liberty Galore": Early Twentieth-Century Dance Halls, Ballrooms, and Cabarets

1. Belle Lindner Israels, "The Way of the Girl," *Survey* 22 (July 3, 1909), 488, 494. The Irving Berlin song is discussed in Mark Sullivan, *Our Times: 1900–1925. Vol. IV. The War Begins, 1909–1914* (New York, 1932), 252; "New York Society and the Turkey Trot," *Life* (February 1, 1912), 254.

2. Michael M. Davis, Jr., *The Exploitation of Pleasure: A Study of Commercial Recreations in New York City* (New York, n.d.), 12; Ruth True, *The Neglected Girl* (New York, 1914), 54; Elias Tobenkin, "The Immigrant Girl in Chicago," *Survey* 23 (November 6, 1909), 103.

3. Julian Street, *Welcome to Our City* (New York, 1913), 10–11.

4. *Variety,* November 28, 1913, 10; December 25, 1914, 7; "All-Night Life in New York," *Vanity Fair* III (April 1915), 50.

5. "Influence of Social Follies," *New York Times,* January 5, 1912, 12. See also Circular from Committee on Amusements and Vacation Resources of

Working Girls, Parks & Playgrounds, Corr., Lillian Wald Papers, Rare Books and Manuscripts Library, Columbia University, New York (hereafter abbreviated as LW-CU).

6. "Dance Hall Law in Operation," *Survey* 26 (April 1, 1911), 12–13; *New York Times,* January 4, 1912, 1. See also Theatrical Investigations folder, Box 150, Community Service Society papers, Rare Books and Manuscripts Library, Columbia University, New York (thereafter abbreviated as CSS-CU); and Elizabeth Perry, *Belle Moskowitz* (New York, 1987), 50–52.

7. *New York Times,* January 5, 1912, 9; January 16, 1912, 13.

8. "How the Castles Built Their Castle," *Theatre Magazine* XIX (March 1914), 126. See also on the Castles, Lewis A. Erenberg, *Steppin' Out: New York Nightlife and the Transformation of American Culture, 1890–1930* (Chicago, 1984), 158–65.

9. Mr. and Mrs. Vernon Castle, *Modern Dancing* (New York, 1914), 177.

10. Cited in Arthur H. Franks, *Social Dance: A Short History* (London, 1963), 176.

11. Samuel B. Charters and Leonard Kunstadt, *Jazz: A History of the New York Scene* (New York, 1981), 24–25, 32–33; Marshall Stearns and Jean Stearns, *Jazz Dance: The Story of American Vernacular Dance* (New York, 1968), 96.

12. Charters and Kunstadt, *Jazz,* 37; Irene Castle, *Castles in the Air* (1958; New York, 1980), 92; Douglas Henry Daniels, *Pioneer Urbanites: A Social and Cultural History of Black San Francisco* (Berkeley, 1990), 148.

13. "Report No. 12," Investigator's Reports 1912, Box 28, Records of the Committee of Fourteen, Rare Books and Manuscripts Division, The New York Public Library (hereafter abbreviated as CF-NYPL); Laurence Bergreen, *As Thousands Cheer: The Life of Irving Berlin* (New York, 1990), 69.

14. Roland Haynes, "Recreation Survey of Kansas City, Mo.," in *Second Annual Report of the Recreation Department of the Board of Public Welfare* (Kansas City, 1911–1912), 32; "Recreation Survey," *Bulletin of the Milwaukee Bureau of Economy and Efficiency,* no. 17 (Milwaukee, March 31, 1912), 13; Juvenile Protective Association of Chicago, text by Louise de Koven Bowen, "Our Most Popular Recreation Controlled by the Liquor Interests: A Study of Public Dance Halls" (Chicago, 1911), 1, Juvenile Protective Association of Chicago Papers, Manuscript Collections, University of Illinois at Chicago (hereafter abbreviated as JPA-UIC).

15. See, for example, "Report of George S. Myers, Dance Hall Inspector" (Cleveland, Ohio, January 1914), 3–6; "Annual Report of the Sub-Division Dance Hall Inspector. Department of Public Service of the City of Cleveland. For the Year Ending December 31, 1914" (Cleveland, n.d.), 4–10; "Annual Report of the Sub-Division Dance Hall Inspector. Department of Public Service of the City of Cleveland. For the Year Ending December 31, 1915" (Cleveland, n.d.), 3–10. On Kansas City, see Fred F. McClure, "Survey of Commercial Recreation of Kansas City, Mo.," in *Second Annual Report of the Recreation Department of the Board of Public Welfare* (Kansas City, 1911–1912), 75–77.

16. On the importance of the parlor for courting and its absence from working-class, immigrant homes, see Mary Kingsbury Simkhovitch, *The City Worker's World in America* (New York, 1917), 31–33; True, *Neglected Girl*, 61–62.

17. Erenberg, *Steppin' Out*, 156.

18. The description of the New York City dance hall is found in, "Terrace Garden—Sat. night, Sept. 16, 1911. Mr. and Mrs. Hastings," Investigative Reports 1912, Box 28, CF-NYPL. I have corrected the spelling and grammar. The behavior described here is similar, if not identical, to that described by other investigators in other dance halls across the country. See, for example, Collis Stocking, "A Study of Dance Halls in Pittsburgh Made under the Auspices of the Pittsburgh Girls' Conference" (Pittsburgh, 1925); and William S. Wollner, "Report on Dance Halls," in "Public Recreation," *Transactions of the Commonwealth Club of California* VIII (June 1913), 273–77.

19. Kathy Peiss, *Cheap Amusements: Working Women and Leisure in Turn-of-the-Century New York* (Philadelphia, 1986), 104–7.

20. Juvenile Protective Association of Chicago, n.p. For an even more exaggerated "melodrama," see John Dillon, *From Dance Hall to White Slavery* (New York, 1943), who uses the files of the Juvenile Protective Association for his source material.

21. Stocking, "Dance Halls in Pittsburgh," 31.

22. Mr. and Mrs. Hastings' report from the "Eldorado—Sat. night, September 16, 1911," Investigative Reports 1912, Box 28, CF-NYPL.

23. Ellen Rothman, *Hands and Hearts: A History of Courtship in America* (Cambridge, Mass., 1987), 289–90; Beth L. Bailey, *From Front Porch to Back Seat: Courtship in Twentieth-Century America* (Baltimore, 1988), 13–19.

24. Sullivan, *Our Times*, 253.

25. "Terrace Garden—Sat. night, Sept. 16, 1911. Mr. and Mrs. Hastings," Investigative Reports 1912, Box 28, CF-NYPL; Wollner, "Report on Dance Halls," 274.

26. Peiss, *Cheap Amusements*, 109–11.

27. Juvenile Protective Association of Chicago, n.p.; Natalie D. Sonnichsen, report from Harlem River Casino, Oct. 26th, 1912, Investigative Reports 1912, Box 28, CF-NYPL; Wollner, "Report on Dance Halls," 274.

28. Stocking, "Dance Halls in Pittsburgh," 17–18; Erenberg, *Steppin' Out*, 134–36.

29. Street, *Welcome*, 10; Erenberg, *Steppin' Out*, 163; Katrina Hazzard-Gordon, *Jookin': The Rise of Social Dance Formations in African-American Culture* (Philadelphia, 1990), 125–26; Stocking, "Dance Halls in Pittsburgh," 20, 36; Chicago Commission on Race Relations, *The Negro in Chicago: A Study of Race Relations and a Race Riot* (Chicago, 1922), 231, 281.

30. Kathy Ogren, *The Jazz Revolution: Twenties America and the Meaning of Jazz* (New York, 1989), 56–86. On Chicago, see James R. Grossman, *Land of Hope: Chicago, Black Southerners, and the Great Migration* (Chicago, 1989), 117. On San Francisco, see Daniels, *Pioneer Urbanites*, 144–45.

On Atlanta, Memphis, and Cincinnati, see William Barlow, *Looking Up at Down: The Emergence of Blues Culture* (Philadelphia, 1989), 192, 205, 276.

31. Hazzard-Gordon, *Jookin'*, 144 (I have rearranged this quotation); Charters and Kunstadt, *Jazz*, 217.

32. Maria Ward Lambin, "Report of the Public Dance Hall Committee of the San Francisco Center of the California Civic League of Women Voters" (San Francisco, 1924), 9; Maria Ward Lambin, "Can Dancing Be Play," *Survey* (July 15, 1924), 460.

33. "Broadway and Parts Adjacent" and "The Business of Dancing," *Survey* (July 15, 1924), 457–58; Stocking, "Dance Halls in Pittsburgh," 12–13.

34. "The Business of Dancing," 457. The original version of this report is found in Lambin, "Report of the Advisory Dance Hall Committee," 10. See also for Pittsburgh, Stocking, "Dance Halls in Pittsburgh," 22.

35. Mary McDowell, "The Foreign Born" (1927), an unpublished version of her autobiography, 16, in "Mary McDowell and Municipal Housing in Mary McDowell Papers, Archives and Manuscripts Department, Chicago Historical Society, Chicago (hereafter abbreviated as MM-CHS).

36. Stocking, "Dance Halls in Pittsburgh," 38.

37. Ogren, *Jazz Revolution*, 79–82.

Chapter 10. Talking and Singing Machines, Parlors, and Peep Shows

1. Cited in Matthew Josephson, *Edison: A Biography* (New York, 1959), 137, 171–72.

2. The most recent and thorough discussion of Edison's work on the phonograph is found in Andre Millard, *Edison and the Business of Innovation* (Baltimore, 1990), 63–87. See also Roland Gelatt, *The Fabulous Phonograph, 1877–1977*, 2d rev. ed. (New York, 1977), 30–32.

3. Josephson, *Edison*, 317–24; Millard, *Edison*, 64–65; Gelatt, *Fabulous Phonograph*, 32.

4. Millard, *Edison*, 80.

5. National Phonograph Association, *Proceedings of the 1890 Convention of Local Phonograph Companies* (Milwaukee, 1890), 163–64.

6. National Phonograph Association, *Proceedings of the 1890 Convention,* 35. On Edison's demonstration musical cylinders, see Josephson, *Edison,* 322–23; Robert Conot, *A Streak of Luck* (New York, 1979), 316; William Barlow, *Looking Up at Down: The Emergence of Blues Culture* (Philadelphia, 1989), 124.

7. National Phonograph Association, *Proceedings of the 1890 Convention,* 34–35, 72.

8. V. H. McRae, "An Important Suggestion," *Phonogram* I (January 1891), 1. See also V. H. McRae, "The Real Mission of the Phonograph," *Phonogram* I (February 1891), 33–34.

9. "The Most Profitable Phonograph," *Phonogram* I (June–July 1891), 138; "The Spokane Phonograph Company," *Phonogram* I (June–July 1891), 140.

10. *Phonogram* I (June–July 1891), 155; "The Musical Industry of the Phono-

graph Among Some of Our Companies," *Phonogram* II (August–September 1892), 185.

11. "Organization and Progress of the Phonograph Companies of the United States," *Phonogram* I (November–December 1891), 241.

12. Gelatt, *Fabulous Phonograph,* 28–29, 46–57; "Phonograph Records by the U.S. Marine Band," *Phonogram* I (October 1891), 226; "A Famous and Artistic Whistler," *Phonogram* I (August 1891), 168; *Phonogram* I (September 1891), 181.

13. National Phonograph Association, *Proceedings of the Second Annual Convention* (New York, 1891), 93; Gelatt, *Fabulous Phonograph,* 54, 73–81; "Bettini Micro-Phonographs and 'Records'" (June 1898), in Rodgers and Hammerstein Archives of Recorded Sound, The New York Public Library (hereafter abbreviated as RHARS-NYPL).

14. Barlow, *Looking Up at Down,* 124–25; Martin W. Laforse and James A. Drake, *Popular Culture and American Life: Selected Topics in the Study of American Popular Culture* (Chicago, 1981), 25–33; National Phonograph Association, *Proceedings of the Second Annual Convention,* 62–63; "The Louisiana Phonograph Company, Limited," *Phonogram* II (January 1892), 10.

15. Conot, *A Streak of Luck,* 310; National Phonograph Association, *Proceedings of Fourth Annual Convention* (Chicago, 1893), 108–11, 113.

16. *Phonogram* I (September 1891), 202; "The Louisiana Phonograph Company, Limited," 10; "The Musical Industry of the Phonograph among Some of Our Companies," 185–87; E. A. Ludwigs, "To the Operator," *Phonogram* III (February 1993), 336. The final quotation is from "The Exhibition Parlors of the Ohio Phonograph Company," *Phonogram* I (November–December, 1991), 249.

17. "The Exhibition Parlors of the Ohio Phonograph Company," 250.

18. "The Exhibition Parlors of the Ohio Phonograph Company," 248–49; National Phonograph Association, *Proceedings of Fourth Annual Convention,* 117.

19. "A Penny in the Slot," *Phonogram* II (January 1892), 25. (I have rearranged this citation.) See the illustration accompanying the article for information on "Roy's Positive Remedy." On X-ray machines, see Josephson, *Edison,* 381–83.

20. On the lecture-hall and lyceum circuit in this period, see Charles Musser, in collaboration with Carol Nelson, *High-Class Moving Pictures: Lyman H. Howe and the Forgotten Era of Traveling Exhibition, 1880–1920* (Princeton, N.J., 1991), 40; John Mulholland, "Lyceums and Lyceumites" (n.p., n.d.), in George De Mott Collection, BRTC-NYPL.

21. On Lyman Howe, in particular, and the phonograph exhibitors, in general, see the video entitled *Lyman H. Howe's High-Class Moving Pictures* (1983) produced by Carol Nelson, with text by Charles Musser, and Musser, *High-Class Moving Pictures,* 15–21, 24–36.

22. Musser, *High-Class Moving Pictures,* 35, 40.

23. Terry Ramsaye, *A Million and One Nights: A History of the Motion Picture through 1925* (New York, 1926), 313; Musser, *High-Class Moving Pictures,* 41–43; Conot, *A Streak of Luck,* 315–16; D. E. Boswell Com-

pany, "Phonograph and Graphophone Records" (Chicago, 1898), 25–29, RHARS-NYPL; M. C. Sullivan, "How to Give Concert Exhibitions of the Phonograph," *Phonogram* III (February 1893), 324.

24. See Charles Musser, *The Emergence of Cinema: The American Screen to 1907* (New York, 1990), 61–62.

25. Josephson, *Edison*, 392; Ramsaye, *Million and One Nights*, 78.

26. G. W. Bromley and Company, *Atlas of the City of New York, Manhattan Island*, 2d ed. (Philadelphia, 1894).

27. Alfred O. Tate, *Edison's Open Door* (New York, 1938), 285.

28. Gordon Hendricks, "The History of the Kinetoscope," in *The American Film Industry*, ed. Tino Balio, rev. ed. (Madison, Wis., 1985), 49. The drawing first appeared in William Kennedy, Laurie Dickson, and Antonia Dickson, *History of the Kinetograph, Kinetoscope, and Kinetophonograph* (New York, 1895).

29. *Phonoscope* I (November 15, 1896), 13.

30. Gordon Hendricks, *The Kinetoscope: America's First Commercially Successful Motion Picture Exhibition* (New York, 1966), 60–61; Hendricks, "History of the Kinetoscope," 50; Ramsaye, *Million and One Nights*, 88. On Bagicalupi, see *Moving Picture World* 29 (July 15, 1916), 399.

31. Robert Kirk Headley, Jr., *Exit: A History of Movies in Baltimore* (University Park, Md., 1974), 2; Burnes St. Patrick Hollyman, "The First Picture Shows: Austin, Texas, 1894–1913," in *Film before Griffith*, ed. John Fell (Berkeley, 1983); Hendricks, *The Kinetoscope*, 61–63; Gordon Hendricks, *Beginnings of the Biograph: The Story of the Invention of the Mutoscope and the Biograph and Their Supplying Camera* (New York, 1964), 30; Musser, *Emergence of Cinema*, 148.

32. Hendricks, "History of the Kinetoscope," 48; Charles Musser, *Before the Nickelodeon: Edwin S. Porter and the Edison Manufacturing Company* (Berkeley, 1991), 42–43. Charles Musser's list is a bit different. He claims that at least three of the films shown in the parlor's opening were produced for women patrons and "appropriately desexualized," *Highland Dance*, which Hendricks included in his list; *Organ Grinder*, a "picture of a happy, harmless Italian street musician"; and *Trained Bears*.

33. John L. Fell, "Cellulose Nitrate Roots: Popular Entertainments and the Birth of Film Narrative," in American Federation of Arts, *Before Hollywood: Turn-of-the-Century American Film* (New York, 1987), 390. See also letters from Raff and Gammon complaining about lack of films, in Raff and Gammon Collection, particularly vol. 6, in Manuscripts and Archives Department, Baker Library, Harvard University, Cambridge, Massachusetts (hereafter abbreviated as RG-HU).

34. Raff and Gammon to Board of Directors, March 26, 1895; to Thomas Lombard, May 31, 1895, RG-HU; Hendricks, *The Kinetoscope*, 142.

35. G. W. Bitzer, *Billy Bitzer, His Story* (New York, 1973), 9–10.

36. Musser, *Emergence of Cinema*, 176; "The Mutoscope" (1897), 7, in Thomas A. Edison Papers, *Motion Picture Catalogs: By American Producers and Distributors, 1894–1908: A Microfilm Edition* (Frederick, 1985), Reel 1 (hereafter abbreviated as MPC-TE).

37. *Billboard* III (April 1, 1895), 3; *Phonoscope* I (November 15, 1896), 10.

Chapter 11. "The Surest Immediate Money-Maker Ever Known"

1 On the Latham brothers, see George C. Pratt, "Firsting the Firsts," in *"Image" on the Art and Evolution of the Film*, ed. Marshall Deutelbaum (New York, 1979), 20–22. On the relationship of the kinetoscope and the screen machines, see Kenneth Macgowan, *Behind the Screen* (New York, 1965), 62–64; Charles Musser, *The Emergence of Cinema: The American Screen to 1907* (New York, 1990), 91, 103–5. On Armat & Jenkins, see letters from Raff and Gammon to Armat, March 9, 16, 1896, in vol. 3, 316, 355, RG-HU; and letter of March 5, cited in Terry Ramsaye, *A Million and One Nights: A History of the Motion Picture through 1925* (New York, 1926), 224–25.

2. Raff and Gammon to Daniel and Armat, n.d. (probably December 1895), vol. 3, 180; to Peter Bacigalupi, February 5, 1896, vol. 3, 212; to L. C. Breyfogle, Chicago, February 26, 1896, vol. 3, 241, RG-HU. On Raff and Gammon's decision to open the vitascope at Koster & Bial's, see Robert C. Allen, "Vaudeville and Film 1895–1915: A Study in Media Interaction" (Ph.D. diss., University of Iowa, 1977), 84–91.

3. "The Vitascope" [March 1896], [reprint facsimile], MPC-TE, reel 1.

4. Raff and Gammon to A. Caswell, April 3, 1896, vol. 2, 30–31, RG-HU.

5. Musser, *Emergence of Cinema*, 122–28.

6. Charles Musser, *Before the Nickelodeon: Edwin S. Porter and the Edison Manufacturing Company* (Berkeley, 1991), 85–86. The Providence ad from June 4, 1896, is reproduced in Musser, *Emergence of Cinema*, 126; Ramsaye, *Million and One Nights*, 277–78; G. P. Harleman, "Los Angeles, Studio Center, Has Pioneer Exhibitors," *Motion Picture World* 29 (July 15, 1916), 416.

7. On Mark and Vitascope Hall, see *Phonoscope* I (December 15, 1896), 11; *Moving Picture World* 1 (December 7, 1907), 645–46; Ethel Hoffman, "Buffalo Saw First Movies in Edisonia," *Buffalo Evening News Magazine*, April 15, 1944, 5; obituaries in Mitchell Mark, "clipping file," BRTC-NYPL. The advertisement was located in the Star Theater Program, October 12, 1896, in theater program collection, BECHS.

8. *Phonoscope* I (June 1897), 7.

9. Robert Brett, *Temples of Illusion* (East Providence, R.I., 1976), 105–8.

10. Ramsaye, *Million and One Nights*, 269–72; "Rock, Smith, and Blackton Were Pioneer Exhibitors," *Moving Picture World* 29 (July 15, 1916), 379; Joseph North, *The Early Development of the Motion Picture: 1887–1909* (New York, 1973), 60. North puts the price Rock paid for the Louisiana rights at $1,500, the *Moving Picture World* article, at $2,500, which sounds a bit high, considering that the price for California was $2,500.

11. Charles Musser, in collaboration with Carol Nelson, *High-Class Moving Pictures: Lyman H. Howe and the Forgotten Era of Traveling Exhibition, 1880–1920* (Princeton, N.J., 1991), 50–51; Musser, *Emergence of Cinema*, 167.

12. Ramsaye, *Million and One Nights*, 271–72; Brown Electric and Machinery Co. to Raff and Gammon, September 28, 1896, vol. 6, folder 6–2, RG-HU.

13. Ramsaye, *Million and One Nights,* 308–10.

14. *Phonoscope* I (December 15, 1896), 13.

15. Maguire & Baucus, Limited, "Preliminary Circular, Edison Perfected Projecting Kinetoscope" (February 16, 1897), MPC-TE, reel 1; F. M. Prescott, "'99 Model Combined Cineograph and Stereopticon" [1899], MPC-TE, reel l.

16. "Life Motion Realism—The Phantascope" [July 1896], 8, 12, MPC-TE, reel 1; Sears, Roebuck, and Company, "Public Exhibition Outlets" [1900], 6, 8, MPC-TE, reel 5.

17. C. Wright Mills, *White Collar* (New York, 1951), 13–33; Daniel Rodgers, *The Work Ethic in Industrial America: 1850–1920* (Chicago, 1978), 37; Chicago Projecting Co., "Catalogue of Stereopticons" [1907], MPC-TE, reel 5.

18. Sears, Roebuck, and Company, "Public Exhibition Outlets," 6–9, 41, 54, in MPC-TE, reel 5.

19. "Armat Motion Picture Company" [1901], 8, MPC-TE, reel 4; Chicago Projecting Company, "Catalogue of Stereopticons" [1907], 2, MPC-TE, reel 6; Sigmund Lubin, "Tents for the Exhibition of Moving Pictures" (n.d.), MPC-TE, reel 3. On tent shows, see also William H. Swanson, "The Inception of the 'Black Top,'" *Moving Picture World* 29 (July 15, 1916), 368–69.

20. Musser, *High-Class Moving Pictures,* 81–83.

21. "Program" for "The Burton Holmes Lectures: Fifth Year," "Lectures and Readings," file, BRTC-NYPL.

22. Musser, *High-Class Moving Pictures,* 53–55, 75–76, 104–5.

23. Stereopticon and Film Exchange, "Stereopticons" (1901–1902), MPC-TE, reel 5.

24. Kleine Optical Company, "Complete Illustrated Catalogue," June 1902; The Cinematograph & Phonograph Co., "Alcohol and Its Victims," Supplement for May 1902; American Cinematograph & Film Company, "Miror Vitae" [1902], 4, MPC-TE, reel 4; Chicago Projecting Company, "Catalogue of Stereopticons," 3, in MPC-TE, reel 6.

25. Selig Polyscope Company, "July Supplement of New Films" (July 1902), MPC-TE, reel 2.

26. Musser, *Emergence of Cinema,* 137–39. On "dumb" acts as closers, see George Gottlieb, "Psychology of the American Vaudeville Show from the Manager's Point of View," in *American Vaudeville as Seen by Its Contemporaries,* ed. Charles W. Stein (New York, 1984), 181.

27. Brett, *Temples of Illusion,* 111–12.

28. *New York Mail and Express,* April 24, 1896, 12.

29. Gordon Hendricks, *Beginnings of the Biograph* (New York, 1964), 46–49.

30. Allen, "Vaudeville and Film," 129; on Harrisburg, see American Federation of Arts, *Before Hollywood: Turn-of-the-Century American Films* (New York, 1987), 90. On increased production of "actualities," see Musser, *Emergence of Cinema,* 232, 236.

31. On Providence, see clipping books, 1894–1941, B. F. Keith's Opera House in Providence, October 1900, KA-UI.

32. George Miller and Dorothy Miller, *Picture Postcards in the United States:*

1893–1918 (New York, 1976), 1–15. I thank William Uriccho for the information on stereographs.

33. International Film Company, "International Photograph Films" (Winter 1897–1898), MPC-TE, reel 1.

34. Musser, *Emergence of Cinema*, 225; Charles Musser, "Another Look at the 'Chaser Theory,'" *Studies in Visual Communications* 10 (Fall 1984), 30.

35. Albert E. Smith, with Phil A. Koury, *Two Reels and a Crank* (Garden City, N.Y., 1952), 55.

36. Ibid., 66–67; Allen, "Vaudeville and Film," 134–41; Charles Musser, "American Vitagraph: 1897–1901," *Cinema Journal* 22 (Spring 1983), 12–14; Edison Manufacturing Company, "Supplement No. 4," May 1898, MPC–TE, reel 1.

37. Cited in Musser, *Emergence of Cinema*, 241.

38. Ramsaye, *Million and One Nights*, 389–91; Musser, *Before the Nickelodeon*, 126–37.

39. Musser, *Emergence of Cinema*, 245, 247.

40. Musser, "'Chaser Theory,'" 31.

41. Edison Manufacturing Company, no. 94, "Edison Films" (March 1900); no. 105 (July 1901), MPC-TE, reel 1; Selig Polyscope Company, "Naval Battles" [1904], in MPC-TE, reel 2; *Keith News*, Providence, January 8, 1906, in clipping books, 1894–1941: Keith's New Theatre, Keith's and Keith's Theatre, August 1900–December 1918, KA-UI.

42. Miriam Hansen, *Babel and Babylon: Spectatorship in American Silent Film* (Cambridge, Eng., 1991), 23.

43. On the "cinema of attractions," see Tom Gunning, *D. W. Griffith and the Origins of American Narrative Film: The Early Years at Biograph* (Urbana, Ill., 1991), 6, 41–43; Hansen, *Babel*, 29, 37.

44. I have taken this interpretation of *Uncle Josh at the Moving Picture Show* from Hansen, *Babel*, 25–29.

Chapter 12. The First Picture Shows

1. "A Visitor's Experience in a Penny Arcade" [April 1907], City Club of Chicago Records, box 9, folder 5, in Archives and Manuscripts Department, Chicago Historical Society (hereafter abbreviated as CCC-CHS). On children and "stools," see clipping from *New York Globe*, March 30, 1906, in CSS-CU. (This clipping is incorrectly labeled "Extract from New York World," box 9, folder 5, CCC-CHS.)

2. Lewis to Kingsley, April 5, 1907; and "A Visitor's Experience in a Penny Arcade" [April 1907], box 9, folder 5, CCC-CHS.

3. Clipping from *New York Globe*, March 30, 1906; Lewis to Kingsley, April 5, 1907, CCC-CHS. On Boston investigations, see S. H. Stone to Kingsley, April 4, 1907, and Frederick B. Allen to Lewis, March 23, 1906, CCC-CHS. On signs advertising peep-show machines, see Walter S. Ufford to O. F. Lewis, April 5, 1906, Box 180, "Theatre Investigations," CSS-CU.

4. Although most accounts of Zukor's 14th Street arcade do not refer to Mark, the corporate listing of the Automatic Vaudeville Company, located

at 48 E. 14th Street, lists Mitchell Mark as president and Zukor as secretary. See *The Trow Copartnership and Corporation Directory of the Boroughs of Manhattan and the Bronx* (March 1905), 45, New-York Historical Society Library (hereafter abbreviated as NYHS). It is difficult, if not impossible, to get all the details right about Zukor's early business dealings, as the only sources are his own interviews and authorized biographies, none of which are particularly reliable on dates. There is disagreement among the sources as to whether Zukor was a partner in Mark's 125th Street arcade and whether he entered the arcade business in 1903 or 1904. On Zukor and the early arcade business, see Will Irwin, *The House That Shadows Built* (Garden City, N.Y., 1928), 3–8, 90–97; Adolph Zukor Interview, Oral History Collection, Columbia University, New York City, 7–8 (hereafter abbreviated as OH-CU); Adolph Zukor, with Dale Kramer, *The Public Is Never Wrong* (New York, 1953), 38–40; Bosley Crowther, *The Lion's Share: The Store of an Entertainment Empire* (New York, 1957), 23. On the section of Harlem in which the first arcade was located, see Jeffrey S. Gurock, *When Harlem Was Jewish, 1870–1930* (New York, 1979), 52–57.

5. On the geography of New York City in general, see Patricia Evelyn Malon, "The Growth of Manufacturing in Manhattan 1860–1900: An Analysis of Factoral Changes and Urban Structures" (Ph.D. diss., Columbia University, 1981), 301–3, 378–84. On Union Square, see Ernest Ingersoll, *Rand McNally and Company's Handy Guide to New York City* (New York, 1904), 112–16; Gerard R. Wolfe, *New York: A Guide to the Metropolis* (New York, 1975), 162–85; John W. Frick, *New York's First Theatrical Center: The Rialto at Union Square* (Ann Arbor, Mich., 1985), 151–58, 169–77; Irwin, *Shadows*, 5.

6. I have learned much about the arcade from photographs in the collection of the Museum of the City of New York. See also Zukor, with Kramer, *The Public Is Never Wrong*, 38–39; Jesse Lasky, with Don Weldon, *I Blow My Own Horn* (London, 1957), 100; Irwin, *Shadows*, 3–5.

7. Upton Sinclair, *Upton Sinclair Presents William Fox* (Los Angeles, 1933), 33.

8. Sinclair, *William Fox*, 33–34. On 14th Street arcade and on Fox, see also Neal Gabler, *An Empire of Their Own* (New York, 1988), 17–21, 65–66.

9. *Trow Copartnership and Corporation Directory*, 526; Crowther, *Lion's Share*, 23–25.

10. On the locations of the arcades in the Loop, see assorted investigators' reports, box 9, folder 5, CCC-CHS; on Baltimore arcade, see Walter Ufford to O. F. Lewis, April 5, 1906, CSS-CU; on Worcester, see Roy Rosenzweig, *Eight Hours for What We Will* (Cambridge, Eng., 1983), 192. The quotation from the manager is from "A Visitor's Experience in a Penny Arcade," [1], CCC-CHS. Herbert Mills, "How to Get Started in the Arcade Business," *Views and Film Index* 2 (July 27, 1907), 3.

11. Mills, "How to Get Started" (July 27, 1907), 3; (August 3, 1907), 3.

12. Roland Lynde Hartt, *The People at Play* (New York, 1909), 120,

13. Charles Musser, *The Emergence of Cinema: The American Screen to 1907* (New York, 1990), 419–21.

14. Marcus Loew, "The Motion Picture and Vaudeville," in *The Story of the*

Films, ed. Joseph P. Kennedy (Chicago, 1927), 286–87; Crowther, *Lion's Share,* 26.

15. Adolph Zukor oral history, 9–10, OH-CU; Zukor, with Kramer, *The Public Is Never Wrong,* 39–40. On Baltimore, see Robert Kirk Headley, Jr., *Exit: A History of Movies in Baltimore* (University Park, Md., 1974), 3–8.

16. On the early picture theaters, see the articles collected in *Moving Picture World* 29 (July 15, 1916), in particular those by J. M. Shellman, "Baltimore Has Long List of Motion Picture Pioneers," 383; B. S. Brown, "Kansas City, Missouri, First Theater Still Running," 381; A. H. Grebler, "St. Louis, Missouri, 'One of Our Best Picture Towns,'" 394–95; George M. Cheney, "New Orleans, Louisiana, Records Wonderful Development," 403; G. D. Crain, Jr., "Louisville, Kentucky, History Covers but Ten Years," 396; Musser, *Emergence of Cinema,* 420, 424–25; *Billboard,* October 13, 1906, 20; Jack L. Warner, with Dean Jennings, *My First Hundred Years in Hollywood* (New York, 1965), 50–57.

17. On New York City, see Robert C. Allen, "Motion Picture Exhibition in Manhattan, 1906–1912: Beyond the Nickelodeon," *Cinema Journal* 18 (Spring 1979), 4–6; on Boston, see Russell Merritt, "Nickleodeon Theaters, 1905–1914: Building an Audience for the Movies," in *The American Film Industry,* rev. ed., ed. Tino Balio (Madison, Wis., 1985), 91–92; on Chicago, Harold Mayer and Richard Wade, *Chicago: Growth of a Metropolis* (Chicago, 1969), 214; on Philadelphia, see *Motion Picture World* I (October 5, 1907), 485, and (October 19, 1907), 521; for Dallas, *Motion Picture World* I (March 23, 1907), 40.

18. Chicago Projecting Company, "Catalogue of Stereopticons, Motion Picture Machines" [1907], 10, MPC-TE. On the costs of operating a nickelodeon, see "The Nickelodeon," *Moving Picture World* I (May 4, 1907), 140; J. M. Shellman, "Baltimore Has Long List," 383–85. In Joseph Medill Patterson's estimate of the weekly costs of an average nickelodeon, he refers to "wage of porter or musician," the implication being that the porter was going to double as the musician, or vice-versa. See his article, "The Nickelodeons, the Poor Man's Elementary Course in the Drama," *Saturday Evening Post* (November 23, 1907), reprinted in *Spellbound in Darkness: A History of the Silent Film,* ed. George C. Pratt (Greenwich, Conn., 1973), 46.

19. James B. Lane, *"City of the Century": A History of Gary, Indiana* (Bloomington, Ind., 1978), 50; Francis V. C. Oliver, Jr., Chief, Bureau of Licenses, to McClellan, December 18, 1908, Mayors' Papers, George B. McClellan, Box MGB 51, Departmental Correspondence Received. Mayor's Office, Bureau of Licenses, Municipal Archives, New York City (hereafter abbreviated as MA-NYC); *New-York Daily Tribune,* December 26, 1908, 1.

20. Patterson, "The Nickelodeons," 46.

21. Lucy France Pierce, "The Nickelodeon," *World Today* 15 (October 1908), 1052–53; *Motion Picture World* I (March 23, 1907), 40.

22. *Motion Picture World* I (April 27, 1907), 119–20; (October 5, 1907), 485; (October 19, 1907), 521; (October 26, 1907), 540. On attempts to ban or restrict pushcarts and peddlers in New York City, see Daniel Bluestone,

"'The Pushcart Evil'," in *The Landscape of Modernity*, ed. David Ward and Olivier Zunz (New York, 1992), 287–312.

23. R. L. Jenne, "Indianapolis Shows Unusual Growth in Ten Years," *Moving Picture World* 29 (July 15, 1916), 412.

24. Roger Brett, *Temples of Illusion* (East Providence, R.I., 1976), 161–64.

25. Clipping books, Providence, R.I., Nickel Theater and Bijou Theater, vol. 1, KA-UI; "The Nickelodeon," *Moving Picture World* I (May 4, 1907), 140.

26. *Film Index* IV (March 20, 1909), 10.

27. Charlotte Herzog, "The Archaeology of Cinema Architecture: The Origins of the Movie Theater," *Quarterly Review of Film Studies* (Winter 1984), 13; Craig Morrison, "From Nickelodeon to Picture Palace and Back," *Design Quarterly* 93 (1974), 7, 9; Brett, *Temples of Illusion*, 154.

28. Hartt, *People at Play*, 122.

29. Charles Musser, *Before the Nickelodeon: Edwin S. Porter and the Edison Manufacturing Company* (Berkeley, 1991), 373–74; Zukor, with Kramer, *The Public Is Never Wrong*, 49; Adolph Zukor, "Origin and Growth of the Industry," in Kennedy, *Story of Films*, 58. See also *Moving Picture World* I (July 13, 1907), 297.

30. Warner, *My First Hundred Years*, 57; Sophie Tucker, *Some of These Days: The Autobiography of Sophie Tucker* (Garden City, N.Y., 1945), 38.

31. John L. Fell, "Motive, Mischief, and Melodrama: The State of Film Narrative in 1907," in *Film before Griffith*, ed. John L. Fell (Berkeley, 1983), 278; John L. Fell, *Film and the Narrative Tradition* (Berkeley, 1986), 12–36.

32. Edison Manufacturing Company, Advertising bill, "No. 201, Edison Film, The Great Train Robbery," MPC-TE, reel 1; Fell, "Motive," 274; Lewis Jacobs, *The Rise of the American Film: A Critical Essay* (New York, 1968), 75.

33. For a description of *Energizer*, see the Biograph advertisement in *Moving Picture World* 2 (January 11, 1908). The synopsis of *The Suburbanite's Ingenious Alarm* is also found in *Motion Picture World* 2 (January 11, 1908), 25.

34. For a fine discussion of the subject of ethnic representation, see Charles Musser, "Ethnicity, Role-playing, and American Film Comedy: From *Chinese Laundry Scene* to *Whoopee* (1894–1930)," in *Unspeakable Images: Ethnicity and the American Cinema*, ed. Lester D. Friedman (Urbana, Ill., 1991), 39–81. The incident in Providence is discussed in *Moving Picture World* I (May 18, 1907), 167.

35. Musser, *Before the Nickelodeon*, 262–63; Thomas Cripps, *Slow Fade to Black: The Negro in American Film, 1900–1942* (New York, 1977), 8–22.

36. *Moving Picture World* I (May 18, 1907), 168.

37. Robert Allen, "Vaudeville and Film 1895–1915: A Study in Media Interaction" (Ph.D. diss., University of Iowa, 1977), 220–21; Milton Berle, with Haskel Frankel, *Milton Berle* (New York, 1974), 55; Barton W. Currie, "The Nickel Madness," *Harper's Weekly* 51 (August 24, 1907), 1246.

38. Walter Prichard Eaton, "Class-Consciousness and the 'Movies'," *Atlantic*

Monthly 15 (1915), 49; Mary Heaton Vorse, "Some Picture Show Audiences," *Outlook* 98 (June 24, 1911), 445–46.

39. Kathy Peiss, *Cheap Amusements: Working Women and Leisure in Turn-of-the-Century New York* (Philadelphia, 1986), 151; Louise Odencrantz, *Italian Women in Industry: A Study of Conditions in New York City* (New York, 1919), 235; Elizabeth Ewen, "City Lights: Immigrant Women and the Rise of the Movies," in Stuart Ewen and Elizabeth Ewen, *Channels of Desire: Mass Images and the Shaping of American Consciousness* (New York, 1982), 96.

40. Peiss, *Cheap Amusements*, 152.

41. Juvenile Protective Association, text by Louise de Koven Bowen, "Five and Ten Cent Theatres—Two Investigations," (n.p., n.d.), JPA-UIC; Edward H. Chandler, "How Much Children Attend the Theatre, the Quality of the Entertainment They Choose and Its Effect upon Them," *Proceedings of the Children's Conference for Research and Welfare* I (New York, 1909), 56.

42. Jane Addams, *The Spirit of Youth and the City Streets* (New York, 1909), 5–6; Research Department, School of Social Economy of Washington University, "The Newsboy of Saint Louis" (St. Louis, n.d.), 9; William Hard, "De Kid wot works at night," cited in David Nasaw, *Children of the City: At Work and at Play* (New York, 1985), 125.

43. Maurice Willows, "The Nickel Theatre," in National Children Labor Committee, Seventh Annual Meeting, *Annals* (Philadelphia, 1911), 96.

44. Nasaw, *Children of the City*, 124.

45. Rosenzweig, *Eight Hours*, 194, 196; William Fox, "Reminiscences and Observations," in Kennedy, *Story of Films*, 302–3. Also on single immigrants and the movies, see Antonio Mangano, *Sons of Italy* (New York, 1917), 6–7.

46. George Esdras Bevans, *How Workingmen Spend Their Spare Time* (New York, 1913), 19–43; *Moving Picture World* 2 (May 16, 1908), 433; Glendon Allvine, *The Greatest Fox of Them All* (New York, 1969), 42; Sinclair, *William Fox*, 36–37.

47. On saloons and movie theaters, see Garth Jowett, *Film: The Democratic Art* (Boston, 1976), 89; Rosenzweig, *Eight Hours*, 191–92; *Moving Picture World* 1 (November 30, 1907), 631; Headley, Jr., *Exit*, 8. On Saxe, see Larry Widen, "Milwaukee's Princess Theater," *Marquee* 17 (Second Quarter 1985), 19.

48. *Crisis* II (June 1911), 53; III (April 1912), 228; VII (November 1913), 323; VII (January 1914), 117.

49. Cripps, *Slow Fade*, 71; *Moving Picture World* 5 (March 5, 1910), 337.

50. *Moving Picture World* I (March 23, 1907), 40; (June 8, 1907), 216–17.

51. *Crisis* III (April 1912), 228; VIII (August 1914), 168.

52. Vorse, "Picture Show Audiences," 447.

Chapter 13. "The Pernicious 'Moving Picture' Abomination"

1. The definitive work on the critics of commercial culture remains Paul Boyer, *Urban Masses and Moral Order in America, 1820–1920* (Cambridge, Mass., 1978). See, in particular, 120, 162–66. The phrase used as

the chapter title is taken from the New York Society for the Prevention of Cruelty to Children, *Thirty-fourth Annual Report* (New York, 1909), 23–24.

2. John Collier, "Leisure-Time, the Last Problem of Conservation," National Recreation Association of America, *Publication 99* (1912), 8, 11.

3. For an excellent discussion of the censorship issue in general and the historical relationship between film and theatrical censorships, see Daniel Czitrom, "The Politics of Performance: From Theater Licensing to Movie Censorship in Turn-of-the-Century New York," *American Quarterly* 44 (December 1992), 525–53; Edward H. Chandler, "How Much Children Attend the Theater, the Quality of the Entertainment They Chose and Its Effect on Them," *Proceedings of the Children's Conference for Research and Welfare* (1909), 56–57; the Ohio Humane Society study is cited in Charles Matthew Feldman, "The National Board of Censorship (Review) of Motion Pictures 1909–1922" (Ph.D. diss., University of Michigan, 1975), 43.

4. Kathleen D. McCarthy, "Nickel Vice and Virtue: Movie Censorship in Chicago, 1907–1915," *Journal of Popular Film* V (1976), 45; *Block v. City of Chicago*, Supreme Court of Illinois, February 19, 1909, cited in 87 N.E. 1011.

5. *Moving Picture World* 2 (May 30, 1908), 473.

6. *New-York Daily Tribune,* December 24, 1908, 4; partial typescript of public hearing, 150, Mayors' Papers, George B. McClellan, Box MGB 51, MA-NYC.

7. On theater fires, see "Looking Backward: The Iroquois Theatre Fire of 1903," *Chicago History* 17 (1978–1979), 238; Czitrom, "Politics of Performance," 537; letters from Frances V. C. Oliver, Jr., Chief, Bureau of Licenses, to Mayor McClellan, December 14, 15, 18, 1908, and partial transcript of public hearing on closing the theaters, dated December 23, 1908, in Mayors' Papers, George McClellan, Box MGB 51, Departmental Correspondence Received, Mayor's Office, Bureau of Licenses, MA-NYC.

8. *New-York Daily Tribune,* December 25, 1908, 1; *New York Times,* December 25, 1908, 1.

9. *New York Times,* January 12, 1909, 5; John Collier, "Cheap Amusement Shows in Manhattan: Preliminary Report of Investigation," January 31, 1908, in Subjects Papers, Records of the National Board of Review of Motion Pictures, Rare Books and Manuscripts Division, The New York Public Library (hereafter abbreviated as NBR-NYPL); John Collier, "Special Report on Cheap Amusements," in *People's Institute Eleventh Annual Report* (New York, 1908), 21–23; Czitrom, "Politics of Performance," 537–39.

10. Robert Fisher, "Film Censorship and Progressive Reform: The National Board of Censorship of Motion Pictures, 1909–1922," *Journal of Popular Film* IV (1975), 142–56; Nancy J. Rosenbloom, "Between Reform and Regulation: The Struggle over Film Censorship in Progressive America, 1909–1922," *Film History* I (1987), 309–11.

11. Daniel Czitrom, "The Redemption of Leisure," *Studies in Visual Communication* 10 (Fall 1984), 3–4; "Admitting Children," *Nickelodeon* II (November 1909), 135–36.

12. Eileen Bowser, *The Transformation of Cinema: 1907–1915* (New York, 1990), 48–49; *Moving Picture World* I (June 1, 1907), 198; Brooks McNamara, *The Shuberts of Broadway: A History Drawn from the Collections of the Shubert Archive* (New York, 1990), 75; Robert Grau, *The Theatre of Science* (New York, 1914), 33–34.

13. For copies of these petitions and handbills, see Box 20, folder 6, Subject Correspondence: Children and Motion Pictures, NBR-NYPL; and Mayors' Papers, James G. Gaynor, Box GWJ 89, folder 3, "Protests," MA-NYC. Gaynor's correspondence on censorship is found in Box GWJ 80, Subject Files, Censorship, MA-NYC. The full text of his veto message was reprinted in *Moving Picture World* 15 (January 11, 1913), 134–36.

14. *Moving Picture World* 8 (March 11, 1911), 539.

15. Raymond B. Fosdick, Commissioner of Accounts, "Report on *Moving Picture Shows* in the City of New York," March 22, 1911, 10–13, in Mayors' Papers, William J. Gaynor, Box GWJ 22, Departmental Correspondence, Accounts Commissioner, 1911, MA-NYC.

16. Neil Harris, *Cultural Excursions: Marketing Appetites and Cultural Tastes in Modern America* (Chicago, 1990), 165.

17. Chicago Vice Commission, *The Social Evil in Chicago* (Chicago, 1911), 247–51; New York Society for the Prevention of Cruelty to Children, 23–24.

18. Harris, *Cultural Excursions*, 169; *Independent* 67 (March 17, 1910), 590. See also Arthur Meier Schlesinger, *The Rise of the City, 1878–1898* (New York, 1933), 244–46.

19. Robert O. Bartholomew, "Report of Censorship of Motion Pictures and of Investigation of Motion Picture Theatres of Cleveland, 1913," filed with Council of City of Cleveland, April 7, 1913, 12–13.

20. *Birdseye's Consolidated Laws of New York, 1909*, vol. 3, 2906–9, 2996–97; *Motography* IX (February 15, 1913), 120.

21. See, for example, on the effect of the new regulations in Pennsylvania, *Film Index* IV, no. 29 (July 17, 1909), 3; Juvenile Protective Association, "Five and Ten Cent Theatres" (n.p., n.d.), JPA-UIC.

22. See, for example, letter to Mayor Gaynor from President Board of Education, May 31, 1910, in Mayors' Papers, William J. Gaynor, Subjects File: Censorship: Motion Pictures, MA-NYC; *New York Times*, November 12, 1911, 8; John Collier, "'Movies' and the Law," *Survey* 27 (January 20, 1912), 1629; final quotation is from "Moving Picture Houses," November 23, 1913, 36, in Magnes Papers, Hebrew University, Jerusalem, Israel (hereafter abbreviated MP-HU).

23. Fosdick, "Report on *Moving Picture Shows* in the City of New York," 11–12. On Cleveland, see Bartholomew, "Report of Censorship," 10, 27–28.

24. *Moving Picture World* I (June 27, 1907), 262–63.

25. John Collier, "The Motion Picture," *Proceedings of the Children's Conference for Research and Welfare* 2 (1910), 116.

26. Richard Koszarski, *An Evening's Entertainment* (New York, 1990), 201–3.

27. Charlotte Herzog, "The Nickelodeon Phase (1903–c. 1917)," *Marquee* 13 (First Quarter 1981), 8.

Chapter 14. Combination Shows, Stars, and Features

1. For an early mention of this phenomenon, see *Moving Picture World* 1 (November 16, 1907), 593. "The 'Small Time' King," *Theatre Magazine* 19 (March 1914), 139–40; Marcus Loew, "Motion Pictures and Vaudeville," in *The Story of the Films*, ed. Joseph D. Kennedy (Chicago, 1927), 287.

2. Bosley Crowther, *The Lion's Share: The Story of an Entertainment Empire* (New York, 1957), 30–31.

3. Thomas Bedding, "Vaudeville Vitiates the Picture," *Moving Picture World* 6 (June 11, 1910), 985; *Moving Picture World* 11 (February 17, 1912), 458. For more temperate criticism of vaudeville by secular commentators, see *Motion Picture News* VI (October 15, 1912), 7, and Richard L. Stromgren, "The Moving Picture World of W. Stephen Bush," *Film History* 2 (1988), 16.

4. Crowther, *Lion's Share*, 32; Mary Carbine, "'The Finest Outside the Loop': Motion Picture Exhibition in Chicago's Black Metropolis, 1905–1928," *Camera Obscura* 23 (May 1990), 16–18.

5. Robert C. Allen, "Vaudeville and Film, 1895–1915: A Study in Media Interaction" (Ph.D. diss., University of Iowa, 1977), 233; John L. Marsh, "Vaudefilm: Its Contribution to a Moviegoing America," *Journal of American Culture* 7 (Fall 1984), 78.

6. "The Price of Admission," *Nickelodeon* 3 (January 15, 1910), 30–31.

7. Miriam Hansen, *Babel and Babylon: Spectatorship in American Silent Film* (Cambridge, Mass., 1991), 60–63.

8. Benjamin B. Hampton, *A History of the Movies* (New York, 1931), 61–62; Adolph Zukor, "Origin and Growth of the Industry," in Kennedy, *Story of Films*, 60.

9. S. L. Rothapfel, "Dignity of the Exhibitors' Profession," *Moving Picture World* 6 (February 26, 1910), 289; Homer W. Sibley, "The Day of the Dump," *Moving Picture World* 9 (August 5, 1911), 273.

10. Charles F. Morris, "The Chicago Orpheum Theater," *Nickelodeon* 1 (January 1909), 4; Charles F. Morris, "A Beautiful Picture Theater," *Nickelodeon* 1 (March 1909), 66; Charles F. Morris, "The National Theater at Cleveland," *Nickelodeon* 2 (December 1909), 169.

11. Larry Widen, "Milwaukee's Princess Theater," *Marquee* 17 (Second Quarter 1985), 20; Douglas Gomery, "Saxe Amusement Enterprises: The Movies Come to Milwaukee," *Milwaukee History* 2 (Spring 1979), 22.

12. Neil Harris, *Humbug: The Art of P. T. Barnum* (Chicago, 1981), 95–96.

13. *Moving Picture World* 9 (July 29, 1911), 185; 10 (November 4, 1911), 362.

14. Russell Merritt, "Nickelodeon Theaters, 1905–1914: Building an Audience for the Movies," in *The American Film Industry*, rev. ed., ed. Tino Balio (Madison, Wis., 1985), 98–99; G. B. Crain, Jr., "Choosing the Location: Success of a Picture Theater Depends Largely upon Building in the Right Place," *Moving Picture World* 21 (August 22, 1914), 1088–89.

15. On the formation of the Trust and the battle with the independents, see Charles Musser, *Before the Nickelodeon: Edwin S. Porter and the Edison Manufacturing Company* (Berkeley, 1991), 433–45.

16. Musser, *Before the Nickelodeon*, 437; Eileen Bowser, *The Transformation of Cinema* (New York, 1990), 103–5. The quotations from *Moving Picture World*, 1909–1910, are cited in Bowser, 105.

17. Musser, *Before the Nickelodeon*, 446–47. The cited reviews are from *New York Dramatic Mirror*, December 9, 1908, 6, and December 10, 1908, 6.

18. Musser, *Before the Nickelodeon*, 393.

19. On changes in "acting" styles, see Roberta Pearson, "'The Modesty of Nature': Performance Style in the Griffith Biographs" (Ph.D. diss., New York University, 1987). See also Bowser, *Transformation*, 89–94; Tom Gunning, *D. W. Griffith and the Origins of American Narrative Film: The Early Years at Biograph* (Urbana, Ill., 1991), 225–26.

20. Richard deCordova, *Picture Personalities: The Emergence of the Star System in America* (Urbana, Ill., 1990), 55–57; Hampton, *History of the Movies*, 83–89.

21. Bowser, *Transformation*, 110–11; deCordova, *Personalities*, 56–61.

22. Gaylyn Studlar, "The Perils of Pleasure: Fan Magazine Discourse as Women's Commodified Culture in the 1920," *Wide Angle* 13 (January 1991), 6–33; Lary May, *Screening Out the Past* (Chicago, 1983), 183–84, 190–99; Bowser, *Transformation*, 113–17; deCordova, *Personalities*, 113–14; Terry Ramsaye, *A Million and One Nights* (New York, 1926), 742.

23. Tino Balio, "Stars in Business: The Founding of United Artists," in Balio, *American Film Industry*, 154–59.

24. Halsey, Stuart & Co., "Prospectus," May 27, 1927, in Balio, *American Film Industry*, 204.

25. Walter Prichard Eaton, "Class-Consciousness and the 'Movies'," *Atlantic Monthly* 115 (1915), 49. On the individual stars, see Richard Koszarski, *An Evening's Entertainment: The Age of the Silent Feature Picture, 1915–1928* (New York, 1990), 259–314. On the developing culture of celebrity, see Richard Schickel, *Intimate Strangers: The Culture of Celebrity* (New York, 1985), 34–61.

26. Koszarski, *Evening's Entertainment*, 193; William Uricchio and Roberta E. Pearson, "Reframing Culture: Consensus, Distinction and the High-Art Moving Picture," unpublished manuscript in author's possession, chapt. 2, 40–42; chapt. 5, 14–15, 21.

27. A. Nicholas Vardac, *Stage to Screen: Theatrical Origins of Early Film: David Garrick to D. W. Griffith* (Cambridge, Mass., 1949), 75, 79; Tino Balio, "Introduction to Part II," in Balio, *American Film Industry*, 110; Uricchio and Pearson, chapt. 5, 15.

28. Albert E. Smith, with Phil A. Koury, *Two Reels and a Crank* (Garden City, N.Y., 1952), 253.

29. On Craft, see Balio, "Introduction," 110–11; Ramsaye, *Thousand and One Nights*, 516–18; David Bordwell, Janet Staiger, and Kristin Thompson, *The Classical Hollywood Cinema: Film Style and Mode of Production to 1960* (New York, 1985), 133. On the showing in Providence, see Bowser,

Transformation, 129. See also the full-page advertisements in *Moving Picture World* 9 (August 19, 1911), 473, and (August 26, 1911), 557.

30. Balio, "Introduction," 110; Ramsaye, *Thousand and One Nights*, 516; advertisements in *Moving Picture World* 11 (February 10, 1912), 500–4.

31. Bordwell et al., *Classical Hollywood*, 130–31; *Moving Picture World* 9 (August 26, 1911), 530; *Moving Picture News* VI (July 20, 1912), 8; (August 31, 1912), 7.

32. Zukor, in Kennedy, *Story of Films*, 62–63; Ramsaye, *Thousand and One Nights*, 596–97; Will Irwin, *The House That Shadows Built* (New York, 1928), 154–65. The quotation is from Irwin, 164–65.

33. *Motography* X (July 12, 1913), 14; George Kleine ledger, "Quo Vadis," 1913, 50, 277–82, in vol. 84. George Kleine Papers, Rare Books and Manuscripts Division, The New York Public Library (hereafter abbreviated as GK-NYPL). On Worcester, see Roy Rosenzweig, *Eight Hours for What We Will* (Cambridge, Eng., 1983), 209; *Variety* XXXIII (January 28, 1912), 15.

34. Robert Grau, *New York Dramatic Mirror* LXIX (July 24, 1912), 13; *New York Dramatic Mirror* LXIX (May 14, 1913), 25.

35. Kevin Brownlow, *Behind the Mask of Innocence* (New York, 1990), 77–78. See also Shelley Stamp Lindsey, "Wages and Sin: *Traffic in Souls* and the White Slavery Scare," *Persistence of Vision* no. 9 (1991), 90–102; Kay Sloan, *The Loud Silents: Origins of the Social Problem Film* (Urbana, Ill., 1988), 82–84.

36. *Variety* XXXIII (December 5, 1913), 17; (December 19, 1913), 12; (January 2, 1914), 14; Sloan, *Loud Silents*, 84; Brownlow, *Behind the Mask*, 80–82; Ramsaye, *Thousand and One Nights*, 618.

37. Thomas Elsaesser and Adam Barker, in *Early Cinema: Space, Frame, Narrative*, ed. by Thomas Elsaesser (London, 1991), 301; Sloan, *Loud Silents*, 82–85. See also reviews in *Moving Picture World* 18 (November 22, 1913), 849; and *New York Dramatic Mirror* 70 (November 19, 1913), 33.

38. *Variety* XXXIII (January 2, 1914), 11; *Motography* XI (May 30, 1914), 369.

39. Richard Schickel, *D. W. Griffith: An American Life* (New York, 1984), 267, 277; *Variety*, March 12, 1915, cited in Schickel, *D. W. Griffith*, 281.

40. See *Crisis* 10 (May 1915), 41; (June 1915), 87; (July 1915), 147–48; (August 1915), 201; (October 1915), 295–96.

41. These quotations are from *Fighting a Vicious Film: Protest against "The Birth of a Nation,"* a pamphlet written by the Boston NAACP chapter and excerpted in Gerald Mast, ed., *The Movies in Our Midst: Documents in the Cultural History of Film in America* (Chicago, 1982), 124. On the reception and protest against the picture, see Thomas Cripps, *Slow Fade to Black: The Negro in American Film, 1900–1942* (New York, 1977), 41–69.

42. Lester A. Walton, "The Ultimate Motive," *New York Age*, March 25, 1915, 6.

43. Koszarski, *Evening's Entertainment*, 198.

44. *Crisis* X (October 1915), 295–96; Schickel, *D. W. Griffith*, 293.

45. Richard S. Randall, *Censorship of the Movies: The Social and Political Control of a Mass Medium* (Madison, Wis., 1968), 18–21; United States Supreme Court, "*Mutual Film Corporation v. Industrial Commission of Ohio,*" in Mast, *Movies in Our Midst,* 142.

46. On the history of censorship and Hollywood, see the special issue of *American Quarterly,* "Hollywood, Censorship, and American Culture," ed. by Francis G. Couvares, vol. 44 (December 1992).

Chapter 15. Waving the Flag

1. *Motography* XI (January 24, 1914), 54.

2. Richard Koszarski, *An Evening's Entertainment: The Age of the Silent Feature Picture, 1915–1928* (New York, 1990), 198–203; *Motion Picture News* X (August 22, 1914), 16–20.

3. Kevin Brownlow, *The War, the West, and the Wilderness* (New York, 1979), 22.

4. *Motion Picture News* X (August 15, 1914), 10–11; (October 24, 1914), 48; David Harley Mould, *American Newsfilm, 1914–1919: The Underexposed War* (New York, 1983), 51–52.

5. *New York Times,* August 7, 1915, 6; *Photoplay* 8 (November 1915), 80–81.

6. Larry Wayne Ward, *The Motion Picture Goes to War: The U.S. Government Film Effort during World War I* (Ann Arbor, Mich., 1985), 39; Craig W. Campbell, *Reel America and World War I: A Comprehensive Filmography and History of Motion Pictures in the United States, 1914–1920* (Jefferson, N.C., 1985), 41, 161; Michael Isenberg, *War on Film: The American Cinema and World War I, 1914–1941* (Rutherford, N.J., 1981), 104.

7. Mould, *American Newsfilm,* 48–50, 146, 177, 180–87; Brownlow, *War West, and Wilderness,* 54, 63; *Motion Picture News* XVI (September 22, 1917), 1925.

8. Isenberg, *War on Film,* 105; *Motion Picture News* XV (April 14, 1917), 2343.

9. *Exhibitor's Trade Review* I (April 28, 1917), 1433.

10. Campbell, *Reel America,* 52–53; *Exhibitors' Trade Review* I (April 28, 1917), 1435.

11. James R. Mock, *Censorship 1917* (Princeton, N.J., 1941), 49–50; *Goldstein v. United States,* Circuit Court of Appeals, Ninth Circuit, May 26, 1920, 258 *Federal Reporter* 908, cited in *Film and Propaganda in America: A Documentary History. Vol. I: World War I,* ed. Richard Wood (New York, 1990), 296; Brownlow, *War, West, and Wilderness,* 81–82. Other writers give a different version of the final sentence. Ward, for example, writes that Goldstein "was sentenced to ten years in the federal penitentiary and fined $10,000" (*Motion Picture Goes to War,* 119).

12. *United States v. Motion Picture Film "The Spirit of '76,"* District Court S. D. California, November 30, 1917, 252 *Federal Reporter* 946, cited in Wood, ed., *Film and Propaganda,* 287–95.

13. Ward, *Motion Picture Goes to War,* 45.

14. Campbell, *Reel America,* 85–89.

15. U.S. Committee on Public Information, *The Creel Report: Complete Report of the Chairman of the Committee on Public Information 1917 1918 1919* (Washington, 1920), 12–21; James R. Mock and Cedric Larson, *Words That Won the War: The Story of the Committee on Public Information, 1917–1919* (Princeton, N.J., 1939), 130.

16. Mock and Larson, *Words That Won the War,* 114–15.

17. U.S. Committee on Public Information, Division of Four Minute Men, "Bulletin No. 28. March 31, 1918. (For Use March 31–April 5, 1918)" (Washington, D.C., 1918), n.p.

18. George Creel, *How We Advertised America* (New York, 1920), 120–25; *Motion Picture News* XVIII (August 17, 1918), 1054–55; (August 24, 1918), 1220, 1228; (August 31, 1918), 1374, 1377; (November 16, 1918), 2944–45.

19. U.S. Committee on Public Information, Division of Four Minute Men, "Bulletin No. 28. March 31 1918. (For Use March 31–April 5)" (Washington, D.C., 1918), n.p. See also on this same subject, "Bulletin No. 36. September 9th, 1918. (For Use September 9th to 14th, 1918)" (Washington, D.C., 1918), n.p.

20. This list is culled from Campbell's filmography of feature films and serials, *Reel America,* 149–91.

21. Ward, *Motion Picture Goes to War,* 56; *Motion Picture News* XVII (March 23, 1918), 1767.

22. Brownlow, *War, West, and Wilderness,* 137.

23. *Exhibitor's Trade Review* 3 (May 11, 1918), four-page advertising insert between 1810–11.

24. Campbell, *Reel America,* 71; *Motion Picture News* XVIII (November 16, 1918), 2948.

25. Campbell, *Reel America,* 98–99; *Exhibitor's Trade Review* 3 (May 11, 1918), 1819–20; Brownlow, *War, West, and Wilderness,* 137, 139.

26. *Exhibitor's Trade Review* 3 (May 11, 1918), 1815.

27. Ward, *Motion Picture Goes to War,* 129.

28. Ibid., 127, 129; Mock and Larson, *Words That Won the War,* 156–57.

29. Steven J. Ross, "Struggles for the Screen: Workers, Radicals, and the Political Uses of Silent Film," *American Historical Review* 96 (April 1991), 347–48; *Motion Picture News* XVIII (December 7, 1918), 3347.

30. Ross, "Struggles," 344, 348, 358.

31. "Most Important Events of the Year," *Wid's Year Book,* 1918, n.p.

Chapter 16. Palaces for the People

1. *Motography* XI (May 2, 1914), 308.

2. *Variety* XXXII (November 21, 1913), 8; Eileen Bowser, *The Transformation of Cinema, 1907–1915* (New York, 1990), 130–31. See also Terry Ramsaye, *A Million and One Nights: A History of the Motion Picture through 1925* (New York, 1926), 678; Abel Green and Joe Laurie, Jr., *Show Biz from Vaude to Video* (New York, 1951), 142.

3. Ben M. Hall, *The Best Remaining Seats: The Golden Age of the Movie Palace* (New York, 1988), 37, 39; *Variety* XXIII (December 26, 1913), 12.

4. Hall, *Best Remaining Seats,* 39–40. Hall refers to Victor Watson as a critic

for the *New York Times,* but Watson was the drama critic for the *New York American.*

5. Benjamin Hampton, *A History of the Movies* (New York, 1931), 170–96, 252–80; Richard Koszarski, *An Evening's Entertainment: The Age of the Silent Feature Picture, 1915–1928* (New York, 1990), 69–94. For a first-hand and very entertaining account of this era of theater building and chain acquisition, see Arthur Mayer, *Merely Colossal: The Story of the Movies from the Long Chase to the Chaise Longue* (New York, 1953), 53–164.

6. David Hammack, "Developing for Commercial Culture," in *Inventing Times Square: Commerce and Culture at the Crossroads of the World,* ed. William R. Taylor (New York, 1991), 45–49; Hampton, *History of the Movies,* 172–73; Harold B. Franklin, *Motion Picture Theater Management* (New York, 1927), 248.

7. Franklin, *Motion Picture Theater Management,* 28–32.

8. Lizabeth Cohen, *Making a New Deal: Industrial Workers in Chicago, 1919–1939* (Cambridge, Eng., 1990), 123.

9. Mary Carbine, "'The Finest Outside the Loop': Motion Picture Exhibition in Chicago's Black Metropolis, 1905–1928," *Camera Obscura* (May 1990), 22–29

10. Paul Morand, *New York* (New York, 1930), 208. See also comments on the new theaters by John Grierson, in his multipart series on moving pictures, "The Industry at a Parting of the Ways," *Moving Picture News* XXXIV (November 13, 1926), 1842–43.

11. B. Andrew Corsini, "The Tivoli," *Marquee* 17 (Fourth Quarter 1985), 5. For program collection of Balaban & Katz theaters listed by theater name (Chicago, Harding, Oriental, Senate, Paradise, Tivoli, Tower, Uptown), see "Programs, 1928," in "Theatres: U.S.: Chicago" folders, BRTC-NYPL.

12. On the Roxy, see facsimile reproductions from *Roxy, a History* in Hall, *Best Remaining Seats,* 78–91.

13. Koszarski, *Evening's Entertainment,* 41–42; Hall, *Best Remaining Seats,* 174–76; A. J. Balaban, as told to Carrie Balaban, *Continuous Performance: The Story of A. J. Balaban* (New York, 1942), 51. For particular programs featuring jazz, see "Programs, 1928," BRTC-NYPL.

14. Lawrence Levine, *Highbrow/Lowbrow: The Emergence of Cultural Hierarchy in America* (Cambridge, Mass., 1988), 104–46, 219–31; the passages cited are from 134, 146, 226.

15. Charlotte Herzog, "The Movie Palace and the Theatrical Sources of Its Architectural Style," *Cinema Journal* 20 (Spring 1981), 17–18.

16. Robert Bagley, "Loew's State Theatre: St. Louis, Mo.," *Marquee* 10 (Fourth Quarter 1978), 3.

17. David Naylor, *American Picture Palaces: The Architecture of Fantasy* (New York, 1981), 118. The *New Yorker* cartoon is reproduced in Hall, *Best Remaining Seats,* 123. For descriptions of existing and restored palaces, see David Naylor, *Great American Movie Theaters* (Washington, D.C., 1987).

18. On the Syracuse theater, see Hall, *Best Remaining Seats,* 113; on Loew's,

Ohio, see Naylor, *American Picture Palaces*, 120; on 72nd Street Theater, see Hall, *Best Remaining Seats*, 126.

19. Marshall Field and Company, *Fashions of the Hour* (October 1921), 23, CHS.

20. For Los Angeles, in particular, see Karen J. Safer, "The Functions of Decoration in the American Movie Palace," *Marquee* 14 (Second Quarter 1982), 3. On the prevalence of Oriental motifs in the palaces, see Nick Browne, "Orientalism as an Ideological Form: American Film Theory in the Silent Period," *Wide Angle* 11 (October 1989), 26.

21. George Rapp, cited in Hall, *Best Remaining Seats*, 136.

22. "Every Seat Is a Good Seat in all Balaban & Katz Theatres," *Balaban & Katz Magazine* I (August 3, 1925), 10; "The Reason Why Balaban & Katz Theatres Do Not Reserve Seats," *Balaban & Katz Magazine* I (July 27, 1925), 10.

23. Roy Rosenzweig, *Eight Hours for What We Will* (Cambridge, Eng., 1983), 213. For a somewhat different interpretation, see Cohen, *Making a New Deal*, 120–23.

24. Ernest Dench, *Advertising by Motion Pictures* (1916), cited in Robert Sklar, *Movie-Made America: A Cultural History of American Movies* (New York, 1975), 45–46.

25. Franklin, *Motion Picture Theater Management*, 30; Andrew R. Heinze, *Adapting to Abundance: Jewish Immigrants, Mass Consumption, and the Search for American Identity* (New York, 1990), 216. On attracting a female audience, see Miriam Hansen, *Babel and Babylon: Spectatorship in American Silent Film* (Cambridge, Eng., 1991), 119–20; Gaylyn Studlar, "The Perils of Pleasure? Fan Magazine Discourse as Women's Commodified Culture in the 1920s," *Wide Angle* 13 (January 1991), 7.

26. Koszarski, *Evening's Entertainment*, 30; *Balaban & Katz Magazine* I (August 3, 1925), n.p.; Beth Brown, "Making Movies for Women," *Moving Picture World* (March 26, 1927), 342.

27. Lloyd Lewis, "The De Luxe Picture Palace," *New Republic* 58 (March 27, 1929), 175–76.

28. J. Victor Wilson, "Metropolitan Movies," *Photoplay* XV (December 1918), 42–43.

29. Hector Arce, *Groucho* (New York, 1979), 103.

30. *Triangle* 1 (January 8, 1916), 1; Butterfly Theater postcard (1916), reproduced in John Margolies and Emily Gwathmey, *Ticket to Paradise: American Movie Theaters and How We Had Fun* (Boston, 1991), 8; "Keeping Cool at Our Theatres," *Balaban & Katz Magazine* I (July 13, 1925), 10.

31. Erving Goffman, *Behavior in Public Places: Notes on the Social Organization of Gatherings* (New York, 1963), 131–36.

32. On the Balaban & Katz ushers, see Douglas Gomery, "The Movies Become Big Business: Publix Theatres and the Chain Store Strategy," *Cinema Journal* 18 (Spring 1979), 29–31; Josef Israels II, "The Movie Usher and How He Got That Way: A Closeup of Our Newest Paragon of Politeness," *Liberty* (April 28, 1928), in "Theatres: Ushers," clipping file, BRTC-NYPL; Hall, *Best Remaining Seats*, 165.

33. On the Rialto, see Hall, *Best Remaining Seats,* 50. On the Avalon, see Naylor, *American Picture Palaces,* 77. The information on Balaban & Katz comes from the advertisement reproduced in Gomery, "Movies Become Big Business," 30. On Roxy, see *Brooklyn Daily Times,* November 23, 1921, in Scrapbook MFL 1523, BRTC-NYPL.

34. *The Fundamental Principles of Balaban & Katz Theatre Management* (Chicago, 1926), 17–20; Franklin, *Motion Picture Theater Management,* 135–36.

35. George M. Fredrickson, *The Black Image in the White Mind: The Debate on Afro-American Character and Destiny, 1817–1914* (Hanover, N.H., 1987), 276–77; Joel Williamson, *A Rage for Order: Black/White Relations in the American South Since Emancipation* (New York, 1986), 78–86.

36. Chicago Commission on Race Relations, *The Negro in Chicago: A Study of Race Relations and a Race Riot* (Chicago, 1922), 318–19; Charles S. Johnson, *Patterns of Negro Segregation* (New York, 1943), 75.

37. *Moving Picture World,* October 4, 1913, 147, in Bowser, *Transformation of Cinema,* 9–10; E. Franklin Frazier, "Recreation and Amusement among American Negroes" (1940), research memorandum prepared for Carnegie-Myrdal study, *The Negro in America,* 28, 59, 69–70, 89, in SC-NYPL.

38 Albert Mehrabian, *Public Places and Private Spaces: The Psychology of Work, Play, and Living Environments* (New York, 1976), 221–22; Arthur S. Meloy, *Theatres and Motion Picture Houses* (New York, 1916), 3.

39. Lewis, "De Luxe Picture Palace," 175–76.

40. U.S. Committee on Public Information, Division of Four Minute Men, "Bulletin No. 28. March 31, 1918. (For Use March 31–April 5)" (Washington, D.C., 1918), n.p.

41. Franklin, *Motion Picture Theater Management,* 33.

42. Lewis, "De Luxe Picture Palace," 176.

Chapter 17. Decline and Fall

1. Garth Jowett, *Film: The Democratic Art* (Boston, 1976), 190–93, 260–61. The Rorty citation is from p. 261. On changes in moving-picture theater architectural programs during the 1930s, see Lary May, with the assistance of Stephen Lassonde, "Making the American Way: Moderne Theatres, Audiences, and the Film Industry 1929–1945," *Prospects* 12 (1987), 89–124.

2. Robert W. Snyder, *The Voice of the City: Vaudeville and Popular Culture in New York* (New York, 1989), 158–59.

3. Nancy Banks, "The World's Most Beautiful Ballrooms," *Chicago History* (Fall-Winter 1973), 209–12; Marshall Stearns and Jean Stearns, *Jazz Dance: The Story of American Vernacular Dance* (New York, 1968), 315–34.

4. Charles C. Alexander, *Our Game: An American Baseball History* (New York, 1991), 155, 158; Benjamin G. Rader, *American Sports: From the Age of Folk Games to the Age of Spectators* (Englewood Cliffs, N.J.,

1983), 208–9; Bruce Kuklick, *To Every Thing a Season: Shibe Park and Urban Philadelphia* (Princeton, N.J., 1991), 62, 73–76.

5. Lee O. Bush, Edward C. Chukayne, Russell Allon Hehr, and Richard F. Hershey, *Euclid Beach Park Is Closed for the Season* (Fairview Park, Ohio, 1978), 51–56, 151–56, 197–98; Judith A. Adams, *The American Amusement Park Industry* (Boston, 1991), 69–70. On Kennywood, see the video documentary produced by WQED, "Kennywood Memories" (Pittsburgh, 1990).

6. Lucy P. Gilman, "Coney Island," *New York History* 36 (July 1955), 284–86. See also newspaper clips in "Amusement Parks: U.S.," clipping file, BRTC-NYPL. I have learned a great deal about Coney in this period from *Coney Island: A Documentary Film* (1991), directed by Ric Burns, written by Richard Snow.

7. Adams, *Amusement Park Industry*, 70; Burns and Snow, "Coney Island"; Murray Schumach, "Hoopla and Thrills Still Pack 'Em In," *New York Times Magazine* (July 14, 1946), 16; Harry Gilroy, "Everything's Atomic in Screamland," *New York Times Magazine* (August 7, 1947), 14, 59; Alexander, *Our Game*, 210; Neil J. Sullivan, *The Dodgers Move West* (New York, 1987), 39; Peter Golenbock, *Bums* (New York, 1986), 188, 194. See also 1948 photograph of Municipal Stadium in Cleveland in *The Sporting News, Take Me Out to the Ball Park*, rev. ed. (New York, 1987), 103.

8. On the changing racial composition of the nation's cities, see Jon Teaford, *The Twentieth-Century City: Problem, Promise, and Reality* (Baltimore, 1986), 98, 109–10, 115–61; and *Report of the National Advisory Commission on Civil Disorders* (New York, 1968), 236–47.

9. Cyril Dostal, "Paradise Misplaced," *Cleveland Magazine* (September 1977), 128–29. On Kennywood Park, see WQED, *Kennywood Memories.* On Oklahoma, see *New York Times*, June 16, 1966, 35; July 5, 1966, 22; on Baltimore, *New York Times*, September 6, 1959, 31; July 4, 1963, 1; July 6, 1963, 4; August 29, 1963, 14; September 1, 1963, 41; June 2, 1965, 31; Todd Gitlin, *The Sixties: Years of Hope, Days of Rage* (New York, 1988), 132–34. For an imaginative fictional representation of the events in Baltimore, see *Pink Flamingos*, a film by John Waters.

10. Alexander, *Our Game*, 227–28, 237; see also photograph from County Stadium, September 1958, in *The Sporting News, Take Me Out to the Ball Game*, 151.

11. The best biography on Alan Freed, from which this summary is taken, is John A. Jackson, *Big Beat Heat: Alan Freed and the Early Years of Rock & Roll* (New York, 1991). On Freed's early life, see 1–45. Charlie Gillett, *The Sound of the City: The Rise of Rock and Roll*, rev. and exp. ed. (New York, 1983), 13.

12. Arnold Shaw, *The Rockin' 50s* (New York, 1974), 104–11; Jackson, *Big Beat Heat*, 76–77.

13. Jackson, *Big Beat Heat*, 86.

14. Robert C. Toll, *The Entertainment Machine: American Show Business in the Twentieth Century* (New York, 1982), 114–15; James Lincoln Collier, *Benny Goodman and the Swing Era* (New York, 1989), 180–84.

15. Edith Evans Asbury, "Rock 'n' Roll Teen-Agers Tie Up the Times Square Area," *New York Times* (February 23, 1957), 1, 12; Ed Ward, Geoffrey Stokes, Ken Tucker, *Rock of Ages: The Rolling Stone History of Rock & Roll* (New York, 1986), 107–8, 124; Gerri Hirshey, *Nowhere to Run: The Story of Soul Music* (New York, 1984), 16–22.

16. James Haskins with Kathleen Benson, *Nat King Cole* (New York, 1984), 138; Leslie Gourse, *Unforgettable: The Life and Mystique of Nat King Cole* (New York, 1991), 176–78; *Newsweek* 47 (April 23, 1956), 31–32; Jackson, *Big Beat Heat*, 168.

17. Gillett, *Sound of the City*, 17–19; Jackson, *Big Beat Heat*, 128–31; *Time* 67 (June 18, 1956), 54; 68; (July 23, 1956), 34; Jess Stearn, "Rock 'N Roll Runs into Trouble," *New York Daily News*, April 12, 1956, 12; "Rock-and-Roll Called 'Communicable Disease,'" *New York Times*, March 28, 1956, 33.

18. Gertrude Samuels, "Why They Rock 'n' Roll—And Should They," *New York Times Magazine* (January 12, 1958), 16; Edith Evans Asbury, "Rock 'n' Roll Teen-Agers," 12; Edith Evans Asbury, "Times Sq. 'Rocks' For Second Day," *New York Times*, February 24, 1957, 76; Stearn, "Rock 'N Roll," 42.

19. "Boston Common to Hoot Mon Belt They Rock 'n' Riot out of This Veldt," *Variety*, May 7, 1958, 1, 58; Ward et al., *Rock of Ages*, 175–76; Jackson, *Big Beat Heat*, 193–99.

20. See articles and editorials in *Variety*, May 7, 1956, 1, 58; May 14, 1, 41, 46; *Time* 71 (May 19, 1958), 50; Ward et al., *Rock of Ages*, 176–77; Jackson, *Big Beat Heat*, 200–5.

21. Jackson, *Big Beat Heat*, 202–3; Ward et al., *Rock of Ages*, 206–8. On the "threat" of juvenile delinquency in the 1950s, see James Gilbert, *A Cycle of Outrage: America's Reaction to the Juvenile Delinquent in the 1950s* (New York, 1986). On "teenpics," see Thomas Doherty, *Teenagers & Teenpics: The Juvenilization of American Movies in the 1950s* (Boston, 1988).

22. For figures on decline in moviegoing, see Jowett, *Film*, 475; Gary R. Edgerton, *American Film Exhibition and an Analysis of the Motion Picture Industry's Market Structure, 1963–1980* (New York, 1983), 28, 47. On Cinerama and the like, see Tino Balio, "Introduction to Part IV," in *The American Film Industry*, rev. ed., ed. Tino Balio (Madison, Wis., 1985), 427–33. My figures on consumer price index come from U.S. Department of Labor, Bureau of Labor Statistics, *Handbook of Labor Statistics* (Washington, D.C., June 1985), 350; U.S. Department of Commerce, Bureau of Census, *Historical Statistics of the United States: Colonial Times to 1970*, Part I (Washington, D.C., 1972), 165; U.S. Department of Commerce, Bureau of the Census, *Statistical Abstract of the United States: 1991* (Washington, D.C., 1991), 478. The figures on average admission prices come from Edgerton, *American Film*, 27, 47; *International Motion Picture Almanac: 1992* (New York, 1992), 22a.

23. James L. Baughnan, *The Republic of Mass Culture* (Baltimore, 1992), 35–36, 74–75. On the Supreme Court decision, see Michael Conant, "The Paramount Decrees Reconsidered," in Balio, ed., *American Film Industry*, 537–73; Edgerton, *American Film*, 1–25.

24. On drive-ins, see Edgerton, *American Film,* 32–33; Jowett, *Film,* 351–53.
25. Kenneth Jackson, *Crabgrass Frontier: The Suburbanization of the United States* (New York, 1985), 274–76.
26. *Report of the National Advisory Commission,* 266–77; Teaford, *Twentieth-Century City,* 134–36; Eric H. Monkkonen, *America Becomes Urban: The Development of U.S. Cities and Towns, 1780–1980* (Berkeley, 1988), 225–26.
27. David Naylor, *American Picture Palaces: The Architecture of Fantasy* (New York, 1981), 177–78, 207; Meyer Berger, "About New York," *New York Times* (February 28, 1958), and other newspaper articles in "Theaters: U.S.: New York: Roxy," clipping file, BRTC-NYPL. On Midland theaters, see John Tibbetts, "The Midland Celebrates," *American Classic Screen* (January–February 1978), 34; and article by John Quinn in *Variety* in "Theatres: U.S.: Kansas City: Midland," clipping file, BRTC-NYPL.
28. David Naylor, *Great American Movie Theaters* (Washington, D.C., 1987), 72–73.
29. *International Motion Picture Almanac: 1970* (New York, 1970), 56a; see also 1972 edition, 42a.
30. Sullivan, *Dodgers,* 39; Golenbock, *Bums,* 560–61; Kuklick, *To Every Thing a Season,* 131.
31. For information on these ballparks, see *The Sporting News, Take Me Out*; and Lawrence S. Ritter, *Lost Ballparks: A Celebration of Baseball's Legendary Fields* (New York, 1992); Steven J. Riess, *City Games: The Evolution of American Urban Society and the Rise of Sports* (Urbana, Ill., 1989), 234–37. On demolition of Polo Grounds, see Ritter, *Lost Ballparks,* 166.
32. John F. Kasson, *Amusing the Million: Coney Island at the Turn of the Century* (New York, 1978), 106. On Disney's comments, see Richard Schickel, *The Disney Version: The Life, Times, Art and Commerce of Walt Disney* (New York, 1968), 263–64; Bob Thomas, *Walt Disney: An American Original* (New York, 1976), 202–3, 225; David Mamet, "A Time for Mickey Mouse," *Playboy* 36 (August 1989), 110; Garry Cooper, "The World That Was at Belmont and Western," *Chicago Tribune Magazine* (May 16, 1976), 24.
33. Alan A. Siegel, *Smile: A Picture History of Olympic Park, 1887–1965* (Irvington, N.J., 1983), 163; "Amusement Park in Jersey Denied License Renewal," *New York Times,* May 12, 1965; Adams, *Amusement Park Industry,* 71–77.
34. Martin Tolchin, "Coney Island Slump Grows Worse," *New York Times,* July 2, 1964, 33.
35. Hugo John Hildebrandt, "Cedar Point: A Park in Progress," *Journal of Popular Culture* XV (Summer 1981), 95; "Amusement Parks Ride to Boom—or Bust," *Business Week,* April 9, 1966, 32; Bush et al., *Euclid Beach Park,* 265–66.
36. Adams, *Amusement Park Industy,* 164; Frederic Jameson, "Postmodernism, or the Cultural Logic of Late Capitalism," in *Postmodernism: A Reader,* ed. Thomas Docherty (New York, 1993), 80–81. On Conneaut Lake Park, see Lee O. Bush and Richard F. Hershey, *Conneaut Lake Park: The First 100 Years* (Fairview Park, Ohio, 1992).

37. "Sons of Disneyland," *Newsweek*, May 21, 1973, 90; Edwin McDowell, "Travel Industry Looks at Approach of Summer, and Smiles," *New York Times*, May 31, 1993, 8; David W. Francis and Diane DeMali Francis, *Cedar Point: The Queen of American Watering Places* (Canton, Ohio, 1988), 132; Adams, *Amusement Park Industry*, 107, 146.
38. Margaret Crawford, "The World in a Shopping Mall," in *Variations on a Theme Park: The New American City and the End of Public Space*, ed. Michael Sorkin (New York, 1992), 23.
39. Sharon Zukin, *Landscapes of Power: From Detroit to Disney World* (Berkeley, 1991), 200; the *New York* magazine article is cited in Zukin, *Landscapes*, 200.
40. Edwin E. Slosson, "The Amusement Business," *Independent* 59 (July 21, 1904), 135.

INDEX